ALSO BY PETER WYDEN

Stella

I Remember
(with Dan Rather)

Wall: The Inside Story of Divided Berlin

Day One: Before Hiroshima and After

Bay of Pigs: The Untold Story

The Unknown Iacocca

The Passionate War:
The Narrative History of the Spanish Civil War

Inside the Sex Clinic
(with Barbara Wyden)

Growing Up Straight:
What Every Parent Should Know
About Homosexuality
(with Barbara Wyden)

The Intimate Enemy:
How to Fight Fair in Love and Marriage
(with Dr. George R. Bach)

How the Doctors Diet

The Overweight Society

The Hired Killers

Suburbia's Coddled Kids

Conquering
Schizophrenia

Conquering Schizophrenia

A FATHER, HIS SON, AND
A MEDICAL BREAKTHROUGH

Peter Wyden

Alfred A. Knopf New York 1998

THIS IS A BORZOI BOOK
PUBLISHED BY ALFRED A. KNOPF, INC.

Copyright © 1997 by Peter H. Wyden, Inc.

All rights reserved under International and Pan-American
Copyright Conventions. Published in the United States by
Alfred A. Knopf, Inc., New York, and simultaneously in Canada
by Random House of Canada Limited, Toronto.
Distributed by Random House, Inc., New York.

www.randomhouse.com

Library of Congress Cataloging-in-Publication Data
Wyden, Peter.
Conquering schizophrenia : a father, his son, and a
medical breakthrough / by Peter Wyden.
p.   cm.
Includes bibliographical references and index.
ISBN 0-679-44671-0 (alk. paper)
1. Wyden, Jeffrey—Mental health.
2. Schizophrenics—United States—Biography.
3. Schizophrenia—Treatment.
4. Olanzapine.
I. Title.
RC514.W93   1997
616.89'82'0092—dc21
[B]   97-39621
CIP

Manufactured in the United States of America
First Edition

For Jeff, of course

Contents

Conquering
Schizophrenia

CHAPTER I

The Onset

MORE THAN twenty years ago, I walked into the padded, otherwise bare "rubber room" at Metropolitan Hospital on the Upper East Side of Manhattan and found my twenty-four-year-old son Jeff lying alone in the fetal position on the checkerboard tile floor, next to a pool of urine. He was whimpering, "I want my mommy, I want my mommy, I want my mommy. . . ."

I had just spent more than $125,000 for his care at the Menninger Clinic in Topeka, Kansas, arguably the finest American mental hospital. I had seen mental institutions before. Shortly after World War II, I had worked as a reporter in Wichita and had written investigatory articles about the state hospitals, then known as snake pits. At the Topeka State Hospital, I had found only three frantically overworked doctors for 1,744 psychotic patients. Attendants worked thirteen hours a day, six days a week, for $130 a month (a pittance). The heavily sedated, filthy inmates sat rigid, lined up in rows, staring ahead, and rocking their lives away in silence. It was not an experience to be forgotten, most vivid, the stench.

That hospital was not the worst in Kansas. I remember, too, the State Training School for the "feebleminded" at Winfield, where the smell was the same and there was not one full-time doctor for 1,366 patients. There was, however, sufficient staff to perform many of the 1,992 surgical sterilizations and castrations ordered by the State Board of Sterilization to "stabilize" the retarded and to ward off diseases and even, it was said, baldness.

Jeffrey Wyden, age seventeen

Writers at three of the region's other newspapers took up my cause, and I like to think the chorus of our complaints shamed the 1948–49 session of the Kansas legislature into voting for enough funds to remedy the horrible excesses. Fortunately the professional follow-up was put in the hands of Dr. Karl Menninger of the Menninger Clinic, who was close at hand and a preeminent thinker in his profession, as well as a charmer. But twenty-five years later, the world being a convoluted and small place, he was a fateful negative influence when my Jeff became a Menninger patient. That, however, is getting ahead of my tale.

I must confess that this book is an act of perjury. I had pledged that I would never write it. Over the years, a number of psychiatrists had urged me to produce a chronicle of Jeff's travail. No, I kept insisting, I can't do it. It's too painful, too personal. Gradually, four circumstances changed my mind:

- My stacks of accumulated letters, memos, hospital reports, journal articles, books, and endless memories and notes of conversations with Jeff and his many, many doctors—all evidence of my close and active involvement with his fate. Schizophrenia had become something of an obsession.

- I had learned much that I thought I should share about the disease. Myths needed to be dispelled. Vital new knowledge needed to be disseminated. Promising new diagnostic data had emerged, even if still inconclusive.

- My own role as a manager of Jeff's managers had matured. I was also learning from other parents never to give up on a "hopeless" psychotic, because the disease is forever in flux. One lay guide can make a difference. More information can always be explored and additional alternatives considered.

- Science achieved dramatic advances in schizophrenia treatment within the last five years. One trouble-free revolutionary drug, Olanzapine, is on the market as I write. The next year will see more such medications come into routine use. Might I be producing the first optimistic book about schizophrenia? I hoped so, because I was writing on behalf of 2.5 million afflicted Americans, fifty million worldwide—one percent of the population—not to mention their families, friends, and professional caregivers.

Neither Jeff's mother, Edith, from whom I have been divorced for more than thirty years, nor I had any hint that anything was to go drastically wrong with Jeff's health—not until he was seventeen. Even at that juncture, no grave complications were envisioned by his well-qualified doctors. Edith and I were already divorced and felt no serious concern when I reported from New York on Jeff's childhood to the first psychiatrist he was taken to see, the likable Dr. Vincent J. D'Andrea in Palo Alto, California, who was experienced in dealing with young people and who diagnosed "school phobia." On March 3, 1968, in a five-page, typed, single-spaced letter, I wrote him:

> He was the perfect baby: a calm, contented, somewhat smug and all-knowing gentleman. He always seemed to do everything just right: he ate and slept and displayed the Dr. Spock-appropriate baby behavior at all times in just the right way. He had no colic or other physical problems. Within weeks after birth he was an exceptionally handsome boy and just about everybody, male and female, volunteered comments about his good looks: his big, dark brown eyes, his pale clear skin, etc. . . . He was rarely yelled at . . . and I'm not sure he was spanked even once. In due course, he became, if anything, a bit of a pampered star of the family because he was unusually charming and not only obviously bright but able to display his brightness to advantage. . . . Jeff never made friends very easily, but he always did have buddies, he was always scrappy and active in sports . . . always acquitted himself well physically, was not cowardly and certainly shouldn't be pictured as a Little Lord Fauntleroy. . . . I can think of nothing remotely out of the ordinary about Jeff's childhood up to the divorce.

Even this cheery recitation fails to measure up to my memories of the boy we came to call "the old Jeff." When he was very small, Jeff knew which knobs to twiddle whenever the TV got the shakes. If I lost my way in the car, it was Jeff who would pipe up from the rear: "Daddy, you just have to go back three blocks and turn right."

That long-ago Jeff was organized, analytical, a bit perfectionistic, and he commanded a firm sense of self. He was also very, very funny and responsible. Each morning it was his exclusive job to assemble the family for breakfast. We actually did sit-down breakfasts then, and Jeff's shout while I was shaving—"Daddy, come and eat!"—is in my ear like the reveille bugle of my infantry basic training. For a hectic tour of Europe in the world's most anemic Volkswagen bus, Jeff drummed us troops together, permitting no dallying, worrying about the "preservation of the reservation," while his older brother, Ron, grumbled about "Daddy's pain-and-suffering marathon."

When my book *Suburbia's Coddled Kids* came out in 1962, he was quizzical. I distributed campaign buttons as a promotion stunt, red ones saying "I'm a Coddled Kid," blue ones proclaiming "I'm an Un-Coddled Kid." The ambiguity gave Jeff pause. He had a need to know. He planted himself in front of me and demanded, "Daddy, are we coddled?" I said, "Yeah, maybe a little." He walked away pleased, having known the answer in the first place, and the phrase "How coddled!" became family bywords. It also inspired one of Jeff's early literary efforts. "Humphrey's Cat Goes to Florida" ran exactly 166 words, as its author recorded at the top left corner of the first and only page in his typically precise manner. It was a vacation fantasy that began:

> In the Humphrey's [*sic*] small country bakery on the resort island of Martha's Vineyard, Massachusetts, there lives a cat. This cat, unhappy in the surroundings of this famed resort, finds it necessary to go on a much needed vacation to a well known Miami Beach hotel. This hotel is the Fontainebleau. The cat did not just stay in the hotel. This cat stayed in a penthouse suite, in the right wing of the two-winged hotel. This is the same type of room that Frank Sinatra stays in for a "quick gas weekend." The Humphreys' cat stayed with the family at the $75-a-night hotel, in the penthouse suite, for seven months.

Jeff had never been in Miami. He knew about the Fontainebleau from *Suburbia's Coddled Kids*, in which I had recycled the old yarn about the lady in mink who thrust her thirteen-year-old son at the doorman, demanding that he be carried upstairs, thereby inspiring a dialogue familiar in coddled circles:

"But, madame, can't the child walk?"

"Sure, but isn't it nice he doesn't have to?"

From coddled kids to coddled cats was a small distance, especially for my son, an author's delight. Like his brother, he recited from *Suburbia's Coddled Kids* by the page, with little excuse and verbatim.

When Jeff was eight, the divorce threatened to explode his life brutally. My marriage was no longer salvageable, but my disagreements with Edith had been efficiently hidden from the boys. Knowing that a divorce announcement would hit them hard, I consulted a child psychiatrist in Chicago, where we then lived.

I see Dr. Robert H. Korf sitting before me in his office on North Michigan Avenue, a kindly, elderly personage wearing a weary expression that conveyed

"My God, what trouble I've seen parents make for their children!" Dr. Korf knew his business. He dictated a detailed sequence of hard-nosed directives to take Edith and me out of our preoccupation with our own conflict and place ourselves in the shoes of our kids and their disrupted lives, assuring them that the divorce was in no way their doing and emphasizing the many aspects of their daily routine that would not change. Love and stability would endure for them. Dr. Korf did a good job of explaining; most emphatically, he warned us not to spring the separation and the appearance of a new woman in my life at one and the same time.

That part of the counseling didn't take. Our scene played out at bedtime, and it was cataclysmic; no other word will suffice. Extremely agitated, Edith told the boys about Barbara, my new wife-to-be, of whom they had not yet heard. They reeled. Jeff fashioned a sentence with implications that still burden my conscience:

"Will she be our mommy?" he wanted to know. His brother sat bug-eyed and silent in his pajamas.

Their roles were soon reversed. I could never explain the discrepancy fully, but Ron was able to discuss the family sadness, to rail against it and to treat Barbara at some distance. Jeff and Barbara quickly became good friends, but the divorce was a taboo subject, then and pretty much forever after. I realized that this bottling up of a powerful event could cause trouble, and the weight of my guilt feelings has lessened but never left me entirely.

How justified is it? Divorce is a notorious stressor, for children as well as divorcing adults. How vulnerable is a child to lasting psychological damage? No one can say with certainty. What will trouble me eternally is that many studies have implicated stress as a possible cotrigger of schizophrenia; the speculation runs through the professional literature like drumfire. How important a factor is it? Under what circumstances does it activate vulnerabilities of an adolescent? The doctors know just enough to keep a divorced parent imprisoned with the possibilities.

I was only dimly aware of these storm clouds in 1968. (Schizophrenia still had not yet been mentioned.) In my letter to Dr. D'Andrea I wrote:

> Much as I tried, and always in a pleasant and inviting and certainly non-censorious way, I never was able to get Jeff to say a word about the divorce. Not one single word. . . . Jeff appeared on the surface to be coping so very well with literally everything that I gradually stopped prodding him about the subject. It seemed overanxious to take him to a

psychiatrist to raise an alarm about something that was *not* happening. I suspect now that some or much of Jeff's trouble lies buried right there.

One pretty nice family became two pretty nice families and settled down. Edith had enacted her dream of following the sun to Palo Alto; I had followed mine by moving my magazine-editing career to New York, the center of the industry action. The widening of our geographic distance foreshadowed some problems of identity formation for Jeff years later, but I worked as hard as I could not to allow an emotional distance to grow between the boys in the West and me in the East. What had phones been made for, after all? And notes? And cards? And audiotapes? And silly gags to be traded?

Traffic whizzed back and forth. Jeff found fun aplenty and plunged into the full of it. A private new transcontinental world took shape, filled with further outrageous missions of the Humphreys' cat; a symphony orchestra of musical mice like Wolfgang Amadeus Mozart Mouse and Johann Sebastian Bach Mouse, forever uncatchable by the Humphreys' cat; and two boy adventurers named Hopalong Cassidy Jr., known as Hoppy, and Popalong Cassidy Jr., Poppy, who ballooned around the world in seventy-nine days, not eighty. Who had time for separation anxiety?

Here is a "Dear Daddy" letter dated December 30, 1960, written right after Jeff moved to California: "How are you feeling? Today I am not doing very many action things. The Baylor Bears have a real live bear as a mascot on TV." Another message of the same vintage reported: "When we went to Fisherman's Wharf with Grandpa Wyden and Alice, they bought me a shell." Still another reports: "I got my new math test grade back. I got an 'A—.' " And at about the same time Jeff furnished this evidence of a dogged political passion that he would never lose: "I was given a Kennedy button by a boy in my classroom named Dennis. He's for Kennedy, too. Almost everyone around here is for Nixon, but I still hope Kennedy wins."

On August 11, 1963, came this word from him: "I'm writing to you on my new typewriter. . . . I wouldn't think you had your own typewriter when you were a boy. And such a fancy one! This one is called a Signet, made by the Royal typewriter company. This particular typewriter was imported. It was made in Holland. It is unbelievably coddled! The coddled kids deserve the finest, you know."

Jeff had developed a passion for the comedian Allan Sherman and his records *My Son, the Folksinger* and *My Son, the Nut,* so for his twelfth birthday I wrote him an Allan Sherman serenade that began:

Jeffrey Wyden, Jeffrey Wyden,
How's by you, how's by you?
How's your birthday going?
A party you are throwing?

That's nice, too; that's nice, too.

Is it true you're modeled
After a kid that's coddled?

How is Humphrey's cat?
She's getting much too fat.

How're your table manners?
Are they winning banners?

Now you're an adolescent.
That ought to be quite pleasant—
So are you,
So are you.

The day after his birthday he wrote back: "That serenade you wrote for my birthday was good. If you sent it in to Allan Sherman he'd probably use it the first time he looked at it." As so often, Jeff also tackled a sensitive subject: "I am writing you to ask whether we might be able to work on the boat and get everything but the painting done so we could get the boat finished next time you come to California."

I never let more than three months go by between quick trips to California, but "the boat" was beginning to become a delicate issue. When Jeff at age nine expressed repeated hankering for a boat, I purchased an $80 mail-order kit— the parts of a surprisingly sturdy-looking rowboat for self-assembly. It was a bizarre and foolhardy venture, since I am famous as an unhandyman; the parts seemed overwhelmingly numerous, and the plans bewilderingly complex. As we uncrated the "boat," the dream vessel seemed to fade from reality.

I had not reckoned with my son's determination and organizing zeal. When he wrote to appeal for a final push to get the little monster finished, we had been hammering, gluing, and puzzling in Edith's garage for three years, if, necessarily, with extended intermissions. By this time, I, too, had been seized by an irresistible drive not to concede defeat at the hands of the kit makers, who were surely laughing themselves silly into their—to us unreachable— power tools.

Another year and a half would be required for the product of our mania to begin its truck voyage across the country, at about five times the cost of the original kit. I predicted that it would sink upon hitting the water. Jeff said it wouldn't, and when we shoved it very, very gently into the Connecticut River near our summerhouse in Chester, by God, it didn't! What a triumphant couple of skippers we were as we revved up the Sears outboard motor, bought on installments, and put-putted into exclusive Hamburg Cove that Sunday.

When during the kids' stay with us for summer vacation Barbara found that Jeff enjoyed hanging around the kitchen to help fix meals, he became her exuberant assistant. Together, they produced *The Cook-Along Book*, a unique literary voyage, the "senior chef" cooperating with the "junior chef." The book was an adult hit with the Cookbook Guild.

Jeff marshaled enthusiasm for a team spirit on other occasions. Though neither of my semicoddled children likes to get his hands dirty, when we found the family graves at the Jewish cemetery in Berlin-Weissensee overgrown in weeds, Jeff set about to clean them up.

And what a mimic he was! His JFK imitation became a regular attraction for our adult guests. At a ludicrously costly dinner at a three-star restaurant in France, Jeff stopped the Lucullan show. Barbara had two martinis. Jeff kept filling up the empty glasses with water and sipped with deliberation, preening the while. The French onlookers, tending to literal-mindedness, must have been disgusted at those undisciplined Americans.

Jeff also appreciated the laughable. We once gave a summer weekend party and laid in liberal supplies of the then-popular kinds of hard liquor. The clerk in the liquor department that Saturday morning was enchanted as I loaded up my muscular boys with case after case, and when Jeff was last to stagger away with a case of gin on his back, the man sang out, "Have a good weekend!" That was thirty years ago, but to this day the phrase gets belly laughs in our family. It means: "Watch out! Don't have too many!"

Jeff worked cleverly for his laughs. In July 1963 I received a "Coupon for Happy Day" from him, signing himself as "President of New York Happy Day, Inc." The document, carefully laid out for eventual printing, urged "Read carefully" and began: "Yes, Mr. Wyden, you have been chosen to get a Happy Day. . . . If you are not happy with the date of your Happy Day, please see us. We can postpone it. On Thursday, August 1, 1963, you will personally be waited on by us hand and foot from morning to night. This includes such services as breakfast in bed and others. We hope you fully enjoy your Happy Day."

The dark and light shadings of his days mattered to Jeff even as a small boy. It registered on him which was which. Some years after my Happy Day, he was becoming ever so slightly withdrawn, and Barbara used to try to get him rolling on vacation mornings by challenging him, "Come on, Jeff, it's going to be a big day!" After Jeff had heard this exhortation once too often, he looked up plaintively at her one morning and mumbled in exasperation: "We don't have any more little days, do we?" This plea, too, remains part of our family language.

His eye for dissenting social comment and sarcasm, along with his wish to duck confrontation, likewise developed early. He was plainly declaring himself sick of parental arguments when he delivered a draft copy of a publication he called *Bicker,* with the subtitle *The Everyday Evening Bicker.*

We found tremors of change in Jeff's personality easy to dismiss as normal expressions of puberty and postpuberty turmoil in an adolescent boy. When Barbara and I visited him briefly at the Stanford campus in Tours, France, where Jeff was luxuriating in his junior year in 1971, he officiated as the proverbial life of the party: bubbling French, plotting gags with new friends, too busy to pay much heed to us. We were delighted to have seen him reveal himself outside of the shell that had been enveloping him. It was to be his last—and very temporary—outbreak of sociability.

"Introverted" is as strong a label as I picked to describe him earlier, never anything pathological. In a letter to Dr. D'Andrea in the watershed year of 1968, I reported:

> In the last two years or so, his reticence has become excessive. He has had to take a good deal of kidding about it. I've accused him of being too much of a "strong, silent type" and kidded him about being a CIA agent, as close-mouthed as a professional spy. . . . But he seemed to have no trouble in school, although he never seems to have functioned near the level of his potential. . . . He continued to be so introverted that I spoke with him about it very seriously in private. I told him that everybody has to share his fears and burdens; that I realized kids often find this hard to do with their parents and that this was nothing to be ashamed about. I suggested that he talk to his Uncle Fred, an Oakland internist whom he likes a lot, about any worries he might have. Stoically, he kept maintaining that he had no worries. I knew, of course, that this had to be nonsense, but I didn't say so and there didn't seem to be anything to be done that wouldn't have seemed like a hyper-reaction—again—to something that "wasn't there."

One problem was beyond denial, however: Jeff acted as if girls didn't exist. I wrote the psychiatrist:

My wife and I believe that Jeff is very interested in girls, but cannot remotely conceive of any girl getting interested in him. This is part of his low self-esteem, of which there was no evidence for at least four years after the divorce, but of which there has been plenty of evidence since. When he was fourteen we once talked about jobs available to young people and he said, "Who'd ever want to give *me* a job?" I hooked in to bolster his self-confidence on such occasions, but I don't suppose I ever convinced him. He has never gone to a dance and I wouldn't be surprised if he has never spoken a single personal word to a girl. He was treasurer of his Junior Achievement Group, plays in the band and on the "C" basketball team and can hardly be called an isolate. On the other hand, he almost never does anything on Saturday or Sunday night except watch TV.

Our family and friends said he'd grow out of it. Jeff's creativity was pronounced, though curiously abortive. My son was a hit-and-run artist. He was brilliant with words, but even his beloved *Bicker* magazine consisted of mostly empty pages. He tootled his bassoon with gusto, but for only a short spell. Most intriguing and mysterious was his extraordinary devotion when he produced his ashtray.

While we were living in Chicago before the divorce, Jeff decided to make a black-and-white pencil drawing of an instantly recognizable downtown scene. From his vantage point of the Michigan Avenue Bridge over the Chicago River, he zeroed in on a half-open drawbridge and the mighty skyline of famous office buildings—the Chicago Tribune Tower, the Wrigley Building, and the rest. Dominating this tableau were hundreds of meticulously re-created little square office windows, lined up with the precision of a drill sergeant straightening the rows of an infantry training platoon.

Jeff handed over this highly original artwork with slightly feigned indifference, although the inscription "J. Wyden" in the lower left corner was good sized. Whoever saw the drawing was much impressed and said so. I had spotted a tiny ad in *The New Yorker* for a company in Port Chester, New York, calling itself Young Rembrandts. The headline was seductive: "Your Own Child's Drawing on an Ashtray." I ordered four large, rectangular ashtrays, 10½ by 7½ inches. I still have two of them, although I stopped smoking fifteen years ago. Guests can admire one of them in the living room; the other looks at me from near my desk as I write. The remaining two are with Jeff's mother and brother.

Despite the admiration and the fuss—or, perhaps, self-consciously because of it—the artist almost never again took pencil in hand.

Neither Jeff's introversion nor his extreme shyness with the opposite sex diminished with time. Sometimes it seemed almost as if Jeff wanted to vanish from view altogether. That had been the case when he was still small, and we were tourists in Copenhagen. It was pouring rain, but the boys were impatient and demanded nevertheless to be let out to play in the Tivoli amusement park. Barbara, a responsible stepmother, said she would only relent if the boys got hats.

Dutifully, Jeff, Ron, and I trotted off to a decorous male hat emporium. The variety of available headgear was overwhelming, and the boys dug in. The result was the perfect verification of personalities. The extroverted showman Ron, the future politician, selected a trilby of thick, checkered Scottish wool and placed it cockily off his forehead, Rex Harrison incarnate. Jeff picked a narrow-visor cotton cap of gray so dull that it seemed to make him disappear. He pulled this magic hood down over his forehead as far as it would go.

"Poor Jeff!" That became the family chorus. It has never stopped. And as early as 1968 (when his troubles first grew serious) Jeff dolefully joined the wailing for himself, at least some of the time. I think this was the summer—I have no record for this, so it may have been the summer before—when we were still neighbors of the Humphreys' cat and vacationing on Martha's Vineyard, that I became exasperated at Jeff's simply sitting about, looking lost, doing nothing. With effort, he could be moved into activities—even a class in modern dancing, for which Barbara had registered us all, more or less in desperation—but the pushing that was required to set him in motion was discouraging.

Determined to break the spell—wasn't he supposed to grow out of all this?—I accused him of "moofing," a nonexistent word which Jeff adopted instantly and with affection. How beautifully it fit his lethargy and his low opinion of himself. It even broke his artist's block momentarily. With green crayons he drew a monstrous otherworldly creature, ugly and awkward, which he named Sir Reginald Moof, and presented to me as his self-portrait.

The vacation moofing continued. We shrugged: What harm did it do? Other kids were into rock throwing and worse. Systematic clinical concern about negative symptoms, particularly apathy, the core deficit of treatment-resistant schizophrenics, would not arise among scientists to a significant degree until the early 1970s. Apathy, withdrawal, lack of affect and motivation, slowly turned out to be among the demonstrable manifestations of this condition among psychiatric patients. But how could we have recognized what researchers had not yet fully identified in the scheme of psychopathology?

Recently, whenever I've had conversations with experts about ways, if any, to recognize the onset of schizophrenia at the earliest possible stage, I tell them about Jeff's moofing. Invariably, the doctors smile sympathetically and are quite interested. They divide more or less evenly into two camps: half say the moofing held significance for Jeff's future mental health; the other half say it didn't. None has suggested effective steps that we might have taken if some ingenious psychiatrist at the time had shown prescience.

Slowly, my concerns about Jeff's development grew. My letters to Dr. D'Andrea became longer and still more numerous. Whenever I was in Palo Alto, I would see him briefly, sometimes with Jeff.

The doctor was an agreeable, accessible fellow, middle-aged, soft voiced, more talkative than many of his trade, almost cozy. Edith had been referred to him by Jeff's pediatrician. Both belonged to the Palo Alto Medical Clinic, a group practice affiliated with Stanford Hospital. D'Andrea seemed to like Jeff and was not given to the neutral grunts common among his colleagues.

I was further reassured by our psychiatrist's animated assurances. At the outset, he didn't think anything unusual was wrong with Jeff. The lad was anxious and insecure, sure, but not to a degree worrisome during the adolescent stages of a bright child of divorce. D'Andrea related well to anxious, insecure teenagers. Until not long before, he had been a government psychiatrist serving with one of President Kennedy's most popular innovations, the Peace Corps, which was full of intellectually precocious young men much like Jeff.

Patiently, the doctor took in more ruminations from my frequent letters about Jeff's status:

> He has a love—even a sense of excitement—for history. But when he buckles down to a job—writing a letter, reading a book—he is painstaking and very, very slow. I wonder whether this is part of his inhibitions or something else. In his preliminary SAT tests he performed way, way below the standards of his school grades because he finished so relatively few of the questions. . . . Both his mother and I are deeply involved in bookish professions, but Jeff is, as always, *uninvolved*. This is perhaps the word that characterizes him best. He doesn't want to give of himself. Above all, he is "hassle-phobic" and will do almost anything to avoid noise and trouble. It is as if he would like to trust things and people, and occasionally does, but is always fearful of being suddenly burned.

Burned—so I kept thinking thirty years ago, and still ponder now—by parents who didn't tell him that their arguments hid serious differences and dropped a separation bombshell on him without the cushioning of advance grace. Yes, there's guilt. But mostly I've learned that one has to play life as it lays and deal with the hand given at the moment. So much depends on unalterable circumstances. My infantry platoon leader, Lieutenant Ballard, who was killed during the North African campaign of 1943, had the perfect response when we trainees asked him one of life's unanswerable questions. He would muse: "That depends on the situation and the terrain."

CHAPTER 2

Diagnosis: School Phobia

LATE IN February 1968, Jeff's situation and terrain became unmistakably rocky. He turned visibly and severely agitated and distressed. A rapidly unfolding sequence of events was set in motion, as I reported to Dr. D'Andrea:

> What is so frightening is the suddenness and drastic nature of the change in Jeff's overt behavior. Until last week, he was over-controlled, the calmest kid in the world; now his behavior indicates that he is in total panic. Until last week, he acted like a Mafia man sworn to eternal silence; now he gushes out, apparently, everything he feels and fears. Until last week, he was a model of self-sufficiency; now his mother says he literally clings to her.

Without delay, Edith had taken him to D'Andrea, who diagnosed school phobia, which is ambiguously defined in the literature. In the 1994 edition of the *Encyclopedia of Psychology,* the editor, Raymond J. Corsini, describes the condition as "unwarranted fear of school and/or inappropriate anxiety associated with leaving home." This form of separation anxiety occurs "often in children who are very bright." It is usually fleeting and leaves no lasting damage: "Brief psychotherapy . . . yields consistently positive results." Only rarely do "continued psychological disturbances" occur. In his two-page essay, Corsini saw no need to worry about the possible nature of such distur-bances nor any need to speculate on the cause(s) of this form of anxiety, cer-tainly no hint of fateful future outcomes such as schizophrenia.

Jeff's case of school phobia was, if anything, less florid than the somewhat-cosmic state described in the encyclopedia. He did not at all fear school or leaving home. He had developed an acute but basic case of stage fright, seemingly restricted to panicky dread of getting up when questioned in class, especially in his favorite subject, history, and reciting answers that, iron-ically, he knew to his usual perfection.

The family support net gathered around him at once. Fortuitously, my mother was visiting in Palo Alto. For twenty years she had been employed as an assistant in New York hospitals and doctors' offices, and she was much beloved by Jeff. I promptly conveyed to Dr. D'Andrea her report to me on Jeff's crisis.

Already I had learned a key lesson for managing the managers of a mental illness, not to mention psychoses: Don't assume that word gets around. All too often, helpful information goes unnoticed, unused; it is haphazardly ignored, never to be retrieved. Seemingly, too many fragments accumulate to be sorted through. The doctors, clinics, hospitals, halfway houses, and their helpers are too busy and tend to act as if each day is the first day of the patient's troubles, especially if there are many staff shifts and transfers. But somebody *must*—absolutely must—help pick up pieces and pull together as many of the strands as can be marshaled, for the thread is the patient's life. Though that consoli-dating of information carries no guarantee that doctors will respect it.

So on March 6, 1968, I filled in Jeff's doctor on my mother's recounting of how Jeff had let down his guard in a way my young stoic would have found unacceptable in a doctor's office:

> Jeff's conversations with her were the frankest, by far, that he probably ever had with anybody in his entire life. . . . During the time when he was most agitated he would cry a lot and yell and occasionally hit his fist hard against his head. . . . She says he is keenly aware that his "stage fright" is only a symptom of what he now calls, almost proudly, "my problem." My mother asked him whether he had any idea what might be at the bottom of the whole business and he said he didn't know but sure wished he did. . . . He told my mother he is aware of his trouble relating to his contempo-raries. He said, "I have nothing to offer." My mother sensibly said she thought he was so unwilling to give of himself that she and others often thought he was silent because *he* considers other people to be idiots. He said

he had more trouble speaking up in class because there were girls in the room. "I like girls," he volunteered, but they make him feel uncomfortable.

My mother reported that Jeff, to her considerable surprise, brought up the subject of the divorce, although he only said, "It shouldn't have happened," and that he knew his mother wouldn't get married again because she was too hurt and feared that the same thing might happen again.*

As a doctor's assistant, my mother had learned not to get excessively alarmed by a patient's state, but her grandson's plight upset her. As I reported her findings to the doctor:

He seems completely incapacitated, at least in the history class situation, says he is "gasping for breath" and "just can't go on," and "they're all looking at me" and he says he is furious at himself for not being able even just to read a prepared paper that he has rehearsed at home "when most of the other guys can do it off the top of their heads." Rightly, he asks, "Why can't I?"

That was the heart of what Jeff had earlier defined as "my problem," his stage fright, which he had already identified as only a symptom of what was ailing him. What indeed was behind that symptom?

That was not the type of question Dr. D'Andrea was likely to focus on. He was not used to dealing with schizophrenics. Looking back, I think he saw as his job ironing out kinks in the emotional turmoil of mercurial adolescents, making them functional with minimum loss of time and money, not launching open-ended Freudian fishing expeditions that often produced evidence of past trauma but helped the patient little or not at all in the present. The doctor, I think, had been conditioned not to waste his time suspecting lung cancer lurking in every common cold. Schizophrenia was not on his screen.

He saw a very agitated but essentially healthy teenager and resorted to the correct first line of treatment that threatened no side effects whatever: relaxation exercises to curb the patient's obvious symptom of anxiety. Jeff learned to lie on the floor or on a couch, twice a day for twenty minutes each time, and, successively and systematically, tense and untense various groups of muscles.

The regimen worked instantly, as I reported to the doctor shortly after the exercises began:

* Edith never did marry again. When I gently brought up the divorce with Jeff in 1995, he reiterated verbatim: "It shouldn't have happened," and said nothing more.

Jeff was very cheerful on the phone last night; his mother reported that he is very relaxed and his morale is way up, he is sleeping beautifully. . . . His manner of speaking last night was not only markedly different from his manner during his acute agitation but also very different from his manner previously. He sounded much like the Jeff of four or more years ago. I was startled and delighted, although I suppose that during a period such as now, there may be many ups and downs. Anyway, he sounded much firmer, clearer, literally a bit louder, decisive, confident, and explicit. I'd always had trouble getting him to explain himself in more than monosyllables so I could understand how he really felt. Frankly, I've lectured him about this dozens of times. Last night, with no or little prompting, it was as if he suddenly remembered all these lectures and was somehow freed to comply with them. . . . It was eerie.

It is also eerie to write these lines now because countless times I have witnessed this identical cycle of Jeff's mind clouding and clearing and clouding again, as his psychic pendulum keeps swinging, which it now does at a much slower pace and with far less intensity. "Many ups and downs" indeed had been set in motion, with no resolution or lasting relief.

Jeff's frustrations stayed with me. My wish for him—simply to lighten up, cheer up, and move on—matched Dr. D'Andrea's strategy to forget about elaborate psychic excavations. I did, however, have one grave reservation. In 1960, I had come across a marvelous three-man team of researchers in Los Angeles, two psychologists and a psychiatrist, who had created the world's first suicide prevention center, a working model of the research-and-counseling institutions now available all over the country. I wrote about this ingenious and original work, learning along the way about the phenomenon that is our ninth-ranking cause of death and a leading cause of death among teenagers.

I had no reason to note in 1960 that half of all schizophrenics attempt suicide and that thirteen percent succeed, but in 1968 I remembered one component of panic that had been found common to just about all attempts to end life: the feeling of being hopelessly trapped, cornered, with no way out. That was how Jeff seemed to see his situation before the doctor prescribed the relaxation therapy. And Jeff had indicated to both my mother and me that he was flirting with the idea of putting himself out of his misery in the only known final way. These were my thoughts as I put them to Dr. D'Andrea:

I am aware that it isn't true, as commonly supposed, that people who talk about suicide are the ones who don't do it. This has heightened my anxiety on this score to a state of great fear. Jeff broods so much and has such a good imagination that I can't help but be greatly afraid that he might think himself into an emotional cul-de-sac from which he thinks there is no way out. My hunch is that, unless he has suddenly decided to "lay it on thick" for emotional effect, which is not his style—and has brought up suicide just as a grandstanding signal of his desperation—he might be the kind of careful planner who thought about suicide for some time and actually plans it as he does everything—with great care, precision, and intelligence.

Now his radically improved situation seemed to make such thoughts obsolete. Jeff appeared to have emerged from the depths of his crisis and been transported into a radiant, talkative, almost-reborn state. I had not then understood the term "mania," which was to come up often in subsequent years. I wrote Dr. D'Andrea:

> Jeff is fascinated by you and likes you very much. He says he has decided to become a psychiatrist himself. To my recollection, this is the very first time in his life that he has ever said he wanted to be anything. I don't think he ever wanted to be a "fireman" or something of that sort when he was small. He is dying to ask you whether there might be a summer job for him somewhere in your clinic, sweeping up or something of that sort.

It was the starting point of a search for identity that has not ended yet for my son, now in his midforties. He still talks at times of wanting to become a psychiatrist, although his continual rummaging through college catalogs in search of undergraduate courses suggests that he realizes he would, if and when he is ever able, have to start on a career path by turning back the clock and finishing college first.

His preoccupation and identification with psychiatry were flourishing when I came to Palo Alto for a brief visit in mid-March of 1968. His mania, not then recognized by anyone, much less mentioned, was overflowing. I was overjoyed that my "strong, silent type," my secretive son, was opening up like a flower going into bloom. No more monosyllables, interrogations, mealy-mouthed shying away from expressing opinions. Dikes had burst open, and I loved it. On my return East, I reported this to Dr. D'Andrea, whom I had found very relaxed and pleased about Jeff's progress when I visited him at his office:

Jeff continued to be not querulous, as you suggested, but incessantly talk-ative. He was very dogmatic, insistent, and a bit frantic about everything, displaying enormous intellectual energy—almost as if he felt compelled to make up for a lot of lost time. . . . His concept of "his problem" comes from a paperback he brought me. . . . It is about how to improve memory and contains one chapter about "stage fright." It suggests that at bottom the cause is usually an "inferiority complex" and that's what Jeff says his problem really is. He said he knew it was complicated: "Otherwise they wouldn't call it complex, would they?" He now thinks that psychiatry and talking things over with people [are] something of an "Open Sesame." I wish you could have seen him working on his "List of Fears" for you. I got a lot less worried when I saw him literally face his fears so thought-fully. . . . He said that some of the things he was telling you were "very shocking. . . ." He was amazed and delighted when I did his relaxation exercises with him. Considering his drive to cover a million subjects, his reasoning and concentration were, I thought, very good, although he had trouble listening to my attempts to get in a word edgewise now and then. Sometimes he just said, "Let's not talk about that now" and hopped on to some new set of thoughts.

In hindsight, it is easy to spot further traces of mania and general instabil-ity in this record of personality gyrations, but I was comforted by the thought that Jeff seemed to be finding anchorage in psychiatry, and perhaps a measure of transference to Dr. D'Andrea. I hoped the doctor was becoming something of a substitute father, easy to access locally, not busy in New York.

Barbara extended Jeff's support net. As woman's editor of the *New York Times Magazine,* she told one of the writers who contributed articles to her regular parent-and-child page that Jeff wanted to investigate psychiatry as a potential profession. Barbara wrote to Jeff about her New York writer-friend:

She got so enthusiastic that without telling me she called her husband, who is a psychiatrist, and he was so delighted to hear of a new recruit that he called me and said that if you would like, sometime when you are in town, he'll take you around the hospital for a day, let you sit in on conferences and then turn you over to one of the residents and let you spend a day with him going to class and assessing patients.

Jeff's response ran true to a pattern that even yet keeps him in shackles: when challenged by a real-life opportunity that would require him to take action and venture into new waters, he tends to back off, frequently into freshly provoked ambivalence or retreat. He did not take up the New York psychiatrist on his generous offer and managed, as quickly as he had embraced the profession, to eye his personal practitioner with suspicion. I reported to Dr. D'Andrea:

> While Jeff is reacting to psychiatry and open talk the way a reformed drunk talks about Alcoholics Anonymous, I found his present reaction toward you startling. At some point I said to him, "Why don't you ask your friend Dr. D'Andrea about that?" He said, "He's not my friend." "Oh, what is he?" "Well, he's more of a business associate. After all, we pay him, don't we?"

Not that Jeff had given up on psychiatry. He still hasn't. But he made clear even in 1968 that only hands-on therapy in direct support of people held any interest for him. When I happened to mention an official of the National Institute of Mental Health (NIMH), Jeff's comments were scathing.

"Oh, he's an administrator," he scoffed. "I wouldn't want to do that. I want to work with people and have my own private practice." The last four words recurred often in his conversation that week. The cause of his disenchantment with Dr. D'Andrea was slower to appear.

As issues of psychology came to capture Jeff's attention, so did his reading in the field. His brooding increased, and his anxiety returned after a brief respite. Dr. D'Andrea suggested that he buy a kit to help him perform transcendental meditation exercises at home, and Jeff did these faithfully, twice a day, twenty minutes each. The doctor explored Jeff's frustration about his perceived lack of popularity among his peers and his low ranking in the family power structure, finding food for discussion but not for great concern. His reading and brooding, however, led Jeff into darker directions.

He suggested to the doctor that he might be suffering from schizophrenia. Masking his surprise at this far-fetched hypothesis, the doctor asked Jeff how he had arrived at the thought. As usual, Jeff had read a book (he remembered it almost thirty years later: *Psychology for the Millions*, by A. P. Sperling, a doctor of psychology, published in 1946) and had written a book report about it for one of his classes.

"Why does one college youth develop schizophrenia in response to the struggles of adolescence while another survives it?" was a question in Jeff's reference work, which did not pretend to have an answer. How does the illness make itself known? "In the early stages the schizophrenic shows hypochondriasis, complexes, obsessions and all kinds of compulsions."

Complexes. Obsessions. Compulsions. Jeff found himself on familiar ground. The book offered answers about what was to come. "Later," it said, "these [symptoms] are replaced by a variety of grandiose and persecutory delusions." What did Jeff have to look forward to beyond that stage, according to this author? The outlook sounded catastrophic: "The last stages of schizophrenia are usually marked by degenerative loss of personality and intellectual faculties."

Dr. D'Andrea dealt with Jeff's self-diagnosis by the light of past experience.

"This guy is really scared," he remembered saying to himself, "but I saw no thought distortions. He was oriented. It's a danger sign, but I didn't see *that* level of problem."

It wasn't present, not then.

Unfairly or not, D'Andrea was in danger of being drawn into playing mediator between Jeff's mother and me. Whatever the background, the reasons for my parting from Edith had nothing to do with our children. Compromise would eventually settle the divorce quietly, and I firmly believe it did not connect with the unexpected, dramatic onset of Jeff's illness years afterward. But who could know for certain?

Later, Jeff did become a victim of his parents' split. We were battling over how much time Jeff was to spend in the East. Right or wrong, I had the false notion that Palo Alto was a land of easy living, also that Jeff needed a father on the premises, at least more of the time, along with exposure to the realities of the workaday world.

Having been rebuffed in her scheme to get her stepson acquainted with psychiatry, Barbara arranged for him to work as a summer replacement copyboy at the *New York Times*. But that ploy also fell through. After first agreeing with enthusiasm—Jeff knew the job was a plum, and the newspaper and the pay attracted him—he backed out politely. It was evident that he sensed his mother would be hurt if he were to become beholden to "the other woman." I asked Dr. D'Andrea to step between us and explained my rationale bluntly:

Because of proximity, the comfort and convenience of California, and other reasons, his mother's influence is too pervasive on Jeff. . . . I'm a necessary countervailing influence. If I give way, the problem-producing influences will grow further because it's so cozy and sheltering for Jeff. It seems to me that my role in Jeff's life should increase.

The pleasant doctor suddenly grew unpleasant. He would put up with none of what I had in mind. On April 1, 1968, he wrote:

> I felt there was considerable turmoil on Jeff's part in attempting to meet demands from both you and his mother. The competitive nature of the struggle seems very clear: I think that Jeff is attempting to work out a compromise and does not respond well to pressure either from you or his mother. He needs practice in deciding for himself. . . . What seems to be emerging is a picture of tremendous seduction and pressure from you (for very understandable and human reasons) which must force a contrast between your home and way of life and Jeff's present home and way of life, and probably throws a bad light on his present situation, which then must necessarily cause him to feel conflicted.

Turmoil? Struggle? Seduction? There was much more of this in the same letter, including "a seesaw of competition for affection."

I was absolutely flabbergasted. Having ducked into my own emotional foxhole, I had not remotely guessed at any of these perspectives or the storms I had inadvertently whipped up. Moreover, the normally mild-mannered psychiatrist firmly drew another line into the sandy terrain where I suddenly saw my son fencing for his adolescent soul. The doctor was sticking closely to his patient, refusing to be tugged into the case of father versus mother. His letter laid down the rules:

> As regards my forming some opinion about the suitability of his present home environment, I am not in a position to make such a judgment and doubt that I could be.

I felt relieved, even while absorbing the shock of the doctor's barrage of accusations. If that's how a competent professional saw Jeff's position, who was I to disagree? Besides, his judgment relieved me of considerable responsibility. I had begun to envision the crisis of a court fight for Jeff's custody, one that probably would have ended being costly and unsuccessful; courts in those days rarely awarded joint custody or more than visitation rights to fathers. And wasn't Jeff too close to the age of twenty-one—he was seventeen—to be angling for legal upheavals?

I had put my case forward, and perhaps it served everyone best that I had been slapped down hard. By way of reassurance, the doctor did have good words for his patient:

> Jeff has been coming along reasonably well with his therapy. He has experienced considerable relief of symptoms in almost all situations where he was experiencing anxiety, except in the situation of speaking alone in history. His ability to recite in French and in English classes has improved a good deal. He continues to feel generally well and optimistic about himself and the future.

As further consolation, Dr. D'Andrea acceded to my request that he see Edith, and on May 8 she wrote me about their meeting:

> He told me that he is working exclusively on Jeff's phobias (which he considers pretty well under control). . . . He seemed to have no ideas as to whether Jeff might benefit from sessions dealing with other topics. He said he would try to find out. I did draw the line at his comment that Jeff "would probably find it interesting." I told him I was all in favor of anything that would benefit, but that I would have to draw the line at psychiatry for fun. . . . The good old doc says that he cannot anticipate whether eventually Jeff will become more outgoing.

Having achieved reasonable headway with Jeff's "presenting problem," Dr. D'Andrea had also gotten everyone to calm down and benefit from a policy of accommodation, keeping the lines of communication open, enabling Edith and me to address Jeff's problems jointly. This unspoken agreement remains in operation thirty years later; we often confer on the phone about both of our sons.

I stopped my demands to shift the focus of Jeff's life to the East. Edith enjoyed the resulting peace. And Jeff soldiered on in reasonable comfort, doing his exercises and seeing D'Andrea much less frequently. In 1969, his first college year, he earned good grades at his mother's undergraduate school, the University of Rochester. His interest was shifting to political science, and for one semester during his sophomore year he taught a seminar, "The Kennedys and the Liberal Approach to Politics," attended by some fifty students. He organized a series of lectures by professors whom he recruited, assigned book reports on *The Greening of America*, by Charles Reich, and himself lectured on Theodore White's *The Making of the President*.

But his anxiety was returning. He still had stage fright. He tried a little marijuana to see if it would calm him down, which it didn't. He had trouble sitting still in class. And during the summer recess from Rochester, which he spent with Barbara and me in Manhattan, he organized his own sessions of what he considered psychoanalysis.

The analyst he appointed was me. It was a bizarre scene. For three or four weeks, every night after dinner, Jeff stretched out on the narrow bed in what had once been a tiny maid's room in the back of our old-fashioned apartment and proceeded to pour out—sometimes at a very rapid pace—chapter upon chapter of his life as he viewed it.

We invariably met for a couple of hours or more, usually until I fell asleep and he could no longer shake me awake. What I heard sometimes puzzled and occasionally shocked me. His account of his sibling rivalry with his older brother produced nothing dreadful, but the mutual antipathies he was baring were nastier than I had imagined.

Most startling were his occasional inferential disclosures about his relationship with his psychiatrist. I was too naive to believe that it was possible to be in psychiatric treatment without talking about one's past. It was. Whenever Jeff brought up a delicate subject—his early fears of masturbation, for example—and I asked what Dr. D'Andrea's comments had been, Jeff looked surprised and said he hadn't talked to the doctor about that.

My election to the job of substitute confessor eventually made me a bit uneasy, and I asked two psychiatrist friends whether I might possibly do damage. They assured me to the contrary. In fact, they were enthusiastic and fascinated, and eventually I relaxed because summer was over, and Jeff had calmed down quite a bit.

On his return to Palo Alto to enter Stanford in 1970, Jeff began to see Dr. D'Andrea again for phobias and anxiety, but by the spring of 1972, the doctor concluded that Jeff, while he was handling his life well enough, ought to receive more specialized help. The doctor thought Jeff would do better with someone practicing more specialized versions of the behavior therapy he had been receiving.

Jeff didn't mind. He had turned away from Dr. D'Andrea because he felt he was getting worse. He didn't believe the doctor when he told Jeff he was better and sent him off for the new therapy with a specialist, thinking that the end of all psychiatric treatment was near.

"He practically threw me out of the office," Jeff would remember bitterly. "With medical help like that, who needs to jump off a bridge?"

It was the overture to a cruel theme song that he hears in his inner ear even yet when his mood is low. The lyrics blame Jeff's messenger, his treater, for the message: That he is very ill. Like a medieval courier bringing bad news from the battle, the psychiatrist is beheaded.

This dilemma, I would soon discover, is a common one. Like many of his fellow sufferers, Jeff was held prisoner by perhaps the most hurtful of the many delusions set off in schizophrenia. Self-deception persuades him that the doctor is his enemy, not the disease, which he cannot comprehend.

CHAPTER 3

Meltdown

THE MESSAGE HAD been vague. I had just returned from a business trip in Europe and was told that Edith had called, that Jeff was in the hospital. I left for Palo Alto at once.

The scene within the sprawling, campuslike, modern Stanford Medical Center bore witness to the noisy traumas we see and hear these days on the emotionally unsettling television drama *ER*. Jeff was lying strapped onto a bed, bucking, trying to thrash about, yelling obscenities and fantasies more or less incoherently. Men and women in white dashed back and forth, looking grim. None seemed to notice that I was there, which reflected that my presence was in fact useless to Jeff and everyone else except his mother.

Before they had placed Jeff in restraints, she told me, he had dashed out of the hospital and had to be recaptured by the police.

His meltdown had overwhelmed him during the tour of duty of his second psychiatrist, Dr. X.* I'll call him that because we crossed him off our list of helpers early during the turmoil in that summer of 1972. His involvement

---

* Dr. X was the only one of Jeff's treaters who would not allow himself to be interviewed for this book.

illustrates the helplessness of psychiatrists and the families of mental patients whose illness is serious; the considerable variations of beliefs and practices among psychiatric subspecialties, even if the quality of care is pretty good; the understandable resistance of patients to their medications; and the diagnostic anarchy that so often governs the course of schizophrenia treatment.

I was always suspicious of Dr. X. Jeff disliked him from the start and nick-named him to suggest that he resembled an officer of the Nazi SS. The doctor's colleagues seemed not to like him either. "He's intoxicated with himself," said one of them, "he thinks he's God." Yet I found not a shred of evidence that Dr. X was anything less than a competent, experienced, and qualified therapist. And the doctors who didn't care for him personally knew of no grounds to criticize his work. Behavior modification, his specialty, was not generally a top-rated treatment, but this may have been because some of its adherents did not have medical degrees; Dr. X did. He had done sophisticated schizophrenia research in Europe. He was also generous in treating low-income Medicaid patients rejected by other doctors.

No question: schizophrenia can trap anyone, especially while the disease is still lying in wait.

To Jeff's old diagnoses of school phobia and anxiety there was now added the notion of acute depression. That was Dr. D'Andrea's assessment of Jeff's breakdown. D'Andrea, who had left private practice and had transferred to the Stanford Student Health Center, was in his second-floor office the morning Jeff's suicide (or pseudo-suicide) attempt landed his recent patient in the ground-floor infirmary. The doctor rushed downstairs, where Jeff's wounds were being sutured.

"I was surprised and very upset," D'Andrea said later. "It was a severe crisis and something new in his history. He needed to be hospitalized to find out what was going on."

How serious was the incident, as he saw it then?

"I could see no way leading to a disaster," the doctor told me in 1995, still shaking his head.

I have been able to reconstruct the developments leading up to Jeff's collapse, and the event itself, from accounts of several contemporaneous eyewitnesses and subsequent medical records.*

---

* The eyewitnesses include Edith Wyden, Dr. D'Andrea, Dr. Lorrin Koran, and, very recently, with surprising lucidity, Jeff himself.

"Desensitization" was the explanation D'Andrea and Dr. X offered Jeff as the reason for his malaise. Their strategy for dealing with the problem was behavioral techniques—hypnosis and exercises—which would render him insensitive to the stimuli that set off his fears.

In May 1972, Jeff received an explosive indication that behavior modification would not always lead to the promised land of painless relief for his troubles. The indicator was a movie he saw in downtown Palo Alto, *A Clockwork Orange*, Stanley Kubrick's version of the Anthony Burgess novel, usually classified as science fiction but frighteningly contemporary in execution.* The film was so unsettling to Jeff that he wanted to leave the theater. Spectators sitting next to him made it hard for him to pass, and so he watched how perfectly pleasant doctors used electrified headgear and repulsive images to desensitize Alex, a sweet-looking young hoodlum, out of his antisocial behavior. The scenes came across as very real. The experiment was successful with Alex, although the impact on his life was left ambiguous.

Jeff's identification with Alex became all-embracing. He equated the action of the film with the events of his own life. This was no hallucination. He knew precisely what he was doing: deliberately fleeing from dreaded reality to fiction. In a letter to his brother, Ron, then a congressman, he suggested that he was "spending my life acting out fictional plots."

It was the script's final line, shouted by Alex from his hospital bed, that would become a benchmark in Jeff's future. That day, he found it encouraging. In the years to come, he would refer back to it again and again with his many doctors and with me. Sometimes it became a question, sometimes a nagging expression of worry or impatience, sometimes an outburst of defiance. The catchword, however, never varied.

"Boy, am I ever *cured!*" cried Alex in the movie. Cured! That was Jeff's nirvana then. It still is. How understandable an obsession.

Beginning in the spring of 1972, Dr. X treated Jeff with hypnosis, at first twice a week, then three times. The method had by then attained respectability in medical practice, at least for some cases of such conditions as anxiety. Conventional psychiatrists considered it "stupid" for Jeff's condition, he was gratuitously informed, in a voice of firm authority, by the senior member of his subsequent hospital treatment team. Dr. X felt Jeff also needed medication and prescribed Tindal, a version of Stelazine, an early, powerful antipsychotic.

The medication did not improve relations between Dr. X and Jeff, who

* I did not see the film until 1996 and found its violence and sadism still profoundly disturbing as a social commentary, not only in its connection with Jeff.

was launching his decades-long passive (and later active) resistance against all potent antipsychotic drugs. The endemic difficulty with these drugs is euphemistically known as "side effects," a misleading, almost-mocking turn of language that serves as a smoke screen. For almost all patients, side effects are no sideshow. They are the palpable main event, beginning with dry mouth, drowsiness, and drooling, and usually escalating to much worse. As a result, patients refuse to take the medications and suffer relapses.

Psychiatrists have a forbidding term for the resulting vexation, which bedevils them daily. The conundrum is called compliance. The word would better fit the penal code, which is no accident. Secretly, doctors wish they could ethically and legally compel patients to accept all needed medications—a solution not feasible except for extreme cases of self-destructiveness. In practice, the problem surfaces with titration, determining dosage. Jeff wasn't given enough medication to stabilize his condition. But if he had been, he would have rebelled against the dosage or found ways to sabotage his "meds" altogether, as he so often did in later years.

As the deadline neared for Jeff to register for his senior year at Stanford, his anxiety mounted sharply, and his overall condition deteriorated. In a later report to one of his social workers, I summarized:

> Jeff didn't sleep after a while, spent most of his time pacing, ate nothing but ice cubes. Never had he been anywhere nearly as badly disturbed. Edith kept calling the doctor, warning him, telling him what was happening, and he simply told her to bug off.

Science has progressed since then and has exonerated parents of guilt in the process of triggering or encouraging mental illness in their kids. In the early 1970s, however, it was considered professionally acceptable, even sophisticated, to fend off attempts by parents of patients to participate in a family member's therapy.

Whether Jeff continued to take his prescribed medication that summer is not clear; he may have been carrying on his rebellion against pills even then, perhaps hiding them by "cheeking" and spitting them out later. I learned only that his anxiety kept worsening and that he eventually placed a panicky call to Dr. X, who told him, "You are having a psychotic break."

What Jeff remembers next is walking into his mother's bedroom in his pajamas at about six o'clock one September morning to announce that he had just phoned for an ambulance. He was bleeding. He had taken a sharp kitchen knife and cut himself—"viciously," he recalls. Systematically, he sliced his chest, throat, arms, wrists, abdomen, and both feet.

"So they can see I'm already harmed and they won't harm me any more," he explained.

Who were "they"?

"A coalition of the army, the police, and the psychiatrists" was how he recited his delusions for me in 1995. "They were going to kill all the Jews."

Jeff's recall of the paranoia that had seized him was not precise. "I was practically dead," he told me of the suicide's aftermath. Luckily, his wounds, when I saw them later, required only light, loose bandages. In his "vicious" terror, my son had still managed to be careful with himself.*

I don't know whether Jeff engaged Dr. X in talk about suicide or, indeed, about anything substantive, but Jeff did recall having been impressed late that summer by a suicide episode in the television series *M*A*S*H*. The text that he remembered made him think: "Suicide is painless and brings on many changes."

About two weeks after Stanford Hospital, lacking locked wards, declined to treat Jeff further, he was transferred to Twin Pines Hospital in nearby Belmont on San Francisco Bay.

Twin Pines was a pleasantly appointed private institution equipped with locked wards and a reasonably knowledgeable and decently behaved professional staff that didn't mind using potent medication generously. Under the onslaught of pills, Jeff had calmed down but otherwise had not noticeably improved. He made little sense. Most of the time, he was simply too drugged to be responsive—or to make trouble. More advanced treatment was indicated, and I tackled the search for it with zeal. Fortunately, I was not as helpless as so many other parents are.

One day I sat before a pile of quarters in a phone booth at Twin Pines, dialing and dialing until I ultimately got through to every psychiatrist known to me who might be able to advise Jeff's mother and me where to hospitalize him next.

I phoned Dr. R of New York Hospital-Cornell Medical Center, my own shrewd and bubbly psychotherapist, an authority on family therapy; he had

---

* In 1995 I learned from hospital records that the Stanford staff had correctly diagnosed schizophrenia. I don't remember having heard the word.

known—and liked—Jeff for some years because my sons participated in several of my very informative family group sessions with the doctor.

I solicited counsel from Dr. Bruno Bettelheim at his Chicago institution for autistic children; I had gotten along well with him when I had been his editor for four years at *Ladies' Home Journal,* having persuaded him to write a regular column on child-rearing.

I then called a handful of friends who were well-informed medical writers or editors. Through one of my author friends, a psychoanalyst, I also talked with Dr. Otto F. Will Jr., the director of Austen Riggs Hospital in Massachusetts, one of the best and most reputable treatment centers.

For each consultant I quickly summarized Jeff's recent past, the severity of his breakdown, his current state, and my concern in determining his future treatment.

Dr. Will was the speediest of the delegation, also the most cheerful and emphatic. He was a vastly experienced psychiatrist, but either he didn't believe that Jeff needed his hospital or he had no vacant beds. "Tell him to pull up his balls," advised this authority, offering no details but wishing us well. My conversation with him lasted four minutes.

Dr. Bettelheim reacted in his usual manner, as I had come to experience it: deliberate, courtly, exquisitely sensitive. (Not until after his death in 1990 did it become known that he had an uncontrollable temper and often viciously beat his young, autistic patients.) When I said I wanted Jeff to have the best, the Menninger Clinic in Topeka, he agreed that was a wise choice.

Dr. R, knowing me well, understood immediately that, barring some devastating and unexpected new information, I had really already made up my mind about Menninger. He offered no caveats—nor did anyone else.

In those days, the theoretical orientation of my consultant doctors did not concern me. Today it would worry me that Drs. Will and Bettelheim were steadfastly in the Freudian camp. The late Dr. R, who called his methods "eclectic," was, in truth, a super-Freudian. In my marriage therapy, he had proved wonderfully effective. But he had been trained at Columbia's Psychoanalytic Institute, often resorted to Freudian tactics, and, like Freud himself, had little experience with very sick psychotic patients.

And so Jeff's transfer to Menninger was in total disregard and ignorance of the institution's overwhelmingly psychoanalytic, Freudian bias. It was a fateful error because, even in 1972, when effective (if potentially toxic) medications had been widely in use for more than fifteen years as the only sensible means of treating psychoses, the doctors there did not believe in them. They would prescribe pills only grudgingly, in minimal dosages, or, preferably, not at all. The restraint was strange for an establishment taking pride in its scientific research and advances.

The Menninger predisposition showed itself the moment Edith, Jeff, and I were received by Jeff's "treatment team" on our prearranged arrival. The plane trip from California had been worrying because the folks at Twin Pines fretted about Jeff's hours in transit without medical supervision. They had medicated him heavily and given us several different medications for supplementary dosages as needed. They weren't. Jeff was sleepy and confused but nobody on the plane seemed to take notice, much less get upset.

Our hospital reception committee reacted otherwise. The delegates were monosyllabic, glum, and disapproving, especially of our reserve pill bottles. The principal hospital case summary noted: "He came in taking large doses of Stelazine, Thorazine, Haldol, Elavil, among others."

This is probably just sloppy writing, for if Jeff had been taking "large doses" of all these drugs on our journey from California, he would not have reached Topeka alive. It would be silly to quibble over semantics more than twenty-five years afterward. Noteworthy and beyond dispute, however, was the blatant air of disapproval, if not downright distaste, manifested by these helpers. They immediately held the patient in less-than-high regard; viewed his parents with suspicion that would manifest itself again and again; and displayed open contempt for their fellow professionals at Jeff's previous hospital.

The showing of disapproval and distaste for a victim of psychosis was nothing personal. It was and is a fundamental stance of many, perhaps most, psychoanalytic practitioners. But the fact remains that our greeters at once cut off and withheld appropriate treatment and thereupon blamed the patient for getting worse. According to hospital records, they tried to tranquilize Jeff with wet sheet-packs, Thorazine dosages of unstated size, and evidently nothing else until lithium, long clearly indicated for his manic moods, was added five months later. Jeff's response to his treatment was understandably poor, as the report states in what struck me as a slightly accusing tone:

> Following admission, [the patient] stated that he was "well" and wanted to leave. When this was discussed with him he became increasingly agitated and began pacing, intrusively talking to others, pushing and shoving and occasionally hitting others. . . . He seemed euphoric and unaware of the abrasive, abusive aspects of his behavior.

Although Edith and I were instructed not to visit during Jeff's ninety-day "evaluation" period, our initial reception had left me with an inkling that we had landed in a wrong place. So why didn't I insist on leaving this grumpy and snobbish collective? Why did I permit them, in effect, to refuse treatment to my son? Why didn't I take him elsewhere without delay?

The answer is that this was Dr. Karl's place. How could it be doing serious wrong? If that seems naive in these cynical days, I had better amend and extend my earlier comments about Dr. Menninger's commanding charisma and influence throughout his profession during my days of see-no-evil, hear-no-evil.

In person, Menninger's huge frame and basso profundo made one think of him as a force of nature. His large, rugged face belonged on Mount Rushmore. His warmth enveloped everyone, including the crusty rustics of the Kansas legislature and his enthusiastic admirer and deputy for the cleanup of the state mental hospitals in the 1940s, the brilliant Dr. Franklin D. Murphy. With help from his quieter psychiatrist brother, William, known as Dr. Will, Karl Menninger had unquestionably turned Topeka into the "psychiatric capital of the nation." In the early 1950s, Murphy, then dean of Kansas University Medical School, whom I knew and greatly respected, proclaimed: "Topeka today is probably the greatest psychiatric teaching center in the world." How grateful I was that I could count a great man like Dr. Karl as my friend and that he had created a mecca of psychiatry where my Jeff stood the world's best chance of getting well.

I would have been troubled had I known that when Dr. Karl was a psychiatrist-in-training he had remained so immature that he turned down an opportunity to be psychoanalyzed in Vienna, possibly by Freud. "I don't think that I have the courage to stay away from my mama that long," he wrote in a letter. That was only one indication of the doctor's insecurities. His worship of Freud was the outstanding example of blind subservience that brought Dr. Karl fame and simultaneously ordained misery for my Jeff and schizophrenics around the world. The genesis of this disaster, made public only recently, was in 1934.

Dr. Karl had traveled to Vienna to establish a relationship with Freud. His intermediary was his own analyst, Dr. Franz Alexander, who had also urged Menninger to take a "mistress." Attempting to chat with Freud in the garden of the master's Berggasse residence during their first meeting, Dr. Karl encountered instant rejection. He recalled that he found Freud, who was suffering from cancer of the jaw and detested Americans, "utterly impersonal. I don't believe he had the slightest idea to whom he was talking."

Unaware of his visitor's "narcissism" (Menninger's own word), Freud could not guess that Dr. Karl would not be deterred. He had a mission.

"I was a doctor from the hinterlands of America running a small hospital with my father and my brother," Menninger wrote with uncharacteristic humility, "trying to use some psychoanalytic principles in a psychiatric hospital."

Freud, of course, recognized that Menninger was referring mostly to schizophrenics sick enough to require hospitalization, and his reaction was flatly negative. He said that he "never had success with psychoanalysis on severely mentally ill patients." Dr. Karl was thereupon dismissed, and Freud never replied to his subsequent letters.

Paradoxically, Menninger embraced Freud's thinking. When the master died in 1939, Dr. Karl wrote an obituary in which he described himself as "more Freudian than Freud." A few months later, he wrote to Dr. Alexander: "Freud did not treat me very nicely, as you know, but nonetheless, I think his ideas, his grasp, his formulations are so infinitely ahead of anything else that has been proposed, that I have nailed my banner on his mast, and I'll defend it against assault for the rest of my life."

Serious assaults on Freudian thought would not begin until a revolt within the American Psychiatric Association (APA) in 1974, which happened to be the year Jeff was discharged from the Menninger Clinic under less-than-friendly circumstances. In the preceding decades, Dr. Karl's banner rode high. The country was gripped by what one leading anti-Freudian called Freudomania. The message of salvation by psychoanalysis was delivered by the columnist Walter Lippmann, the anthropologist Margaret Mead, the filmmaker John Huston, the pediatrician Benjamin Spock—and countless intellectuals.

Yet as long as their families had money, schizophrenics like Jeff were treated psychoanalytically by Freudians like Dr. Karl's people at Menninger, in defiance of Freud himself. It's hard to comprehend.

Dr. Karl's ideological leadership was by then long acknowledged by his admiring peers in many controversies within psychiatry, especially the treatment-determining question of diagnosis in psychoses. As late as 1963, he tossed that pivotal problem into the winds, writing: "We tend today to think of all mental illness as being essentially the same in quality, although differing quantitatively in external appearance."

Thus, Menninger was encouraging American psychiatrists in the 1960s to consider all seriously ill patients schizophrenic, a questionable practice at best. While diagnosis was more differentiated abroad, in the United States the psychoanalytic catchall was not subject to grumbling by insiders within the American Psychiatric Association until 1971, and the ensuing decade of organized attack and reform by biological practitioners did not begin to crystallize until later in the seventies.

I was oblivious to all this in 1972. I did not know of Dr. Karl's Freudian bias or his notions about diagnosis. I had not heard of the epic split between biological and psychodynamic psychiatry, didn't even know the applicable terminology; I was not specifically aware of the successes registered by antipsychotic medications beginning in 1955. Nor did I know that, as of the mid-1960s, Dr. Karl had been edged out of the Menninger Clinic's active leadership, not because of his pro-Freudian stand, which largely continues at the clinic to this day, but because he couldn't get along with the rest of his numerous kinfolk.

I was pleased and honored, I recall, to be sitting in his elegantly appointed private bungalow on the Menninger grounds sometime after Jeff entered the clinic. We were on a first-name basis. A few years earlier, Dr. Karl had written a long preface to a book of mine. Now it seemed to me that the seventy-nine-year-old Menninger was bestowing the sum of his wisdom on Jeff.

Sadly, not much was said. I remember slouching afterward to Jeff's pavilion feeling empty, disappointed. I was let down because I had expected to come away with some fresh insight, or maybe I was simply sad and depressed. The frequent, useless trips to Topeka were getting me down. Facing Jeff for so long in his unreachable, demented incarnation was not easy to take.

My world was changing. The money drain for Jeff's treatment, not to mention the incessant travel and other expenses, was serious. The uncertainty about his status—what was really ailing him?—was unnerving. The necessarily intensified intimacy with a long-divorced wife was difficult. And more disturbing adjustments in my relationships and values were to come.

Upon visiting Jeff and the treatment staff in Topeka with me, my psychological mentor, Dr. R, issued a judgment that was plain wrong and that, luckily, my instincts forced me to reject. We were settling into our DC-3 for the journey back to Kansas City and then on to New York when the doctor proclaimed on Jeff.

"Oh, he's a *yiddisher Kopf*,"* he exclaimed. "He's leading them around by the nose." He believed Jeff to be faking much of his illness. I can still hear the

---

* Literally, "Jewish head"; real meaning, "smart-ass."

sneer in his voice. And later, long after Jeff left Menninger, Dr. R gave me additional advice that sounded tempting but could have become ruinous to Jeff. The doctor accused me of having become overinvolved with my son's trouble. "Let the doctors handle it," he said. This would have meant parental abandonment, which, I can say with conviction, no kin of any mental patient should ever, ever fall back upon. To me, disengagement is out, especially with so many psychiatrists performing inadequately.

In Topeka, my loving, bright, amusing son was not just very ill, but he had also turned distant, cold, bitter, insultingly rude, and had acquired other distasteful qualities. It would have been easy to *dis*like him intensely and give him hell all the time.

I had not then come across a letter that Freud wrote in 1928, offering his private reaction to the personality handicaps of severely ill mental patients. To his Hungarian psychoanalyst friend István Hollós, he confided: "Finally I confessed to myself that I do not like these sick people, that I am angry at them to feel them so far from me and all that is human." It helped to know that even the sage, to whom nothing was supposed to be unspeakable, found it hard to speak to people like my Jeff and experienced them as less than human.

More than a quarter century after Topeka, it remains, at times, still a problem: How do you keep on loving a son who can be an unpleasant stranger? And more: back then and still recently, I kept thinking that my long job of raising this son was done. Instead, I am in my seventies, and the task continues.

CHAPTER 4

*What Really Ails
Jeff Wyden?*

SCHIZOPHRENIA. I remember perfectly the occasion when the word, stark and unqualified, seemed to echo off the walls in a psychiatrist's nondescript office at the Menninger Clinic in Topeka during the Christmas season of 1972. The doctor was a spare, pale, soft-spoken type with a neatly trimmed (Freudian?) beard and a melancholic expression that never varied in the two years during which I dealt with him often. I'll call him Dr. Y because I wondered even then why I put up with him.

Schizophrenia, the doctor said. In his formal *Case Summary (Diagnostic)*, dated December 28, 1972, to which I was given access years later, he described Jeff's overarching problem as "Schizophrenia, acute (295.4)."* I had no idea what that meant. I had never heard of anybody who had such an illness. It conjured up the term "split personality," whatever that might entail, and a hopeless outlook.

"What are his prospects?" I asked.

"Not very favorable," said the mournful Dr. Y.

---

* The number matched the code for "schizophreniform disorder" as defined by the generally accepted standard *Diagnostic and Statistical Manual*, or *DSM*.

My uninformed state at that time led me to draw two improper conclusions. In fact, contrary to conventional wisdom, schizophrenia is not related to the very rare condition known as multiple personality disorder, in which victims shift between two or more different personalities. And while the causes of, and a cure for, schizophrenia are unknown, it is eminently treatable. Even before the introduction of the latest drugs brightened prospects considerably, between twenty and thirty percent of patients (depending on what study is consulted) showed long-term improvement—a better treatability rate than for some forms of cancer.*

Nevertheless, the respected journal *Nature* called schizophrenia (in 1988) "arguably the worst disease affecting mankind, even AIDS not excepted." As I became acquainted with the illness, I found myself floundering in an exotic land whose inhabitants were engulfed in constant chaos and terror. They existed in a surreal elsewhere, a location more intricate than one or the other of two entities. The splitting that is usually mistaken as a division of the self is in fact Greek for "splitting of the *mind*." Schizophrenics consequently find it difficult to distinguish between their fantasies (hallucinations) and reality. Imprisoned in their mad, private universe, they are unable to think clearly or manage their emotions.

I used to believe, as most people still do, that schizophrenia is rare. But with fifty million sufferers worldwide, the disease represents a formidable threat. The incidence is much the same everywhere. Men and women are equally affected. So are the white, black, and Asian races. The onset is typically in early adulthood: between age seventeen and thirty in males and between twenty and forty in women. One-third to one-half of the homeless in America are schizophrenics (usually unmedicated). The disease is still something of a social taboo, rarely mentioned and encrusted by stigma. Yet whenever I talk about Jeff's illness without showing inhibitions, it turns out that almost everyone is aware of somebody with a schizophrenic friend or relative and seems relieved to talk about it.

The disease is responsible for 2.5 percent of *all* U.S. health costs as well as most mental hospital beds. The total economic burden for the United States amounts to $32.5 billion a year, which includes treatment, reduced work time, cost of caregiving and other services, and lost productivity due to premature death. It is the costliest disease on earth.

---

* Outcomes would be appreciably better if so many patients did not relapse after going off their medications, as some seventy percent habitually do.

Investigations into the multiple, complex roots of schizophrenia are among the most intensively pursued explorations in contemporary medicine. Most probably, the cause is a bundle of syndromes with differing origins—none as yet fully understood. Structural and chemical brain abnormalities are among responsible factors, probably originating during a mother's prenatal or perinatal periods. Genetic causes are most likely to blame in an unknown minority of cases. Viruses are under suspicion, possibly including those transmitted by house cats. Acute malnutrition has also been blamed.

Because of the many uncertainties, schizophrenia research, until a few years ago, was known as the graveyard of neuropathologists, and to this day severe disappointment remains an occupational hazard for doctors who decide to treat schizophrenic patients. Some thirty percent of them still do not respond to *any* medications. About one-half become noncompliant at least some of the time. About three-quarters eventually discontinue medications unilaterally. And ignorance about many aspects of the illness persists. In a 1996 national survey by the National Alliance for the Mentally Ill (NAMI), fifty-seven percent of respondents said they believe that schizophrenia is caused by parental treatment—a remarkable sign of backward thinking.

In 1972, when I was compelled to start familiarizing myself with this vexatious territory, my mind-set about psychiatrists was two sided. The quiescent part of me was intimidated. Psychiatrists had medical degrees. They had to undergo long training and clinical experience and could therefore be presumed to know what they were doing. Also, as I was quickly learning, these authorities disliked back talk and considered it suspicious. They viewed it as "resistance," which is frowned upon because it denies their supreme wisdom and raises questions in their skeptical minds about the mental health of whoever dared to challenge their pronouncements.

So my respectful layman's self considered it wise to tread with care, to stay on the psychiatrist's benevolent side, because he was obviously a potent influence on what his profession calls "outcome." It is a mild term, yet it means everything: the patient's future and what it holds—sanity or madness, function or dysfunction, independence or dependency, sometimes life or death. A "not very favorable" outcome pronounced by Dr. Y was extremely frightening, for I had learned that every treater's outlook by itself exercises a profound influence on outcome.

All too often, the vitally important factor of "outlook" can be reduced to the simplistic formula of a glass being seen as half full or half empty. I had picked up this kernel of wisdom from Albert Stunkard, M.D., then chairman of psychiatry at the University of Pennsylvania Hospital and later at Stanford. The crucial full-versus-empty formula did not originate with him, of course, but it was revealed to be a cliché of his craft often unknown to patients and their kin.

Stunkard's formula came to mind when I sat slumped before Dr. Y, the depressed prophet at the Menninger hospital: the prognosis, as the treater views it, pretty much determines a patient's fate. The more enthusiastic and optimistic the doctor, the better the patient's chances of recovery. Dr. Y was obviously attuned to this truth. When I blurted out the professional secret that Dr. Stunkard had shared with me, Dr. Y's usual poker face displayed no reaction, but his comeback was instant.

"We'll just have to watch that," he replied smoothly.

In retrospect, I suppose I should have protested more; I should have reminded him that pessimism often turns into a self-fulfilling prophesy and thus into failure. I didn't speak up, I suppose, because I was only beginning to learn the delicate art of managing psychiatric case managers. At times, common sense dictates that these would-be gods need very badly to be managed, much as a parent's resistance can become a projection of a doctor's own resistance. This possibility had barely dawned on me then. But even in 1974, when my money had run out to pay for the pricey Menninger treatments, I somehow mustered enough inner strength (or chutzpah) to challenge the pronouncements of the Topeka doctors. Since then, I have often, on carefully considered occasions, revolted against professional counsel, and have never had to regret such a move.

On December 17, 1974, I sent a bitter letter to Jeff's social worker at Menninger. It was at the time when my son, long grossly undermedicated and still dysfunctional, was about to be discharged from the hospital at my insistence and over the doctor's resistance. To spare myself an unproductive confrontation, I communicated my farewell to the dreary doctor by sending him a carbon copy of the same letter. I had hit one of the lowest of the many low points in the decades with Jeff's illness. The doctor had almost succeeded in getting me down, but I had one final blast left in me.

"Enthusiasm is a quality that I have found distinctly lacking in Dr. Y," I wrote, "and it is a necessary, even vital, ingredient in Jeff's or anybody else's treatment, as I've said over and over again."

I had been learning about psychiatrists, if not about Jeff's diagnosis, which had mysteriously changed since his admission to the hospital. The "discharge summary" said: "Schizophrenia, chronic, schizo-affective type, 295.7," as defined by the *DSM*. I was never notified of this shuffle—"acute" had turned into "chronic." I discovered it when I saw the papers many years after the fact. Nobody then really knew how much difference the change made; nobody knows now, not exactly.

Fresh evidence of the chaos hit me on the phone in May of 1995. I was bringing my friend Skip Pope up-to-date on Jeff's ever-fluctuating status, as I do at least once a month. Skip is as shrewd a clinician and as loyal a supporter as I'd ever found among the fifty or sixty psychiatrists with whom I've come in professional contact since Jeff was first diagnosed as schizophrenic twenty-three years ago.*

I was telling Skip that, to my happy surprise, Jeff seemed lately to have turned somewhat calmer, clearer, and more insightful. I wondered aloud whether perhaps his latest antipsychotic medications had required an unusual length of time to penetrate his system or whether we might be witnessing the first hint that his disease was very slowly beginning just to wear away on its own. Studies had found that—for reasons unknown—this is the fortunate fate of some patients as they reach their midforties.

Skip brushed away these backseat-driver speculations and shook me considerably.

"Oh, you know," he shot back in his accustomed machine-gun delivery, "Jeff isn't really schizophrenic. He has a particularly malignant case of manic-depressive disorder."

I was floored by this strange and sudden news, especially because of its source. His irreverent nickname notwithstanding, he is a specialist's specialist, one of the more widely quoted researchers and practitioners in psychopharmacology, author of some two hundred articles in professional journals, on staff at McLean Hospital and Harvard Medical School all his working life. His full name is Harrison G. Pope Jr., M.D.

Hyperenergetic and precise, Skip was recognized for his writings on the diagnosis of schizophrenia. His best-known paper, written with his friend Dr. Joe Lipinski, "Diagnosis in Schizophrenia and Manic-Depressive Illness," published in the July 1978 *Archives of General Psychiatry*, is considered a landmark, though its estimate that forty percent of alleged schizophrenics are mis-

---

* The precise count of this multitude can no longer be reconstructed. Jeff once compiled a list by name of doctors he remembered actually treating him; his catalog ran to thirty-two.

diagnosed remains controversial.* Jeff's attending psychiatrist in California, for example, does not agree that my son is manic-depressive.

Attention must be paid to Skip. He has treated uncounted schizophrenics and manic-depressives. He is also as accessible and responsive a physician as I have ever known. As my personal outside consultant, he had been counseling me on Jeff's treatment for six years, talking with Jeff by phone, seeing him when other business took him to the West Coast, and talking regularly (and tactfully) with the doctors attending Jeff directly—a delicate act of kibitzing since many psychiatrists, if by no means all, consider themselves to be God and tend not to welcome assistant gods.

In my frequent communications with him, Skip seemed invariably to stand by his fax machine, poised to pounce into action. We have cowritten letters on Jeff's behalf to hospitals and other authorities. We routinely conspire to determine whether he or I should make the first call to another consultant, California administrator, or pharmaceutical company.

So, what was suddenly going on in his mind? The understanding had always prevailed in my family that Jeff was schizophrenic. Belatedly, we had this on high and expensive authority. It became a truth never questioned, like my readily measurable tendency toward elevated blood pressure. Why was my son now supposedly not schizophrenic after all? Had dozens of doctors and hospitals been grossly in error for twenty-three years? How could so many identical accidents have befallen him?

If he was indeed manic-depressive, a less serious and much more readily treated condition than schizophrenia, why did Jeff still require high dosages of clozapine, a dangerously toxic drug, authorized only for "treatment-resistant" schizophrenics? And how come he was, despite recent improvement, still totally and consistently dysfunctional, 100 percent disabled as defined by Social Security law eligibility, unable to perform any work, not even gentle volunteer duties, or to live on his own outside his halfway house?

This may strain credulity, but it is demonstrably true: nobody, not Skip, not any of the other most highly regarded internationally renowned researchers, absolutely nobody, knows precisely what schizophrenia really is or how to diagnose it unambiguously, no matter what profound opinions are tossed

* From Dr. Pope's summary of this paper: "We conclude that most so-called schizophrenic symptoms . . . have remarkably little, if any, demonstrated validity in determining diagnosis, prognosis, or treatment response in psychosis. In the United States, particularly, overreliance on such symptoms alone results in overdiagnosis of schizophrenia and underdiagnosis of affective illnesses, particularly mania."

about, sometimes with vehemence. The cause of the illness is an even less penetrable mystery for which the most illustrious specialists have proposed a bewildering variety of notions, some of them outlandish, for more than one hundred years.

A lot seems to depend on the direction in which a specialist's idiosyncratic subspecialty has led him.

"We just stagger along," said Skip in a moment when he let his guard down a bit.

We aren't simply dealing with a question of labeling and semantics, for this much is beyond dispute: diagnosis, no matter how questionable or wrong, determines treatment, and treatment determines outcome.

"So what do you think about psychiatrists after your years with Jeff?" a friend once asked me.

I thought about Dr. X, Dr. Y, Dr. D'Andrea, and all the rest.

"They're not great," I said, "but we'd be a whole lot worse off without them."

Skip had been correct: they just stagger along as best they can, and that includes the care of famous patients of public high visibility.

He was a young man; bright, personable, but also anxious and listless. He was something of a loner, obsessed with an attractive young woman who would have nothing to do with him and with a brutally violent movie that he viewed sixteen times. A doctor gave him Valium to counteract "stress," and a psychiatrist assured his parents that he was merely immature and would outgrow his quirks without further professional help.

The young patient was not Jeff Wyden, as readers might suspect from the similarities of the two cases. He was John Hinckley Jr., who attempted to assassinate President Ronald Reagan in 1981 and left the White House press secretary James Brady permanently disabled.

In John's hometown, Evergreen, Colorado, in the countryside twenty-five miles west of Denver, his psychiatrist, Dr. John Hopper Jr., had told Hinckley's parents that their son was spoiled. He needed to have his apron strings cut, the doctor counseled, and should be sent away from home permanently. John's father and brother disagreed. They eventually came to believe that John was so troubled that he had to be hospitalized. A struggle with Dr. Hopper ensued. "Don't do it," the doctor warned. "I've worked in these hospitals, and I've worked with people who've come out of them. It makes adjustment to the real world that much harder. If you put him in a hospital, you'll be making an emotional cripple out of him."

The psychiatrist's word carried weight with John's father, Jack Hinckley, a wealthy oilman, so when the distraught son returned once again from his wanderings to the Denver airport, Hinckley Sr. told him: "You can't come home." The scene broke the father's heart at the time and triggered horrendous guilt feelings after the assassination attempt. The father thought his edict became the basis of his son's murderous notions, which was demonstrably untrue. It was a fact, however, as Hinckley's lawyer pointed out at the son's trial, that with the airport encounter John's "last anchor to reality was severed."

While Dr. Hopper's trivializing of John's condition illustrated the capriciousness of diagnosing schizophrenia, the totally contradictory psychiatric testimony at the trial could not have laid bare the conflicts governing this art in more dramatic fashion.

In their book, *Breaking Points*, the senior Hinckleys summarized the key testimony of the principal doctors, all of whom had examined John at length: "Dr. Bear, with the prestige of Harvard Medical School behind him, had concluded: 'It is a psychiatric fact that Mr. Hinckley was psychotic.' Dr. Dietz, equally of Harvard Medical School, had testified: 'Mr. Hinckley has not been psychotic at any time.' " Dr. Sally Johnson, a government psychiatrist, diagnosed that Hinckley was afflicted with only a relatively mild "personality disorder." Dr. William T. Carpenter Jr. testified that the defendant suffered from the slowly developing devastating illness then called "process schizophrenia," with a notoriously poor prognosis.

Of the expert witnesses, Dr. Carpenter, director of the Maryland Psychiatric Institute, was by far the most experienced in schizophrenia research and care. Indeed, he was the most punctilious and respected of the specialists in the diagnosis of schizophrenia. Carpenter had spent forty-five hours with the defendant before the trial and three days testifying on the witness stand.

John Hinckley was found not guilty by reason of insanity in June 1984. When his parents went on their speaking tour on behalf of the National Alliance for the Mentally Ill (NAMI), they pointed out that $170 a year was spent on every cancer patient for cancer research, $150 for every heart patient, and $7 for every mental patient. As of summer 1996, John Hinckley was still indefinitely confined to St. Elizabeth Hospital, a government mental institution in Washington, and had never been granted leave. However, he held a job in a hospital ward and, according to his attorney, had not been given any antipsychotic medication for some time.

During the first two years of his hospitalization, Hinckley survived three suicide attempts. His obsession with Jodie Foster continued; a search of his hospital room in 1987 uncovered fifty-seven photos of her. His hunt for fame, however notorious, also did not subside. In 1995 he participated enthusiastically in an arrangement that would eventually yield him television exposure with Barbara Walters and a book. Proceeds from this "intellectual capital" would go to James Brady, the still-disabled Reagan press secretary, and two others injured in the attempted assassination.*

The publicity enjoyed by the patient was consistent with his latest cheerful and surprising diagnosis. Hospital psychiatrists told the *New York Times* that Hinckley merely suffered from "a narcissistic personality and delusions of grandeur." The verdict of hopeless deterioration from process schizophrenia had evaporated as if it had never appeared in the record.

And still, uncertainty about Hinckley's fundamental state continued. In the summer of 1997, a federal judge denied him the privilege of unescorted visits to his family's home because "he has deceived those treating him in ways too numerous to recount."

Also controversial, still today, are the circumstances surrounding the tragic misdiagnosis of another notable personage: Rosemary Kennedy, sister of President John F. Kennedy. At seventy-seven, she is alive in a near-vegetative state in a rural Jefferson, Wisconsin, nursing home, more than fifty years after a needless, mutilating frontal lobotomy secretly ordered by her immensely wealthy, dictatorial father, Joseph P. Kennedy.

From childhood on, Rosemary offended her father by being different— unable to keep up with the activism and competitive exuberance rampant in her family. She had trouble with her baby spoon. She was slow in school, starting in the first grade. She was retarded. Her father banished her from home, out of his sight, to be cared for by family friends.

Beginning at twenty-one, the same age when Jeff's difficulties broke open, Rosemary experienced dramatic behavior changes. She was no longer her sweet self. According to her aunt, she had "wild moods," "tantrums, then rages." She was "pacing up and down" and became "a wild animal, given to

---

* The connection between schizophrenia and violent behavior is receiving increasingly methodical investigation. A worldwide 1996 study found that schizophrenic patients were five times more likely than people in the general population to have been convicted of violent crimes. A Finnish study concluded that the risk of committing a homicide was about ten times greater. Drugs and alcohol were implicated as important exacerbating factors. So, crucially, was the absence of medication.

screaming, cursing and thrashing out at anyone who tried to thwart her will. Every day there would be one terrifying incident after another: physical fights where Rosemary would use her fists to hit and bruise people." In the summer of 1941, on the porch of the family compound at Hyannis, Massachusetts, she suddenly hit and continued to kick her tiny, white-haired grandfather, Honey Fitz, until she was pulled away.

In 1988 the research psychiatrist Dr. E. Fuller Torrey would write: "Rosemary Kennedy apparently had developed a psychosis, either schizophrenia or manic depression psychosis, in addition to her mild retardation." Whatever the diagnosis, in 1941 her condition was threatening enough to Joe Kennedy's sense of invulnerability and the presidential ambitions he was nurturing for his sons. Firm steps had to be taken, especially since Rosemary had a full figure, pleasant features, and was in danger of getting pregnant.

"She was the most beautiful of all the Kennedys," recalled Ann Gargan, Kennedy's niece. "She had the body of a twenty-one-year-old yearning for fulfillment with the mentality of a four-year-old. She was in a convent in Washington at the time, and many nights the school would call and say she was missing, only to find her out walking around the streets at 2 a.m. Can you imagine what it must have been like to know your daughter was walking the streets in the darkness, the perfect prey?"

Rosemary's father enlisted Dr. Walter J. Freeman and Dr. James W. Watts, the most prominent and publicized practitioners of what was rapidly becoming a fashionable treatment for severe mental disorders. It is unclear what Kennedy really thought was ailing his daughter, for the doctors never listed mental retardation as appropriate to be treated by frontal lobotomy. They did treat schizophrenia and other psychoses. By "cutting the matter of each frontal lobe" of the brain, the two operators said they relieved "mental symptoms," allowing "the personality to appear in purer form." Changes in "energy and intelligence" were said to be negligible. Retardation was nowhere mentioned in the large literature on lobotomies.

"Psychosurgery" was a term introduced by a Portuguese neurologist and diplomat, Dr. Egas Moniz, brilliant, haughty, driven to be world famous. He had achieved stature as the father of angiography when, unexpectedly, at age sixty-one, his career took another turn. It happened at the Second International Congress of Neurology in London in August 1935. A doctor from Yale University was describing an operation on the frontal lobes of an agitated female chimpanzee. The Yale professor was concerned with the monkey's learning capacity, but Moniz was fascinated by emotional changes that the Yale man also reported: the monkey had become calm and cheerful.

Moniz returned home and shortly thereafter, assisted by a local neurosurgeon, he performed his first prefrontal lobotomy on a mental patient in a Lisbon hospital. Within a year, the surgery was popular in more than half a dozen other countries, and in 1949 Moniz was awarded the Nobel Prize. He had pioneered the ultimate tranquilizer—relief for patients whom no treatment had helped before.

While abstracting French articles for the *Archives of Neurology and Psychiatry* in the spring of 1936, Dr. Freeman came across Moniz's first summary of his work in a Paris medical journal, describing the successes of the revolutionary new surgery. Freeman believed in decisive action. He shared the report with Watts, communicated with Moniz, and decided to start performing the operation as a team with Watts upon return from their summer vacation.

By the time Joseph Kennedy asked them to operate on Rosemary in the fall of 1941, the pair had undertaken sixty-six prefrontal lobotomies. All told, Freeman performed or supervised about four thousand of the more than forty thousand lobotomies performed in the United States between 1936 and the late 1950s, many of them on schizophrenics. Fatalities were less than two percent, and while most patients were said to have "recovered" or "improved," the vast majority became dysfunctional zombies—like Rosemary Kennedy.

Full details of her surgery remained a closely guarded secret. Even Rose Kennedy, Joe's wife, did not know for years that surgery had been performed on the daughter to whom she had dedicated her 1974 memoir, *Times to Remember*. Rosemary was not otherwise mentioned publicly by the family, but a book by Ronald Kessler finally broke the security barrier in 1996. In *The Sins of the Father*, a biography of Joseph Kennedy, Kessler disclosed that he had taped a candid interview about Rosemary's operation with Dr. Watts on October 13, 1994, shortly before the doctor's death.

Rosemary was only mildly sedated, the doctor told Kessler. "We went through the top of the head. I think she was awake . . . I made a surgical incision in the brain through the skull. It was near the front. It was on both sides." Kessler reported: "The instrument Dr. Watts used looked like a butter knife. He swung it up and down to cut brain tissue."

The extent of the cutting was determined by what surgeons call the empirical method, meaning rough *estimate*. "I would make the incisions," Dr. Watts told Kessler, "and Dr. Freeman would estimate how much to cut as she talked. He talked to her. He would say, 'That's enough.' " Dr. Freeman had been asking Rosemary to recite the Lord's Prayer or count backward. When she became incoherent, the doctors stopped.

Among physicians, lobotomies aroused a furious debate. In May 1940, an editorial in the *Medical Record* called the procedure "radically wrong . . . meddlesome surgery . . . a violation of the Hippocratic oath," which ultimately became the prevailing medical opinion. At the time of Rosemary's surgery, however, the profession largely rallied to support Drs. Freeman and Watts. They were denied permission to do the operation at the government's St. Elizabeth Hospital, but the profession's great arbiter, Dr. Adolf Meyer of Johns Hopkins University, held that "available facts are sufficient to justify the procedure in the hands of responsible persons."

What lent the most legitimacy to psychosurgery (until the late 1950s, when tranquilizers and neuroleptics made lobotomies clearly unnecessary) was an editorial in the *Journal of the American Medical Association* published in the year of Rosemary Kennedy's surgery, 1941. It held that lobotomy was justified when chances of remission were remote.

Remission from what? Mental retardation was nowhere mentioned in the lobotomy discussion. What, then, was wrong with Rosemary? In his interview with Kessler, Dr. Watts confirmed that retardation was not in his mind when he operated. He believed that the patient was mentally ill. "It may have been agitated depression," the doctor ventured, using a term long discarded. He was not asked about schizophrenia.

The surgery was a disaster. According to Rosemary's mother, Rose, it "had the effect of leaving Rosemary permanently incapacitated." Ann Gargan elaborated: "You could see by looking at her that something was wrong, for her head was tilted and her capacity to speak was almost gone. There was no question now that she could no longer take care of herself."

Her father always maintained a diagnosis of mental retardation. "Joe orchestrated an elaborate cover-up," Kessler wrote in his biography. The father told historians that Rosemary taught retarded children. Later he told *Time* magazine that she suffered from aftereffects of spinal meningitis. The Kennedys made themselves the angels of mental retardation. They became prominently identified with the cause and financed research with gifts of up to seventeen million dollars at a time.

Kessler elicited the truth from Dr. Bertram S. Brown, a former director of the National Institute of Mental Health, and, as special assistant to President Kennedy, executive director of the President's Panel on Mental Retardation.

"There was a basic attempt to deny that the sister had any mental illness, meaning crazy," Dr. Brown told Kessler. "There was a hatred of psychiatry, because mental retardation was more acceptable to them."

No doubt Rosemary Kennedy was slightly retarded, but the records make clear that she also became schizophrenic in her early twenties. The radical behavior changes recorded at that time are too suggestive to believe otherwise.

The diagnosis for Marilyn Monroe is less firmly documented, but evidence exists that she, too, suffered from schizophrenia, along with other conditions.

Of the several serious Monroe biographies, *Goddess,* by the British author Anthony Summers, digs into her life most deeply and with the most insight. His work benefited from having been researched in the 1980s, almost a quarter of a century after Marilyn's death, and its reportorial energy brought forth frankness from contemporaries who knew the anguished actress intimately and remained fascinated by her tragedy:

- Photographer Milton Greene: "She was going out of her mind."

- Screenwriter Nunnally Johnson: "Monroe is something of a zombie. Talking to her is like talking to somebody underwater." Years later Johnson again imagined her "ten feet underwater. . . . You can't get through to her."

- Historian Arthur Schlesinger was struck by the same qualities: "One felt a terrible unreality about her—as if talking to somebody underwater. . . . She was most agreeable . . . then she receded into her own glittering mist."

- Hal Schaefer, a musician friend: "She struck me as . . . not being altogether in this world, not all there."

- Author Kenneth Tynan: "Monroe was not far from being a madwoman."

- To Billy Travilla, her dress designer, she said: "You know, I'm losing a piece of my mind each day. My brains are leaving me."

Throughout her crises, her adoring public and her profit-hungry film-maker employers willed Marilyn to be brilliant, witty, and well. For a 1956 *Time* cover story, the magazine's Hollywood reporter, Ezra Goodman, spent weeks interviewing old friends, teachers, colleagues, and psychiatrists. *Time* ignored most of the downbeat facts and instead marveled at her talent, even though Goodman felt that anyone less popular would be "ending up a schizophrenic in a state mental hospital."

The diagnosis of schizophrenia seemed to fit symptoms described by some of Summers's eyewitnesses: withdrawn from reality, depressed to the point of despair; chronically suicidal; neglectful of her person because of absent self-esteem; torn by paranoid delusions. All these burdens were superimposed on Marilyn's addictions: prescription drug abuse through massive doses of uppers and downers, promiscuity, and alcohol.

Schizophrenia was constantly on the mind of her principal doctor, Ralph Greenson, the Los Angeles psychoanalyst who treated Monroe during the two years before her pill overdose suicide in 1961. Greenson was an effusive, theatrical character, outlandish for a psychoanalyst and thus controversial among his peers. Born Romeo Samuel Greenschpoon in Brooklyn, he received excellent training at Columbia and in Berne, Switzerland. During the war he served as chief of the neuropsychiatric service at an army hospital in Colorado, later sharing his experiences with his friend Leo Rosten, who converted him into the hero of a hilarious best-seller, *Captain Newman, M.D.*

Like many of Monroe's friends and colleagues, Greenson was moved by her exceptional infirmity. He had grown wealthy analyzing many neurotic stars, but the thirty-four-year-old Monroe struck him as especially pitiful, a "fragile waif." Her case consumed him. His sessions with her sometimes lasted four or five hours, and he often analyzed her seven days a week. "I had become a prisoner of a form of treatment that I thought was correct for her, but almost impossible for me," the doctor would write to a colleague. "At times I felt I couldn't go on with this."

At no time would he venture a definitive diagnosis for the records. Nor did he ever prescribe Thorazine or Stelazine, effective antipsychotics that had been in use for several years, though very rarely then by psychoanalysts. He treated her psychoanalytically as if she was schizophrenic, even though Freud himself, as we know, had long ago ruled out psychotic patients as too inaccessible for his methods. After Monroe's death Greenson described her in a letter to another psychiatrist as ailing from "extremely weak psychological structures . . . ego weakness, and certain psychotic manifestations, including those of schizophrenia."

Categorizing her as a permanent psychiatric emergency, Greenson made dramatic concessions to her condition, unusual departures from psychiatric practice, most especially from psychoanalysis. He opened his home to Marilyn and welcomed her into it like a daughter. He asked his family, especially his daughter, to befriend her. Often, he had the patient stay for dinner with his wife and children and made himself available virtually around the clock for house calls to the hospital-like protective environment that he organized for the Monroe home. While the residence was clearly not suicide-proof, it was more secure than the psychiatric hospitals in which Marilyn had been periodically confined, sometimes in restraints.

Greenson's widow later said that the doctor adopted Monroe to provide a little of what she seemed to need most: security, a sense of belonging. As Freud had predicted, it didn't work, and after Monroe's death Greenson became a target of considerable criticism. Psychoanalysis was still ruling his profession, especially in the affluent entertainment colony, but biological psychiatry was beginning to make inroads, and its practitioners seized the opportunity to criticize a leading rival.

Dr. Robert Litman in Los Angeles offers insight into the medical side of Monroe's diagnostic riddle. Litman was the psychiatrist member of the triumvirate who in 1960 created the first of the world's suicide prevention centers, now in use in many jurisdictions. A year later the team was assigned by the Los Angeles County coroner to perform a "psychological autopsy" of Monroe. Litman investigated her case management by the many psychiatrists who had tried to control her condition over the years. He traced her treatment to its beginnings in New York, where some of her doctors viewed her as "borderline," a still officially accepted state defined as very nearly psychotic. Others classified her as suffering from "pseudo-neurotic schizophrenia," a definition so loose that it is no longer employed. An unadorned schizophrenia diagnosis was discussed by several of the doctors, and her psychoanalyst, Dr. Marianne Kris, said it was a "possibility."

"The prominent symptoms were anxiety and compulsiveness," Litman explained, "but underneath the anxiety was a breaking up of thought and feeling."

"At bottom, wasn't she really schizophrenic?" I asked him years later, "with Greenson barely keeping a lid on the illness by his intensive attention and confining her to what was really a private hospital?"

"It's possible," said Litman carefully, but he preferred the "borderline" diagnosis.

I said I was surprised. "Well, she didn't have hallucinations," he began. "She had no social dysfunction, no flattened affect or other negative symptoms, and she was functioning, working."

I cited the testimony of delusions from the many intimates interviewed for *Goddess* and reminded Litman of the heroic—and often futile—nonstop efforts required to keep Monroe haltingly at work on her films.* Whereupon he delivered an epitaph for Monroe: "Diagnosis is such a pseudo-science, we don't really know anything."

No wonder Jeff Wyden's diagnosis kept shifting.

---

* More than forty years after his divorce from Marilyn Monroe, the playwright Arthur Miller, eighty-one, was still ruminating about the mental state of the star he had nursed through the making of her most memorable movies. He was inclined to believe the belated diagnosis that schizophrenia had held sway underneath all her ailments. The idea was not new to him.

"I often wondered about that," he once told me.

What, in particular, caused him to wonder?

"It was the sharpness of the shift in her moods. She could turn around on a dime."

Why had he not pursued his suspicions?

"It was hopeless. It was as though what she internally determined was not related to the outside."

It was as telling as any description of schizophrenia.

CHAPTER 5

The Godfather:
Emil Kraepelin

THE CAPRICIOUSNESS of the disease reinforced my resolve to understand what was happening to Jeff, to acquaint myself with all evidence I could muster. What was the history of this phenomenon? Who were the pioneers, the heroes, the villains, and what did they think? Why were even the questions about its treatment—not to speak of answers—so vague? My reading led me to a strange genius and to a few answers, but mostly to more questions.

It is a commonplace that schizophrenia usually strikes with little or no warning in the late teens or shortly thereafter. To this day, nobody knows why. The characteristic onset of the disease was documented at the turn of the century. Together with a cornucopia of other basic data then unknown, the telltale evidence emerged from thousands of six-by-nine, case-record index cards scribbled by an obscure psychiatrist at the Munich University Hospital: Emil Kraepelin.

Kraepelin died in 1926, but in the minds of today's schizophrenia researchers he is very much alive, a daily reminder of what they have discovered and all that remains inscrutable about the elusive target in their lives. The professor's austere likeness, his handlebar mustache bristling in the manner of his idol, Otto von Bismarck, "the Iron Chancellor," occupies the lonely spot of honor in Cleveland above the desk of Dr. Herbert Y. Meltzer, a ranking contemporary schizophrenia authority. The same picture commands a similar position over a leading scientist's workplace in Germany. And other manifestations of Kraepelin's continuing influence abound.

He is a stalking presence wherever the schizophrenia establishment assembles. At the 1995 convention of the American Psychiatric Association, a featured speaker displayed the professor's portrait as the first slide of his talk. Another lecturer started with a famous group photo of some obviously deranged mental hospital inmates; Kraepelin had used this shocking image to illustrate his own talks almost a century ago. In the prepared texts delivered at such gatherings, the name of this godfather is dropped as if he were in the hall.

As the principal founder of biological psychiatry, Kraepelin was first to categorize schizophrenia as a physical condition, a brain disease, not the emotional-based "psychosocial" or "psychodynamic" state proposed by his arch-competitor, Sigmund Freud. The conflict of these titans—nature versus nurture—became a great intellectual battle. For more than half a century, the father of psychoanalysis reigned supreme, but Kraepelin—and hard physical science—won out in the end. Never reluctant to deliver a firm diagnosis, he defined the outcome as the "victory of scientific observation over philosophical and moral meditation," and preponderant psychiatric opinion came to agree that Kraepelin's role in setting the direction of his profession was seminal.

"Thanks to Kraepelin, the working methods of psychiatry began to acquire an organization along lines similar to the methods practiced in clinical medicine," wrote Dr. Adolf Meyer, the Swiss-born head of psychiatry at Johns Hopkins University, for decades the grand old man of psychiatry in America. And a weighty British textbook flatly delivered this judgment in 1969: "Modern psychiatry begins with Kraepelin."

Even his detractors felt compelled to praise him. In a still-authoritative 1966 history of psychiatry, Dr. Franz G. Alexander, an early Freud disciple and for twenty-five years head of the Chicago Institute for Psychoanalysis, downgraded Kraepelin as a "rigid and sterile codifier of disease categories" and accused him of "organic bias" and "inability to think in psychological (motivational) terms." Yet on the same page, Alexander lauded Kraepelin's "medical approach of detailed observation, careful description, and precise organization of data," concluding: "Without this orientation psychiatry could never have become a clinical, disciplined specialty of medicine."*

---

* A measure of Kraepelin's method: in 1908 alone, he produced index cards describing 721 cases.

Another historian of Freudian partisanship, the psychoanalyst Gregory Zilboorg, accused Kraepelin of practicing a "psychiatry without a psychology" and scoffed that the old German professor "did not want to know *what* the patient thought when he was ill, but *how* he thought." Nevertheless, Zilboorg was impressed that Kraepelin brought "the physiological laboratory into psychiatry and psychiatry into the laboratory."

In keeping with his interests and skills, Kraepelin did not bring warmth or empathy to his research and teaching. Kurt Kolle, who began studying psychiatry at Munich University in 1920, became a professor there and one of Kraepelin's successors; he found the master "small, compact, squat" and his teaching "sober, dry," a "disappointment." Alma Kreuter, a researcher who knew Kraepelin at the university some years before his death, says that the great man looked like a "little clerk from the finance bureau," with the reputation of an oddball (*komischer Kauz*)—hardly the picture of the quintessential German professor whom the philosopher Nietzsche described as second only to God.

Kraepelin was well aware that he was hardly a people person. "I have felt myself more or less lonely all through my life," he wrote. Even his immediate family did not enjoy his intimacy. His 1919 memoirs coolly describe correct relationships with some five hundred colleagues but fail, even once, to name his daughter Toni, a psychiatrist who for many years was his principal personal assistant and administrator.

The professor's grandson, Dr. Hans-Peter Dürr, a physics professor at the Max Planck Institute in Munich, born three years after Kraepelin's death, was accustomed to tales of Kraepelin acting as "the terror" of his family. Dürr's mother told him that the grandfather's treatment of family members had been "merciless," especially new family members. All young people who married into the clan were psychiatrically "evaluated," as if the professor were continuing his daily office routine of classifying his psychotic patients.

"It was as if the difference between the sick and the sane was only a matter of their background and schooling," said Dr. Dürr. "It was terrible. Whoever couldn't tolerate this treatment was classified as 'weak.'"

Within the immediate family, the patriarch was unbending as well. "When my mother spoke of her father, the relationship emerged as distant," Dr. Dürr told me, and the cold treatment extended into the family hour at the dinner table. "For each meal, one topic was assigned for discussion, usually something historical."

The worldwide scholarly eminence Kraepelin achieved among his peers, beginning in the first decade of the century, rested largely on his one major formal work, his *Text Book* (*Lehrbuch*), which underwent nine reinventions over a period of forty years, bespeaking the author's snowballing understanding of psychotic illnesses. The first edition, a conventional compendium of 385 pages, was published in 1883, and his outlook on the future of his specialty was bleak. When a promising researcher called on him, Kraepelin inquired what the young psychiatrist planned to investigate.

"Brain anatomy of the psychoses" was the reply.

"Then I must give you a bad prognosis," said the older man, "for anatomy can contribute nothing to psychiatry."

That was before Kraepelin's index cards with their minute clinical observations began to pile up. The ninth edition of the *Lehrbuch*, published posthumously in 1927, had exploded into two volumes totaling 2,425 pages.

Over the years, Kraepelin had personally examined enough psychotic patients to pinpoint the patterns of their symptoms as well as some of the chemical and physiological abnormalities of their diseased brains. The overarching result of this Herculean effort was the professor's differentiation between two major categories of psychotics, their diagnosis and prognosis. For the first time, doctors learned from him how to distinguish between manic-depressives, whom Kraepelin considered curable, and schizophrenics—he condemned them by labeling them as afflicted with dementia praecox*—whom he pigeonholed not only as hopeless but genetically dangerous to the German nation.

Behind this negative outlook loomed Kraepelin as ideologue. His pessimism was fused with a fanatical nationalism, and he became one of the earliest proponents of "racial purity" and the concept of a German master race. He confessed his passions readily. "My whole heart belonged to my fatherland," he wrote, "and I willingly flung away cool objectivity of judgment when it was a matter of defending German interests."

Rule by democratic means was illusory and abhorrent to him. "True popular rule is entirely impossible," he wrote in 1919, visualizing someone like Hitler years before the Führer materialized even as a minor Munich street

---

* The term means "premature deterioration of intellectual faculties" and is no longer in use. The Swiss psychiatrist Eugen Bleuler introduced "schizophrenia" in 1911.

haranguer. "Invariably the masses submit to individual leaders who by virtue of certain qualities have risen to the top. They are true leaders; those led by them are left with only the appearance of sovereignty. It is not they who decide, but rather the superior leaders who understand how to *force* [emphasis added] the others to follow."

"He would have welcomed Hitler," said Alma Kreuter. Hitler attempted to legitimize his philosophy by embracing the guidelines of eugenics (racial hygiene), and Kreuter identified Kraepelin squarely with this now-discredited pseudo-science. "Racial hygiene was emphatically his way," she said.

Kraepelin made no secret of his thinking, which Germans then described with the now-taboo label of *völkisch*, a perversion of populism. In his lecture hall, his student Kurt Kolle, the future professor, witnessed "lively demonstrations pro and con the gnarled old man" when he vented his political views. Student outbursts were uncommon in the German universities of that era. In Kraepelin's auditorium they boiled up "often."

Kraepelin's Weltanschauung found ready entry into his professional practice. He routinely condemned "degeneracy," "degenerates," "inferior species," and "life-incompetents," stopping barely short of endorsing the Nazi death sentence: "life unworthy of living," the official rationale behind the Holocaust and its campaign to wipe out the "unfit."

"I could believe that he sympathized with National Socialism," said his grandson, Professor Dürr. "His nationalism was very extreme."

Anti-Semitism was a prime motivator for most of the eugenicist physicians. Its underpinning was "scientific": the presumed inferiority and degeneracy of the Jewish "race," a notion to which Kraepelin subscribed as the "hygienic *Führer* of the *Volk*," as a British historian described him.

"Among the leaders of current and past upheavals one finds a surprising number of people who in one way or another fall outside the bounds of normality," Kraepelin wrote in 1919. Comprising this curious collection of the deranged were "dreamers and poets, swindlers and Jews." He singled out Jews for their "frequency of psychopathic predisposition."

It must be rated one of the ironies of pioneer psychiatry, then, that Kraepelin's most influential financial backer was James Loeb, one of his patients, an American Jew. (Kraepelin also tolerated some Jewish coworkers.) Their relationship brought out the professor's talent as a determined administrator, adroit at the art of large-scale fund-raising. His no-nonsense manner proved convincing to men who controlled large pools of money.

Loeb, a scion of the immensely wealthy Kuhn Loeb banking interests, was a tragic figure: once brilliant and charming, he was thwarted by his dictatorial father, slowly slipped into depression and finally into long episodes of severe manic-depression. Loeb hoped for treatment from Freud and evidently stayed for a time in his house. When psychoanalysis failed to help him, he enlisted Kraepelin, who administered a dietary treatment for what the professor diagnosed as epilepsy. It was a disaster. A Loeb relative recalled: "His mind became blunted, so that he really thought only of eating and drinking. He was still very amiable, but the entire quick-witted man was no longer there."

Though Loeb became increasingly withdrawn, most of his functions slowly returned. He did not hold Kraepelin's treatment failures against him. Instead, following a casual conversation in 1911 in which the professor pointedly admired the generosity of American foundations and their grants for scientific research, Loeb guaranteed a contribution of the then-enormous sum of half a million prewar gold marks toward the professor's dream: his own psychiatric research institute in Munich.

Smoothly, Kraepelin converted Loeb's donation into seed money and leveraged it, tapping more millions from the chief of the Krupp steel clan and the Bavarian government. Construction had to await the end of the war, but eventually Kraepelin took up residence in an adjoining villa, and in 1925 Loeb engineered the institute's financial push over the top. He persuaded another American Jew, Abraham Flexner, the most influential science educator of his time, to interest the Rockefeller Foundation, and it contributed the final $2.5 million.

Loeb was not the only patient of consequence to embrace both arch-rivals, Kraepelin and Freud. If Freud did not cure Loeb, he succeeded with his celebrated four-and-a-half-year psychoanalysis of Sergei Pankejeff, a colorful and totally dysfunctional patient on whom Kraepelin had simply given up, although he was only very severely neurotic. Pankejeff, a handsome and wealthy young Russian aristocrat, became famous in the psychiatric literature as "the Wolf Man" because of a shattering dream in which he saw himself terrorized by six white wolves perched above him in a tree, threatening to devour him. By 1914 the great analyst as well as the patient considered the Wolf Man "cured."

For years, Kraepelin conducted his feud with Freud by seeming to ignore the objectionable Jewish upstart in Vienna, who had not even attained the rank of professor. Freud, in turn, privately called Kraepelin a "coarse fellow." He considered the professor an enemy, not merely a critic, and their professional views could hardly have differed more profoundly, although both came from the same petit bourgeois Germanic culture.

Both were born in May 1856, within eleven days of each other, in rural villages near Berlin and Vienna, respectively. Kraepelin's father was a music teacher; Freud's was an impecunious wool merchant. Both sons pursued psychiatric careers with unusual diligence and passion, but Kraepelin, preoccupied with pathology of the brain, dismissed Freud's methods of free association and dream interpretation as unscientific. He rejected the search for the deeper meaning of sex as disgraceful and unworthy of serious discussion. He seemed to hope that Freud would shrivel away; his 290-page memoir fails to mention him even once.

By the time of his textbook's 1909 edition, Kraepelin felt compelled to launch an attack, formally and in print. He called Freud's methods "peculiar" and "torturous." He attributed psychoanalytic successes to the "relentlessness of the procedure" and the "power of suggestion exercised by the doctor's medical authority." Moreover: "Whether the continual, relentless pushing for embarrassing sexual revelations is really always so harmless must be doubted for the time being."

By his 1915 edition, Kraepelin's guarded ruminations had escalated, and his views of Freud's sexuality theories triggered a "most insistent warning." Freud's "monstrous" insistence on "reading the most disgusting sexual aberrations out of harmless experiences" now struck him as "reprehensible" and loaded with "harmfulness." Whoever gave credence to Freud's stress on hysteria simply "can't be helped."

Inside Kraepelin's office practice, Freud came under continual clinical assault, which the freshly accredited psychiatrist Helene Deutsch—eventually to become one of the immortals of psychoanalysis—experienced firsthand when she came to work for the professor in 1914. Deutsch had three strikes against her: she was a woman, a liberated feminist at that; she was Jewish; and she spoke German with the reviled accent of her native Poland. She recalled with distaste Kraepelin's "comic-German standoffish bearing" at her initial interview.

"So! You want to do psychological work. What knowledge do you have of the subject?"

"None at all, Herr Professor."

"So! Then it will not be possible for you to work here."

"I just want to learn, Herr Professor."

"So! How long do you want to stay?"

"Half a year."

"Too short a time, far too short."

Nevertheless, the professor turned her over to a research assistant for an assignment, and it quickly became clear why the hospital needed more help. Many of the doctors spent as much time as they could spare—Deutsch would do the same—conducting tests by which Kraepelin kept attempting, unsuccessfully, to discredit Freud's theory of the link between thought and feeling. Using a stopwatch, Deutsch elicited pleasant and unpleasant word associations from depressed and nondepressed patients. Her results were inconclusive, but her attitude was firm.

"I am supposed to act as though I did not know that there is a subconscious, and finally bring evidence against Freud," she would recall. She felt as if she were directing "weapons against myself" and was sickened by the anti-Freud hostility that surrounded her. She likened its intensity to religious fervor. Kraepelin's staff seemed to say: "It is a sacred duty to fight these dangerous and fateful teachings."

These days, reputations of some hallowed names in mental illness have been severely damaged: Freud; the partisanship of Karl Menninger; the ferocity of Bruno Bettelheim; the obscurantism of Adolf Meyer; the drug addiction of R. D. Laing; Carl Jung's flirtations with the Nazis; and the CIA dirty work of Ewen Cameron in Canada. A brilliant 1995 paper in the *British Journal of Psychiatry* by Professor Michael Shepherd of the London Institute of Psychiatry concluded: "The leading figures in the history of psychiatry exhibit far too much clay below the ankles. Kraepelin is one among many." The article was aptly entitled "Two Faces of Emil Kraepelin."

The master's appalling bigotry is only one aspect of his tragedy. In placing biological psychiatry on the medical map, he was simply ahead of his time. Treatment was lagging far behind discovery. While psychotics were no longer kept in chains or confined to closed, cagelike body baskets in filthy insane asylums, therapies in the early twentieth century remained inhuman and mostly useless. Pressure bandages around the head were supposed to shock the body into brain activity. Emetics and purgatives were administered to stimulate healthful physical reactions. Deliberate malaria infection was deemed promising, as was prefrontal lobotomy. At Kraepelin's death in 1926, protracted warm or cold baths were choice treatments, as were sedatives like chloral hydrate. The cruel and dangerous technique of inducing insulin shock in schizophrenics was still a year away.

Nobody was envisioning successive generations of effective neuroleptic drugs. The practice of biological psychiatry—and the medical vindication of Kraepelin—were still more than thirty years distant.

CHAPTER 6

The Menninger Wars

GIVEN THAT the Menninger Clinic's cofounder, Dr. Karl Menninger, having described himself as "more Freudian than Freud," it was hardly surprising that his staff initiated Jeff's hospital treatment by prescribing psychoanalytically oriented therapy in February 1973.

From the start, the half-hour sessions slipped past my son like so much wind. "The patient attended fairly regularly," his record reported, "but seemed unable to stay through the period of time until eventually he was only coming for ten or fifteen minutes." Even Dr. Karl's people seemed unaware that Freud considered psychotics too ill to be reached by talk therapy. "Throughout these sessions," the Menninger notes recalled, "the patient had massive difficulty in reflecting on the emotional significance of his emotional life, being unable or unwilling to reflect on the past or to explore the details of his present relationships."

Nevertheless, the talk "therapy" sessions, for which I was charged an extra fee, continued for seven months. Much of the time was spent with Jeff and his doctor staring at each other without a word. Still, when the sessions finally ended in September, it was not because they were considered to have failed. "It was felt at that time that in order to work with this patient he would need to be hospitalized for an extended period of time, which did not seem within the patient's financial capability." According to the hospital, then, Jeff's "resistance" and my inadequate income were to blame for the fiasco, not the choice of treatment.

Money was a frequently discussed ingredient of Jeff's Menninger treatment. The staff clearly did not approve of his parental resources. "Throughout the stay the family's finances have been in question," the treatment report stated reprovingly. "Father's view was that he would arrange for whatever was needed, mother's view was that they could not afford that." Evidently the staff would have liked to believe me: "The patient's father continued to reassure us that there were enough finances to last through the following summer."*

I felt even then, however, that for the Menninger administration the real problem was something else: I was not to be trusted. When I later read their records, I learned how right I had been, and not merely about their doubts concerning my earning power. While the personnel were critical of "mother's pessimism" but mustered some credit for "father's optimism," in the aggregate they considered me wanting.

"The father gives the impression personally of attempts to be seriously concerned about his son," the report stated, in fragile syntax, "but actually simply not being able to muster up an effectively responsible attitude about it all."

This judgment would account for the air of almost-palpable disapproval that hung like smoke over the room where I met at frequent intervals with the senior caregiver, Dr. Y. The two younger social workers who managed Jeff from day to day seemed somewhat more accepting of me, as well as of Jeff, but I supposed that their attitude mattered little to the Menninger hierarchy.

While I stuck to my financial commitment, Dr. Y probably noticed that my heart was not with him. Why should it have been? The place was too triste. The treaters were too sour. The attitude toward medications seemed to me, even then, at best curiously tentative. Most especially, why couldn't they have *liked* my helpless Jeff at least a little? Shouldn't that have been part of the mental hospital's covenant with a psychotic young man, especially considering the prevailing price of more than fifty thousand dollars a year—a huge investment in those years?

The issue of my alleged flightiness remains intriguing after twenty-three more years of life with Jeff. No doubt the Menninger people picked up on my reservations, although these did not concern my son's situation, but *them*. I suppose they expected me to sell my house to pay their bills, as some people do. I might have given up my home, all right, but not to hand the proceeds to

* That was to be mid-1974. Actually, I took Jeff from Topeka in December of that year.

people who had shown themselves, over nearly two years, neither effective nor humane.

To bankrupt oneself or not? This question is often at the core of the schizophrenia equation for families. Whatever one's answer, this is a shaming disease—to patients if they retain sufficient awareness and invariably to family members. The literature calls it a poor man's disease. Wrong. It is an impoverished man's disease; it usually leaves all but the very rich penniless in the end, whatever the medical outcome.

Asking myself again how I could have stuck with the hospital for such an extended time, it became clear that the Menninger public relations skills kept working on me. I remembered Walter Cronkite going to Topeka for a special CBS program on this illustrious place; how its name kept turning up in films and magazines; how the brothers Menninger were cited like deities. Neither I nor the general public nor the broad psychiatric profession had become aware that the hospital's refusal to join the sharp turn toward biological psychiatry, to nod toward Kraepelin, not Freud, had caused its reputation among knowledgeable specialists to slip.

"Menninger's popular image as a center of excellence outdistanced its ebbing professional fortunes" was the elegant phrasing of Professor Lawrence J. Friedman in his 1990 biography, *Menninger—the Family and the Clinic.* Even by the 1990s, however, word had not spread sufficiently. In a three-year survey of 2,400 doctors, *U.S. News and World Report* found that the Menninger Clinic was ranked second place nationally among psychiatric hospitals, right after McLean (Harvard Medical School).

Jeff was not enamored of his Menninger confinement, and his handlers were distinctly unhappy with him. I found him lost in his own world, shut off, monosyllabic, mostly unreachable. He snarled a lot, a new trait, and often would not concede that he was ill. Throughout his stay, he kept setting new dates when he hoped to be "cured" and leave the hospital. This struck me as evidence of strength and a resolve to overcome his trouble. His caretakers interpreted this as further proof of his removal from reality.

The tone of their case notes conjures up a willfully unruly child in need of a spanking. For three weeks following his admission, he "was almost completely out of control. His discontrol [*sic*] took the form of marked hyperactivity, restlessness and hypersensitivity to the environment. That is, he would approach almost anyone who made any motion around him, coming very close to them, and begin a badgering, intrusive, hostile, demanding questioning which contained much sarcastic mocking . . . frantically testing limits and seeking control. He struck several people, threw coffee on another."

With time, Jeff got worse: "Eventually it was necessary to have male staff with him around the clock. . . . At the high point of his *manic* [emphasis added] behavior he was standing on the conference table."

For all of 1974, Jeff's condition bounced about wildly in the typical toboggan pattern of schizophrenia out of control. In December 1972, the clinical notes read: "The patient was extremely hyperactive, markedly suspicious and unpredictably combative . . . he assaulted two female nursing staff . . . he became more uncontrollable." Now: "On 12/26/74 he became explosively violent and assaulted three patients. . . . The patient was in restraints."

Simultaneously, Jeff's battle against loss of control when under powerful medications—a rebellion that began when he resisted even mild drugs during treatment with Dr. D'Andrea—had reached a new level.

"On the day after admission he requested that his medication be cut down . . . and within 24 hours he became rapidly more unmanageable." The medication, Thorazine, which Jeff called "Horrorzine," was indeed reduced, leaving Jeff worse. Surely the problem was the dosage. The hospital notes mention a frugal 400 milligrams a day; a subsequent independent evaluation that I commissioned at Stanford Medical Center recommended 800 to 1,600 milligrams for Jeff, depending on his manic state. No matter. Without offering details or any explanation, the case notes recorded: "During the middle six months of 1973, the patient was gradually taken off of [*sic*] medication."

Thorazine, the baby that the Menningers were tossing out with the bathwater after handling it as warily as if it were an experimental treatment, had actually proved itself on an impressive scale, though its side effects were atrocious. The drug, invented in 1954, represented a breakthrough: the first effective antipsychotic medication, the birth of biological psychiatry in practice. But by the 1970s it had counteracted psychoses so dramatically that it had all but emptied the largest mental hospitals in the United States and Europe. Nothing like it had ever been known.

The genesis of Thorazine was characteristic of the helter-skelter evolution that created a sizable family of dramatic antipsychotics, the neuroleptics, which are said to act by blocking dopamine nervous receptors in the brain.

Typical of the early pioneers, Thorazine's inventor was a man with no reputation to speak of, Dr. Henri Laborit, thirty-seven, a provincial French naval surgeon eager to ease the surgical pain of sailors on whom he performed operations. His lack of connections in Paris and its elitist medical establishment guaranteed his obscurity. A voluble, dashing enthusiast, Laborit was born in French Indochina, trained in the naval service at Bordeaux, was wounded in World War II combat at Anzio, and began his pain research at a naval hospital in Tunisia. In 1951 the navy, impressed by the "euphoric quietude" Laborit had induced in his patients with a new medication, first called 4560 R.P., transferred him to its Val-de-Grace Hospital in Paris, prestigious for research since 1795.

The drug, chlorpromazine (CPZ), eventually to become known as Thorazine, was intended for use against surgical shock. In 1952 Laborit published his findings and appended this prescient afterthought: "These facts let us see certain indications for this drug in psychiatry."

The interest among pharmaceutical manufacturers was mild, and for years Laborit remained a nonperson in the medical press, although he was a relentless lobbyist and kept buttonholing colleagues in the hospital cafeteria. The psychiatrists snubbed him, so Laborit recruited his own highly qualified guinea pig and administered an injection of CPZ to a friend and colleague, Dr. Claudia Quarti, a psychiatrist, who reported: "I felt incapable of being angry about anything, irresistibly optimistic. . . . After about a week . . . my mood was of perfect euphoria, unaffected by the little traumas of daily life."

Within a year, enthusiasm nevertheless cooled. Thorazine's side effects were daunting: sedation, tremors, rigidity, involuntary body movements, and facial twitches. Sometimes the drug produced masklike faces and almost always a slow gait that became known as the Thorazine shuffle.

Jeff's records mention no reactions to the drug, and I remember nothing remarkable until much later when the dosage was greatly increased at other hospitals. At the Menninger Clinic, the staff acted for about half a year as if antipsychotics did not exist, not even for a common, though frightening, condition that they had spotted and recorded for Jeff: strong mood swings from mania to depression and back, for which an excellent medication had long existed.

They finally availed themselves of lithium, greeting the use of this by-then-routine medication in the spirit of discovery. The case notes relate: "In the fall of 1973, we decided to try Lithium. The patient had begun to be a bit more active and outgoing from his period of withdrawal. Unexpectedly, he accepted the Lithium rather well and from that period on there seemed to be a reduction in the extremes of swings from depression to euphoric hypomania."

That Jeff's reaction was "unexpected" is strange, because lithium had been one of psychiatry's stellar success stories, with obscure origins twenty-five years earlier.

"An unknown psychiatrist, working alone in a small chronic hospital with no research training and negligible equipment." So the ebullient Dr. John F. J. Cade, thirty-seven, described his status at the Repatriation Mental Hospital in Bundoora, Australia, as of March 29, 1948. On that day, he injected lithium carbonate, a salt commonly available and cheap but considered dangerous and disreputable for the preceding forty years, into a "wizened little man of 51," hospitalized for five years as manic-depressive.

Dr. Cade was following a hunch. Earlier, lithium had relaxed his excitable guinea pigs. He was not aspiring to a cure, merely a hint at a cause for the up-and-down emotional spirals that terrified tens of millions, fifteen percent of them suicides like Vincent van Gogh and Ernest Hemingway.

As Dr. Cade described his patient, "He was amiably restless, dirty, destructive, mischievous and interfering. He had enjoyed preeminent nuisance value in a back ward for all those years and bid fair to remain there for the rest of his life." As a "by-product" of his experiments with lithium, however, within weeks, the patient was out of the hospital and back at his job.

Unfortunately, cardiac deaths from lithium were reported in the United States at about that time, and the Food and Drug Administration made its use illegal. Lithium did not become the widely publicized and stunningly effective standard treatment for "bipolar" (also called manic-depressive) illness until 1970, well before Jeff entered Menninger.

Dr. Cade had conjectured correctly a generation earlier what the difficulty had been: other doctors had administered the salt in excessively high dosages. In the United States alone, well over 250,000 adults now take the medication safely at any one time, although occasionally kidney damage and other serious complications can develop. It is still not entirely clear why it took Jeff's doctors a year to discover the medication he obviously needed and still takes more than twenty years later.

CHAPTER 7

The Revolutionaries

I WOULDN'T HAVE believed it at the time, but 1946 to 1948 would turn out to be vintage years for the care of schizophrenics and patients afflicted with other then-hopeless psychotic disorders. Longtime warehousing in state hospitals had been the unalterable fate for the vast majority, and their neglect in these places had long been a scandal ripe to be broken open by disturbers of the status quo.*

Notable among the earliest of the postwar revolutionaries were pioneering writers, now largely forgotten but wielding considerable influence at the time: Albert Q. Maisel (*Bedlam*), Mary Jane Ward (*The Snake Pit,* an autobiographical novel), Albert Deutsch (*The Shame of the States*), and, most enduringly, Mike Gorman. Gorman was so stung by what he observed in the hospitals that he turned himself into, arguably, the twentieth century's most potent reformer on behalf of the "mad" among us, and certainly the loudest.

At the age of thirty-six, a new reporter for the *Daily Oklahoman* in Oklahoma City, he wrote in 1946 of his initiation into the nauseating world of mental hospitals: "I barely managed to get out of the building before I threw up." When he returned to his office, he looked up "schizophrenic" and "psychotic" in the dictionary. His follow-up report, reflecting his conversion to

---

* The tradition originated with an undercover exposé, "Ten Days in a Madhouse," by Nellie Bly, in the *New York World* in 1887.

activism, appeared in the *Reader's Digest* under the title "Oklahoma Attacks Its Snake Pits."

Gorman and his fellow crusaders mobilized the national conscience, persuading state legislatures and federal health authorities to make record appropriations to reinvent the snake pits and launch more research. Soon drugmakers developed antipsychotic medications, and lobbyists and doctors tried to counteract the initial resistance against them. Then the families of the mentally ill banded together and became a powerful force for their afflicted kin.

To learn more about Jeff's illness, I wanted to know what these advocates were like; what they found out about schizophrenia; and how they succeeded on behalf of people like my son. Eventually I met with many of them and learned much. I never talked with Mike Gorman, who died in 1989, but it became clear how he succeeded. He and people like him made their impact mostly for the very reasons why mainstream mental health spokesmen shunned them. Alan Gregg, president of the Rockefeller Foundation, called them "unmanageably determined and perhaps even reckless in obtaining their objectives"—the precise qualities required.

Gorman was a tall, heavyset former advertising writer from New York, equipped with little patience, a big Irish temper, and flamboyant language. On his first swing through the Oklahoma hospitals he lost seventeen pounds and found "a witches' brew . . . more gruesome than the Black Hole of Calcutta." His elevation in 1953 to executive director of the National Mental Health Committee in Washington served to rev up his passions further.

The prevalent old-school resistance against biological psychiatry made him livid. In one of his formal addresses, he excoriated the negative appraisals of the government's principal evaluator on the new medications as "drivel." That half of all U.S. hospital beds were occupied by mental patients struck Gorman as outrageous and, worse, unnecessary. In his book *Every Other Bed*, published in 1956, barely two years after the introduction of Thorazine, Gorman wrote, "You can't fight a raging epidemic with an overstuffed couch." To him, the deficiency was obvious: "Insight is not enough." Nor did he hesitate to blame the "incantations of the psychoanalysts, with their ritualistic excommunication of the deviationists."

By then, Gorman called on articulate "deviationists" to help him lobby congressional committees for more funds for mental health research. One of his most effective allies was an unconventional psychiatrist from Baltimore, Dr. Frank Ayd Jr.—short, outspoken, known for ferocious energy—and one morning in May 1955, Gorman watched as the doctor startled a Senate committee with his flair for the dramatic.

That very day at 1:30 a.m., Dr. Ayd testified, he had been called to the home of a thirty-year-old woman who was demolishing furniture in her agitation. A single injection of chlorpromazine (Thorazine) calmed her for uneventful transfer to a hospital. The doctor then told the senators about schizophrenic twin sisters. One was hospitalized for eighteen months in the early 1950s at a cost of $3,000. When the other sister suffered a similar psychotic break in 1955, she was treated with Thorazine for one week in a nursing home and another eleven weeks at home at a total cost of $325.

Ayd had been shaken when he experienced the "living hell" of chronic schizophrenics whiling away their years. He had recently come out of the navy and had begun treating patients unsuccessfully with insulin coma, electroshock, and hydrotherapy at the Perry Point, Maryland, Veterans Administration Hospital. In 1952 the pharmaceutical house Smith Kline Beecham invited him to write articles in psychiatric journals about Thorazine, which he had started using with startling success. Ayd quickly recognized that a new era was at hand, and he began churning out findings on hundreds of patients whose lives had been salvaged.

Many of his colleagues remained unconvinced, however. "I have only one recommendation," said the chairman of a conference where Dr. Ayd read one of his papers. "Hurry up and prescribe this drug while it still works!" This skeptic was certain that Thorazine was made effective by the power of suggestion and was therefore only briefly of value.

"I was persona non grata," Ayd told me, "I was the medicine man. I was called a quack. I couldn't get privileges at psychiatric hospitals."*

He was not dissuaded. Applying his congeniality and missionary zeal, he rallied impressive international support. In 1957, in Milan, Ayd was one of the few American psychiatrists involved in launching the International College of Neuropsychopharmacology. In 1958, in Rome, he helped to persuade the pope to address the college's first convention and to invest the Vatican's enormous prestige in the principles of biological psychiatry—a triumph for the new science.

That same year, at a private dinner in New York, Ayd forged a lifetime mutual support alliance with Dr. Paul Janssen, president of the Janssen Pharmaceutical Company. The tall, beefy Belgian physician, pharmacologist, entrepreneur, and bon vivant had just invented R1625, marketed as Haldol and still the world's most widely prescribed antipsychotic forty years later. Eventually he would have seventy-seven pharmaceutical inventions to his credit.

---

* Dr. Ayd became an elder statesman of psychopharmacology, publisher of the *International Drug Therapy Newsletter*, and columnist for *Psychiatric Times*.

When I met him in 1995 at the Janssen laboratories and manufacturing plant in the tiny town of Beerse, an hour's drive from Antwerp, Dr. Paul (his universal sobriquet) was officially retired from executive functions but remained a forbidding figure. He reigned from a huge corner office, wearing his starched white laboratory coat like a royal robe, still a commanding figure for sixteen thousand employees.

"I grew up with an obsession," Dr. Paul said in almost accent-free English.

His father was a country doctor who also manufactured patent medicines under the formidable business eye of Paul's very strict mother. Paul's fellow students and professors at medical school made it their sport to ridicule the family nostrums, which left Paul furious and determined the direction of his life. "Research was my goal, not a means," he explained. "I was going to try to beat the world record for pharmacological creativity."

At twenty-one, he took a year off to learn research methods in America. During his observations at Cornell Medical School in New York, he lived at the YMCA and earned the $1.50 he needed for daily support by winning four or five games each evening at the Manhattan Chess Club. And in 1953, with a $1,000 loan from his father, he formed a research laboratory in his hometown with a crew of chemist friends, none older than twenty-seven.

Hunting for patentable new compounds seven days a week, Janssen discovered antipsychotics because of his love for bicycle races, a popular sport in Belgium. Some of the best racers were chronic amphetamine (pep pill) abusers, which caused them to suffer from symptoms almost indistinguishable from paranoid schizophrenia. After overcoming some hurdles, Janssen developed a medication resembling Thorazine and effective at dosages up to one hundred times lower when used on mice.

Late one night in 1957, Dr. Paul had an emergency call from a doctor at the University Hospital in Liège. "You have to come," the friend said. His eighteen-year-old son, ill with paranoid schizophrenia, was in the grip of a terrifying acute psychotic breakdown. Janssen injected the young man with ten milligrams of his experimental new medication, and the impact was nearly instantaneous. The patient calmed and went to sleep. Notwithstanding a few subsequent setbacks, the young man became a successful architect, married, and had three children.

Within a few weeks of the emergency in Liège, five psychiatrists at its University Hospital began trials with eighteen patients varying in age who were given a hundred intravenous doses of two to five milligrams of Haldol. The results were nothing short of startling.

"The drug was said to be obviously and highly effective as a psychomotor sedative within five to fifteen minutes and for about three to five hours," Dr. Janssen would report. "Tolerance was excellent." The usually noisy and disorderly hospital ward had turned into an island of calm, but most psychiatrists in Belgium and surrounding countries, wedded to Freudian psychotherapy, remained unconvinced about psychobiology.

"It was a threat to their incomes," Dr. Janssen recalled, "and so they ridiculed the whole thing."

As his productivity intensified, so did his caustic feelings about the ritualistic skepticism that tended to greet each new innovation. "When the obvious facts can no longer be denied, the general feeling changes," he said in a speech at an international congress. "There must be something to it, but the whole story is much less important than we were once led to believe: at this stage, the usual rumors start spreading about all kinds of mysterious dangers. Smoke is being produced and people start looking for a fire."

Janssen blamed the "thalidomide tragedy"* for the air of suspicion that handicaps pharmaceutical novelty, not stopping to concede that this tragedy had proved all too real. "Nobody trusts anybody anymore," he said. "Rumors about side effects are immediately believed by everybody, and even rumors of side effects can kill drugs."

He was exaggerating, and it was not the only time that he did so. When I asked him for his views on Olanzapine, Sertindole, and the other rapidly approaching new medications competitive to his own, his verdict was unhesitating, unsmiling, and emphatic. All were without value, he said, and none would even make it to the market. As a prophet, he would prove to be fallible.

Withal, Janssen was a trailblazer. Haldol was a dramatically effective antipsychotic, certainly, though the side effects made many patients jittery and dysfunctional (including Jeff). In 1961 his company was bought by the American giant Johnson & Johnson (sales fifteen billion dollars a year) for thirty-three times its annual net earnings.

The practical application of the new inventions posed unprecedented difficulties, and nobody was more acutely aware of the opportunities and risks than the thirty-eight high-ranking psychiatrists from hospitals, medical schools,

---

* This sedative was withdrawn in 1961 after eight thousand European children had been born severely deformed.

and federal and state agencies who assembled at New York's Barbizon-Plaza Hotel on November 12 and 13, 1960. Responsible for the welfare of hundreds of thousands of mental patients throughout the United States and Canada, they had gathered to settle on common standards for practicing the new biological psychiatry.

Commonality had been eluding them. Indeed, the doctors addressed each other like generals representing the same army, yet ignorant about their own guns and even about one another. They could barely communicate meaningfully in those early days of psychopharmacology.

"We had all these new drugs coming, and we didn't have a common language," remembered Frank Ayd, seventy-six, one of the most active speakers at the sessions, and the 102-page transcript of the talks supported his contention. How useful were the new drugs, really? How should they be tested? How should they be applied with patients? How could the enthusiastic claims of drug manufacturers be checked?

Most of the best-qualified practitioners in the field were present in the room—Drs. Heinz Lehmann, Henry Brill, Paul Hoch, Nathan Kline—but none claimed to have firm answers. "We couldn't talk to each other," said Ayd. It was this conference that gave birth to the American College of Neuropsychopharmacology and led to policies that allowed doctors to begin using the new medications safely and to best effect.

The tenacity of the resistance encountered by these pioneers was awesome. Their opposition, the talking therapists, couldn't face reality. "They were very unhappy and weren't able to believe what was taking place," recalled Brill, who operated the huge New York State mental hospital system. "At the time, no one in his right mind was using drugs," said Lehmann, a research innovator from McGill University in Montreal. "In the mental hospitals, we found a heavy atmosphere of custodial care," reported the corporate product manager for Thorazine. "Anything else meant money, more than the $2.50 per day that most institutions were spending on their patients."

The unofficial anchor of the conference at the Barbizon-Plaza was Dr. Jonathan O. Cole, the psychiatrist director of the Psychopharmacology Service Center (PSC), formed in 1956 at the National Institute of Mental Health in Washington. "He was the captain of the ship," said Ayd. Cole was that rare gem: an antibureaucratic bureaucrat with a sense of humor. He also possessed the inexhaustible patience and the people skills required when psychopharmacology came to coexist with the sluggishness of government rule-by-committee.

Cole commanded some degree of control over the pace of progress because he had money raised by Gorman, Ayd, and their lobbyist allies: two million dollars a year. Unhappily, Cole found almost no sympathetic peers within government, so little agreement was reached in the early years on how to distribute his money. "I could hardly spend it all," he told me. Along with bureaucratic squabbles, the fragility of the new science itself held Cole back.

"We prepared a list of all psychopharmacological drugs and appropriate dosages, which we were very shaky about," he recalled. "It doesn't tell a guy what to do, but it kind of tells him which end is up, if he is well enough informed to utilize it." Not until the year following the Barbizon-Plaza conference could he launch the first large-scale controlled study of antipsychotics. Tracking 344 schizophrenics at nine hospitals, his investigators found the drugs effective for ninety-five percent of patients.

The next step ahead came in 1963, when the Swedish pharmacologist Arvid Carlsson, a professor at the University of Gothenburg, pointed the finger of suspicion at a ubiquitous neurotransmitter called dopamine. Ever since, Carlsson's "dopamine hypothesis" has dominated the investigations into the still-elusive multiple causes of schizophrenia and guided the trial-and-error process of lurching toward new medications. In the decades since, the hypothesis was adopted as gospel throughout the international schizophrenia establishment.

Carlsson is a laboratory genius who thought about his experimental rats in terms of human needs. What troubled him principally, from the beginning, was the cluster of schizophrenia characteristics that make up the one most stubborn underlying riddle of the illness—the heartbreaking slowing and dulling of the mind that became known collectively as negative symptoms. The problem, identified by Kraepelin in 1896, was not named generically until the early 1970s, when researchers came to appreciate its obstinacy and complexity.

Carlsson singled out this perplexing phenomenon as a motivating force for his continued labors on the dopamine receptors. The most refractory of the numerous negative symptoms is the patient's lack of motivation, the inability to engage in constructive activity of any kind ("diminished sense of purpose"). This force would eventually keep my Jeff benumbed.

"It takes away the rewards system, which is the life force," said Carlsson. "Why should you take on the job of living if there is no driving force left? If there is no pleasure, why bother?"

Carlsson's personal reward system was mobilized by the failure of his profession to figure out, for eleven years, why chlorpromazine (Thorazine) works. At that point, he fed the medication to his laboratory rats and wrote a prescient four-page paper in a Scandinavian pharmacology journal about his observations and the implications of the results: Thorazine blocked the flow of dopamine in the brain. An excess of this neurotransmitter, he predicted, would turn out to be one of the major causes of psychotic disorders. Thorazine, Haldol, and several new antipsychotic medications have since proved him correct.

Dopamine originates deep in the brain stem, within clumps of some hundred million cells that together measure less than a grain of sand. These cells form nerve fibers that fan out to billions of cells all over the brain. In the decades since Carlsson's original detective work, dopamine has become identified as a modulator in a remarkable catalog of human behavior. With too much dopamine, people hear voices, and their thoughts become disorganized; with too little, their movements freeze and Parkinson's disease develops.

Carlsson's 1963 paper gradually proliferated into a dopamine industry. Five receptor subtypes were discovered—D1, D2, D3, D4, and D5—and all came into play in the development or manufacturing of recent and emerging antipsychotics. (For example, clozapine—of which more later—was found to act on the D2 and D4 receptors.)

This cascade of findings spawned attempts at fine-tuning in laboratories throughout the world, and nearly a decade ago, Carlsson entered into a development partnership with one of the most highly regarded of the American authorities, Dr. Carol A. Tamminga, a research psychiatrist and second in command at the prestigious Maryland Psychiatric Research Center in Baltimore. Together, they worked on a new drug that Tamminga described as "a conceptual jump": a milder-than-usual pill developed by Carlsson.

"It slows down the release of dopamine," Tamminga said. "It acts as a roadblock *and* a tollgate." Carlsson added: "The principle is not to knock the [dopamine] system out."

The drug was called Minus Triple P, or Preclamol. Taken once a day, it proved effective for twenty schizophrenic patients in Baltimore. Tantalizingly and inexplicably, its action ceased after one week. "We don't know the mechanism," Tamminga said. The researchers altered the dosage, gave the drug twice a day, added a second medication, and were hoping for better results.

As the scientists foundered at their tasks, the stressed families of the afflicted felt increasingly thwarted at theirs. They saw themselves ignored and powerless. At a minimum, they wanted their voices to be heard. Perhaps they could help to speed up a more favorable outcome for their kin. Action got under way with one spontaneous phone call.

"Let's organize," said Harriet Shetler.

"Yes, let's organize," said Beverly Young.

And so they did, with historic and lasting results. Following up their spontaneous call to action, the two Madison, Wisconsin, friends, and mothers of schizophrenic sons, corralled a handful of similarly burdened local housewives in November 1978 and formed the Dane County Alliance for the Mentally Ill (AMI). (The name was chosen because *ami* means "friend" in French.) All the mothers held the same fervent hopes: a better life for their afflicted children through more and improved research; a measure of relief from the tensions and pressures that the disease had thrust onto themselves, their spouses, and their other children; and, at the least, some company in their misery.

"That was my family," said one of the earliest members. "I felt I was no longer alone."

The pervasive feeling of isolation was not restricted to Wisconsin. Bev remembered how one of their members brought to one of the early meetings a newsletter from another local organization, Parents of Adult Schizophrenics, in San Mateo County, California, in the southern suburbs of San Francisco. Formed in 1974, it was one of dozens of similar self-help groups springing up all over the country.

"It was like an awakening," said Young. She and her friends perceived the clusters as a force of families waiting to be galvanized, and from September 7 to 9, 1979, at the Wisconsin Center in Madison, her group was host to 268 delegates from fifty-nine like-minded organizations. The National Alliance for the Mentally Ill was born. Over the years, it expanded into what the *New York Times* called "one of the nation's fastest-growing pressure groups." By 1996 it had 140,000 members organized in 1,100 chapters.

The idea was not new. Advocates for the mentally ill first organized in 1846 with the Alleged Lunatics' Friends Society, formed in London by John Thomas Perceval. A nobleman and son of a former prime minister, he had been hospitalized for three years because he was "living in heaven and hell" and hearing "command hallucinations." Released "against medical advice," he spent the next twenty years protecting the civil liberties of psychotics and exposing negligence, greed, and corruption endemic in the "asylums."

For his courage, Perceval was rewarded by being called deranged and told that his sympathies with the insane were of "very morbid character and his judgments weak." At the time, the "mad" were no longer being practically scalped to let their evil spirits escape from the brain, a scene painted in 1490 as *The Cure,* by Hieronymus Bosch, an artist, admittedly, with an eye for the macabre. Nor were they any longer chained or caged in small crates or sold as slaves. But bedlam still flourished in Perceval's day.

The London asylum that would become the synonym for any "madhouse" was the Bethlem Hospital, and it became famous not only as the scene of sights and sounds of torture and outlandish behavior but also as a popular tourist attraction. The engraver and satirist of cruelty, William Hogarth, recorded an unforgettable tableau of out-of-control inmates being inspected by smiling highborn ladies in hoopskirts. They were enjoying bedlam as a sideshow.

In the United States, mental patients did not acquire an articulate champion until 1909, when Clifford Beers, a Connecticut businessman who had been hospitalized with manic-depressive psychosis, founded the National Mental Health Association (NMHA). He had lately published a widely acclaimed autobiographical work, *A Mind That Found Itself,* with an introduction by William James.

"*Uncle Tom's Cabin* had a decided effect on the question of slavery of the Negro race," Beers reminded readers. "Why cannot a book be written which will free the helpless slaves of all creeds and colors confined today in the asylums and sanitariums throughout the world?" As acute a social critic as Albert Deutsch welcomed the work as "the beginning of a great crusade and a new era in the management of mental ills."

It wasn't to be. Fear, stigma, and frustration born of hopelessness engendered by the failure of available treatments caused the NMHA to concentrate on lobbying for the worried well ("Have you hugged your kid today?" was its poster slogan) and to subordinate the needs of the psychotic. This misguided focus was still paralyzing helpers in the 1970s, when Dr. John Spiegel, president of the American Psychiatric Association, toured the nation and asked psychiatrists about the ten most significant problems of their profession. The fate of chronic mental patients, last on his list, was met by a "numbing silence."

Silence was not a NAMI tactic; noise was. The movement had much in common with the frustrated hero in the movie *Network* who shouted into the night that he was "mad as hell" and wasn't going to take it anymore. Year after year,

NAMI campaigners kept up their loud demands for more research and lobbying dollars; for more tolerant federal and state laws; for relief from economic ruin, especially equal insurance treatment, so that schizophrenia would be considered like diabetes or any other long-term illness. Perhaps most comforting for its parent members, the organization worked to overcome the awful stigma encouraged by the psychoanalysts who held mothers and fathers responsible for the schizophrenia of their children. "Mental illness is a brain disease" became NAMI's mantra.

Given its relatively intelligent, largely white-collar, middle-class membership, NAMI had little difficulty in maneuvering to cement advantageous alliances. Beginning in 1980, the newly established MacArthur Foundation, with an eye for deserving but neglected causes, provided an initial grant of $78,650. The next year, it contributed $200,000 and in 1984 another $300,000.

NAMI's collaboration with the NIMH was immediate and close. The same held true of its relationship with the pharmaceutical industry. There was muttering about a "psychopharmaceutical complex," but NAMI members had learned firsthand that their kin would face a poor future without the medications produced from research funds appropriated by the companies out of their profits.

As the new drugs stirred hope for the improved outcome of treatments, schizophrenia became a less feared subject and more mentionable in the media. NAMI barrages on behalf of the mentally disabled found increasing acceptance. More parents were admitting publicly, stigma notwithstanding, that they had a schizophrenic relative.

In 1983 NAMI emerged in the national conscience. Dr. E. Fuller Torrey, the NIMH schizophrenia specialist whose sister suffered from the disease, praised NAMI on Phil Donahue's talk show. The organization had never been discussed on national television before. That year, Torrey published the first edition of his excellent book *Surviving Schizophrenia,* which listed addresses and phone numbers of NAMI chapters throughout the country; he also turned over his royalties to the organization.

The NAMI national convention in St. Louis during August of that year scored a publicity coup: for the first time, the parents of the country's most famous schizophrenic, John Hinckley Jr., spoke publicly, pledging to travel to where NAMI chapters were located and help spread its word. Jack and JoAnn Hinckley had established a fund-raising organization and were devoting themselves full-time to proselytizing on behalf of brain-ill patients like their son. This articulate couple proved to be popular speakers. "Mental illness must come out of the closet, too," they preached, "and we who are closest to it will have to start."

That year, the government spent just $7.35 per person annually for research on the mentally ill, compared with $203 for cancer. There were still only thirty thousand NAMI members. In the next decade, though, NAMI membership almost quintupled, and the NIMH research budget tripled under the leadership of Laurie Flynn, who took over as NAMI executive director in 1984.

Flynn's biography promised nothing unusual. She had served on boards and committees for causes in health and in child welfare. She had been executive director of the North American Council on Adoptable Children and cochair of the Maryland Commission on Women's Health. However, her curriculum vitae omitted two qualifications. She was noisy and visible.

Of course there was more to her role than appearing as a convincing expert witness before every convention, congressional committee, and television program that would hear her. Cheerful and popular, she persuaded every big name in mental health to do active service on the NAMI advisory board. She organized a "helpline" and, within a year, it fielded 175,000 inquiries from callers in need of assistance in caring for their sick kin.

Political savvy helped Flynn to recognize that the new generation of antipsychotic drugs would produce still-greater opportunities for cooperation between NAMI members and the pharmaceutical industry. The companies needed to recoup their huge research investment by selling their drugs on a vast scale. Like Prozac, the medications would generate considerable new income. So Flynn persuaded nine companies to pledge fifteen million dollars for a national antistigma drive.

"Open your mind," the campaign literature kept repeating. "Mental illnesses are brain disorders."

Flynn also understood the ways of Washington and was able to maneuver two political arch-opponents, Senators Pete Domenici of New Mexico and Paul Wellstone of Minnesota, to cosponsor NAMI's key legislation for the relief of families: the bipartisan measure to achieve equal insurance treatment (parity) for the mentally disabled. Domenici was chairman of the Senate Budget Committee and one of the most conservative of Republicans. Wellstone was one of the most liberal of Democrats. Flynn got the two to meet on common ground: Domenici had a schizophrenic daughter; Wellstone had a schizophrenic brother.

Flynn's personal life matched her career path. With her husband, Joe, she was raising a daughter, Shannon, and seven multiracial children, some adopted, including retarded youngsters. And shortly after Flynn joined NAMI, Shannon, seventeen, a senior and honor student in high school, was diagnosed as schizophrenic.

"I didn't know how mental illness would affect me," her mother told me. "But the identification gave me a lot more passion for my work. I said, 'This is kismet.' "

Others would have called it a catastrophe. Shannon was hospitalized in a catatonic state, mute and unresponsive, the disease having made itself known eight weeks earlier. "I was starting to shut down," Shannon told me. She couldn't sleep. Her fellow students terrified her: "People were evil; they were reading my mind." She couldn't stop pacing. She eyed her safety razor—it seemed to invite suicide.

Discharged from the hospital when her parents' insurance ran out after thirty days, Shannon became reasonably stable on Stelazine and was able to graduate from high school with the highest award. The family's hopes were soon dashed. Schizophrenic crises took Shannon twice to hospital emergency rooms, then back for a longer hospital stay. Released on clozapine, she could tolerate the drug for only two weeks. It sedated her; she kept falling asleep in the subway.

In 1994 came a new drug, risperidone, and a new life for Shannon. I spoke with her at her full-time job in the Experimental Therapeutics Branch of the NIMH, where she led a support group of patients. She had been taking risperidone for two years. She had gained weight, but lived in her own apartment, traveled independently to visit relatives, had been admitted to graduate school, and radiated her mother's sunny cheer.

It was Dr. Paul Janssen who, at the age of nearly sixty, had invented risperidone (trade name Risperdal). It was another reasonably safe and effective antipsychotic and was launched with a glitzy thrust unusual for a prescription medication. According to the marketing literature, it was for the newly sane person "waiting to emerge" from the mist of madness. The drug was Johnson & Johnson's fastest starter ever, reaching $100 million in sales within less than a year of its public debut.

It was the first in a new class of compounds that blocked the cell firing of both dopamine and serotonin neurotransmitters (receptors) in the brain. While it was not different enough from clozapine to fall within the medical category of "atypical," meaning a truly new drug, it was the first major new antipsychotic in thirty years and attracted commercial interest. "Schizophrenia—a Major New Market Opportunity" read the top headline across the drug industry newsletter from Merrill Lynch in November 1994. "The market for schizophrenia drugs appears to be underserved and highly dissatisfied with existing drugs," the securities analysts had discovered. Their conclusion was seductive: "Currently a one billion dollar market but the potential to be an estimated $3–5 billion market by 2000."

Janssen and his Belgian chemists had known for some time that a drug combining dopamine and serotonin antagonists (blockers) could successfully deal with psychosis. By 1981 they synthesized the first drug to meet that specification, R52245, Setoperone. It proved inferior to Haldol, its cousin, and its chemical properties made it difficult to work with. So the researchers turned to R55667, Ritanserin, which they created in 1982. In a double-blind study,* it was found especially useful for negative and affective symptoms. They linked it with the positive effects of Haldol, and this led them to develop R64766, which would become known as risperidone.

The drug worked beautifully for many patients, including Michael B. Laudor, thirty-two, who had graduated in three years summa cum laude from Yale and soon thereafter spent eight months with schizophrenia in the psychiatric hospital of Columbia; despite his severe handicap, he graduated from Yale Law School. It was an inspiring comeback, and he was writing about it in a book for which movie rights were sold for $1.5 million. Risperidone had helped significantly, but its side effects were keeping him prisoner.

"I feel that I'm pawing through walls of cotton and gauze when I talk to you now," Laudor said to a writer from the *New York Times*. "I'm using sixty or seventy percent of my effort just to maintain the proper reality contact with the world."

With risperidone, EPS symptoms (severe muscle spasms and contractions) were minimized, although they increased considerably when the dosage had to be elevated beyond six to eight milligrams a day. Among the side effects were insomnia, agitation, dizziness, sleepiness, and rapid heartbeat. Orthostatic hypotension—low blood pressure and feeling faint or light-headed when standing or sitting up quickly—was not uncommon, at least during the start-up period. The drug worked well and very quickly after the onset of the illness, but its usefulness over the long term and in refractory (difficult to treat) patients was in question.

Laudor had the great benefit of a brilliant intellect, gritty determination, supportive colleagues and family, a relatively brief acute phase of the illness,

---

* "Double-blind" means that neither patients nor evaluators know who is getting what medication or placebo. For Olanzapine, some "triple-blind" tests were run, meaning that the organizers, too, were kept ignorant. Only the computers were all-knowing.

and onset at a time of his life when he had already processed and banked much intellectual capital. Very few schizophrenics were ever so lucky, yet Laudor's case was far from unique. As I look back, it turns out that I have identified a remarkable number of schizophrenics who fought their way to reasonably normal health. Their records are inspiring; some are downright astounding. I wish I had known about them years ago; still, they offer solace.

CHAPTER 8

The Restored

AMONG THE reborn I have talked with is Mark Vonnegut, the forty-nine-year-old son of Kurt Vonnegut, the novelist. In 1975 Mark published an autobiography, *The Eden Express,* an inspiring and terrifying book. In 1,400 pages it detailed his six years as a dropout, followed by three breakdowns with hospitalizations for schizophrenia.

When I phoned him in 1996 in suburban Boston, he was practicing pediatrics. His voice sounded strong and cheery, and he spoke of his memories with the precision of a clinician. "Electroshock scared me to death," he said, "but it helped me. I also had Thorazine, Haldol, and lithium. I still take lithium."

His road back was long and torturous. After his graduation from Swarthmore, Vonnegut established his own commune in a valley one hundred miles north of Vancouver ("No cops, no Nixon, no nothing"), and there he descended into madness. He heard strange voices, "mostly bearers of bad news." He failed in his attempt to drink a gallon of Clorox because he was "so confused I couldn't do a decent job of it." He threw rocks at windows. He thought he was black. The sun was exploding. The air looked liquid. There wasn't enough oxygen for everybody. "The devil was taking over." He thought his girlfriend was dead, that his father had killed himself. His voices were sabotaging his chess games. ("Concede. Your position is hopeless.")

His fantasy experiences became internalized. When he began reciting *Moby Dick* from beginning to end, or so he had planned, he felt as if he were actually losing a finger to a harpoon and that a companion lost half a foot. On another occasion, holding out his arm for shots, he inquired, "Is this going to be more like a square dance or more like a clambake?"

Shortly after he finished his autobiography, an interviewer, Otto Friedrich, asked the author what he thought had saved him. Vonnegut said: "I knew enough about textbook psychiatry to know, in my lucid moments, that I was a paranoid schizophrenic, that I was suffering episodes of increasing severity, with shorter and shorter time in between. And that, as a textbook case, I was pretty much slated for this for the rest of my life. And that gave me a hell of a lot of resolve." Friedrich concluded that this resolve had been pivotal, although the recovering patient himself gave most of the credit to his medications, electroshock, large doses of vitamins, and the steadfast support of his parents.

At the time, Vonnegut had managed to start medical school. He had applied to twenty of them, and only Harvard had accepted him in the face of his psychiatric past. "Since I was applying to Harvard, they said I couldn't have had schizophrenia," said Vonnegut. They did give him "unusual" psychiatric tests. He had no trouble passing these or graduating from medical school.*

The value of insight derived from psychotherapy had been dismissed by Vonnegut, at least for a case such as his. "That's OK because it sounds nice," he once said. "Who could be against insight? Who could be against motherhood? But clinically, it has zero effectiveness." Resolve—that was his most powerful asset.

So many other schizophrenics I met had inspiring experiences to share.

- Dr. Frederick J. Frese had become a professional caregiver helping patients still struggling with the disease. He was a psychologist, well into his fifties, diagnosed with paranoid schizophrenia thirty years before while he was an officer in the Marine Corps. He was hospitalized ten times over the next decade. Although he still suffered

---

* Had Vonnegut truly been afflicted with schizophrenia? He was still inclined to believe so, although his good response to lithium could indicate that he might actually have had a case of "bizarre bipolar" disorder. To me, this doesn't seem likely, given his florid history. As a doctor, Vonnegut was troubled by the uncertainty. "Diagnosis by [later] outcome is an unsatisfactory business," he said.

occasional relapses, sometimes for several weeks, he served for fifteen years as director of psychology at Ohio's Western Psychiatric Hospital; held a faculty appointment at another hospital; was married and the father of four children; and served on the national board of NAMI. He was taking risperidone.

- Dr. Carol North, a St. Louis psychiatrist, wrote an eye-opening autobiography, *Welcome, Silence,* about the years when she was an off-and-on college student. Often hospitalized for schizophrenia, she told her doctors, "Someone is trying to kill me. I am not in this world. I'm in another world. . . . My thoughts were stolen away." She nevertheless retained a sharp ear for useless lines spoken by her psychoanalytically oriented doctors: "What was your childhood like?" or "When I ask you about sex, you look frightened. Am I right?" And the final diagnosis: "What's wrong with you is that you have a scared little girl inside you. You have a badly beaten child ego state."

  Determination paid off for North. She was able to place herself in the hands of doctors who were working experimentally with renal dialysis. The method rarely worked for schizophrenia. For her illness, which was considered atypical, it worked dramatically.

- Lori Schiller, thirty-seven, decided to become a full-time missionary to work against schizophrenia. She was fifteen when she first heard voices screaming, "You must die! Die! Die!" Somehow she managed to graduate from Tufts, but the following year her parents, comfortably situated in the upper-class New York suburb of Scarsdale, persuaded her to enter the first of several mental hospitals where she spent a total of seven years. Her voices commanded her to kill her doctors, her family, herself.

  Successively, she was given Prolixin, Thorazine, Haldol, Mellaril, and twenty electroshock treatments. Nothing decreased her agitation and confusion, even when dosages were doubled and tripled. The worst remedy was the "quiet room," eight by eight feet, with nothing but a mattress, where she was to calm down. Finally, clozapine turned her functional, and she wrote a book that was admiringly reviewed, *The Quiet Room: A Journey Out of the Torment of Madness.*

  At last report, Schiller was taking twenty pills a day, worked as a counselor in a halfway house, and taught a class on schizophrenia for staff and patients at New York Hospital. She had converted her illness into a teaching tool. "If I can help just one person look into the avenues that make them well, it will be worth it," she told Amanda Bennett of the *Wall Street Journal.* "I want to help people the way they helped me."

- Linda Woods was thirty-eight when she appeared among the one hundred "Neediest Cases" in the *New York Times* during the 1995 Christmas season. For twenty years, she was in municipal psychiatric hospitals, refusing pills because she thought they were poison. She assaulted nurses and often escaped, fearing she would become ill like her fellow patients. Her "brain storms"—as she called them— tormented her: "One thought comes, then another. One says yes, another says no, another maybe. . . . One time it got so bad I couldn't decide whether to sit down or not."

   Ultimately, an agency counselor persuaded Woods to try Prolixin, and she found her life turned profoundly around. "I take my medicine and all my problems just float out the window," she said. Woods lived at the YWCA, did volunteer work for Brooklyn Hospital, and had her life planned into 2002: by then she expected to be a geriatric or psychiatric nurse.

These stories, each in its time, gave me solace. I was also buoyed somewhat by learning that, although schizophrenia's course over decades is so often disastrous in unpredictable ways, it can eventually turn benign—miraculously and, again, unpredictably. Dr. Fuller Torrey has written about how the disease wanes for some sufferers in their forties, and then becomes "significantly less severe" for them in their fifties and sixties: "We do not understand why this is so and there are, of course, exceptions," he wrote, "but schizophrenia represents one of the few conditions in life for which aging is an advantage."

A stunning example is Professor John Forbes Nash of Princeton, winner of the Nobel Prize in 1995. While still an undergraduate at Carnegie Tech, Nash was already shaping some of the foundation underlying game theory. At twenty-one, he wrote a twenty-seven-page Ph.D. thesis on the subject and became a professor at MIT. Not much later, his lectures no longer made sense. He abandoned his classes and wrote bizarre letters to public figures. In 1959, at thirty, he was confined with a schizophrenia diagnosis at McLean Hospital in suburban Boston.

Freudian therapists dominated treatment at the time, and Nash's wife was pregnant, so his illness was interpreted as "fetus envy." Eventually, the professor wandered aimlessly around Europe, certain that he was spied upon. He tried to renounce his citizenship, was hospitalized three more times, and then stalked around Princeton like a ghost, looking vacant and disheveled and hunting for secret messages in the numbers on blackboards.

The remission came gradually and, according to close friends, without help from drugs or other treatment. "It's just a question of living a quiet life," thought his wife, who divorced Nash more than thirty years ago but let him live in her home. A quiet life—but not disabled. He started working again at the age of sixty-six, after a lapse of thirty-six years, in his abstruse subspecialties of mathematics.

While the experiences of Nash and the others who recovered are not offered as conclusive, available clinical testimony seems sufficiently voluminous to warrant cautious optimism.* Routine supporting documentation has long been published as the final article in every issue of the NIMH official quarterly, *Schizophrenia Bulletin,* under the title "First Person Account." I have often found these contributions encouraging antidepressants. They were clearly composed by patients themselves, and their ability to do so was of itself some proof of sanity. I have studied these narratives for some twenty years. Most of the authors remained troubled to a greater or lesser degree, but all were once very ill and had become functional by the time they set down their experiences.

At the time of writing in a 1989 issue, for example, Esso Leete, after an illness of twenty years, worked as a medical transcriber in Denver. In 1991 Patricia J. Ruocchio, who used to think she was real while the rest of the world was not, wrote articles for the *New York Times* and the *American Journal of Psychiatry.* In 1992 Roberta L. Payne, who once drew weird monsters and believed herself abducted by alien beings, was employed as an editor in Denver. In 1994 Jeffrey DeMann—who had fantasized that his mother told him, "Die quickly now!"—had developed the terrible muscle spasms called tardive dyskinesia; still, he now was a clerk for a Grand Rapids grocery chain. By 1996 a one-time Detroit college student who felt the government was bugging his clothing, had earned his paralegal diploma and was a law librarian in New York.

---

* One of the most scornful and dismissive words in the medical lexicon—as I learned in decades of conversations with doctors—is "anecdote." When doctors are asked to listen to a case history, particularly one with a cheerful outcome, they like to invoke this term as a polite squelch. Even Dr. Fuller Torrey had a sign over his desk with the warning: "The plural of anecdote is not evidence."

As the effectiveness of new drugs improved, so did news of restored patients. Eventually, the anecdotal chorus on behalf of Olanzapine—I will write about this drug extensively later—grew progressively more convincing. And the cracks in the glaciers have been widening for some time. Dr. Courtenay M. Harding, a psychologist at the University of Colorado School of Medicine, researched the records of 369 severely ill patients discharged from the back wards of a state mental hospital in Vermont during the 1950s. Half were schizophrenic. They were given therapy, job opportunities, and social support in their communities. The most effective medications were still not available, yet two-thirds of the patients had "improved considerably or had fully recovered" twenty-five years after discharge, according to the study Harding published in the *American Journal of Psychiatry* in 1987.

Contrary to much of the still-prevailing conventional wisdom, schizophrenia is anything but a predictable malady.

CHAPTER 9

"An Arrogant View of Their Mission"

Diagnosis. The art or act of identifying a disease from its signs and symptoms.

—*Webster's Medical Desk Dictionary*

THE LONG-BREWING WRANGLE ABOUT diagnosing psychosis approached its climax in the fall of 1972, when Jeff had been trying to elude his overtaxed handlers at the Stanford Medical Center and a historic experiment was secretly taking shape in the nearby Stanford Department of Psychology. Coincidentally, this was happening just before the signpost for my son's prospects, his own diagnosis, was switched from "Schizophrenia, acute" to "Schizophrenia, chronic, schizo-affective type." I was unaware of the Stanford experiment until years after the outcome was published, in 1973, in the prestigious journal *Science* under the title "On Being Sane in Insane Places."

The author, Dr. David L. Rosehan, a member of Stanford's psychology and law faculties, had become disturbed about the vagueness of psychiatric diagnosis and wanted to expose the equivocations and their consequences.

Although he found his method "distasteful," he organized a team of eight infiltrators who presented themselves at eight hospitals in five states, complaining that they heard voices saying "empty," "hollow," and "thud."

The pseudo-patients, three women and five men, were sane. Three psychologists (plus Rosehan) participated, along with a pediatrician, a psychiatrist, a painter, and a housewife. All were diagnosed as schizophrenic on admission and kept hospitalized for up to fifty-two days. They were administered Stelazine, Thorazine, Compazine, and several other medications—2,100 pills in all, of which only two were swallowed. Not one of the intruders was seen as such by hospital personnel, although thirty-five patients voiced suspicions ("You're not crazy, you're checking up on the hospital"). All the "patients" were eventually discharged with the potentially damaging label "schizophrenia in remission."

The resulting uproar reverberated for years. The nation's psychiatrists were profoundly stirred up, none more so than the triumvirate of ambitious young professors who were just then plotting the revolution that fueled a decade-long fratricidal duel of the biological psychiatrists against their psychoanalyst brethren.* Medical historians would call the trio's campaign a "signal event for American psychiatry," "a fateful point in the history of the American psychiatric profession," and "a profound reframing" leading to the "remedicalization" of their craft.

The issues warranted such strong language. It was the time when feelings were heated, and a textbook by an influential psychoanalyst, Professor Silvano Arieti, dismissed medications for schizophrenia: "One can no more treat so deeply an ingrained and emotionally internalized state of mind by drugs than one can take a pill to learn or unlearn French." A president of the American Psychiatric Association (APA) announced that Freudian thinking "had brought the profession to the edge of extinction," and victims of schizophrenia like Jeff were at particular risk. In 1971 a team of three respected authorities reported in the *Archives of General Psychiatry*: "Because of the overly broad definition of schizophrenia used in the United States, considerable numbers of patients . . . were being misdiagnosed and therefore incorrectly treated."

* I wish to acknowledge assistance in this discussion from three research projects: "Neurosis, Psychodynamics, and DSM-III," by Ronald Bayer and Robert L. Spitzer, *Archives of General Psychiatry*, February 1985; "DSM-III and the Transformation of American Psychiatry: A History," by Mitchell Wilson, *American Journal of Psychiatry*, March 1993; and *The Selling of DSM*, by Stuart A. Kirk and Herb Kutchins (Aldine de Gruyter, 1992).

When Dr. Theodore Millon cast the first stone in the mid-1960s, he was professor of psychology at Northwestern University. In a groundbreaking volume, he had classified all personality disorders into fifteen types, and by 1996 his ultimate inventory would cover seventy-five varieties spread across 818 pages. He became the theoretician of the rebels, eventually moving on to Harvard.

Political leadership was the role of Millon's friend and Northwestern colleague Dr. Melvin Sabshin, professor of psychiatry and chairman of the Council on Research and Development of the profession's power base, the APA.* The imposingly huge Sabshin, a smooth diplomat, a good infighter against bureaucracy, widely known and liked, became medical director and principal strategic thinker of the APA.

Millon, Sabshin, and their fellow committeemen (this would be almost totally a male war) brought in as a tactician a recruit eager to be drafted, Dr. Robert L. Spitzer of Columbia University. As chairman of the APA's Committee on Nomenclature and Statistics, he would labor for twenty years to drive, lure, tug, and cajole his Freudian colleagues to acquiesce reluctantly to modern diagnostic definitions and treatments.

"Appeals to reason were often overshadowed by appeals for votes and power," he recalled.

What triggered hostilities was a revision due for the APA's catalog of mental ills, the *Diagnostic and Statistical Manual (DSM)*. *DSM-I* had been published in 1952, *DSM-II* was negotiated by 1968, and by 1971 Millon was bursting with impatience because of its imprecision. He was pushing hard for a radical revision to be known as *DSM-III*, and all parties involved knew they would not be tinkering with a fusty academic treatise; they would be altering a seminal document known as "the bible" and "the official map of American psychiatry's clinical jurisdiction."

DSM-II had been a molehill: a small spiral notebook, 150 pages, costing $3.50. *DSM-III*, a mountain that would not emerge until 1980, ran to 500 pages at $35, and its 25 advisory committees employed more than 250 consultants to identify 182 disorders. *DSM-II* required only one paragraph to delineate schizophrenia; *DSM-III* devoted a dozen pages to it.

The conflict over *DSM-III* would be an all-out dispute about substance,

---

* Brain power aside, the APA represents a lobbying force of scope. Its 1995 membership was forty thousand; its annual budget, twenty-six million dollars.

not semantics, and it would reveal the doctrinaire partisanship so difficult to reconcile with the profession's new goal of scientific objectivity.

Millon possessed an effective lobbyist's two principal assets: persistence and connections. Throughout the late 1960s, while writing his first classic book, *Modern Psychopathology*, he kept grumbling to his friend Sabshin about the inadequacies of *DSM-II*. Sabshin became interested, so in 1971 Millon gave him a memo deploring the guide's "total lack of creative innovation" and urging appointment of an APA review committee to work toward a *DSM-III*.

In April 1974, Sabshin, having just become the new APA medical chief, and Millon held an all-day planning meeting with Spitzer, the research psychiatrist, who seemed to them ideally qualified to lead the push to reform American psychiatry. The candidate's professional qualifications were sound, and he had been eager for the job for years. He possessed the requisite level of energy and political skills, including a thick skin. He also was a veteran of this turf, having worked as a consultant on *DSM-II* and engineered the settlement of its most hectic Donnybrook: an epic (and finally successful) effort to dislodge homosexuality from the list of pathology and the attendant stigma.

By September, Spitzer's *DSM-III* task force of five psychiatrists was hard at work. All had been selected by him for their biological orientation and their disdain of such Freudian "etiological assumptions" as the unconscious. Ultimately, the leadership of the task force would number fifteen psychiatrists, but new members would be added only in minimal increments over the years as Spitzer surrendered ground, inch by inch, yielding to pressure to make his group more nearly representative of the profession, yet always making certain that he would stay in control and that his philosophy would prevail.

Psychoanalytically oriented doctors were admitted to membership in the task force only to quit in frustration or disgust. Some analysts departed silently, others with bitter blasts at Spitzer and his confreres. Thousands of pages of resentful letters piled up. The doggedness of the deadlocks that developed over an array of specialized issues was without precedent in the world of such normally dispassionate clinicians.

The first countermoves mounted by a special committee of the American Psychoanalytic Association against the Spitzer team, beginning in 1976, were relatively measured, if sweeping. The analysts' initial review held that the proposed *DSM-III* classifications, "bad as they were," were not primary issues. The entire thinking behind the diagnostic labels, which the Spitzer team had called "atheoretical," was perceived as "superficial" by the Freudians.

Worse was the prevailing bias diagnosed by the analysts: "Only those items were included that could be proven statistically, which was—we felt—in a not so subtle way, an antianalytic stance."

The assault intensified with an editorial in the *Journal of the American Academy of Psychoanalysis* entitled "Retreat from a Psychiatry of People." It charged that the only reality recognized by the proposed new manual was what was "scientific, behaviorist and measurable," to the exclusion of "psychiatry as a humane, open, and socially progressive force."

The tone of the debate sharpened when a New York practitioner, Dr. Howard Berk, attacked the Spitzer group's "loosely conceived and untried changes." Berk said: "Change can be destructive, as is vulgarization and wide and peremptory extirpation of large parts of the living language of a people, of a science, of an art."

On the strength of these sentiments, Berk was appointed chairman of a liaison committee of the APA with five of its most alarmed state societies, and in this role he released an emphatic cri de coeur. The profession would suffer grave damage, he warned, "if a rigid exclusionism were allowed to paralyze the creative and intuitive activity of that large part of psychiatry that lies outside the conceptual pale of the task force," which Berk found "narrow, strictured, one-sided," and suffering from "linguistic and conceptual sterility."

In mid-1976 he focused on the concept that would, in the end, lie at the heart of the whole war: "DSM-III gets rid of the castles of *neurosis* [emphasis added] and replaces it [sic]with a diagnostic Levittown."

As hostilities escalated, some of the biggest names in American psychoanalysis weighed in, employing harsh terminology. The renowned Dr. Otto Kernberg said he had wondered whether Spitzer's effort might be dismissed as a "joke," but had come to believe it was a catastrophe: "It is a straitjacket and a powerful weapon in the hands of people whose ideas are very clear, very publicly known, and the guns are pointed at us."

By 1978 a former APA president wrote to the chairman of the Council on Research and Development: "I do not know who determined that this small group of people should try to reorganize psychiatric thinking in the United States, but I am . . . concerned that they have such an arrogant view of their mission and are not willing to incorporate some of the things which we have learned over the past seventy years."

Spitzer knew that the status of the Freudian concept of *neurosis*, which he considered meaningless, was shaping up as the make-or-break question of the project. Powerful APA board members were rejecting his work, as his postmortem would record later, "because they were committed to the perspective of the pro-neurosis forces, others because of their concern about the politically divisive impact of adopting DSM-III without the concept *neurosis*."

Further protracted negotiations yielded a compromise remarkable in that it accepted as well as rejected "neurosis"—the bread and butter of psychoanalysis since Freud began to treat neurotics. While "neurotic disorder" won acceptance, "neurotic process" was rejected. It was, said one of Spitzer's loyalists, "a minor capitulation to psychoanalytic nostalgia."

Spitzer had won his marathon. When a motion to approve *DSM-III* in its entirety achieved acceptance by an overwhelming majority at a formal session of the APA's assembly, he was honored with a standing ovation.

Like most champions of causes, Spitzer had arrived at his belief in biological psychiatry by way of personal experience. His famous analyst critic, Dr. Otto Kernberg, had diagnosed him correctly, charging during the debate that Spitzer had "extremely strong negative feelings about psychoanalysis." As part of his training, Spitzer had undergone personal analysis with an unhappy outcome. The sessions had stretched across ten years and then slowly faded out "with many problems unresolved." Five subsequent years as a psychoanalytic practitioner further increased his disenchantment with Freud as a problem solver.

Becoming a full-time research academic at Columbia, Spitzer took on diagnostic anarchy as psychiatry's most vexing ailment, and his opponents on the *DSM-III* task force continued to annoy him when their battle was over.

"They never said what the alternative was," he said.

I asked him what might finally be done about the prevailing anarchy.

"The extent to which there is anarchy is hard to study," he said somewhat uncomfortably.

Isn't the genie still out of the bottle and aren't the newly standardized criteria vague, even arbitrary?

"Sure, sure," Dr. Spitzer said. "They're a kind of a reference point."

Kind of a reference point, still eluding firm grip as the year 2000 was closing in.

Even Ted Millon, the champion classifier, was getting impatient, going so far as to diagnose a distressing resemblance between the treaters and the treated. In his 1996 opus, *Disorders of Personality,* he chided his colleagues for stick-in-the-mud inertia as if Spitzer and his twenty-year war had never taken place.

"Like patients who are unable to extricate themselves from their past, perpetuating and fostering new difficulties as a consequence," he grieved, "so too does the profession of psychiatry find itself unable to break its old though admittedly poor classificatory troubles."

CHAPTER 10

The Shattered

ALONG WITH the euphoria induced by the comebacks of so many, I had to absorb the heartache triggered by the destroyed, especially the suicides.

Many schizophrenics who attempt to take their own lives do not succeed. Those who do tend to be depressed males suffering from relapsing-and-remitting cycles of the illness. They possess lucid insight into what is wrong with them, and the discrepancy between their past and current level of performance is great and of itself depressing. In these ways, Michael Wechsler was typical.

Wechsler, seventeen and precocious, was a Harvard student and under psychiatric care. "I'd been taking tranquilizers," he once said, "and one day I finished the bottle—thirty-four times the regular dose." Although he had been formally diagnosed early as "psychotic" and self-diagnosed as "nuts," he quickly put on his shoes, went to the Harvard Clinic, and had his stomach pumped.

At eighteen, still in Cambridge but hospitalized, he was more determined to kill himself: "I started strangling myself—with shirts, a razor cord, whatever I could get my hands on. . . . I tied a guitar string pretty tight around my neck." He was always discovered in time.

In other respects, Wechsler was atypical. Many schizophrenic suicide victims are secretive and live as social isolates; they succeed in doing away with themselves before anyone has any warning. A meticulous Finnish study in

1994 found that death-bent patients saw their psychiatrists within ten days prior to the event and failed to mention their intention. Wechsler, however, talked freely to his doctors and communicated well with his highly intelligent, loving, and tenaciously supportive parents: his father, James A. Wechsler, was editor of the editorial page of the *New York Post*; his mother, Nancy, was a prominent attorney who specialized in publishing matters.

Perhaps because Michael was able to draw on other favorable personal assets unusual to schizophrenics, the disease was not definitively diagnosed until about six years after its onset in 1960. He was a delightful, outgoing young person who held various jobs, at least intermittently; had experienced and enjoyed sex with women; wrote publishable poetry; and played the flute with skill. He also occasionally experimented with drugs, including LSD.

His psychiatrists, in the aggregate, served largely as agents of confusion, rather than clarification. There were eight of them over nine years, whom the parents identified only as Dr. First through Dr. Eighth. Some practiced individual therapy on Michael, some group therapy; some demanded parental involvement, others refused to talk to the parents and would not return phone calls. Their therapies ranged from Freudian analysis, to years of (traditionally painful and unsuccessful) insulin injections to induce shock, to medication.

Michael underwent three stretches of confinement in mental hospitals. From one of these he escaped eight times within a year so that the institution declined to care for him further. He hated the hospitals and often refused to cooperate with their rules. Thorazine, the most widely used major antipsychotic available at the time, made him listless and drowsy and caused him to gain weight, so eventually he secretly refused to swallow the medication, a bit of sabotage that long went undetected. There was no record of efforts to administer other drugs.

Much of the time his endlessly forbearing parents cared for their son at home. I came to compare their lot with the periods when my son lived with me and confess that I could not have endured even briefly what the Wechslers went through for years. Michael played the flute on top of a car in the garage. He paced up and down the hall all day and into the night. He complained that his "skin was too tight." He reported feeling "as if I were not really there" and once thought his mother was an FBI agent.

His moods fluctuated erratically. Once he simply wept through an entire session with one of his therapists. At other times, he was the sunniest of companions. When he departed from one of his hospitals, his fellow patients presented him with a testimonial headed "We'll Miss You."

At irregular intervals came more suicide attempts. Once Michael's father frantically pulled his son back as he dangled from their ninth-floor apartment house window.

Still, Michael held a job and was planning to return to Harvard, when, in April 1969, at age twenty-six, he wrote a poem that began:

> One has the choice to live or die
> One has the choice to fall or to fly. . . .

One morning shortly afterward, he took his life.

Maxine Mason was diagnosed as schizophrenic in 1964, at fifteen, and taken to the first of her innumerable hospitalizations. In the ambulance she asked her mother, "Is there no place on earth for me?" In 1982 that question became the title of an enormously moving book, which expanded a four-part series in *The New Yorker,* covering Mason's life and illness. In the book she was called Sylvia Frumkin, to protect her privacy. The author was a Pulitzer Prize winner, Susan Sheehan, who became Maxine's friend and champion.

Mason was a wildly manic, brilliant, obese, and forever-monologuing patient; Sheehan described her verbosity as "Joycian." Mason's life was a thirty-year war against her medications and the psychiatrists who, sometimes hapless and often wrongheaded, didn't know how to handle their armamentarium. If I had not had comparable experiences with my son, I would have found Mason's misadventures difficult to believe.

Her torment commenced with one of her early doctors, a resident at St. Vincent's Hospital in Manhattan, who gradually lowered her Thorazine dosage from two thousand to four hundred milligrams daily, beginning as soon as she appeared "more organized." Mason thereupon worsened and swallowed the contents of a bottle of shampoo; the doctor called the cause of the deterioration "obscure." According to a specialist in psychopharmacology who years later reviewed the records for Sheehan, the relapse wasn't mysterious at all. The dosage should have been raised, not reduced, until the symptoms were firmly in remission, not just slightly improved.

The following month, Mason was transferred to Creedmore Hospital in Queens Village, a New York State institution for chronic patients. A resident doctor there lowered her Thorazine to two hundred milligrams, a move described by Sheehan's consultant as "irrational and incompetent." One possible explanation: Creedmore in the 1960s had a reputation for undermedicating, much as Menninger's did when Jeff was there in the early 1970s. Mason proved the consultant correct, refusing to wear shoes, snatching food from other patients, and running up and down the hallways.

About two weeks later, a staff psychiatrist scribbled on her chart, "Patient did not show much improvement on drug therapy . . . and, therefore, she will start a series of ECT [electroshock] today." The electroshock treatments, which Sheehan's expert adviser considered counterindicated, were first welcomed by Mason's parents as "nothing short of a miracle," much as I would later react to Jeff's ECT results, but the "miracle," even after it was frequently repeated, did not last, just as it did not endure for Jeff.

In 1967 it was decided to try insulin shock treatments on Mason, although they had by then come to be considered obsolete and dangerous; they often jumbled the metabolism of patients for life. Mason detested the insulin and begged for an end to it, which was granted after forty comas and a weight gain of thirty-two pounds. Then she was put on Haldol and Valium.

Early during her acquaintance with the madwoman for whom she developed exquisite empathy, Sheehan was struck by a comment about her friend, which had resonance with me, given my own experience with Jeff.

"Many psychiatrists—those she encountered, at least, and I don't think her case is uncommon in this respect—don't take the time and trouble to study the case histories," Sheehan's consultant told her. "No treatment she received over a period of thirteen years bore any logical relationship to a previous treatment. You get the impression that the psychiatrists pulled a drug out of a hat and gave her too little of what they pulled out, or that they dumped the contents of the hat out on a tray and gave her too little of several drugs."

By 1978 Mason was at Hillside–Long Island Jewish Hospital, improving only slightly on lithium, Thorazine (2,800 milligrams), and Stelazine (90 milligrams). She developed elevated liver enzymes, a common and dangerous side effect, and began treatment instead with a new drug called Moban, on which she remained psychotic. She danced on tables, broke her glasses in a rage, and spoke in such a frenzy that she ran out of breath.

Hillside could not keep her. Admitted to Creedmore for the tenth time, she was prancing around the day hall and taking off her blouse. She wore no bra or shoes. "Creedmore is Universal Studios," she announced. "This isn't schizophrenia, it's terminal acne. . . . I'm planning to go back to school to do sixth grade. I want to relive my childhood. . . . Being a mental patient is really my profession. . . . God talks to me a lot. The voice is an imp in my head."

The ensuing fifteen years saw Mason whirl through rounds of further hospitalizations, occasional jobs, disruptive scenes on the streets and subways, and a period with the born-again-Christian movement, accompanied by disenchantment with her medications. Mostly she refused to take them or she "forgot."

During 1991 to 1992, Mason spent more than a year in Bellevue Hospital at a cost of $381,625, paid by Medicaid and Medicare, and began taking clozapine (Clozaril). "I think Clozaril helped her as much as any medication currently available," her psychiatrist said. "I wish she had kept taking it." But once she was transferred to Fountain House, a model board-and-care facility, she stopped the medication, assaulted staff, consumed entire jars of mayonnaise, and was sent to her last institution, Rockland Psychiatric Center, a state hospital where parts of the movie *The Snake Pit* were filmed.

She weighed 247 pounds and announced, "I am a star. I'm Dr. Mason. I'm the head doctor on these grounds." Sheehan read the hospital record. "It is a litany of Maxine hitting and being hit, of Maxine biting and being bitten, of pills she swallowed and refused to swallow," her indefatigable chronicler wrote in February 1995, for a *New Yorker* article entitled "The Last Days of Sylvia Frumkin."

Maxine Mason died of cardiac arrest caused by bleeding from an untreated stomach ulcer, and Sheehan was sadly reviewing some of the many letters from her friend: "She was the only person who ever wrote letters to our cat, enclosing coupons for cat food and inquiring after Fearless Fosdick's well-being."

CHAPTER 11

Freud Is Dead,
Freud Lives!

ALTHOUGH THE biological psychiatrists wrestled Sigmund Freud to the
ground with seeming finality in the 1970s, the venerable professor will never
fade away, and only the other day Jeff and I were talking about him.

He is not a far-out subject for us. My son has been ill for so long that he has
almost of necessity been touched by just about every fashion in contemporary
mental treatments.

It turned out that when Jeff first talked to Dr. D'Andrea about school phobia in the late sixties, my inquisitive teenager had been reading up on the subject. That was his custom. His fears seemed rooted in an inferiority complex,
and Jeff suggested this to his doctor, "I guess we'd better get out old Freud."

"Oh, I don't think we're going to need him," the doctor said. He was no
fan of lengthy Freudian excavations. He also figured that my son had no need
for deep therapy. Jeff didn't, not at that time anyway, so Freud was left at rest.
He was evoked again when Jeff was in poor shape and disillusioned about all
civilization, including Freud and psychoanalysis, and the Menninger Clinic
after his psychotic break.

The clinic's analyst asked him to free-associate. Jeff demurred.

"This stuff can't work," he remonstrated.

"Things will come out," coaxed the analyst.

"But it didn't happen," Jeff recalled as he reminisced about his brief encounters with the pioneer who remained the most exalted name in psychological healing.

In March 1980, while he was briefly out of the hospital and living in one of the many halfway houses where he sat around bored and lost, Jeff decided he wanted to become "a psychoanalyst and vitamin therapist" and that he should enter psychoanalysis. I suspected he was simply lonely.

After consulting the San Jose Yellow Pages, he contacted a psychoanalyst, Dr. Philip Stein, for an appointment. The doctor sounded Jewish to Jeff, and he had been thinking that someone of his own faith seemed most likely, somehow, to bring sympathy to his needs. Stein charged seventy-five dollars per session, and Jeff saw him three times. He paid for the first meeting himself; I paid for the others. I didn't wish to undercut any remotely reasonable undertaking that spurred him into activity.

The ruminations and intellectualizations helpful in psychoanalysis were bound to attract Jeff, but I also suspected that he hoped to enlist this form of treatment as an ally in his war against medications. While more and more psychoanalysts were using drugs cautiously to assist them with their therapy, the biological specialists remained scornful of analysis. "Since it often makes the patient worse, it can be said to be the non-treatment of choice," wrote E. Fuller Torrey.

Wanting to deal with his "repressed childhood memories," Jeff was preparing for an extended stay with Dr. Stein. Aware of my finances, my son tried to prepare me gently for the investment. "I do not at this time believe," he wrote, "I will need Dr. Stein, if I consult him twice a week, as he recommends, longer than two years." Showing himself to be an adept lobbyist, he added: "Did you know that you are the finest father a young man could possibly want?"

Too bad that my pocketbook did not measure up to my character. With regret, I informed Jeff that we could not afford Stein. Jeff did not protest. It was never clear whether he was being thoughtful or had already lost interest. He did share the principal message that he took away from the doctor. "He told me I was into indignation," Jeff said, which seemed perceptive, if not too helpful.

Like many alleged incurables—the pilgrims to the shrine at Lourdes come to mind—Jeff exhausted more of his expectations in another shopping trip for a miracle. This time he pinned his hopes on Arthur Janov's primal scream therapy.

"I thought it was the easy way out," he told me not long ago without bitterness.

His Pied Piper was not Janov, the Beverly Hills psychologist whose noisy technique of driving for catharsis in troubled souls was in vogue in the 1970s among wealthy entertainers, if not with conventional therapists. Jeff felt he was following in the footsteps of John Lennon.

In later years, my son became a trifle apologetic about his hero worship, but in the time when he was hungriest for support he admired Lennon inordinately. The psychedelic quality of some of the Beatles' music appealed to him, as it did to millions of the world's young. Lennon, in particular, was special for Jeff. He found solace in the singer's adaptability, his perseverance over adversity, and, especially, John's overcoming of a breakdown much like Jeff's own, a recovery for which Lennon gave all the credit to Janov. The affinity for Lennon preceded the serious phase of Jeff's illness, but not by much. It started in 1969 when my son spotted a full-page picture of the singer and a long interview about his travails in *Rolling Stone*. The following year Jeff bought Janov's best-seller, *The Primal Scream,* and noted the blurb on the cover. It was a newspaper quote predicting that Janov would "wield as much influence as the early writings of Sigmund Freud." Other reviews made similar comparisons.

A friend had sent Lennon the book while he was living in Ascot, England. "Just the title made my heart flutter," John recalled. It reminded him of how the Beatles screamed themselves to fame. He invited Janov to Britain, where John and his wife, Yoko, screamed themselves hoarse for three weeks and then followed Janov to continued "treatment" at the Primal Institute in California. The idea was to scream away the pain of childhood, the struggles against parents, and other Freudian ballast. The Lennons were enchanted, pronounced themselves "liberated" of their neuroses, and Jeff, impressed, phoned Janov's institute to enroll. He was promised an application form and was told the cost was six thousand dollars, payable in advance.

"The patient's first primal scream usually came when presented with the bill," Fuller Torrey has written. Jeff was sane enough to swallow hard and forgo the Janov treatment. Still, his abortive exploration seemed to have left him with the comfortable feeling of having made an effort to bond with Lennon and an up-to-date incarnation of Freud.

The master's status was still lofty. When my son presented his "inferiority complex" to Dr. D'Andrea for repair, he was pursuing a mainstream of thought that still governed many troubled souls, especially in Freud's principal sphere of influence, the United States. "For no other system of thought in modern times," observed the dean of culture critics, Alfred Kazin, "except the great religions, has been adopted by so many people as a systematic interpretation of human behavior."

Freud himself would have found this eminence startling. He did not publish his first important book, *The Interpretation of Dreams,* until he was forty-three. When he explained his discoveries at meetings of the Vienna Medical Society, the reaction was derision. "My dear sir," he remembered a venerable surgeon exclaiming, "how can you talk such nonsense?" Another distinguished colleague called Freud's work "a scientific fairy tale."

As Bob Spitzer and his biological partisans battled, the popular worship of Freud's treatment methods was diminishing; it had even become a minority position among psychiatrists. By the 1990s, anti-Freud polemics had become staple literature. It was reported that Freud napped or wrote correspondence during sessions; that he simply ignored some of his patients' testimony; that he slept with his sister-in-law and counseled a patient to leave his wife so Freud could cadge donations from the man's wealthy mistress. His classic diagnoses in some of his most celebrated cases were being second-guessed and ridiculed by revisionists. In fact, ridicule had become a preferred weapon against him.

"Freud took two pieces of Vermont folk wisdom and turned them into a science," scoffed Dr. Thomas Gutheil, professor of psychiatry at Harvard Medical School, in 1992. "The first was, 'There's a whole lot more to folks than meets the eye.' This became known as the theory of the unconscious. The second was, 'Keep your mouth shut and you might learn something.'"

Yet, even this scornful critic gave Freud credit for a revolutionary turn in the physician-patient relationship. He changed the position of the doctor from that of an authority figure issuing orders to a more receptive role: "Freud said, 'Let the patient talk and tell his story.'"

Gutheil's observations appeared in a *Time* magazine article with the title "Is Freud Finished?" The writer exemplified another Freudian concept: ambivalence. Something *was* noteworthy in Freud's techniques even while the old doctor was being trivialized as a Vermont soothsayer. As Gutheil notes, "'Let the patient talk and tell his story' is Freud's most powerful contribution to modern culture." Ten million Americans a year would hardly be seeking psychological counseling of one type or another if Freud had not invented his fundamental technique for people to work on their personal problems.

It seems fair to assert that Jeff would never have been talking with Dr. D'Andrea in the first place if Freud, back when his peers still considered his notions to be nonsense, hadn't coaxed a few neurotics onto his couch in the 1890s. Furthermore, the idioms that Jeff invoked—as patients still do all over the world each day—was the old language of Freud. For as Peter Gay, one of the doctor's biographers, noted: "It is commonplace that we all speak Freud today, whether we recognize it or not," including our quotas of "Freudian slips."

If D'Andrea had found it advisable to take Jeff up on the suggestion to apply Freudian ideas to help my son out of his "inferiority complex" and other problems in 1968, they could have invoked quite a few additional concepts pioneered by the master and the theoreticians who came to embrace these and related terminology:

Phobias were the symptom that drove Jeff into therapy to begin with.

Sexuality was the issue that kept him from asking a girl for a date.

Self-esteem and *ego* were clearly qualities that Jeff lacked for many years.

Neurosis was the condition that afflicted him, and *psychosis* was where he was headed.

Obsession drove him to fantasize about a phantom girlfriend and the curative powers of vitamins.

Unconscious was the arena where Jeff's demons began their mischief in the sixties.

Separation anxiety was what he felt when his parents divorced.

Angst (Freud's German word that is usually and too limply translated as "anxiety") was the force that overshadowed his life.

The Freudian saturation of American culture has never ceased. In the 1940s, Ingrid Bergman was the psychoanalyst who cured Gregory Peck's trauma in *Spellbound*. In the 1950s, makers of hit films like *The Caine Mutiny, The Shrike, Fear Strikes Out,* and *The Three Faces of Eve* used Freud as their reference library. Henry and Clare Boothe Luce were psychoanalyzed, and the emotional journeys of these and other media barons trickled into any number of outlets that helped to shape popular psychology.

In the ensuing years, *Portnoy's Complaint* could hardly have existed unless Philip Roth had consulted Freud—a practice that persisted into the 1990s. *Psychology Today* featured "Re-Examining Freud." *Newsweek* ran "Dreams on a Couch." When Joel Steinberg and Hedda Nussbaum were accused of having beaten their adopted daughter to death, their childhoods were blamed. Kitty Dukakis attributed her drug and alcohol addictions to her rejecting mother.

Freud's ideological stranglehold was the more remarkable considering the master's abominable manners toward his perpetuators. His curt dismissal of Karl Menninger was no isolated pique. Another devotee, the inventor of Gestalt therapy and spiritual father of the encounter movement, Dr. Fritz Perls, told Freud he had come especially from South Africa to pay his homage. The master countered: "Well, and when are you going back?"

Some of the most forceful criticisms of Freud were published in 1992 by Dr. Torrey, *Freudian Fraud: The Malignant Effect of Freud's Theory on American Thought and Culture.*

The label "malignant" is in large measure overdrawn except insofar as it suggests long-term impact. However, three particulars in Torrey's indictment are weighty: (1) Freud's philosophy did encourage narcissism; (2) it stimulated personal irresponsibility; and (3) Freud's denigration of women is unacceptable.

These sins were troublesome enough to soil the reputation of even a giant among thinkers. Furthermore, Torrey didn't bring up the master's—to me unforgivable—bias against schizophrenics. Assuredly, Freud's vividly expressed revulsion of them was more tragic than his own interpretation allowed. He trivialized his rejection as "a curious sort of intolerance." In fact, it was a violation of the Hippocratic oath.

Withal, I detect more fallibility in Freud than fraud. His handicaps as a healer frustrated him, and they were severe. Medical knowledge available in his time was, after all, very sketchy. Freud was trained as a neurologist, and practitioners of this specialty were not permitted to treat patients in the hospitals of old Vienna. He had little occasion to see schizophrenics.

Yet he was sufficiently steeped in hard science to know that the inability of emotionally deadened patients to "form a positive transference" to a psychotherapist was not just due to the limitations of psychoanalysis. He realized that biological problems were implicated. He called them "organic factors" and considered them influential in "half of the problems of psychiatry."

While medications to deal with these factors did not then exist, he wished that they did. "Freud's fondest dream was to see the psychological factors about mental functioning in illness and in health linked to the chemical and physical architecture of the brain," wrote the Johns Hopkins brain specialist Dr. Solomon Snyder, no devotee of the master.

"Fraud" or not, Freud retains a remarkable ability to provoke controversy. Thus, late in 1995, a petition from forty-two scholars forced the Library of Congress to postpone an exhibit to be called "Freud: Conflict and Culture." The announcement coincided with the winter meeting of the American Academy of Psychoanalysis, entitled "Is There a Place for Psychoanalysis in Contemporary Culture?" The profession's critics accused the national library of wishing to help pro-Freudians "polish up the tarnished image of a business that's heading into Chapter 11."

Feminists among the protesters objected to Freud's view on masturbation and clitoral orgasms. Freud's granddaughter Sophie, a professor of social work, wanted it known that some of his work was "obsolete." Historians said that the exhibit was to forestall new anti-Freud disclosures likely to come with the release of more of his papers in the year 2000. Some broadsides were global. "His major edifice is built on quicksand," said Frank Sulloway, a science historian.

Nowhere in the debate could I find concern with the problems currently posed by the decline of Freud's depth psychology techniques, although some thoughtful authorities said they were worried about the issue: Would the financial restrictions of managed care drive longer-term therapy out of the medical market?* In the push to pills and quick fixes, were medical schools turning out enough dual-track psychiatrists capable of undergirding their medications with adequate psychotherapy? Was psychotherapy in danger? Was psychiatry regressing to limit itself to cataloging in the way of Emil Kraepelin?

"The careful description of symptoms is often taken to be an adequate or even proper assessment of the patient," cautioned Dr. Mitchell Wilson, a historian with the Joint Medical Program of the University of California, Berkeley. "It remains for the psychiatric profession to decide whether it has lost something crucial in the process of refinding its medical identity."

I had a parallel question. Never mind what may have *caused* an inferiority complex, if indeed he had one; once Jeff's pills accomplished their mission, how would he be guided to find his way to reenter the real world's bustle after a hiatus of a quarter century?

---

* Recent studies reveal a persistent and profound trend by managed-care companies to offer incentives to therapists to use drugs while discouraging and penalizing the use of more costly, longer-term talk therapy, even when unmistakably indicated. A survey in the *Harvard Review of Psychiatry* warned: "Managed care might become one more example of the tradition of neglect and abuse of the mentally ill."

At that, Jeff was lucky never to have fallen into the hands of actively—even aggressively—harmful healers. The nagging frustration induced by the stubborn resistance of his disease drove some unconventional medical minds to impose treatments that were of themselves, in fact, forms of madness. These psychiatrists could not tolerate being defied by nature.

CHAPTER 12

Antiheroes

"MILTON, ARE YOU still slapping schizophrenia patients?"

Dr. Milton Wexler of the Menninger Hospital in Topeka was being asked half in jest by a colleague visiting in the 1940s, Dr. Bert Lewin, about research to replicate the work of Dr. John Nathaniel Rosen, a psychiatrist practicing on Fifth Avenue in New York. Rosen had greatly impressed Karl Menninger, who had asked him to visit the Menninger Hospital to present his cases and was seriously thinking of inviting him to join the staff.

Rosen called his techniques "direct analysis." They included the beating of psychotic patients. Wexler had actually once become so provoked by an obstreperous patient that he had hit her, as Rosen probably would have done. His friend Lewin had heard about it; hence his black joke.

"Bert, you know I don't do that," Wexler protested.

"I know you don't, but think what a marvelous practice you would have if you did!"

Before the advent of antipsychotic medications, desperation and impatience were so great among psychiatrists and the kin of the afflicted that Rosen enjoyed an enviable practice. Dr. Karl's enthusiasm for his work was a boost for Rosen's reputation, and it had been sparked by an article by Rosen in the fall 1947 issue of *Psychiatric Quarterly*. Excited, Dr. Karl sent copies to his brother, Will, cofounder of their clinic, and five of their fellow leaders, along with a memo dated November 14, 1947.

"I think this is a most extraordinary and most important phenomenon," Dr. Karl declared. "It is important first that he has actually done something, namely to take thirty-seven incurable, hopeless [schizophrenia] patients and cure thirty-six of them. I don't care if they stayed well a week, a year, a month, or a day, he temporarily cured them to the satisfaction of the hospital authorities. . . . We ought to hear all about this, and hear about it soon. I think it may revolutionize the whole practice of hospital psychiatry."

The same day, Dr. Karl sent Rosen an invitation to lecture for a week in Topeka. The letter congratulated Rosen for his therapeutic results ("little short of a miracle") and effervesced: "I very much envy our colleagues at Chestnut Lodge who have so recently had the opportunity of hearing you."*

Difficulties caused by Rosen's practices first came to the attention of Will, then president of the American Psychiatric Association, in October 1949. The Baltimore relatives of a psychotic patient reported that the doctor had "guaranteed" to "cure" him for fifty thousand dollars.

On October 15, in a memo to his brother, Karl, Will called such a promise "reprehensible" and added firsthand information about Rosen: "I have heard him make the statement repeatedly that he had cured everyone he had treated." Will cautioned his brother, "I don't share your enthusiasm for him."

Dr. Karl continued to support Rosen. Faced with the Baltimore family's complaint to Will, Karl wrote Rosen to compliment him again on "a unique and very promising and hopeful method of treatment"; reiterated that "we want you very, very much [on the Menninger staff], as I have told you, at least I do"; and suggested exculpation: "I can't really bring myself to believe that you offered to give these people a written guarantee of cure." He complimented Rosen on his "warm and impulsive nature," alluded collegially to notoriously bothersome "disappointed relatives," and suggested that the doctor take up his troubled relationships with his personal analyst. Menninger did warn Rosen that unless he changed his methods, "you are really going to be in a bad spot, and so are we."

This admonition notwithstanding, complaints continued to arrive in Topeka. "Another doctor wrote us that he was charging the patients $10,000 a month," Dr. Karl reported to a psychiatrist in Rochester who was inquiring in 1951 on behalf of a patient. Dr. Karl by then called Rosen's work "experimen-

---

* These and some of the other documents cited in this chapter were kindly made available to me by a member of the Menninger family who manages the hospital archive, with the understanding that they would be published to clarify the history of the relationship between Dr. Karl and Dr. Rosen.

tal," but did not turn his back on him or drop his own role of patron saint. "He was doing some things quite unique and occasionally rather startling in results," he reported. "I thought perhaps he was claiming too much for it, but without such optimism he could not succeed at all."

Implicit approval by the Menninger establishment of Rosen's "unique" methods was signaled in May 1950, when Rosen's predilection for using violence and indignities as treatment modalities showed up in an item in the nationally circulated *Bulletin of the Menninger Clinic*. It amounted to a certificate of respectability.

In the article, the doctor presented the case of Joan, a twenty-five-year-old schizophrenic mother of two, who was brought to him in a catatonic state and refused to stay in the treatment room. When she made a dash for the door, the doctor brought his "direct therapy" to bear: "I grabbed her, pulled her back in again and forced her down on the couch. While I held her wrists, Joan squirmed, kicked and wrestled violently. . . . The struggle lasted about *half an hour* [emphasis added]. . . . Very often at the end of this type of struggle, the patient seems closer to reality."

Joan, like *all* of Rosen's patients, was made ill by not having been loved in childhood, he explained. What to do? "You become the patient's parent and the patient becomes your child. The patient is re-living the infantile period and you are afforded the opportunity of bringing him [*sic*] up all over again."

Soon, Karl Menninger was joined by other Rosen advocates. When the conventional medical publishing house Grune and Stratton brought out Rosen's primer, *Direct Analysis: Selected Papers*, in 1953, Dr. Leon Stone, a distinguished psychoanalyst, reviewed it in the *Journal of the American Psychoanalytic Association*. He praised Rosen's "courage," "intuitive resourcefulness," and "passionate dedication." He described the doctor's case histories as "moving" and his therapy as "heroic." "There is an unreserved, uninhibited involvement with the patient," Stone found, "fearless, exuberant, loving, authoritarian, at times combative and punitive, but always strong and affirmative." Evidently the reviewer had been impressed by Rosen's self-descriptions, such as his improbable claim that he once spent ten hours a day with a psychotic patient for two months and four hours daily for the next seven.

In 1959, at fifty-seven, Rosen appeared overtly to be a fatherly, dignified type. His "combative and punitive" techniques moved into the mainstream of his profession that year with his appointment as associate professor of psychiatry at Temple University Medical School in Philadelphia, which administered research financed by the Rockefeller Brothers Fund. Rosen treated members of the Rockefeller family, which resulted in referrals to other wealthy clients.

At Temple, his godfather was Dr. O. Spurgeon English, chairman of the psychiatry department and author of a standard psychiatry textbook. English later said that psychiatrists all over the country, including the Menninger brothers, approved of his hiring Rosen. He created a special institute for Rosen's work, made available two buildings, and eventually reported that the doctor was successful in two-thirds of his cases.

English wrote a foreword for *Observations on Direct Analysis: The Therapeutic Technique of Dr. John Rosen,* a 1959 book by a Temple colleague, Dr. Morris W. Brody. The book approvingly quoted Rosen as telling patients, in front of professional observers, "If you continue to act crazy I will crack your skull open" and "I will knock you through that wall in a minute." Brody later said that he was present on one occasion when Rosen hit a female patient because she insisted that she was hearing voices.

As Rosen grew older, his threats increasingly escalated into vicious brutalities that he practiced upon psychotic patients and that ultimately emerged in the newspapers and the courts. Sally Zinman, a college English instructor whose father paid the doctor five thousand dollars a month, had her breasts and vagina fondled by Rosen. An aide, an ex-marine, stripped her and held her down while Rosen beat her, according to testimony by a Rosen assistant, "with his fists on both her face and breasts."

Throughout the 1960s and 1970s, the doctor's stature nevertheless grew. In 1968 he was the hero of the best-seller *Savage Sleep,* by Millen Brand, which was based on Rosen's work. In 1971 he received the Man of the Year award from the American Academy of Psychotherapy.

Rosen's difficulties with the law began when Zinman hired a private investigator; and another patient, Janet Katkow, who had been in his care from 1970 to 1979, sued him and went public with accounts of her therapy.

"He then proceeded to lie down and take off his pants and boxer shorts down over his penis and he commanded the Plaintiff to suck on his penis," Katkow's complaint stated. It quoted Rosen as explaining to the patient: "This is what it is all about, this is when a baby is at peace, when it is sucking." Allegedly, there were hundreds of such sessions, always followed by Katkow vomiting, and once Rosen caused her to perform cunnilingus with another woman, saying he would "beat the shit out of her" if she refused.

The complaint charged: "Defendant also stated 'your insides are rotted,' that she was 'hopeless,' and told her that she should kill herself."

After five years of investigation, the Pennsylvania State Board of Medical Education and Licensure accused Rosen of sixty-seven violations of the Pennsylvania Medical Practices Act and thirty-five violations of regulations of the Medical Board. Rather than face trial, Rosen surrendered his medical license on March 29, 1983, when he was eighty-one years old.

Many of the foregoing facts were assembled by Jeffrey Moussaieff Masson for his 1988 book *Against Therapy*. In 1986 Masson telephoned Dr. English, who had retired. English said that the charges against Rosen were not relevant to the effectiveness of his techniques.

"Dr. English no longer saw psychotic patients," Masson wrote, "so he didn't use Rosen's methods, but if he did, he would continue to use them."

Long before Rosen's day, at a time when standard treatments were all but nonexistent, another—a more conventional researcher, a psychiatrist with first-rate credentials and professional backing—committed physical mayhem upon helpless psychotics on a far more extensive scale.

It is not easy to convey the bankrupt state of psychiatry then. "Our therapeutics is [*sic*] simply a pile of rubbish," declared Dr. C. G. Hill in his presidential address to the American Medico Psychological Association annual meeting of 1907. It was the same year that the charismatic Dr. Henry A. Cotton, only thirty-one, after two years of study with Emil Kraepelin and Alois Alzheimer in Munich, was appointed superintendent of the Trenton State Hospital in New Jersey. From there he would radiate international influence and controversy for almost three decades, contending that hidden bacterial infections were the underlying cause of psychosis.

"The insane are physically sick," he stated flatly, and "psychoanalysis will in time be superseded by gastric analysis."

Commissioning an unprecedented avalanche of gastrointestinal operations, Cotton ordered colectomies performed on hundreds of psychotic patients in the practice of his "surgical bacteriology." The stomach, duodenum, small intestine, gallbladder, and colon all were suspect, as was the urinary tract, also the cervix, and an obscure section of the bowel that Cotton labeled "the wisdom tooth of the gut." The admitted mortality rate was about twenty-five percent. Confusingly, the claimed recovery rate ran eighty-five percent.

Teeth were Cotton's initial and favorite target. "Without exception," he held, "the functional [acute] psychotic patients all have infected teeth." Between 1919 and 1920, Cotton's staff extracted more than four thousand teeth; six thousand in 1921. "If we wish to eradicate focal infections, we must bear in mind that it is only by being persistent, often against the wishes of the patient," he wrote. If results were disappointing, "We have not been radical enough," he insisted, and all previously unsuspected teeth—and the tonsils—would also have to be pulled to achieve "detoxification."

Ambitious, articulate, and publicity wise, Cotton worked assiduously to become widely known. He wrote numerous articles, gave lectures at Princeton, and wrote a book, *The Defective, Delinquent and Insane: The Relation of Focal Infection to Their Causation, Treatment and Prevention,* with a foreword by Dr. Adolf Meyer.

Cotton was Meyer's protégé, having trained at Johns Hopkins and having started his career as one of the great Swiss-born professor's assistants. Cotton frequently quoted from his mentor's "endorsement" in the book's introduction. "He appears to have brought out palpable results not attained by any previous or contemporary attack on the grave problem of mental disorder," Meyer wrote.

It was like the approval of celestial authority and produced handsome returns. Between 1916 and 1921, private, paying admissions at Trenton rose by forty-five percent, and the widely circulated *Review of Reviews* published a glowing report by Burdette Lewis, the New Jersey commissioner of institutions and agencies, that drummed up still more business.

"New Jersey's experience has made the old-fashioned asylums, camouflaged as hospitals, as extinct and out of date as are the prison grottoes of Old Venice, or the old Bethlem Hospital for the Insane," Lewis wrote.

Inevitably, a backlash of skepticism hit Cotton. In 1923 a carefully controlled study showed that patients who underwent Cotton's surgery did not improve faster than an unoperated comparison group and that some patients who were readmitted and discharged appeared repeatedly as "cures." The influential Dr. William Alanson White wrote that he could "not conceive how such results can be accepted by the scientifically trained mind" and called Cotton's work "profoundly unfortunate." Another critic warned: "If the craze for violent removal goes on, it will come to pass that we will have a gutless, glandless, toothless . . . witless race."

Outside evaluation seemed likely, and so the hospital's board, seeking to short-circuit trouble, asked Meyer to take on the task. Meyer agreed to supervise, but deputized an assistant, Dr. Phyllis Greenacre, who later acquired a major reputation as a New York therapist, to spend more than a year combing through the details. After she had worked for five months, Meyer wrote his brother without his customary circumlocutions: "The investigation of the material of Dr. Cotton discloses a rather sad harvest. His claims and statistics are preposterously out of accord with the facts."

Worse, a legislative commission made headlines in 1925 with two months of testimony from ex-patients and ex-employees about appalling conditions in Cotton's hospital. Andrew Scull, professor of sociology at the University of California in San Diego, who published his meticulous investigation of Cotton's career in 1990, reported that the eyewitnesses told of "brutality by hospital attendants, unexplained deaths, patients dragged kicking and screaming into operating rooms," and other abuses.

Most noteworthy were not Cotton's demented theories or his delusions of grandeur but Meyer's manipulations to back him at the risk of being himself exposed for doing wrong. He not only suppressed Greenacre's findings—permanently, as it turned out—but went to remarkable lengths to conceal them actively.

Meeting privately with Cotton and Greenacre in Baltimore during January 1926, Meyer received final confirmation of the devastation wrought by his protégé. Cotton was claiming a cure rate of eighty-seven percent; Greenacre found a general rate of twenty percent and a death rate among the treated patients approaching forty-three percent. "Thorough treatment, including abdominal operation, is not only dangerous to life, but ineffective in the cases of those who survive," Greenacre's never-circulated report concluded.

In Meyer's notes of the discussions, Professor Scull recorded, "Cotton emerges as truculent and unyielding, at times incoherent and verging on irrational."

Back in Trenton, Cotton modified his intestinal operations but "became even more aggressive" about dental extractions. In 1930 a visitor reported, "I felt sad seeing hundreds of people without teeth. . . . They suffer from indigestion, I was told, not being able to masticate the ordinary food which they get."

When Cotton celebrated his twentieth anniversary at Trenton, Meyer sent word applauding his "most creditable and noteworthy achievements," and when Cotton died in 1933, Meyer wrote the obituary in the *American Journal of Psychiatry*. It mentioned that Cotton had been controversial, but lauded his work as "a most remarkable achievement of the pioneer spirit . . . an extraordinary record by one of the most stimulating figures of our generation."

To Mrs. Cotton, Meyer wrote that her husband had died "like a soldier in action."

As fourteen million television viewers saw and heard, Dr. Peter R. Breggin was telling Oprah Winfrey what a patient should do in a psychiatrist's office: "If that person offers a drug, don't even say, 'No, thank you.' You can take the prescription and go. Don't fight about it. Don't get in trouble. But go. Don't take the drugs!"

What happens to people who do? he was asked.

"They very likely come out with permanent brain damage," Breggin advised Oprah and her audience.

Breggin had begun agitating on behalf of his point of view in the 1970s, and by the 1980s he was considered, in his words, "a force in the arena." If my son had been watching the show on the afternoon of April 2, 1987, I'm confident he would have stopped taking his medications. He would have been impressed by Breggin's credentials and personality and would have eagerly followed this Pied Piper's call to sabotage his treatment.

Quite a few patients did, and the mental health authorities were asked to lift Breggin's license. "People across America are notifying AMI offices that, as a result of having viewed this show . . . their ill family member has discontinued drugs," Laurie Flynn wrote when she suggested action to the state medical officials of Maryland, where Breggin practiced psychiatry. In fact, the small Montana Alliance for the Mentally Ill chapter notified the director of *The Oprah Winfrey Show* that seven patients were rehospitalized in Montana because they followed Breggin's television counseling. An eighth, a young man, committed suicide "because of what he heard on your show."

No action was taken against Breggin. The Maryland authorities listened to him at a closed-door hearing and wrote Flynn that they "identified no legal violation or ethical impropriety on the part of Dr. Breggin." Aside from that conclusion, they declined accountability because "this entire matter is essentially a freedom of speech issue."

Breggin was not lacking supporters. "There is nothing that he said that I would not agree with after thirty years of training therapists," wrote Dr. Jay Haley, a distinguished family therapist. "Dr. Breggin is the conscience of American psychiatry," wrote Dr. Bertram P. Karon, author of *Psychotherapy of Schizophrenia*. And Breggin's friend Dr. Loren Mosher concluded, "Nothing Dr. Breggin said was irresponsible."

The root issue was Breggin's basic agenda: this psychiatrist was campaigning against psychiatry itself, especially biological psychiatry. Schizophrenia is not a brain disease, in his view, so psychiatrists do more harm than good. The doctors give patients drugs when love and psychotherapy are all they need. The result, in his view, is disaster: "Psychiatry has unleashed a plague on the world, with millions upon millions of damaged patients. It is the worst doctor-induced catastrophe in the history of medicine."

Breggin was no quack. He had been a teaching fellow at Harvard Medical School and a full-time consultant for NIMH. He maintained a flourishing practice in Bethesda, Maryland, and had appointed himself director of something he called the Center for the Study of Psychiatry, whose studies were conducted in his office. He had written several books and stacks of articles for professional and lay audiences. His was a warm, pleasant-looking, pleasant-sounding persona, and he had a knack for making the most outlandish assertions seem reasonable.

All this made the doctor seem sympathetic to troubled victims like Jeff, rendered gullible by the side effects of the medications. *The Oprah Winfrey Show*, seizing on controversy, asked Breggin to be a guest again on August 17, not long after his don't-take-drugs counseling had triggered complaints about patient rehospitalizations as well as massive criticism of him. This time Oprah matched him in debate against Dr. Paul Fink, then president-elect of the American Psychiatric Association.

Sensing a populist issue suitably inflammatory for the mass audience, Breggin attacked Fink with one of his regular charges: the conspiracy of the "psychopharmaceutical complex" combined with the APA's "conflict of interest" in accepting funds from the big drug firms to pay for research and professional education.

BREGGIN: The Psychiatric Association is not beholden to the patients now, it's beholden to the drug companies. And we need a "Psychogate" investigation . . . about the millions of dollars being channelled through the American Psychiatric Association.

WINFREY: Well, Dr. Fink is fuming now. . . .

BREGGIN: Can you deny what I just said? . . .

FINK: No, I can't deny that we get millions of dollars of support from the drug companies. I also can't deny that that seems to be tangential to the issue of whether the drugs are of value, and they are.

BREGGIN: Your scientific meetings are funded by the drug companies.

FINK: . . . That's irrelevant. . . .

BREGGIN: You're a psychiatrist, you understand self-interest. If you go to a convention and everywhere it says, "Supported by this drug company, supported by that drug company"—

FINK: I don't understand. I don't understand.

What the sputtering Fink failed mostly to understand was the potency of Breggin's trading on public fear: fear of incomprehensible psychotic illness; fear of psychiatrists, their confusing talk and practices; fear of hurtful drugs; and disgust with the greed of big business.

Breggin had been playing off those fears in his books for years, though they had failed to catch fire. Suddenly, in 1987, his appearances on *Oprah, Today,* and other shows lent his ideas credibility for millions, as only television can. In 1991 Breggin published his blockbuster *Toxic Psychiatry,* accusing his own profession of most forms of evil known to civilization, including genocide.

The considerable publicity generated by this work had barely abated when fate and the Eli Lilly company handed him a bonanza: the billion-dollar success and controversy triggered by Prozac. Riding on the coattails of Dr. Peter Kramer's best-seller, *Listening to Prozac,* Breggin countered with his response, *Talking Back to Prozac.* The chapter entitled "Pushing Drugs in America— the Long Financial Tentacles of Eli Lilly" contained such subsections as "Lilly Hides Prozac-Induced Suicidal Ideation" and "Conflict of Interest on the FDA Advisory Committee."

Since then, vilification of Breggin by respectable authorities has reached a degree of hostility that would incinerate the hardiest of polemicists. Not Breggin. The head of NAMI called him "ignorant." A former head of NIMH called him an "outlaw." The president of the APA called him a modern-day "flat-earther." Their target was unsinkable.

"Like a slick lawyer," said an article in *Time* magazine, "Breggin has answers for every argument." The piece applauded Breggin's skill at exposing weaknesses of psychiatry, such as the tendency of some doctors to prescribe too many drugs for too long and in excessive dosages. The *Time* writer deplored that "calmer voices [than Breggin's] never seem to make it onto 'Oprah.'"

I asked Breggin whether he thought schizophrenia was a brain disease.

"Absolutely not," the doctor said quietly, "schizophrenics are not sick people."

I didn't tell him about my twenty-five years with Jeff.

Even the *New York Times* had come to consider Breggin a force in the arena. On March 9, 1995, its editorial page published a long lead letter from him with the headline "Psychiatry Doesn't Help Mental Health Cause": "Even the most violent patient is more likely to benefit more from a skilled, caring person than from a pill," he claimed.

Breggin enlisted unfortunate psychotics—some recovered, many struggling in various stages of illness—whom he called "psychiatric survivors." They were people living marginal existences who considered themselves abused by psychiatrists. They more or less successfully resisted medications and hospitalization in favor of an alternative known as the "self-help movement," many of whose crusaders were highly intelligent and dedicated people—sometimes well organized and invariably powerfully motivated. A leader among them was Judi Chamberlin, whom Breggin had brought along as an insider and fellow debater on *Oprah,* where she helped scuttle Dr. Fink of the APA. Among other relevant questions, she asked him: "How can you have a scientific debate as to whether drugs are good or bad if the drug companies are underwriting the discussion? It skews everything."

Chamberlin was hardly typical of the ailing, often-relapsing schizophrenics fighting to stay afloat with well-intentioned assistance from self-help groups.* Much of their work was courageous and admirable; still I was thankful Jeff evidently never heard of them. Breggin was their guru. His no-drugs philosophy was their bible—clearly dangerous for Jeff and most others diagnosed with severe mental illness. For some ex-patients like Chamberlin, they probably did no harm, but such adherents were a minority. The test was, once again, the individual diagnosis.

Chamberlin had somehow wound up in Bellevue Hospital where she was "brain-disabled by neuroleptics," according to Breggin. As she recalled it: "They took somebody who was going through a depression reaction to losing her baby and made a 'schizophrenic' out of her. . . . I was

---

* The best-known organization is the National Association of Psychiatric Survivors (NAPS), P.O. Box 618, Sioux Falls, SD 57101. Among long-experienced writers in the field was Sally Zinman, one of the successful litigants against Dr. John Rosen. She coauthored *Reaching Across: Mental Health Clients Helping Each Other,* published in 1987 by the California Network of Mental Health Clients, at 1722 J Street, Suite 324, Sacramento, CA 95814. The movement's principal periodical was *Dendron,* published at P.O. Box 11284, Eugene, OR 07440, by David Oaks, a Harvard graduate recovered from five hospitalizations in mental institutions. Chamberlin was the author of the book *On Our Own* (1978), as well as a comprehensive, well-organized history, "The Ex-Patients Movement: Where We've Been and Where We're Going," in *Journal of Mind and Behavior* 11 no. 3/4, (1990): pages 323–36.

being de-humanized." After hospitalizations in six different institutions, she managed to find a psychologist who treated her with respect, which led to the end of her illness. Clearly, she had not been schizophrenic.

Germany was the most fertile territory for Breggin's theories, his most articulate supporter being Peter Lehmann in Berlin, who in 1986 founded the publishing house Anti-Psychiatrie Verlag. He wrote *Der Chemische Knebel* (*The Chemical Gag*), now in its third edition, a potpourri cataloging probably every collectible negative fact, case history, journal and book citation of outrage, real or rumored, about antipsychotics. I do not recommend this volume, with its 1,157 footnotes, to readers with fragile stomachs.

In another book, *Instead of Psychiatry* (1993), Lehmann, a bright man in his late forties who held a teaching certificate, rendered an account of his "escape" from schizophrenia, hospitalization, and "poisoning by neuroleptics." Recovery was due to the support of a self-help group and dealing with his "crazy beliefs" by writing a book manuscript. Four years later, he went "crazy" again, believing he was in charge of a "world revolution" and "hunted by all the world's intelligence agencies combined." This time, he wrote, he attributed his comeback to long talks with two sympathizing friends, one male and one female; a full bottle of red wine, consumed as a tranquilizer; and the knowledge that his self-help group stood ready to support him. It all steadied him enough to publish more books. "I see few problems," he concluded, "in living as lively a life as possible, and, when necessary, helping things along by a shot of craziness."

Lehmann had been onstage at Berlin's prestigious Technical University in September 1988 when Breggin appeared there to deliver an address unveiling the genesis of his ideas. "I am fifty-six years old. I am a Jew," he began, and his familiarity with the Holocaust, he said, enabled him to appreciate the situation of psychiatric patients. At the age of nine he had seen newsreels about concentration camps and heard about them from an eyewitness, an uncle who had participated in their liberation as an American soldier. The scenes became fused in his mind with the pitiful figures he saw and the odors he smelled in the Massachusetts mental hospitals where he worked as a volunteer while a student at Harvard.

In his mind, a continuum evolved from his subsequent studies, so Breggin informed the Germans. "How many people know that psychiatry paved the way for the Holocaust?" he demanded. First came the German psychiatrists in the 1920s who wanted to "destroy life unworthy of life," who advocated euthanasia and sterilization for the retarded and other unfortunates. Beatings with resulting brain injuries turned even pre-Hitler mental institutions into death camps everywhere, including the United States. "Death by starvation was not uncommon."

In recent times, Breggin said, medications became "far more poisonous" than those available before the war, although "modern psychiatry does not basically differ from the pre-war psychiatry that led to the Holocaust." Drug-caused tardive kinesia turned into tardive dystonia and proliferated into hopelessly regressive "tardia dementia," a condition, he said, that he had "developed" himself (I've not noted it elsewhere).

Greater catastrophes were in the offing, according to the doctor. The cost of maintaining chronic mental patients was leading "more and more" to thoughts of "murdering sick people," to the reintroduction of new sterilization laws, lobotomy, and other "barbaric" treatments. "Humans are being turned into objects."

Breggin had the inside word. He was a Jew, and he knew how the Holocaust got started.

The nagging frustration induced by the stubborn resistance of the disease kept hounding the psychiatric profession and drove some unconventional minds to impose treatments that were, in fact, forms of madness. These doctors could not tolerate being defied. And so John Rosen tried to beat schizophrenia out of his patients. Henry Cotton tried to root it out by their teeth. Peter Breggin dealt with the intractability of the illness by denying its existence ("Schizophrenics are not sick people").

Most troubling was the profession's reluctance to deal with these colleagues for what they were.

And then there was Dr. D. Ewen Cameron, chairman of psychiatry at Canada's McGill University and former president of the APA. Schizophrenia was his leitmotiv. It possessed him. He was absolutely determined to discover its cure and win the Nobel Prize.

He issued his declaration of war in 1938, when he was director of research at the Worcester (Massachusetts) State Hospital, publishing a pioneering investigation in the *American Journal of Psychiatry* into the earliest (prodromal) manifestations of the condition. In 1958 he wrote in the *Journal of the Canadian Medical Association* how he reduced adult patients to the mental level of fourteen-year-olds by ordering them to undergo frequently repeated *daily* electroshock treatments of unusual potency. By 1962, writing in *Comprehensive*

Psychiatry, he advocated still more intensive disassembly of personality with his own technique of "de-patterning."

Some of his patients were kept asleep for as many as sixty-five days and subjected to repeated recorded messages, a brainwashing technique that Cameron called "psychic driving." Some were fed megadoses of LSD. And not long before the doctor's death in 1968, he was routinely treating schizophrenia by supervising surgery for the long-discredited frontal lobotomies. Some of the patients were reduced to incoherent babbling and permanent hospitalization. Years later, expert psychiatric testimony branded as "torture" many of the illegal manipulations conducted by Cameron for the Central Intelligence Agency on at least fifty-three patients, mostly women.

Cameron's peers hardly condemned him upon his death. On September 23, 1968, the eulogy in the *British Medical Journal* declared: "Ewen Cameron by his work and example helped not only many psychiatrists become much better doctors, but directly and indirectly helped hundreds and hundreds of patients, both personally and through those he had inspired and taught." The *American Journal of Psychiatry* also carried a glowing obituary accompanied by a full-page picture of the doctor's kindly face.

Jeff and I were not helped, however, by the good fortune of having eluded maniacs like Cameron.

CHAPTER 13

Out of It

I WAS LOSING control. Jeff was eager to leave the confining environment of Menninger, which I had found demeaning and futile and could no longer finance. While Jeff realized that he was not functioning normally—he volunteered on the phone from the clinic that in his own way, he, too, felt "out of control"—he had yet to concede that he was afflicted by any real illness, much less a terribly serious one. And I did not yet recognize his Catch-22: his continuing fierce resistance to medications, which *had* to lead to more illness. The Menninger doctors had never made clear to him or to me that without pills, Jeff didn't have the slightest chance at a life outside a hospital. As Fuller Torrey put it: "If a person does not believe he/she is sick, why take medication?"

All this was still as foreign to me as some alien civilization. So were these statistics: eighty-one percent of schizophrenics suffer from "impaired insight"; as many as seventy percent who do accept medications stop taking them within two years. And I never fathomed that the act of taking neuroleptics represents for the user a surrender, a defeat; he is defining himself as mentally ill, not merely troubled—a wrenching internal break with one's past.

Hindsight, all hindsight. Not knowing much about the disease and nothing at all about the pivotal role of the medications, I decided that Jeff should be exposed to something fresh, something new for him: family therapy. That was the buzz in psychiatry in the 1970s, and I had witnessed a dramatic demonstration of the results this technique could achieve. And maybe I, too, feeling increasingly trapped, had come to deny Jeff's illness, or at least its seriousness.

A young, talented woman editor of my acquaintance had been victimized for all of her thirty-plus years by her dictatorial father, a house painter, as brutally gruff a parent as I have ever met. He infantilized my friend, told her she was a failure, that she should forget her career and move back into the parental home. He terrorized her out of the self-esteem for which she had labored successfully at her job. Her distress was great.

I enlisted my former therapist, Dr. R, and was allowed to sit in as he and a young female cotherapist chaired two meetings with the extended family of my friend. I don't know how they managed to lure the father into showing up, but he did. It quickly developed that he had no idea of the deleterious effect of his behavior and how deeply—if all too quietly—his daughter and the rest of his family deplored its harsh impact. He never became warmly loving after this confrontation, but his terror tactics ceased. Dr. R had brought about a quick and drastic change in a rigid, primitive father. I extrapolated that my bright but troubled Jeff might loosen up under gentle family pressure as well. At this time Jeff was still undermedicated and carrying on at his most obstreperous worst.

"I am very sorry that you were unwilling to conduct a conversation with me on the phone tonight," I wrote to him in Topeka on December 20, 1974, after he hung up on me. "I do know that the environment and treatment you have had in Topeka for more than two years have not worked. If they had, you would not feel so 'out of control' that you feel compelled to slug a nurse and break her nose."

I proposed a trial stay in New York, perhaps thirty days, and some family meetings with Dr. R, whom Jeff liked, and my mother, whom he adored, along with me and other members of our clan. To my surprise, Jeff was willing to put up with the hated New York winter weather to gain friendly, noninstitutional company. He seemed to enjoy the family sessions with Dr. R, which did nothing to help with his condition. I had been so naive: schizophrenia could not possibly yield to family therapy, in the manner of my editor friend's father, who had merely behaved badly. It was absurd, like using aspirin against lung cancer.

Like Freud, whose work had influenced him at the (then psychoanalytically oriented) New York Psychiatric Institute of Columbia University, Dr. R had hardly ever had contact with a schizophrenic patient. Unlike the master, however, my doctor was not intimidated by his inexperience. With medications, he worked, like the Menninger crew, as a minimalist. Jeff and I experienced the results at home in the small Manhattan apartment he and I were now sharing. There, my son had become all but unrecognizable, more angry and violent than I had ever seen him. I imagined that he even *looked* evil.

Twice he hit me hard in the face with the flat of his hand for trivial reasons I cannot recall. Once he moved into a cheap neighborhood hotel where the management called the police because he decided that the furniture was his enemy. Another time he was so agitated that I took him to the Payne Whitney Psychiatric Hospital. They looked him over, refused to admit him, and sent a bill for fifty dollars for this nonservice.

At least our flier into family therapy resulted in no residual damage. The same can't be said for my next initiative. It left psychological burns that had not healed twenty years later. Not knowing what I was doing, I pushed Jeff into the minefield of mega-vitamins.

Shortly before, I had given up magazine editing and had become a book publisher. One of the first ventures in my increasingly hectic swim for survival was called *Mega-Nutrients for Your Nerves*, by Dr. H. L. (Hank) Newbold. This big, smiling, brassy psychiatrist ran a booming East Side practice in New York and had received sound and conventional training at Duke University, the University of Chicago, and the University of Minnesota. Personal health problems sidetracked him into the relative wilderness of nutrition. He wrote a book called *Vitamin C Against Cancer*, elaborating on the notions of the Nobelist Linus Pauling, but Newbold's true and abiding enthusiasm, and that of his followers, was reserved for what he considered the healing properties of huge vitamin dosages for mental illness, including schizophrenia.

I found Newbold appealing. Like all successful psychiatrists, he exuded optimism and persuasive argumentation. So did the book he wrote for me. Other psychiatrists and qualified nutritionists had grown wary of the claims put forth by vitamin enthusiasts. They charged that clinical proof of efficacy was lacking. I did not know of the critics then, and if Newbold had read them, they had not discouraged him.

As late as 1993, in a reworked version of his book, he detailed exactly how niacin should be administered to schizophrenics; how a woman patient of his who was "almost incapacitated by schizophrenia" took on a demanding full-time job after six months of his "nutritional therapy"; and how "wheat products are toxic for many patients suffering from schizophrenia."

Newbold decided that Jeff was allergic to wheat and grapefruit and prescribed a string of supplements that Jeff to this day recites fervently as his mantra: "dolomite, niacin, zinc, and yeast." In reasonable dosages, these and other supplements favored by Newbold are not known to do harm and may make some patients feel more energetic. Some of his ideas no doubt have value for some patients. However, I have yet to see solid evidence of therapeutic value for schizophrenia.

Jeff, on the other hand, was not only sold on this hypothesis; for decades, he lobbied hard for the idea that vitamins and supplements are actually superior to antipsychotic medications and that he should be taking them rather than the prescription drugs. The reasons for his preference are not obscure: vitamins do not cause unpleasant or downright disabling side effects and don't brand him as a mental patient.

The vitamin-supplement regimen cheered Jeff and gave him a sense of mastery and, eventually, an air of authority. Appended to one of his letters of that period I found this note: "P.S. If you're depressed, and hence grouchy, etc., may I suggest you try niacin capsules (such as 100 mg. twice or three times a day) or brewer's yeast tablets or powder—the latter can be used with tomato juice to hide the bad taste, as per your needs."

Dr. R, always fast to embrace creative alternatives, had offered no objections to my trying out Newbold's methods, never suspecting that we might be embarking on a fateful, long-enduring mistake. And Newbold sincerely believed in his recommendations. I alone have reason to feel guilty for having led my son up the vitamin path.

Jeff was "decompensating," as doctors like to say. It meant that he was going crazier, disintegrating, actually frightened out of his wits, unable to get rest, to sleep at night, to reason, unmanageable at home, even when I took large chunks of time away from my struggling new business. He was unable to focus on the consequences of his actions, and, since he constantly smoked cigarettes, I lived in dread that he might burn down our apartment house. The elevator men were beginning to view me as a failed lion tamer.

Since I couldn't afford a private psychiatric clinic at hundreds of dollars per day, my only ready alternative was Metropolitan Hospital, the enormous public institution in Harlem. This was the memorable refuge where I found Jeff incontinent in the "rubber room." The doctors were decent, overworked, knowledgeable, and did not hesitate to inject the antipsychotic Haldol in large enough dosages to stabilize Jeff and qualify him for early discharge, and so

Jeff's obvious next stop late in 1975 was California, where his mother unhesitatingly consented to let him again live in his own carefully preserved room in her large Palo Alto house and where, as a legal resident, he was entitled, in case of need or when Edith simply could not manage, to fall back on a much more humanely developed medical safety net than the New York area offered.

The need arose quickly and never ceased. It revolved like a kaleidoscope: the emergency ward of the area's largest general hospital; the psychiatric hospitals in San Jose and Fremont; several board-and-care homes; a halfway house; back to Edith for a while; and the streets, always the streets, Jeff wandering aimlessly through darkness, dodging traffic, dazed, his mother pleading with the police department to find him, which they invariably did, eventually, after a night or two, to deposit him in handcuffs, yelling defiance at his supposed enemies, the cops, once again with the emergency crew at Valley Medical Center, where he was becoming a well-recognized regular: ten times until 1981.

I was becoming one of their regulars, too. Valley Medical was where I would most often find Jeff on my visits, rarely more than two or three months apart. Its psychiatric wards were busy; the turnover was rapid, the atmosphere not nearly as depressing as in the many longer-term hospital wards where I became a regular later, where psychotics would be housed, heavily drugged, shuffling along for months or years. Valley Medical was an island in the madness where a sense of movement prevailed, an air of the walking wounded getting better, preparing to leave—even if only temporarily—to escape these walls bursting with an overflow of the disabled.

There I met Dr. Rick Robinson, harassed, loping, emaciated, alert as a terrier, never with a spare moment, never lacking for a new move forward, a biological psychiatrist who deployed medications with unusual flexibility, a sense of nuance, whose impatience seemed not to tolerate what I most feared: atrophy, loss of hope, resignation. Rick was a gift to my mental state as well as Jeff's. He soon went into private practice where we held on to him for a decade until Jeff fired him for the last of several times. Jeff ultimately fired almost all his doctors. He could never understand why they resisted "curing" him.

But he and I were permanently stuck with each other. "How do you stand it?" I was sometimes asked by friends when they wanted to know how Jeff was faring. "You can't fire a son" was my standard comeback. I guess Jeff figured out at some point of our journey that he couldn't fire me either.

That didn't help my chronic anxiety in managing his managers. The required judgment calls were exquisitely difficult to render. "Where's my M.D. degree?" I often said to myself. And "Who appointed me God?" Sometimes instinct whispered, "I don't dig that doctor. I don't trust him." Or common sense would contradict a professional judgment. And always the dilemma: Should money be invested over there or over here? How was I to know if even the experts didn't?

The problems would not be mine alone. As I approached sixty, I began writing periodic letters to my older son, Ron, to help him prepare for the inevitable days when he would have to make decisions about his brother's care. November 18, 1977, is the date of my first guidance about psychiatrists. Ron had lately graduated from law school.

"I have always felt it useful to listen to [the caregivers] very closely," I wrote.

> But it's also wise to question them very, very closely to get the rationale behind what they're advising (and to get it in plain English) and also to find out how firmly they believe in the opinion or advice they happen to be dishing out. Sometimes they are not as sure as they sound. Sometimes they fly in the face of the facts or your own firmly rooted opinions. Do get a second opinion or a third or a fourth, but remember that outside consultants may not know as much relevant history as you do. . . . Use your own good common sense to make the ultimate judgment according to your own gut feeling.

None of this is to suggest that I ever pictured Jeff in a free-fall descent toward hopeless incurability. Through all his torment, he managed to hold on to a sharp edge of self-assertion. Was my insistence upon perpetual optimism for his future edging into perversity? I could see that his ingenuity in sabotaging his medications—hiding them in his mouth to spit them out later, flushing them down the toilet, faking the act of swallowing—was self-destructive. It was also, I thought, a gesture of independence, of wanting to be his own master, not to be, as the sociologists say, other-directed.

I saw the life force in him as quite unquenchable, and this seemed crucial in assessing him as a possible suicide risk. Suicide hangs over all schizophrenia like a permanent thundercloud. It is the leading cause of death for all patients like my son. The literature on this subspecialty is extensive. Every practitioner must factor the hazard of self-destruction into every moment of every patient's life.

I had learned something about suicide from the "red blanket" cases I saw as a journalist in 1960 at the Los Angeles Suicide Prevention Center. I knew that potential suicides nearly always emit cries for help, often disguised and in need of decoding. I knew that it isn't true that people who talk of suicide tend not to go through with it, and that suicide is a natural sequel to depression.

Jeff's schizophrenia had an unmistakable overlay of manic depression, mania being his most blatant and frequent symptom. I could easily hear it coming on, usually over a few days, on the phone. Jeff rarely called when he was reasonably in control. When he was manic, he called every day, occasionally more than once. He would report that he was feeling great, on top of everything in the world, his voice booming, his speech pressured, then explosive, uninterruptible. It was like trying to talk back to machine-gun bursts. When I followed up with his treaters, they had rarely begun to increase his medications to deal with these phases. More often, I was their early radar.

Phases of depression could be plotted along Jeff's way, too, but they came much less frequently and were not as readily pinpointed. His normal communications were monotone. When asked for an opinion, his standard response was "Oh, I dunno." I never did get used to the persistent neutrality. It was hard to separate from clinical depression, and suicide, I had learned, might be next.

In Jeff's lowest moods, he more than once or twice made the point that his life rested in his own hands. His standard opening into the subject would be "I'm worried about my future" or sometimes "What's going to happen to me?" or "When am I going to be cured?" From there, he sometimes moved on to "I really want to put an end to all this," coupled with exclamations of disgust at exactly how many years he had by then been ill.

I always reported these utterances to his doctors and asked them to investigate. Invariably, they reported back with the riskiest prognosis of all: they did not believe Jeff was suicidal. "He isn't the type," one of them said, as if there were a suicide "type."

When I could summon the nerve, I'd ask Jeff straight out, "Do you really want to harm yourself?" The response would never be direct. He always launched into tirades of very old, very specific complaints: the "street hasslers" at Westwood Hospital who beat him up because they didn't like his "Stanford Jewish" looks, or some psychiatrist who had counseled him ten years earlier to just "be patient," to which Jeff would now add, "No pun intended. I guess." Complaining about ancient slights had become Jeff's favorite sport, so when he activated such a litany I concluded he wasn't about to do himself in. It would stop him from venting his indignation.

In short, I never became too seriously concerned that he might commit suicide, although it was forever on my mind that at least ten percent of schizophrenics succeed in doing so (the corresponding figure for the general population is one percent). I always considered him too tough to give in. His suicide gestures—at least two were recorded—were acts of manipulation, not intended death. That was evident from the care he took when he slashed himself so gingerly at the time of his first big breakdown and again in 1975 at the residential care facility when he tied a vacuum cleaner cord into a noose and swung it across a roof beam, keeping an eye out to make sure he would be caught.

"They expected me to be responsible for myself and I couldn't handle that" was his elegant explanation to the staff, according to the record. To me, years later, he confessed otherwise. He was maneuvering to get off his detested Prolixin and judged, correctly, that he would be rehospitalized at Valley Medical Center, where he hoped (and succeeded) to persuade the staff doctor to give him something else.

Jeff's mother insisted that his tricks made him his own worst enemy. I thought he was his own best friend. I respected his wit and spunk in standing up to the doctors, who were not exactly ego poor. Jeff made one of them so mad about his insistence to get "cured" that the doctor exclaimed: "You're going to be ill forever!"

Jeff replied, "Don't I even get to die?"

Another doctor on another occasion tried, for the umpteenth time, to confront Jeff with the prospect of trying out for a volunteer job.

"That's *your* obsession," said Jeff.

You've got to be alive and kicking to be a smart-ass.

Caught in the revolving door of relapse-and-remission, followed by more relapse-and-remission, Jeff had twice been in and out of Westwood Manor in Fremont, California, a public hospital where he spent a lot of his time in restraints during the late 1970s. "I get the impression that Jeff is worse than at any time in at least a year and that he is worse than he was before he re-entered the hospital recently," I wrote to the director, Dr. Harold Wollack. In my search for an explanation, I cited speculation of my family therapist, Dr. R, that Jeff might be suffering from "process schizophrenia," an antique concept no longer in use because it hypothesizes an inevitable brain deterioration that experts have dismissed as unproved.

Wollack did not believe in the pessimism of process schizophrenia. He was locked in a struggle with Jeff that seemed to hold promise to the doctor but prompted Jeff to hark back and identify once more with Alex, the guinea-pig hero of *A Clockwork Orange*. Wollack was administering injections of Thorazine, which were painful to Jeff. He wanted the shots to stop, so when the doctor wielded the needle on one occasion, Jeff was ready with a cri de coeur.

"I'm cured, praise God!" he yelled, like the hero in *A Clockwork Orange*.

"You're not cured yet," the doctor corrected, a needle hitting the buttock, as it would, periodically, again and again. And this was not the only sequence of hurt and frustration that befell Jeff at Westwood. The other drama lasted a lot longer and revolved around a woman we'll call Annie.

She was his dream woman for at least fifteen years and may still occupy that spot; I don't dare ask. She was a pretty, young recreation therapist on the staff at Westwood, not at all seductive, no friendlier than someone in her position was supposed to act, accessible but not in the slightest intimate. She and Jeff sometimes talked, but the conversations were never particularly personal. Annie was simply cheerfully present; that was all.

It was enough. Starved for emotional female response from someone of his own age, Jeff fell for Annie, and he fell very hard. Unfortunately, he fantasized that she cared for him as well. Although he received no acknowledgment of any of his overtures, she was his vision, a classic schizophrenic delusion, a fixture in conversations with me, with his mother, with all his doctors, with anybody who would listen, year after year. Annie had said such and such to so-and-so, he reported; Annie had looked at him; Annie this and Annie that. . . .

The letters to her that I saw were respectful, surprisingly impersonal. Mostly they reflected preoccupation with his anxieties. His obscure citations from the Scriptures or a recollection of a scene from *A Clockwork Orange* would be preceded by, "I don't want to worry you." His most strongly expressed yearning for his love object was engagingly old-fashioned and reticent: "I believe, as I've brought up before, that you and I could get along well."

Jeff didn't mind that he lacked the opportunity to spend much time alone with Annie. Nor did it trouble him that she was anchored within her own crowd, the establishment, the hospital staffers, his sworn enemies, whose outlook often offended his own. He could even forgive Annie the time when she snubbed his hero, John Lennon.

He was enjoying himself when someone played Lennon love songs one afternoon on the hospital record player in the rec room. Annie and two of her colleagues made a joke about Lennon and laughed. Jeff protested. They didn't stop, so he left.

Nevertheless, his preoccupation with his love object increased after he left Westwood and the town of Fremont. For years he saw to it that she could not forget him. He wrote her many letters. They were imploring and tender for the most part, but once he threatened to harm her. No disciplinary measures discouraged him. He phoned her, first at her job, then at home—nobody is more adept at ferreting out home phone numbers than Jeffrey Wyden. She remained a commanding presence in his head, a larger-than-life obsession. Twice he hiked all night from San Jose along the railroad tracks over the bridge across San Francisco Bay to Fremont, only to be rebuffed in his attempts to catch a glimpse of his adored Annie and to find himself transported back under guard.

His doctors gently pointed out, year after year, that he was wasting his energy, not to mention his affections. His mother argued the same, as did I. Jeff's persistence never flagged. Finally, I told him that I wasn't going to listen to further talk about his phantom. I said she wasn't real to me, and I wouldn't collude with unreality. He paid no attention. In 1994, at last, as a new medication seemed to gain hold of his system, Annie faded slowly from his routine conversations. I'm convinced that she still has not vacated his heart. My own memory keeps the case notes from the Menninger Clinic alive—"empty of people and feelings" they called Jeff.

Beginning with Jeff's Westwood days, lithium was a great source of turmoil. He had been taking it for more than four years, as he repeatedly pointed out, against mania and depressions. For reasons never clear to me—again, I didn't want to set off problems by inquiring—Jeff never resisted taking this simple natural salt, at least not as stubbornly as the other "meds," which he dismissed with the epithet "meds, shmeds." No doubt he experienced lithium as relatively benign because its side effects were not grossly objectionable.

It was a salt, though, and it left him forever thirsty. "I have to go to the bathroom to urinate about every twenty minutes," he wrote on March 12, 1978, "because I drink about three gallons of water a day." The incessant drinking turned his whole life into "a bleak picture." He therefore hoped "to get out of Westwood in six weeks." The time limit was an illusion, but Jeff needed to hold on to it as evidence of his determination to make progress, with hope to get well, not to fall victim to open-ended disability, the abyss. Time limits kept alive his hope to be "cured."

The lithium problem, unhappily, was not readily put to rest and never would be. While thirst was a side effect that he could manage on his own, the pounding of the drug on his kidneys could lead to serious trouble. Sometime after leaving Westwood, one of Jeff's frequent checkups revealed permanent damage to that vital organ. A renal specialist consulted by Jeff's mental health system ordered lithium stopped. I was alarmed. Jeff's manic-depressive condition was known to leap out of control without this medication. I arranged a consultation with the head of renal services for Stanford Medical Center and explained to him the stakes involved.

We were in luck. Considering the importance of the drug for Jeff's total health, the risks were considered acceptable. The lithium was reinstated. The episode showed me yet again how crucial the constant full feed-around of information could be. The local renal consultant had likely never been briefed on the consequences of his prohibition. Grateful for the easy outcome of another potential disaster, I never asked what happened. I had done my job as communicator and keeper of Jeff's historical memory.

"Chance favors the prepared mind," said Louis Pasteur when he was asked to account for his apparent great luck in his creation of scientific miracles. While I am no scientist, I did encounter luck and was prepared to make the most of it. Luck had sent Jeff for three new hospitalizations to the excellent Stanford Medical Center, instead of his usual pit stops, and the chief of his ward, Dr. Lorrin Koran, was obviously the right man for a critical job for which I was prepared but unqualified.*

Something had to be done to draw from the experience of past years the medications and dosages that had been found to serve Jeff best. The cycles of his perpetual relapses had to be slowed down; and each new team of treaters had to be kept from looking questioningly at Jeff when they first confronted him and then acting, as so often, as if this were the first day of the first year of his illness. My son needed a great deal, but he didn't need to be reinvented,

---

* I was not alone to spot Dr. Koran's talent for tackling complex subjects requiring a commanding overview. In 1987 the American Psychiatric Association commissioned him to survey his entire profession. The resulting book was called *The Nation's Psychiatrists*.

especially not with constantly fluctuating notions about treatment. Most urgently, he needed a sense of direction and order, and so did I.

The introduction of a qualified authority figure would also help, for Jeff was increasingly turning into what we called a "guardhouse lawyer" in the World War II army: an untutored jailbird who thought he commanded all legal expertise needed to defend his cause on his own. Like these losers, Jeff was beginning to tell his ever-new doctors which medications he should take and in what dosages. The older and more fatigued the doctors were, the more they would give in to his clever importunings. He would have been so much better off if he had been a less glib spokesman for himself.

Koran, professor of psychiatry at Stanford Medical School, who was very tall, spare, and laconic, with a welcoming face cocked in the listening mode, diligently gathered information from Jeff's former and current doctors and the pharmacopoeia of all his medications. He requisitioned records, interviewed therapists, traveled to Valley Medical, and analyzed notes from twenty-one institutions. On March 10, 1981, he delivered a case summary of five single-spaced pages that constituted a unique encyclopedia of Jeff's illness. It diagnosed "schizoaffective schizophrenia,"* noting his mood disorder, particularly his behavior when manic.

I felt almost comforted when I read the doctor's clinical description of the behavior I knew so well. He confirmed that I wasn't going over the edge myself:

> His affect is very irritable, occasionally euphoric, and he is very argumentative, intrusive, and grandiose, stating in January 1979 at Santa Clara Valley Medical Center that he is God and in August 1979 that he has had a successful advertising career inventing jingles. . . . In August 1976 while hospitalized at Stanford he said, "I feel a lot happier, more excited when I'm sick." His motor behavior is marked by hyperactivity, with pacing, psychomotor agitation, and occasionally assaulting nurses and other patients. He has required seclusion during many hospitalizations and restraints at times. There is one mention of "thought broadcasting on TV and radio" and a history of having "heard voices giving simple com-

---

* Researchers first described "schizoaffective disorder," a mixture of features seen in schizophrenia and mood disorders, as long ago as 1913. The name was coined in 1933 by Dr. Jacob Kasanin of the Rhode Island State Hospital in a presentation to the American Psychiatric Association, but did not come into general use as a descriptive label until the 1970s. The condition is considered somewhat less grave than unqualified schizophrenia.

mands," and a note that he heard "voices screaming at me" in August 1979.*

The document listed a step-by-step, seven-point program of six drugs recommended for future use. While the doctor never dropped a word of explicit criticism, it was obvious that he considered many of the past treaters to have been cowardly or ill informed or both. "His physicians should not hesitate to treat him with . . ." was his most censorious phrasing.

Would Jeff ever be "cured"? The verdict was not encouraging: "Jeff's prognosis remains guarded because he still doesn't accept that he has an illness and frequently fails to take his medications. However, recent studies suggest that schizoaffective patients have a much better recovery rate and social outcome than other schizophrenic groups."

In a word, my son's outlook would remain grim unless he could make peace with his pills or be maneuvered into an armistice.

Having paid Stanford five hundred dollars for Dr. Koran's herculean effort—a remarkable bargain—I was determined to see Jeff's attending doctors make use of the findings. The document's outstanding assets were its obvious authoritative sweep, its brevity, and the fact that it was typed. I have never seen Jeff's case records assembled in one place and cannot imagine the height of the stack. But it's obvious doctors cannot wait until records make their way from one center to another; that every institutional psychiatrist has another patient waiting and another and another; that even a glance at the most recent page or two from the paper pile would be too much if there were handwritten scrawls to be deciphered.

While Jeff was having his fantasies, I was having mine. With Koran's report, I thought that a new state of order had been declared, and I could

---

* In November 1995, voices made news. Research laboratories in New York and London pinpointed sounds originating in the brain of schizophrenic patients. Patients lying in the brain-imaging device were asked to press a button whenever they heard the voices that upset them. The researchers believed that this behavioral-technical tool had enabled them to track schizophrenia to specific deep brain structures that might be treatable with medications of the future.

Although the hearing of voices rates as an unequivocal symptom of schizophrenia, only a minority of sufferers from "acoustic hallucinations" have the disease. As many as two to four percent of all people (depending on what study is considered) habitually hear strange voices. According to studies that began in the mid-1980s, this phenomenon can be set off by traumatic events of ordinary life. Although the emotional stress of nonpsychotic victims can be severe, many, fearing they will be called crazy, seek no help. Only one-third see psychiatrists. Counseling is available from the Weerklang Foundation, organized by Dr. Marius Romme, a psychiatry professor at Limburg University in Holland, and Paul Baker, a public health worker in England, founder of the Hearing Voices Network.

picture my son's illness being dealt with effectively. He was seeing Al Scopp that spring, a psychologist who did talk therapy with Jeff, and who dispensed vitamins and supplements without excessive promises, but was not qualified to deal with prescription medications. I wrote him what to tell Jeff about the Koran report:

1. How painstaking a review has been conducted, how many doctors and records were consulted. PURPOSE: to give him confidence in the process that has been conducted in his behalf, that it's not just another doc giving him the by-guess-and-by-gosh treatment.

2. Study-in-continuity shows he is in fact improving. PURPOSE: I'm sure he cannot perceive this long-term uptrend and he needs and deserves some good news.

3. Control over his medications is now firmly established so that he has a dependable footing to operate from. PURPOSE: get him off the feeling of doctor-floundering which he must be experiencing.

4. Assure him that a large component of his problems is definitely chemical and this portion at present is only controllable chemically. PURPOSE: to try to influence his excessively psychological orientation, as evidenced by his continuing hankering for psychoanalysis.

5. For future medication questions, a knowledgeable, fully informed consulting authority, Dr. Koran, is now established and available to Jeff, no matter who his day-by-day helpers may be. PURPOSE: to give Jeff a life raft when he is tempted to tinker with his medications.

6. Challenge him that the way is now clear for him to help himself, that only he can really do this, once the meds clear the way. PURPOSE: to influence him to give his best.

I sought help from Dr. Koran's memory the other day. The weight of Jeff's medical history was pressing in on me and I must have shown it.

"He might not have survived without you, he was so disorganized," the doctor said quite unexpectedly. "You were his advocate."

I said that advocacy was surely what Jeff required as much as anything else, and that advocacy and more advocacy was a key nutrient for others like him, but that it might look awkward if I said so in the book.

"You can quote me," the doctor said quietly. I received his gift as a balm.

Rereading this pipe dream fifteen years later, I am impressed with its logic and clarity. I also recall that it accomplished absolutely nothing.

Jeff's condition was, shall we say, disorganized. So were most of his treaters. The bright-eyed six-point plan for Dr. Scopp was simply naive. I had counted in vain on the collaboration of the doctors in charge of Jeff's medications. By and large, though, they resented help. At the time, the doctor in charge on behalf of the county mental health system was a particularly harassed, monosyllabic, sad, and physically handicapped psychiatrist who had already made clear to me that he had no interest in the views of his patients' families.

I hoped that he might be impressed with Koran's two months of work, by its high quality, and by the Stanford sponsorship. So on March 16, 1981, I wrote this man:

> I understand that Dr. Koran's report has been completed and that copies have been sent to you. . . . Since so often in Jeff's illness the problems have been aggravated by communications failures, I'm eager to confirm that you have in fact received the medication review and would be greatly relieved to hear that you may be finding it helpful with Jeff's current problems. It's heart-breaking to hear how miserable he sounds, sometimes very high, other times depressed, with greatly changed speech patterns.

Did the doctor receive the Koran report? If so, had he read it? If so, was he applying it? If he was and if he had absorbed Koran's strong advocacy of lithium in adequate amounts for the manic depression, why were Jeff's moods still swinging wildly? I never got answers because I could never establish contact with this doctor again. I suspect he didn't wish to be second-guessed by Koran, an outsider, or by an intruder like a father.

In time, I learned that the proud and overloaded doctors, the fluidity of the disease, and the eccentricities of my son were not the only forces working against Jeff and me. I had been making the mistake of trying to bring logical reasoning to bear on the obstacles to recovery that he kept erecting. Common sense is often not the wavelength of a schizophrenic. My reality was not his reality. He couldn't connect with my life.

I had been placed on thyroid medication and advised that I would need to take it always. My condition was controllable but not curable. When I drew the parallel with Jeff and his medications, the logic didn't click for him. Further proof of the dilemma emerged in early 1983 when I sent him this note:

For Jeff

Doctors who treat non-existent illnesses lose their licenses.

Hospital administrators who admit and treat well people get fired.

Public guardians who sign themselves responsible for well people get fired.

Judges who approve such public guardians get impeached.

Budget directors who OK hospitalizations for people who aren't ill get fired.

Social Security administrators who approve disability checks to people who aren't disabled also get fired.

Families who for years pay for treatment of illnesses that don't exist have got to be crazy themselves.

Physically fit adults who are willing but *unable* to finish their education or hold a steady job or make their own living may possibly be faking an illness. Much more likely: they are really ill.

I got no response.

I was still consulting Dr. R in New York about Jeff's misery and was still under the spell of the behavior change I had seen the doctor achieve in family therapy with the dictatorial father of my magazine editor associate, and had not given up on talk therapy. It seemed to fit Jeff's inclination to ruminate and intellectualize.

Dr. R recommended an old friend of his, Tom Ferreira, a psychiatrist who practiced in the Silicon Valley. Jeff had lately been discharged after seven months in one of his regular hospitals, Crestwood. Rick Robinson was now overseeing the medications. Rick agreed that psychotherapy would strengthen Jeff's efforts to make it "on the outside."

So I went to see Ferreira, whom I liked. When he said cautiously that he would think about the case, I followed up with a letter on February 15, 1983, enclosing a copy of the Koran report, which I was circulating wherever it seemed promising to do so, and appealing to this elderly, gentle practitioner as ardently as I knew how.

"I'm growing increasingly desperate (the word is carefully chosen) at the possibility that he may be so far removed from the real world that a re-entry may no longer be feasible," I confessed. "In a rare moment of self-perception some time ago he said to me, 'Sometimes I think I can't even tie my shoe laces anymore.' "

I closed with an affirmation that my money and my will would remain where my mouth was and that my expectations for my son were not excessive: "I am deeply involved in this, totally committed to doing anything remotely reasonable to break the cycle of Jeff's re-hospitalizations and to drag him, kicking if necessary, into some sort of life in the real world where he can have a little fun and do something, most anything, other than sit around on a mental hospital bed."

Gently, regretfully, the doctor declined. He didn't think he could be very helpful. It was a rare case of candor.

While pondering what other help I might recruit, it seemed time to shore up the support of my own family defenses and not commit the sin of which I was accusing everybody else: failure to communicate what I had learned about Jeff's needs and limitations. The key helper in our clan and shepherd of Jeff's long-term future was obviously his brother, Ron, then recently elected congressman from Portland, Oregon, a most dedicated family advocate. I wrote him in Washington:

> His non-sick behavior needs to be encouraged and reinforced, and this is best done by reassuring him constantly. This is not a matter of giving him semi-phony pep talks but simply giving him attention, not treating him as if he isn't there or is a permanent mental patient. His self-identification as such a chronic patient is by now one of the worst things going against him.

I then offered a somewhat rosy assessment of Jeff's current situation, telling Ron (in part):

1. Jeff is very, very lonely and feels his loneliness very much. He needs every friend, every warm human contact he can get, whether he sounds receptive or not.

2. Jeff is NOT malingering, as I and you and even Dr. R sometimes thought. He's just been in the hospital seven months and with the crowding and budget pressures, the system keeps a patient in the hospital not even an hour longer than necessary for his safety.

3. The doctors agree that with the knowledge of his case now assembled, plus some luck, it IS possible to keep him out of hospitals; to be functional; to work. . . . There is no reason to give up. You could influence him not by talking at him, much less lecturing, as I used to do notoriously, but by *listening* to him, closely and sympathetically, not judgmentally, which I am also now finally learning. . . . An occasional

"hmmm" or a quiet, "Why do you think that?" is helpful. It is NOT helpful, except in extreme cases, to give advice!! Jeff is "other-directed" enough. The doctors tell me it's better to throw the ball back in Jeff's court when he asks for direction. ("What do YOU think?")

"Silences with him are productive," I advised. "Important thoughts dislodge from him very, very slowly. His mind does not function like ours. Listen! Ask yourself: What's he getting at? There's no point in you or me being doctors. He's got doctors. But there are often hidden messages in what he says and asks. Don't try to divine what they are. Let it go into your mental file or ask, 'Jeff, are you saying that . . . ?'

"Keep in mind that Jeff can be a master manipulator," I wrote. "He's famous for it among his doctors. When he throws out a problem, remember who 'owns' it. Usually, he does, not you. Keep asking: 'What do you think?' which flatters him by conveying that you *care* what he thinks, that you assume he *has* an opinion, that you *are* interested in his views. In extreme cases, I say to him, 'Jeff, I'm not your doctor and I'm not God!' "

CHAPTER 14

"So Many Wonderful, Wonderful People"

I'M ALSO NOT a millionaire. Like most relatives of schizophrenics, I was left broke when insurance ran out. Inevitably, the pressure to pay bills, and then more and more bills, mounted. It would be years later, in the fall of 1996, that I would finally have my say about this in Washington, bonding in troubled fatherhood with a Republican senator who seemed to have little in common with the Wydens, Democrats all. He was one of the many people who have taken an active interest in schizophrenia because of a family connection; it's a notable fraternity.

Whenever talk on Capitol Hill turned to cutting the budget in the 1990s, and then cutting it by still more tens of billions of dollars, Senator Pete V. Domenici appeared on television with the mien of the Grim Reaper. Lean, ascetic, thin-lipped, the Republican from New Mexico, chairman of the Senate Budget Committee, was the picture of unyielding austerity.

His looks matched the well-known conservative politics of this Italian immigrant grocer's son. The appearance was, however, deceiving. Underneath the stony facade, according to a longtime Domenici staffer, beat "the biggest bleeding heart you ever saw." Most particularly, it bled for the mentally ill, including a daughter, thirty-two, one of his eight children. Despite lithium, Thorazine, and Trilafon, she had been dysfunctional, off and on, for fifteen years.

"There are many symptoms of manic depression and some of schizophrenia," the senator, sixty-two, said in explaining her condition at a public ceremony not long ago, "but this is not exactly diagnosable." Those labels sounded much like the varying verdicts passed on Jeff over the years.

Budget-cutter or not, Domenici was determined to use his considerable influence to ease the hardships of our children's kind and the pain of their families—"so many wonderful, wonderful people," as the senator told me, eyes shining with surprising passion through thick horn-rims. "I'm a conservative who believes in helping those who can't help themselves," he said.

Domenici was blazing angry when I called on him in the summer of 1996. He had just led—and won—the fight in the Senate to require insurance companies to deal with the mentally ill as they deal with cancer or diabetes patients, but the House refused to go along with his view that patients like his daughter and my son were entitled to equal rights. Domenici felt vulnerable. Not long before the Senate vote, he and his wife, Nancy, had rushed to New Mexico to see whether their ailing daughter needed rehospitalization.

"The mentally ill are always seen as bad people who commit murders," the senator bristled. "Stigma? The word is too mild. We're fighting an illogical fear!" Blindness to the advances of modern treatments was the source of the opposition's resistance, Domenici was convinced: "They're stuck in another age."*

He also questioned his adversaries' economics. "If they'd analyze the data," he told a *Washington Post* interviewer, "they'd realize that they'll save money if they take care of people with schizophrenia and depression." Increased worker productivity would make up for additional expense.

Domenici had not remained a lone senatorial crusader after he and his wife encountered Paul and Sheila Wellstone at a NAMI meeting. Paul, the Democratic senator from Minnesota, had given a talk about the discrimination against a "very good friend of mine" who was schizophrenic. It was later that day that he told the Domenicis he had referred to his brother, Stephen, schizophrenic since the age of eleven. And the Domenicis then talked about their daughter, and the couples have enjoyed friendly contact ever since.

* After heavy legislative wrestling by the senator, the first step toward parity was signed into law on September 26, 1996; most health plans would have to observe identical limits for physical and mental illnesses beginning in 1998.

Lobbyists call the two senators "the odd couple of health care" because Wellstone, a former college professor, votes as liberal as Domenici votes conservative. While they agree on virtually nothing else, they cosponsored the bill for parity of insurance rights, and both have spoken at NAMI conventions. "The personal has overridden the political," Wellstone said. For the NAMI high command, the two senators naturally hold the rank of archangels. My son, Ron, of course, supported them.

Nancy Domenici is a small, somewhat shy woman whose activist involvement with the NAMI board of directors clearly did not come easily. She was torn between her eagerness to bolster the cause while protecting the privacy of her troubled daughter. When I talked with the Domenicis, neither parent uttered their daughter's first name, and Mrs. Domenici preferred to talk about the "wonderful constituency" of the NAMI families. She touched only obliquely on her role, and the senator's, as morale boosters. "People open up to us, and we want them to share with us," she said. "You almost need to put halos on them [the NAMI families]. They have seen the bottom of life."

Her ill daughter in New Mexico was doing better—again. The young woman had a new part-time job and was thinking of getting a car. No one could be certain if the remission would last.

Schizophrenia is a ruthless leveler, sparing no one, including longtime friends. I have known Bob Litman, a California psychiatrist-investigator, for thirty-five years. A week after I was talking with him about the psychological autopsy of Marilyn Monroe, I received a letter from his wife, Connie, identifying herself as a psychiatric social worker. We had never met. Her husband had told her about my book and my son, she wrote, and she wondered whether she could help other parents by telling me about their own son, Joe, thirty-four. He was schizophrenic, too. I was flabbergasted. How could I possibly not have known that I shared such a significant fact of family life with a man I had known for so long and thought I had known well?

I had long taken notice that Bob often seemed subdued, even defeated. There were long pauses between his sentences. His head habitually hung a bit low. His smiles were brief. I had found such neutrality common among therapists and supposed that it was an old-fashioned technique for inviting communication from others. It now occurred to me that I had never even known that Bob was married.

Along with Connie's letter came nine single-spaced pages of notes, memories about Joe. She had worked on these for years, rewriting and remembering life with her son. Once she had thought of publishing her efforts, and Joe had encouraged her. Eventually, the pain of recollecting had become "too searing," and she abandoned the plan to go public. If it would help my book, I was welcome to use whatever I chose.

Even the saddest gifts can be beyond price; this was one of them, and I told Connie so when I thanked her.

Joe had been a very bright child, but pensive and "always frightened." Only in recent years did he mention that he had been so scared because he heard strange voices in his head "from the beginning." He attended several nursery schools, always refusing to leave the house after a few weeks. He chewed holes in his T-shirts. His father walked many evenings with him in the hills above their suburban home. That calmed Joe because there were no people about.

When he was thirteen, he began sneaking out of his home around midnight. Once the police brought him back at dawn. He had been walking in the hills, talking to himself, and looking for "the androids." His parents decided he was simply eccentric and would grow up to be a science fiction writer. In their hearts, they knew they were deluding themselves, because his bizarre actions continued. When Joe returned from a dance, he said he would not attend any more public events because "the agents" were following him.

In the 1980s, Joe fled in terror from three colleges and two hospitals. When Connie took him to Sequoia National Park, he knocked on her hotel room door and said he would jump off the balcony because the androids had landed. They were going to kidnap him and take him to another dimension. Computers were his best friends. He understood and loved these nonhumans.

Transferred to a third hospital, Joe called home to say goodbye because the agents were closing in on him. An hour later he was found unconscious, lying in his blood, his wrists slashed.

"Our family of six unravels," Connie's notes reported. Joe's oldest sister was becoming an internist, the next oldest a rabbi. The third and youngest sister stayed out of classes for ten years before returning to college. Much of the time during her dropout years she spent crying for Joe.

"I feel estranged from them," Connie wrote about her healthy children. "Later, they tell Bob and me they felt abandoned by us. Bob and I, who love each other, are quarreling mindlessly."

After another year with his parents, two years in a large group home that collapsed of staff dissension and lack of money, and two more stays at a fourth hospital, Joe finally received clozapine and lived, much improved and no longer frightened, with two other recovering schizophrenic young men and a counselor in a private cooperative setup in the mountains, six hours from Connie and Bob. Joe's current care system was costly—I lacked the nerve to ask how much—and even though their fortunes appeared to have turned for the better, Bob and Connie felt worse.

"We're both old," Connie wrote me. "A few months ago, during an angiogram, I thought, 'Who'll take care of Joe?'"

When I visited with the Litmans several months later, in 1996, they remembered more about their puzzlement concerning Joe's condition when he was about twenty. Connie had challenged Bob then.

"You're the big doctor," she recalled saying to him. "How come you can't fix it?" Retrospectively, she said to me: "I just had highly unrealistic expectations."

Bob had only then begun to admit to himself what they were facing: "Probably classic schizophrenia—I hope not." He was well aware that his most proficient colleagues "couldn't manage the disease." Why should he be expected to do better?

Fifteen years later, even the most benign of the government's assistance agencies seemed to have turned against Joe. The Social Security authorities sent him a "notice of action": his SSI (Supplemental Security Income) payments were being discontinued. He was said to be receiving unauthorized income from somewhere, which wasn't true. They sent him many pages of incomprehensible bureaucratese offering "three ways to appeal." I saw the papers and couldn't understand them either.

Bob and Connie hired an SSI lawyer who eventually got Joe's assistance reinstated. Connie pointed out that few people knew that such specialists existed. Although I had gone through an SSI scare with Jeff, I certainly didn't. Still, like Jeff, Joe had retained a gallows humor about the sharp edges of the outside world.

"Are they going to deport me?" he asked his parents.

Along with much bitterness, they conveyed a sense of relative relief. Joe had cut down to smoking two packs of cigarettes a day. He weighed 240 pounds, 70 pounds under his maximum. And he delivered a startlingly insightful talk about his illness at a local church. ("Schizophrenics talk to themselves, make strange gestures, and often have poor bathing habits. People simply don't want to be around a schizophrenic.")

The Litmans were elated about Gary, Joe's counselor, who had a lengthy record of caring for convalescing schizophrenics. The mountain environment he had fashioned for Joe fulfilled requirements that I had identified as crucial to recovery only after more than twenty years of watching over Jeff. The group had to be very small. The counseling attention had to be intensive, seven days a week, around the clock. Above all, the patients had to be kept busy constantly, letting up for little more than sleep. Sheer activity seemed to be superb medicine, and I made a note of that.

Joe turned out to be wonderful, a giant bear, surprisingly light on his feet, overwhelmingly quiet, but easy, gracious, well organized in conversation with our restaurant's waiters and me. He was looking forward to working with computers, he said.

A week later, Connie phoned me in Connecticut. A place could be made for Jeff in Joe's mountains, she said. I hope I thanked her enough, but I felt it was too early for Jeff to be without his accustomed doctor in northern California.

The gesture of hospitality more than made up for a strange void I had noticed. Neither Joe nor his parents had asked me about Jeff. I suppose they felt, from personal experience, that I would find talking about my son "too searing," as Connie had put it when she first wrote to me.

In my reply, I had said that I guessed being parent to a schizophrenic was indeed a "cause." Connie had written back: "Bob and I are old and feel we should get Joe 'into the system,' whatever that means. This whole thing really does feel like a 'cause,' as you wrote."

As we were saying goodbye at his car in Los Angeles, I felt Bob's hand ever so lightly on my lower arm. From anyone else, this would have been a meaningless brush. From this very private man, it felt like a benediction.

Dr. E. Fuller Torrey reported in his classic family manual, *Surviving Schizophrenia*, that "many schizophrenia researchers, including myself, began working in this field primarily because we had a family member affected with the disease." Torrey's sister, fifty-five, has been ill since age seventeen. Recently she has fared better and been stabilized on risperidone, living in an upstate New York group home and enjoying enduring male companionship. The doctor keeps in close contact, wishing for still better things for her, hoping he may yet engineer a great coup in his field. Already, he has overseen enough research to keep a fair-sized institute going, and he exercised control in an idiosyncratic way.

"He's our conscience," said Dr. David Pickar of the NIMH, one of the most respected specialists and authors on schizophrenia.

Until 1988, Torrey had knocked about in NIMH and invested decades in epidemiological hunches, churning out books investigating schizophrenics in Ireland, Bosnia, and on minuscule Pacific islands. The books never gained much attention.

Nobody could determine why so much schizophrenia occurred in certain beautiful but dirt-poor southwestern Irish counties or what could be done with sixty afflicted natives' spinal fluids, which Torrey was still hoarding in his office freezer a decade later. Enough money was never available to investigate why schizophrenia broke out in tight clusters around America. Torrey knew of more than twenty-five such outbreaks that suggested infection as a cause of the disease.

"Epidemiology was almost totally ignored at NIMH," he told me with his usual, barely suppressed scorn. A grand sweep eluded him, but he refused to ignore obscure leads. Many in the establishment dismissed him as a laughable odd duck, a troublemaker who insisted on bringing up inconvenient subjects.

His brilliant but widely ignored book *Nowhere to Go: The Tragic Odyssey of the Homeless Mentally Ill* traced the origins of today's epidemic of the homeless, at least one-third of whom are schizophrenic, to the first 433,000 patients who were disgorged by state hospitals in the 1960s because Thorazine and other new antipsychotics had restored them to some measure of stability. "The community" was supposed to have taken charge of these fragile convalescents and ensured that they kept up their medication. The community, by and large, did no such thing. There were few facilities, fewer doctors, and not nearly enough funds. Typically, the area around San Jose State College, near Jeff's halfway house in San Jose, became overrun with destitute ex-patients discharged from nearby Agnews State Hospital. I still see homeless, obviously deranged people stagger around Jeff's neighborhood whenever I visit.

In July 1988, a somewhat mysterious multimillionaire mail-order businessman named Theodore R. Stanley of Westport, Connecticut, read *Surviving Schizophrenia* and found it opinionated but helpful and lucid. Stanley headed the Theodore and Vada Stanley Foundation (assets exceeded thirty million dollars, recent annual income eight million dollars), and he decided, in partnership with NAMI, to finance more intensive research into serious mental illness.

"We chose Fuller Torrey to lead our effort based on the picture we got from his book of a compassionate and intelligent leader in the field," Stanley wrote me. "That he might have been regarded by some as a maverick was of little consequence; aren't such people usually the real leaders in every field?"

With effective control over millions of dollars each year, Torrey could influence, to a significant degree, the choices of research directions that would be nurtured. He continued his basic research with patients at St. Elizabeth's Hospital, in Washington, D.C. His headquarters was still his terminally cluttered ground-floor cubbyhole, where he officiated amid his jogging clothes, looking like a harried gym teacher. Over his desk hung a sign warning "Just because I'm paranoid doesn't mean they're not after me."

Among his envious fellow professionals, Torrey was recognized as the ugly duckling that had turned into a swan, and even he, impatient with external trappings, couldn't resist a bit of glee. "People are calling up about grants who were happy to fire me twenty years ago," he said.

Torrey's research grants financed such specialized studies as "Biochemical, Ultrastructural, Molecular and Functional Changes in Glutamate Synapses in Rat Brains," but he had also ordained the establishment in 1994 of the more immediately practical Stanley Specimen Bank at St. Elizabeth's. It collects postmortem brains of schizophrenics—a perennial, crucial shortage for the study of schizophrenia.

Also in 1994, Torrey helped create the world's first Neurovirology Laboratory at Johns Hopkins University, headed by Dr. Robert H. Yolken, director of pediatric infectious diseases at Hopkins. As of 1996, the laboratory had sponsored two three-day symposia to investigate the possible link between viruses and schizophrenia as well as other severe mental disorders. Viruses had been under suspicion as schizophrenia instigators since 1925, Torrey noted, when Karl Menninger, not yet in psychoanalytic training, uncovered thirty-nine cases of schizophrenia at Boston Psychopathic Hospital. He believed those illnesses to be "the psychic manifestation of a viral encephalitis" (the finding was never replicated).

Following World War II, there was a statistically significant increase of schizophrenia in western Holland among young people whose mothers were in the third trimester of pregnancy during a terrible wartime famine when cats and dogs were eaten. Drawing on this and a variety of other hints, Torrey and Yolken teamed up in 1995 to produce the article "Viruses, Schizophrenia and Bipolar Disorder" in *Clinical Microbiology Review,* a respectable though hardly mainstream publication for schizophrenia researchers.

Farmers, Torrey explained to me, who kept their cats in their barns to chase mice reported no schizophrenia. However, in urban centers, where cats lived in houses, ate off people's plates, and jumped into bed with small children, it was possible they might transmit viruses. This stimulated excitement in Torrey and Yolken.

Later in 1995, the team wrote a carefully hedged article entitled "Could Schizophrenia Be a Viral Zoonosis Transmitted from House Cats?" which was published in *Schizophrenia Bulletin,* the official NIMH quarterly. The editors flagged the contribution as controversial, followed it by a rebuttal, and the authors accompanied it by a footnote assuring readers that they need not change their behavior toward cats.

"One of the authors continues to own two cats," it said. "The other author continues to allow the neighbor's cat, who believes she owns all houses in the neighborhood, to visit regularly." It was not made clear why the doctor-authors' cats enjoyed presumed immunity from schizophrenia.

As an inquisitive Los Angeles graduate student of psychology in 1993, Meggin Hollister wondered if the Rh-negative blood of her mother, Patsy, could have been dangerously incompatible with the Rh-positive blood of the fetus that became her older sister Annick. Psychiatrists had advised Patsy not to worry about this when she was pregnant with Annick. Now, a talk by a researcher on genes and schizophrenia made Meggin think that the psychiatrists were wrong because Annick, thirty-four, had been schizophrenic for eighteen years.

Determined to investigate, she asked her dissertation adviser for permission to research her suspicion for her doctorate paper. "Meggin wanted to do this for months before I said OK," remembered the professor. "It was just too much of a long shot."

Two years later, after digging through the unusually complete medical records compiled in Denmark, Meggin perched anxiously in front of her computer in a crowded laboratory, watching her final statistical analysis emerge.

"Oh, my God," she would remember thinking, "the implications!"

Out of her findings, Meggin, thirty-one, produced what the *Archives of General Psychiatry* called a "landmark study." Published in January 1996, it carried an introduction by Dr. Richard Jed Wyatt of NIMH. "Perhaps the most important clinical implication is that some forms of schizophrenia may be preventable," he wrote. (I will discuss this later.)

For Meggin and her family, this was the first really good news since Halloween of 1977, when the police called to report that they had found Annick, vice president of her sophomore high school class, howling at the moon, insisting she saw God. Brought home, disheveled and ranting, she cut her wrists as Meggin burst into her room. Ever since, Meggin had not been the only family member struggling in a state of constant mobilization against schizophrenia.

Since 1989 the senior Hollisters helped transform adversity by working six days a week in the drafty warehouse of an organization they founded: NARSAD Artworks, which reproduces and sells art by the mentally ill, including their daughter.

"They're an extraordinary family," said Constance Lieber, president of the National Alliance for Research on Schizophrenia and Depression (NARSAD), the nation's largest donor of mental health research funds. "They have turned adversity into something positive." NARSAD awarded Meggin a sixty-thousand-dollar grant for further research to solidify her findings.

Annick, who became a talented painter, lived in a board-and-care apartment complex and worked as a clerical volunteer at the Los Angeles Zoo. Her thoughts remained erratic at times, but the pleasures she took from life, her pride in Meggin's work, and the caring of her family had brought her serenity.

Serenity was not given to Jay Neugeboren, on the other hand, and neither was a benign view of NARSAD. Neugeboren, a novelist and college professor in Massachusetts, and the sole psychological support of his older brother Robert, fifty-three, a schizophrenic for decades, had seen one of the group's full-page ads in the *New York Times*, celebrating "the many urgent scientific projects that are paving the way for better treatments and the cure we all hope for."

"Robert and I have been hearing talk about 'breakthrough cures' for more than thirty years now," Jay wrote in his memoir, *Imagining Robert*. "What upset me in the *Times* ad is not the possibility that Robert's condition is chemical, but the belief that so many people have in its corollary: that if the condition is chemical, it can be corrected with chemicals. Oh how easy it would be for everybody."

Neugeboren became angry when he read about NARSAD providing funds to 315 doctors in seventy-eight leading research centers because for him this largesse conjured up a devastating scene. "What I also see, but more vividly," he wrote, "is my brother, in a room by himself hour after hour, day after day, trembling from medications and fear and loneliness."

Where was simple attention to ordinary human needs? And what, Neugeboren wanted to know, would happen if, one day, cause and cure were in fact to be discovered for schizophrenia? "What then will we do about the life that has come before and will continue after the moment of diagnosis and medication, and of how the fact of having this condition has affected an individual's history?"

Jay, his brother's keeper, was understandably mired in memories of Robert's more than fifty hospitalizations; his incessant changes of diagnoses (similar but more multifarious than Jeff's); the nine different types of psychotherapy; the eight medications dispensed merely to minimize the side effects; the incessant struggle against the pills, the pills, the pills.

Once Jay had asked Robert what made him go off the pills. After a long time, Robert answered: "No answer." Silence was also the answer when their father, whom Robert once threatened to kill, asked a doctor, who refused to continue treating Robert because he stopped taking his pills, "So where, doctor, is the pill to make him want to take his pills?"

"It is as if, I often think," Jay reflected, "the very history of the ways in which our century has dealt with those it calls mentally ill has for more than thirty years now been passing through my brother's mind and body."

His brother's and my son's.

Jay asked Robert why he had not gone under.

"I just wanted to survive and persist," said Robert, which is, I guess, what kept my friend still able to survive and smile as well.

I did not share Jay's pessimism. Evidence was accumulating that the biological breakthroughs he ridiculed were, in fact, real and valuable. I had been looking into some of them and was impressed.

CHAPTER 15

Clozapine I:
The Twenty-Five-Year Marathon

THE ASSOCIATED PRESS story in the *New York Times* of May 15, 1987, was short and buried deep inside the paper. It carried the guarded headline "Test Shows New Drug to Be of Help for Some Severe Schizophrenics." The text was equally unexciting. The medication being reported on at the annual meeting of the American Psychiatric Association in Chicago was called clozapine. The often used (and abused) word "breakthrough" was not in evidence.

I had never heard of clozapine, and the news of its appearance under these circumstances was not especially inviting. The story mentioned "a potentially fatal side effect," a blood disease. The drug had reportedly been tested on only 125 severe schizophrenics, a relatively tiny sample. It was still "experimental," therefore not authorized for general use. Here was another item for my capacious "pending" file.

As so often before and since, I was too uninformed to know what I was reading. From the account in the *Times*, I could hardly be expected to know that clozapine was not new at all, that it was more than just promising, and that its emergence would signal a crucial turning point for my son and tens of thousands like him.

After nearly two decades of Jeff's illness, and without planning or awareness of what I was reaching for or why, I had been recruiting a variety of skills for Jeff's medical support system. Rick Robinson at the Valley Medical Center introduced Jeff to the nuances of the medications. Robinson had guided me to Andy Abarbanel, who connected with Jeff, employing his own imaginative psychotherapy. Larry Koran's overview of the field had indicated to me that he was the right authority to extract a measure of order from the treatment maze that had entrapped Jeff for so many years and kept inducing his constant relapses and rehospitalizations. I had developed confidence in this tested crew, and I especially appreciated their liking for Jeff, a significant step toward his eventual improvement. But still missing was a technical commander qualified to shape strategy. I had an ensemble waiting for a conductor.

Abarbanel, sensing this need, turned to one of his former teachers at McLean Hospital. The best teachers mark their best students for life, and Andy was thus affected by Skip Pope. In April 1990, then, with Jeff vegetating among stupefied peers milling about at Crestwood Hospital, Andy proposed Skip as a "consultant."

I knew that consultants can be languid rubber stamps, but in Skip I was acquiring something quite different. He was consistently up-to-the-minute on the latest news, and in schizophrenia—so Skip informed me on April 8, 1990—*the* news was clozapine. The FDA had just authorized its general use for "treatment-resistant" schizophrenics. Jeff fit that specification all too neatly, because of his body's resistance to past medications and the vehemence with which he refused to swallow his "meds."

I had been told that Pope was somewhat manic in his manner, but possessed of a brilliant mind, and was as surefooted as anyone in psychopharmacology. I was also pleased to remember that one of Skip's papers from the *American Journal of Psychiatry* had been quoted by Koran in his 1981 white paper on Jeff's history. Skip's decades with Harvard Medical School and McLean were also persuasive. Surveys consistently rated it the nation's premier mental institution. On its 240-acre campus, it maintained two clinical staff members for every patient. It boasted more than a hundred principal research investigators, and no private psychiatric hospital received more government research grants. And Pope was a star on its list of "well-known specialists."

His entry into my life was, well, staggering. The very first of our innumerable phone conferences clarified why his former fellow students had likened his style to a "trip." I experienced it as a blitz. In rapid fire, he rattled off characteristics of clozapine vastly different from what I had learned from the *Times* article.

The medication was in fact revolutionary, the first major neuroleptic drug advance in thirty-five years. While it produced little or no benefit for about forty percent of treatment-resistant patients, it yielded improvement for the rest. For about ten percent, the recovery was so radical that it amounted to rebirth. Extrapyramidal (muscle spasm) complications were minimal or nil. The potentially fatal side effect, agranulocytosis, which kills the white blood cells needed to fight infection, could, with luck, be spotted by weekly blood tests and promptly reversed.* Skip told me he had first started working with it in 1974. If I'd known him then, I might have saved Jeff half a lifetime of anguish. The thought was and is profoundly depressing.

Skip turned out to be but one voice in an unusual chorus of exultation about clozapine. "The benefits are overwhelming," declared a spokesperson for the FDA, not known for overstatement.

The story of how Jeff came to try the drug, as well as the tale of clozapine's genesis and stormy early days, is relevant and cautionary.

When I talked with Pope that April day in 1990, clozapine was theoretically available to Jeff. But Jeff's detestation of all "meds" was a formidable barrier. Skip sent me a carefully tailored letter, to be forwarded to Jeff. Crisply, he described two patients whom he had just helped "to resume active lives studying and working outside the hospital." He detailed how "clozapine has been dramatically successful in a large number of patients who had previously had very poor results with conventional drugs like Thorazine, Stelazine, Haldol, etc." He offered himself as an "adviser" and volunteered to talk with Jeff by phone and answer his questions, which he shortly did. Disgusted with the muscle contortions induced by Haldol, which he was then taking, Jeff surrendered with minimum grumbling.

The nervousness of Jeff's bureaucracy in Santa Clara County, California, and my difficulties with the clozapine manufacturer, Sandoz Pharmaceuticals, a multinational giant with forty thousand employees, were the next roadblocks. Since the cost and the risks attendant to the brand-new medication were clearly making the county officials reluctant, I decided on a more direct approach. A friend of mine knew a research doctor at Sandoz headquarters in Basel, Switzerland, and I phoned the doctor to inquire where one could buy

---

* Like all good news, the trivialization of agranulocytosis was a relative matter. Between February 5, 1990, and December 31, 1994, 386 clozapine-induced cases of the disease were reported in the United States, and twelve patients died despite blood monitoring.

clozapine. The suggestion left her speechless. I asked whether she could give me the name of anyone in the company to whom I could present my request. She reacted as if I had been guilty of a gross sexual advance. I was forced to fall back on the county fathers.

For the fragile sheltering arm of Santa Clara County, burdened by a destitute population of four thousand psychotic dependents, clozapine was no manna from heaven. The nervousness of the mental health system's psychiatrists, social workers, and pharmacologists, whom I found scurrying, red-eyed, in windowless cubbyholes, was understandable. The fatalities were worrisome. Too many overadvertised "miracle" drugs had let them down in the past. And the financial demands of Sandoz left these good people spluttering.

The role of money in dealing with schizophrenia had been very much on my mind since I had become too poor to pay for more than Abarbanel, Pope, frequent trips to California, and other not-so-incidentals. Furthermore, my son had been reduced to a second-class or maybe third-class citizen. He had been certified as one hundred percent disabled under the strict definitions of the Social Security Act. Unable to deal with the most mundane details of daily existence, he had landed under the wings of a conservator, a sensible and cheerful counselor, Henry Russell, with whom I had had many useful meetings and phone talks. Still, as a ward of the county, his care was subject to limits.

I had become fond of Russell's Mental Health Department colleagues on ramshackle Santa Clara Street in the thick of the Vietnamese shop signs of downtown San Jose. They were grossly overworked: Dr. Michael Kerschenbaum, Jeff's empathetic attending psychiatrist, cared for 175 (later 240) patients. Russell's headquarters was a receptacle of the unwashed, addicted, unsorted underclass—really a welfare office where the caregivers managed, on the whole, to operate with friendly faces, no minor achievement, considering the chronic crowding, understaffing, and constantly shrinking budgets.

In my decades of wrestling with schizophrenia, I had come to recognize the disease as an endurance contest. The budgets were not made of money alone. They also represented human perseverance, the willingness never to let up, enough resilience to keep playing the unending game of knock-the-head-against-the-wall. And thus far, the illness had outlasted all convalescence programs I had had personal contact with.

I had expected better. As long ago as March 1986, the *New York Times* had run an exceptional, deeply researched, four-part series entitled "Advancing on Schizophrenia." I found it mesmerizing, full of news, and mostly discouraging, but there were two exceptions. The *Times* had discovered superior residential treatment-and-convalescence programs, one in Boulder, Colorado, the other in Madison, Wisconsin. Both reported an unusual rate of recovery.

The Maitri system in Boulder then cost up to $9,850 per patient per month, about as much as care in a good hospital, because treatment personnel were in contact with patients around the clock. The Madison program cost only $15,000 a year. Both demonstrated that recovery could be stimulated by persistent close attention through trained and sympathetic social workers.

Jeff was firmly rooted in California. It would have been difficult, perhaps impossible, and probably inadvisable, to try breaking him loose from his accustomed environment, his treaters, the proximity of his mother, the great climate, and little amenities that he enjoyed in his home turf.

My hunt in California for a facility that approximated those in Boulder and Madison proved fruitless. I heard of several projects, but all had disappeared, usually for lack of money. Sometimes, burnout of the organizers and treaters, a common manifestation in every phase of schizophrenia care, was to blame. Once I heard of a program under Veterans Administration auspices in Los Angeles. It was said to be achieving gratifying progress in adjusting patients to the demands of society. By the time I learned of this, it was no more.

But in 1988, right in Jeff's neighborhood in San Jose, in a downtrodden residence on Virginia Street, the mental health functionaries of Santa Clara County had managed to create the Virginia Street Project. It was modeled after the Madison system and offered the same therapeutic environment.

The process to gain admission into Virginia Street resembled the competition for a scholarship place in a top prep school—only the qualifications were reversed. To gain entrance into the project, you had to be in certifiably terrible shape, the worst, excepting only the hopelessly warehoused souls roosting in the back wards of the last state hospitals.

Jeff made the necessary low grade, all right. We hardly celebrated his condition, but we did his admission, and my first encounter with the project's psychiatrist-director was more than I would have dared asked for. I remember the scene well.

"Give us your son's illness," said the smiling, well-scrubbed young man.

"Boy, am I ever ready!" was my response.

Jeff was showered by attention. Instead of moping alone and in silence, he was surrounded by helpers—trained, buoyant contemporaries—throughout his waking hours. He blossomed. The style rubbed off on me as well. I relaxed. How glorious it felt to give my son's illness to these upbeat new helpers!

But not for long. One day there was a rumor that Virginia Street would close, for budgetary reasons. The program had been underwritten by the Robert Wood Johnson Foundation, based in Princeton, New Jersey, and it had lost interest. Long afterward, when the project vanished, I called a doctor there to inquire why. Schizophrenia? It was a bottomless pit, hopeless.

The Virginia Street Project never died officially. It just vanished. There was no announcement. The pink-faced director moved on to other duties in another town. He had never said so, but he was giving my son's illness back to me.

In Europe, meanwhile, clozapine was being profitably sold at prices ranging from $1,600 to $3,200 per patient annually. In America, the Sandoz marketers set their fee at $8,944, regardless of dosage. The outcry from institutions and consumer groups was immediate, but Sandoz explained that they were not selling pills alone. They were offering a Clozaril Patient Management System, or CPMS. The package included weekly blood tests to be administered exclusively by a partner whom Sandoz retained for the occasion: Caremark, then a Chicago subsidiary of Baxter International.* Its inventors described this arrangement as public-spirited insurance, motivated by concern for patient safety. Later, an investigating senator, David Pryor, Democrat of Arkansas, called it an "extraordinarily creative but morally bankrupt profiting scheme."

In New York, the Sandoz maneuver infuriated Vera Hassner Sharav, an irrepressible retired librarian with a schizophrenic son who needed clozapine. In May 1990, she and fourteen other mothers picketed the New York hotel where members of the American Psychiatric Association were attending a clozapine panel demonstration.

"Clozapine is priced obscene! Clozapine is priced obscene!" the mothers chanted.

Mobilized by the tireless Sharav, a board member of the Alliance for the Mentally Ill in New York State, the media reacted sharply. Sandoz found itself denounced in front-page articles in the *New York Times* and the *Wall Street Journal*. ABC's *20/20* and NBC's *Inside Edition* did critical pieces. "Way Out

---

* The leading purveyor of home delivery systems for injectable medications, Caremark led a colorful corporate life. In June 1995, it culminated with a guilty plea in a federal kickback investigation and fines of about $159 million for civil and criminal damages.

of Reach" was the title of an article in *Time* magazine. Psychiatric institutions and public health authorities issued outraged statements. The *New England Journal of Medicine* denounced the Sandoz scheme as monopolistic.

The New York board of the National Alliance for the Mentally Ill put the problem succinctly: "Right now there are thousands of people who are suffering because they can't get this medication." Thousands—with Jeff among them. As of October 1990, only seven thousand Americans were taking clozapine.

The bottleneck concerned a point of public policy—the economic stranglehold that is likely to bedevil the cost of treating schizophrenia into the next century. Not only was the Sandoz scheme, as Sharav would write later, an attempt "to manipulate the market under the guise of protecting patient safety." Worse: "It was actually a plan to profiteer at the American taxpayer's expense."

The great majority of consumers in the schizophrenia marketplace, like Sharav and myself, are inextricably beholden to the good graces of the taxpayers; more than eighty percent of schizophrenics and their families, like us, cannot possibly muddle through decades of the attendant financial catastrophe without some public aid.

State governments felt the clozapine squeeze quickly. A federal judge in Kansas ordered the state Medicaid program to pay for the drug. The Pennsylvania authorities budgeted two million dollars for it and organized a lottery to determine who would receive its healing power. Striving for an equitable solution, one state attorney general after another filed antitrust suits against Sandoz until thirty-three such actions were lined up in the courts.

Sandoz could mount only an oblique defense. A full-page ad in the *New York Times* and seven other major newspapers, entitled "Politics vs. Patient Safety," argued that "CPMS was designed to save lives." The company failed to explain why only Caremark was qualified as a lifesaver, and it threatened summarily to boycott all of the nation's schizophrenics and their doctors.

Six months after Skip Pope had told me of clozapine's approval and the FDA had pronounced the drug's benefits as "overwhelming," Jeff still wasn't receiving it. I was bombarding his impecunious and jittery California caregivers with begging calls and letters. Skip supplied them with technical data about its efficacy. But Sandoz had succeeded in simultaneously offering and restricting the blessings of its creation.

Jeff's mother, meanwhile, was becoming perturbed. She was reading clozapine's critics. So on October 5, backed by data from Pope, I wrote her that improvements resulting from clozapine often became noticeable after three to four weeks; the risk of agranulocytosis was extremely low after three months; drowsiness was the drug's most common side effect, so that it is given at night; seizures occurred, but only at high dosages, and they could be managed with another drug, Dilantin; drooling and bedwetting were handled by Cogentin. Weight increase was rarely serious.

Edith and I had consoled each other for years with fantasies of magical new drugs that would give us back "the old Jeff." Now that time seemed close.

On October 5, the clozapine barrier came down for Jeff at last. I had been pushing his county guardians by offering to pay the required $8,944 myself. This startled the bureaucrats. Special meetings of the leadership were called. Finally, having heard enough good things about clozapine, they gave their assent.

Also on October 5 came a letter from a "reimbursement coordinator" at Caremark that had nothing to do with reimbursement. It was a cheery greeting for me as a cash customer: "Caremark, Inc., welcomes you to our CPMS therapy program," it began. "As we pride ourselves in providing quality products and service to our customers, we feel that you will be pleased with the program chosen to support your son's health care needs."

I *was* pleased. I kept thinking about that blessed ten percent of Caremark clients who were substantially reborn. And I tried to suppress negative ruminations about the company's holdup tactics. The exorbitant price was definitely not excessive for the rebirth of my son.

About the time I began sending a weekly $172 check to the Caremark reimbursement coordinator, the antitrust suits against Sandoz yielded an agreement that separated the Swiss manufacturer from the pricey Chicago supplier of the blood tests. Sandoz was also muscled into an agreement to refund $21 million. On April 15, 1991, Caremark sent me a "Dear Customer" letter to "update" me "regarding the changes" and in due course I received a check for several hundred dollars.

Our county fathers in California promptly started buying clozapine at newly reduced rates for the patients who needed it most.* They also arranged for routine blood tests at neighborhood laboratories. And yet at Crestwood Hos-

* In May 1994, only fifty thousand patients were getting clozapine in the United States. Its high cost was keeping tens of thousands of others on the less-effective medications with greater side effects. In California alone, sixty thousand should have been getting clozapine.

pital, Jeff was still showing no discernible change in his state after several months on the wonder drug.

At first, I thought the shifting diagnoses of Jeff's illness might be at the root of his nonresponse. Clozapine, after all, had been licensed by the FDA only for refractory sufferers of pure schizophrenia. If Jeff had the schizo-affective condition, as had come to be commonly supposed, would clozapine still be helpful?

Skip Pope had a documented answer. He and seven colleagues at McLean had published a survey showing that the drug appeared "equally effective and perhaps superior, in the acute and maintenance treatment of patients with psychotic mood disorders and schizoaffective disorder." So we were on track.

The core problem seemed to be the question of dosage: How much clozapine would it take to seize hold of Jeff's system and turn around his illness or, at least, blunt it? The relevant numbers confused me. Various studies had pegged the average daily effective dose of clozapine at about 400 milligrams. By March 1991, Jeff's intake had gradually been increased to 550, with still no sign of impact.

On March 5, 1991, Pope wrote that he was "disappointed" that Jeff's response had not been "more robust" (a favorite locution of psychopharmacologists). Lack of response was "quite rare," in his experience. He hoped that Jeff still "may ultimately be a clozapine responder."

At McLean, Skip reported, some nonresponders had found the drug kicking in only at 850 or more milligrams, 900 being the manufacturer's specified maximum. (On the phone later, Skip revealed that McLean had treated a frail young woman successfully with 1,100 milligrams. A huge truck driver needed only 150.) Skip mentioned caveats. At over 550 milligrams, "the risk of seizures begins to increase significantly," although "coverage" was possible with an antiepileptic drug, Valproate, which Jeff was already taking. Sedation and light-headedness might become troublesome. On the other hand, "even though dosage increases [of great magnitude] are rarely effective when using conventional neuroleptic drugs, I have seen some fairly striking changes in a few clozapine patients under such circumstances."

Since even Pope made no specific recommendation, I called Dr. David Pickar, a research psychiatrist who had worked with hundreds of schizophrenics at the Experimental Therapeutics Branch in the federal government's National Institute of Mental Health. I had met Pickar years before and found him accessible and outspoken. He had a brief and defiant response, which I remember well. "I'd push the clozapine," he snapped. When I raised doubts, he repeated himself still more firmly.

My learning curve was turning erratic. Never yet had the volatility and eccentricity of Jeff's disease or its unpredictable interaction with the neuroleptics become so apparent. The facts were grim but absurdly simple. Anything might work. Anything might fail. All patients had intrinsically personal reactions to any intervention. There were no true experts.

"We just stumble along," as Pope always said, and many of his colleagues over the years volunteered similar fulminations. Frustration was the permanent bottom line for the treaters; pain ruled for the treated.

Since Jeff's status has never achieved stability, much less repose, change often comes daily, and it has been part of my job to make sure that the continuing flow of intelligence about him never slows. I cannot know when a phrase or brief sentence muttered by a doctor or social worker might contain some hint for action or for follow-up inquiry. The required level of constant alertness is of itself quite tiring.

On March 19, 1991, I reported to Pope on Jeff's first hospital visit by his mother in three months; she had undergone serious surgery. She was cheered, which was uncommon. She had found our son "considerably changed for the better," I told Pope. "He talked sensibly, showed interest in the outside world, discussed a book he was reading." There was cautious speculation by the hospital personnel that he might be transferred to a halfway house before long.

His improvement might not have impressed anybody but a parent in search of hope. Jeff still insisted that clozapine, lithium, Valproate, and his other medications were not as valuable to him as the vitamin supplements he hankered for, especially niacin and dolomite. He still fantasized about his delusional relationship with Annie, now many years off his horizon.

In my letter, I asked Pope about the risk of relapse on clozapine. After Jeff's thirty or more hospitalizations, this was never far from my mind. No, said Skip in our subsequent phone conversation; once clozapine worked, patients remained improved. But the drug didn't seem to work for Jeff as well as it might, I said. At this point Skip suggested that 800 to 900 milligrams should be tried.

That never happened. As soon as Jeff's dosage was pushed beyond 550 milligrams, he vomited. It was an idiosyncratic phenomenon, unlisted in all compilations of side effects. Understandably, my son then went into his rebellion mode. A drug to deal with the vomiting was administered. It didn't help. The clozapine dosage was lowered to 400. Jeff's circular pacing continued along his hospital's grounds, paved with cigarette butts.

"The first thing was that I stopped pacing," said Kevin Buchberger. "One day I was pacing; the next day I wasn't." To me, this modest recollection was a dazzling vignette. Its protagonist, a grinning, apple-cheeked former mental patient, spiffy in a plaid wool shirt and a new windbreaker, now in a hurry to get back to his job as produce manager in a large Cleveland supermarket, was relating a triumph. It could happen!

I didn't know what to say to Kevin. I had been watching Jeff as he paced in circles year after year, round and round, for half his life—in his hospital, in my motel room, round and round, unable to cease until fatigue flung him onto a bed. Awake, he was too restless even to watch television.

The pacing was a classic symptom of psychosis, one of the least painful for the afflicted, but one of the more disturbing for the observer. The sight of his exercise in agitation always brought home to me the meaninglessness, the futility, of Jeff's existence. If all the energy and mileage he invested in pacing could have been directed, say, to cooking hamburgers instead, there wouldn't have been a hungry soul in town. Kevin offered hope that pacing was not to be Jeff's main activity for the rest of his life.

Kevin, thirty-six, schizophrenic for a decade, was telling me about his savior, clozapine, and other unexpected happenings in his life. We were talking where his rebirth had taken place, beginning in 1987—in the Laboratory of Biological Psychiatry at Case Western Reserve University Hospital in Cleveland.

Pacing had been the least of Kevin's problems. He couldn't sit still. He couldn't stop smoking. His hands shook. He couldn't concentrate enough to read. His vision was blurred from the Stelazine, the Navane, the Prolixin that didn't help. "Demons were following me around, taking my soul," he recalled. A golden beam of light that he believed had haunted an executed murderer would not let him go: "I felt trapped." He barely survived swallowing a vial of pills.

Kevin was sharing a house with friends these days and seeing a girlfriend. He took art courses at Cayuga Community College and played on a volleyball team. He saw his psychiatrist only once every two months, and his clozapine dosage had been reduced at least slightly, from nine hundred to eight hundred milligrams. He had been off cigarettes for ten months.

"I feel so good, I can't believe it," he said, hurrying off, apologizing that his boss needed him.

Brandon Fitch had been waiting to see me, and I shared with him what his friend Kevin had told me about how he stopped pacing. Brandon, twenty-two, immediately grasped my wonder at the turnaround produced by clozapine.

"Each of us has a bit of an epiphany," he reflected, and he proceeded to relate his own to me.

Brandon had been diagnosed schizophrenic at the age of eight, and Cleveland's upmarket Beecher Place Mall with its Saks Fifth Avenue store, where his mother often took him, had been one of the places where he felt most uncomfortable. Six months after starting to take clozapine at the age of eighteen, he was there again and suddenly stopped himself.

"I think something has changed," he remembered telling himself. "I'm enjoying myself! People aren't staring at me and saying, 'He looks like a creep!' "

Brandon had been a severely depressed loner from infancy. He tolerated no playmates and sometimes wept uncontrollably for long periods and without apparent reason. In school, he believed that his classmates could see through his clothes and that famous personalities would glare at him from magazine covers. Music played constantly in his head.

His first child psychiatrist diagnosed school phobia—the same catchall label that was initially pinned upon Jeff. Brandon was a brilliant student, yet his fear of teenagers became so intense that he had to be tutored at home. Beginning at age thirteen, he believed that Czar Nicholas II of Russia lived in his house. Lenin and Trotsky also were in his retinue.

"They would peer at me," Brandon told me. "I felt their presence. They could read my thoughts. I was a bottomless well of anger and at times in absolute agony." Fortunately, his belief in God kept him from committing suicide before and during seven hospitalizations. "I wanted to get into heaven" was how he said he avoided suicide while he was herded in and out of his hospital stays.

Brandon was still experiencing occasional bouts of depression and lived at home, but he felt released from his demons and put in full workweeks as program annotator for the Cleveland Philharmonic Orchestra and lecturer for the United Way Speakers Bureau. As a role model for recovered schizophrenics, he addressed an audience of 2,500 at an annual convention of the National Alliance for the Mentally Ill.

I had first seen Brandon's name in the summer of 1992, when he was chairman of a dinner dance at his hospital. The event was reserved for recovered schizophrenics. It was the crowning scene of a *Time* cover story called

"Awakenings" about the therapeutic triumphs of clozapine. The hospital's psychiatrists and social workers were sponsoring a prom for their patients and graduates, most of them in their thirties. It was to celebrate redemption, and to make up for a graduation they had missed.

The article related the stories of Brandon Fitch, Kevin Buchberger, and numerous others, such as Daphne Moss, who used to be suicidal and was convinced that her parents were witches. She was living in her own place and had become a part-time schoolteacher. The report also told some of the story of clozapine itself: how it worked and which scientists were responsible for it.

The medication was not merely the first major innovation introduced in psychopharmacology in decades; its very mechanism of action—still not fully understood by 1996—was novel. While clozapine is not chemically related to its predecessor, Thorazine (generic name chlorpromazine), all drugs that belong to the family of neuroleptics work by blocking, slowing, or stimulating biochemical messengers in the brain. The organ functions like a complex switchboard. Incoming perceptions are sent along signal paths. Then appropriate feelings, thoughts, and actions are dispatched in response. Schizophrenics, however, are likely to react to messages in dozens of ways, all of them inappropriate.

Thorazine worked principally by blocking dopamine, one of the many messengers darting through the brain. This was the action discovered by the Swedish biochemist Dr. Arvid Carlsson, in 1963. Doctors came to believe that an excess of dopamine was *the* cause of schizophrenia, a belief that turned out to be too simplistic. Clozapine likewise inhibited the transmission of dopamine, at least somewhat; primarily, however, it blocked another neurotransmitter, serotonin.

While perhaps no medical innovation experienced as many frustrating ups and downs as clozapine, one particularly ambitious and impatient American researcher experienced the hurdles as an intriguing scientific challenge: Dr. Herbert Y. Meltzer, a mercurial psychiatrist who headed psychopharmacology at Case Western Reserve University Hospital.* In 1975 the managers of Sandoz's U.S. subsidiary in New Jersey asked him to conduct the first large-scale human trials of the drug. They were eventually postponed, but Meltzer had already been ensnared by the potential of the drug. Here was a compound that helped with the most serious problems of his most desperately ill patients.

Soon, colleagues called him "Dr. Clozapine" and by the 1980s he was the

---

* In 1997 he moved to Vanderbilt University in Nashville, Tennessee.

obvious principal "investigator" to run the clinical trials that I had seen reported by the Associated Press in 1987. Within his sober, scientific account covering parts of the drug's trials, Meltzer permitted himself to stop and marvel: "The story of Clozapine has brought enough twists and turns, despair and hope, tragedy and triumph to Sandoz management, healthcare policymakers, scientists, psychiatrists, as well as patients and their families, that at times it seems more the product of an imaginative screenwriter than reality."

Perhaps only the puzzle of schizophrenia could keep a network of researchers, commercial enterprises, and government regulators so insistently dedicated to one difficult drug's survival.

CHAPTER 16

Clozapine II:
Death and Resurrection

DR. JUHANA IDÄNPÄÄN-HEIKKILA was fond of the formality practiced by the old-time European medical authorities. Belatedly, he had adopted
their ways. His manner and speech were arch. His cuff links glistened. His
hand-knotted bow tie sat straight and immovable. His staff made certain that
his appointments schedule remained inviolate to the minute.

One Friday afternoon in the summer of 1975, the doctor's world of perfection was derailed. He had been serving as a host to colleagues at an international medical convention in Helsinki, and this had kept him away from his
office at the National Board of Health across town. Returning on that Friday,
July 25—he never forgot the date—he found on his desk news of mortal
peril. Six Finnish hospitals were reporting a total of seven deaths from agranulocytosis in schizophrenic patients. The victims were among sixteen who
contracted the disease while taking clozapine, sold in Europe as Leponex.
The following Monday, two more patients died. Since only 2,800 Finns were
taking the medication, this sudden, clustered, and unprecedented outbreak
was considered an epidemic, one that could spread rapidly throughout the
world.

Fortuitously, Sandoz representatives from Basel were still in Helsinki for the pharmacology meeting. Idänpään-Heikkila summoned them to his office for an emergency conference where he said, "Let's stop it immediately."

The Sandoz reps agreed but were privately disturbed on several counts. The worldwide publicity damage and legal culpability resulting from fatalities were obvious. Once banned in Finland, clozapine would survive nowhere, and the probable demise of the medication represented a significant financial loss to Sandoz. Moreover, that this eruption was the only one in the world seemed to them bizarre; they didn't care for the Finnish doctor's haughty manner, nor did they trust his reporting system. All sorts of errors or exculpatory factors might still emerge.

More than 450 pharmacies and hospitals in Finland had long been linked in a national telephone notification system, and all were called by the National Board of Health before nightfall that same evening. Inevitably, the "confidential" news leaked to the press and television.

The Finnish authorities launched an immediate investigation and reported results in the British journal *Lancet* in the autumn of the same year, 1975. A more sweeping study by two Swiss and two Finnish researchers, assisted by investigators representing five medical specialties, was published in 1977 in *Acta Psychiatrica Scandinavia*. The findings of both teams were exhaustive and inconclusive.

The suddenness and simultaneity of the onset were never explained. Neither was the geographic concentration of the outbreak: all the involved hospitals were clustered within a relatively small area in the southwestern part of the country. All the deceased patients had been taking the drug for no more than three months. All died of secondary infections, usually developing fever, tonsillitis, and finally pneumonia.

A study covering fifteen of the sixteen affected families dug through six generations for possible genealogical factors and found no answers. The 1977 investigation concluded: "It must be assumed that this side-effect occurs only in individuals with a particular predisposition, but the absence of characteristic signs makes prior recognition of such persons impossible." The "side-effect" was death.

Idänpään-Heikkila became director of drug management and policies for the World Health Organization (WHO) in Geneva and stood above the lingering controversy. Mysteries were offensive to him. "There is no mystery," he told me, bristling. "We just don't know enough."

In any event, the nine deaths in rural Finland would keep clozapine from Jeff for fifteen years.

Sandoz was not unaccustomed to controversy surrounding mind-altering medications. The company's official histories don't mention it, but Sandoz introduced the world to what a historian called "the chemistry of madness."

The era began quietly in midafternoon, on Friday, April 16, 1943. Uncharacteristically, Dr. Albert Hofmann, a senior research chemist at Sandoz headquarters, decided to go home early. He was feeling dizzy and was "seized by a peculiar restlessness." Barely balancing his bicycle, he reached safety but was dazed.

"I lay down and sank into a kind of drunkenness which was not unpleasant," he reported later. "There surged upon me an uninterrupted stream of fantastic images of extraordinary plasticity and vividness and accompanied by an intense kaleidoscope-like play of colors."

Hofmann had, in effect, invented the century's most controversial mind drug, LSD, the psychedelic that turned on (and endangered the sanity of) a generation. Actually, Hofmann had first synthesized lysergic acid diethylamide in 1938 while investigating ergot, a ryegrass fungus. That work resulted in the development of Sandoz medications that greatly reduced the pain and blood loss in childbirth.

The mind-exploding properties of LSD lay undiscovered until that fateful Friday afternoon when Hofmann was again working with the substance and evidently absorbed an amount through his skin that was minute but sufficed to induce the effects he reported. Sandoz, in business since 1886, was prepared. The company had learned to manage promising properties conservatively but with an eye toward potential profits. LSD's "profound psychoactive effect" showed such potential.

Its possible benefit for psychiatry was that it could induce "model psychoses" for the close study and, it was hoped, eventual treatment of schizophrenia. By 1947 Sandoz was marketing twenty-five-microgram tablets of LSD to European research institutions. By 1960 more than five hundred scientific papers about the drug were in print.

For a time, it was an exciting subspecialty. Some of the most distinguished researchers of schizophrenia hypothesized that its hallucinations might be triggered in the body by an LSD-like substance, so that the drug might lead them to the cause or causes of the disease. At Johns Hopkins University, Dr. Solomon Snyder, chairman of neurosciences, tried LSD just once and was intrigued. He constructed a rating scale to analyze the thought content of psychiatric patients in his hospital who had ingested psychedelic drugs. LSD-induced visions were found to be remarkably similar to the specters produced by schizophrenia, but Snyder discovered little else.

In Britain, Dr. R. D. Laing, psychoanalyst, guru, and best-selling author (*Knots, The Divided Self*), organized a commune, mostly of psychotics, and shared therapeutic six-hour acid-dropping sessions with his patients. He called himself an "LSD therapist" and achieved "varying degrees of success," according to his son and biographer Adrian Charles Laing. The elder Laing also liked cocaine, and used alcohol in great excess. He grew increasingly disorganized, sometimes dysfunctional, and eventually his medical license was revoked.

By 1966 Sandoz had abandoned the LSD business even for research purposes. The former Harvard professor Timothy Leary, LSD disciples in the Haight-Ashbury communes, and countless other hippies all over the world eventually demonstrated that Hofmann's invention was an acid that induced schizophrenic symptoms, and, for that reason alone, socially undesirable and unsafe. It had nevertheless made its inventor a star. He was appointed head of all Sandoz pharmaceutical and chemical laboratories.

LSD was the company's untypical wild side. The original prosperity of its founders, Edouard Sandoz, a manager in a dye manufacturing works, and Alfred Kern, a chemist specializing in colors, came from an unpleasant, black, odorous mass called coal tar, once regarded as a useless residue. By the late nineteenth century, chemists had found ways to transform this tar into synthetic dyes of brilliant hues, thus contributing to the birth of the modern fashion industry.

By 1917 Sandoz had established its first British and American manufacturing subsidiaries. Its pharmaceutical division had already begun researching ergot. The chemicals division was making artificial fibers. A factory went up in Brazil. Antibiotics were produced by a newly acquired Austrian company. Purchase of an American seed firm brought entry into that profitable industry. Alkaloids, artificial sweeteners, and hospital supplies were added. The 1967 acquisition of the barely profitable Dr. A. Wander Ltd. of Bern presented Sandoz with a leading position in nutrition products.

Tucked away in the amalgamation process with the Wander firm, fortuitously, was clozapine. The negotiators in the merger talks probably never heard of it. Expansion-minded Sandoz managers had their eye unfalteringly on an auspicious Wander monopoly: Ovomaltine (sold in the United States as Ovaltine), a malt nutrition supplement, a favorite staple for a generation of children and parents. The merger protocol showed that officials talked about this product "almost as in a church service."

The division prospered. In the 1990s, Sandoz added to it the American Gerber baby foods enterprise, among other companies, so that its total sales multiplied, exceeding fourteen billion dollars by 1994, about one-half from drugs. At that, Sandoz was the smallest of the three firms that made Basel the European capital of the pharmaceutical industry. The competitors were Ciba-Geigy and Hoffman-LaRoche, all having branched out from the dyes industry and all having been attracted by the unique chemistry of Basel itself. It was a patrician and cosmopolitan center, half the size of nearby Zurich but even wealthier. Settled in Roman times in the northwestern corner of Switzerland, at both the German and French borders, it was a magnet to chemists, engineers, and financiers from both these neighboring countries.

Medications for schizophrenia were a sideshow for the pharmaceutical divisions of these giants, albeit very profitable and prestigious. So, following the adventures of Hofmann and, more particularly, the discovery of chlorpromazine (Thorazine) in France during the early 1950s, the sizable Swiss talent pool of biochemists and research psychiatrists was strongly motivated to advance further into neuroleptics.

According to conventional wisdom, chlorpromazine and its chemical family were supposed to work only as antihistamine and antiparkinsonian agents. The serendipitous discovery of their antipsychotic properties by the French surgeon Henri Laborit triggered a massive hunt into the thousands of vaguely related tricyclic compounds.

Clozapine, first identified as HF 1854, surfaced in 1958, not at Sandoz but at the Wander firm in Bern, the Ovaltine makers. It was one of several experimental substances that seemed to display antipsychotic characteristics. It was spotted among 1,900 compounds laboriously synthesized by a research chemist bearing an unfortunate name: Dr. Jean Schmutz. Animal trials proved productive, but mostly for alleviating pain. Early tests on twelve human schizophrenics were inconclusive: about one-third improved, but one-half worsened.

Prominent among the researchers who closely tracked these and other experiments at centers throughout central Europe, on the lookout for new antipsychotics without disabling side effects, such as the Thorazine shuffle, was Professor Hanns Hippius at the Free University in Berlin, later director of the psychiatry clinic at the University Hospital in Munich.

Without Hippius, clozapine probably would never have come to market. He was an effervescent research psychiatrist and administrator, multilingual, full of curiosity, popular with colleagues in several countries, a star who also managed to work well as a team man. After World War II he was among the first of the non-Nazi German doctors to develop contacts abroad, and thus he became a cofounder of the International College of Neuropsychopharmacology. In Munich, he occupied the same big corner office that once was the domain of Emil Kraepelin, where Hippius discovered the lost manuscript of the old master's autobiography in a desk drawer. He and his associates edited and published it. By then Hippius had been head of the German Society of Psychiatry and Neurology.

His ebullient ways and distinguished biography were critical elements when he made himself, along with Herbert Meltzer in Cleveland and a few others, a charter member in a band of clozapine loyalists who believed in the drug's value and refused to waver for a quarter of a century. It was a question of science, primarily, but also of a contributing factor not often found—but useful—in science: plain faith. The roadblocks would have disillusioned a less ardent group.

According to Hippius's theory, the compound produced by Schmutz should have worked merely as an antidepressant. But new trials in the 1960s disclosed, to Hippius's embarrassment, that it acted as a neuroleptic. Moreover, it seemed that clozapine, though fully effective as an antischizophrenic medication, had no extrapyramidal (parkinsonian) side effects whatever. Hippius was stumped.

"This finding was almost unbelievable," he wrote later, "because at that time it was part of psychopharmacological dogma that extrapyramidal effects went in tandem with anti-psychotic efficacy." More than a paper correction was required. "The Wander company, the manufacturers, found themselves in a bizarre situation," Hippius reported. "They were hesitant to introduce the drug, not because of its effectiveness, but because it lacked an adverse side-effect!"

Agranulocytosis did not stand in the way then. It was not considered an excessive risk because Hippius had discovered in 1958 that the disease was detectable early and reversible. Weekly blood examinations could do the job and could even be suspended after sixteen weeks, so Hippius judged, because any danger beyond that point was deemed negligible.

By 1966 clozapine was available from Wander, but nobody wanted it. As Hippius reported: "The final judgment, especially amongst pharmacologists, was that a drug without extrapyramidal side-effects cannot be a real neuroleptic!" Based on favorable new clinical trials in Austria and Germany, however,

Hippius kept up his lobbying for the drug in German, Dutch, and even Mexican medical publications—to no avail.

"The response to our efforts was weak," he wrote. "Pharmacologists and clinicians were too wedded to the notion of an inseparable connection between anti-psychotic efficacy and extrapyramidal effect." The drug was stuck in its pipeline.

Enter, in a whirlwind, Dr. Nathan S. Kline of New York, research psychiatrist and force of nature. Here was a rambunctious, charismatic charger who relished his self-selected role as his profession's most unrestrained disturber of the peace. "I have a kind of obsessive curiosity about everything," he told a historian in the 1970s. "Whatever goes on, I like to stick my rather long nose into it."

The doctor also had an appealing way with words that enabled him to evoke the ecstasy of "Eureka!" moments in science.

"You have forged a passkey which might open innumerable closed doors!" he said in a lecture. "I will never forget Linus Pauling in a meeting at McGill [University] describing the creative process. He rubbed his hands in pure sensual satisfaction and his baby-blue eyes positively glittered. 'Just think,' he said, 'I know something that no one else in the whole wide world knows—and they won't know until I tell them.' "

In 1952 Kline became director of the 8,500-patient Rockland Research Institute at Rockland State Hospital, about an hour north of New York City. There he introduced tranquilizers into the United States. Next, Kline delved into antidepressants, becoming the key researcher for the development of Iproniazid. In the first year following its introduction, a record-breaking 400,000 patients were treated with the drug, according to the FDA. Unfortunately, too many of them developed femur fractures, jaundice, and male baldness. Henceforth, for the rest of his life (the doctor died in 1983), Kline was the enfant terrible of his government overseers.

His competence as a healer, his maniacal appetite for work, and his devotion to his patients were not questioned. In his private practice on the Upper East Side of Manhattan, the doctor and his assistants sluiced an average of seventy-five patients through the office every day. Yet Kline insisted that each case be properly written up and cataloged before the lights went out at night.

This doctor had faith, too, and it was transferrable. He was convinced that the medications he dispensed in such large quantities did more than appease his grandiosity and relieve his patients. He believed that the pills also reduced some of the public's disdain for the mentally ill, a prejudice he resented.

All told, he did much to encourage the new biological way of thinking in psychiatry.

"The fact that a condition is treated with medication," he liked to say, "somehow guarantees in the public mind that it is a genuine illness."

Beginning in the early seventies, Kline purchased clozapine in quantity directly from Sandoz in Switzerland. He found the drug so useful for his schizophrenic patients that it quickly became his treatment of choice. In the United States, such imports were subject to detailed outcome reports by FDA protocols on medications known as INDs (investigational new drugs). Kline, the ultimate free spirit and antibureaucrat, thought this paperwork unnecessary. He helped little in the government's attempts to keep track of every one of his pills.

At least one psychiatrist called at his stylish Manhattan office in the hope of cadging a few samples of the new wonder drug clozapine, whereupon Kline gaily tossed an envelope full of the pills across his desk. On the other hand, a 1974 request for a progress report from the FDA yielded a two-line letter from Kline and a journal reprint discussing three hundred patients, but not the mandatory FDA forms. The Washington authorities became annoyed. Kline promised to make amends but never did, which caused the FDA to request that Sandoz not send Kline any more clozapine.

"This precipitated the great luncheon meeting that is legend at FDA," according to an agency executive's testimony before a congressional investigative committee chaired by Senator Edward M. Kennedy. "The doctor came in on a chartered plane and brought a catered lunch for officials of the Bureau of Drugs and Neuropsychopharmacology, with his attorney . . . and made numerous assurances which again, of course, were not complied with."

Kline had become an immovable object confronting the irresistible force of the United States government. The feud lasted for several years. Once, Kline called the commissioner of the FDA and demanded: "Commissioner, could you tell me why I should not go on television in five minutes and tell the country what an awful job the FDA is doing and why they are not letting me treat my patients?" Another time, according to congressional testimony, the doctor "threatened to land a helicopter on top of the Parklawn [FDA headquarters] building . . . with most of the prominent people in his practice, and let them tell the Commissioner . . . what they thought of the idea of terminating the IND."

Fortunately, by the time Kline was compelled to sign a consent decree terminating his authority to administer investigational drugs, clozapine had become firmly entrenched as an international therapeutic property. That had happened in 1973, when Sandoz, seeking to maximize its asset, hired a New Jersey clinical psychologist, Dr. Gilbert Honigfeld, to bring it to the American market.

Honigfeld, a precision-tool, time-conscious organizer, had become a great supporter of clozapine, along with Meltzer and Hippius. He had worked with psychiatric drugs at leading New York university hospitals and had just published an encyclopedic desk-reference volume surveying these medications. Along the way, his mentors had exposed him to clozapine. The drug's lack of parkinsonian side effects impressed him greatly. When Sandoz interviewed him for the development job at its American plant in East Hanover, New Jersey, he accepted at once, even though he was offered more money elsewhere.

Honigfeld was a conservative realist and never lost sight of the one pitfall of his chosen specialty. Throughout his years working with clozapine, his enthusiasm was tempered by his knowledge that *most drugs fail* at some unpredictable stage before reaching the market, and sometimes afterward.

He had just commissioned the first large-scale U.S. clinical trials—only two hundred Americans at this point were using clozapine regularly—when the tragedy struck in the countryside of Finland. Honigfeld was hardly consoled by the small number of fatalities: he immediately understood the stark statistical extrapolations if the drug were to be used worldwide.

"I thought the drug was dead," Honigfeld said. "It was just too toxic. I thought it was history." And so, at first, did Sandoz management. But nobody had taken the patients sufficiently into account. Clozapine was withdrawn from the many schizophrenics who were already taking it in Europe, and there were numerous relapses with serious consequences. Doctors and hospitals were much disturbed. Pressure was intense on Sandoz, especially from the large German market, to keep the medication available. Its future might yet become viable because the precautionary blood tests, not heretofore in use, could presumably head off the agranulocytosis.

To deal with the crisis in Germany, Dr. Botond Berde, the Hungarian-born scientific director of Sandoz, met in Berlin with Hippius, who was greatly agitated because he believed passionately in clozapine. "I think he would have gone to the barricades for it," Berde remembered twenty years later. When Berde returned to Basel, he persuaded his management to make clozapine available on a carefully restricted, "compassionate need" basis, case by case, to the most severely ill patients in Switzerland, Germany, Sweden, and Denmark.

In the United States, Honigfeld began using clozapine again but very sparingly, monitoring fifteen severely ill patients who had never been taken off the drug. Quickly, pressure for "compassionate" use mounted. As he remembered: "Doctors were calling and saying 'This stuff is dynamite! We'll do anything! We'll do blood tests every day!' "

Actually, the reliability of the blood tests in routine clinical use was still an open question in Honigfeld's mind. As far as he could tell, they worked neatly only on paper. "We wanted to predict vulnerability," he said. "Who's going to live? Who's going to die? We started tearing our hair out."

Bellevue Hospital in Manhattan was one of some twenty experimental centers throughout the country designated by Sandoz where Honigfeld was permitted, case by case, to make clozapine available to doctors whom he knew and who could document that a particular patient was not being helped by any other medication. When a research psychiatrist named Lou Gerbino returned to Bellevue late one morning in 1978 with a weekly blood sample, it showed a frighteningly low blood-cell count. The doctor left his office on the run. The blood came from a woman over sixty, of Eastern European Jewish extraction—warning signs of particular vulnerability. She lived on lower Third Avenue, not far from the hospital.

Startled at seeing her doctor at her door, she submitted to having her temperature taken. It registered a suspicious one hundred degrees. Gerbino asked her to come with him to the hospital.

"Why?" asked the patient. "I'm not sick."

Feeling hard-pressed for time, Gerbino forgot his bedside manner.

"You will be," he snapped.

Bundled off to Bellevue, the patient was isolated and given a triple antibiotic. Her blood count bounced back within eight days, and Honigfeld took Gerbino into his heart forever. "He told us that the disease is really reversible," Honigfeld said. "We had an early warning radar."

By 1981 Honigfeld was controlling treatment for more than one hundred successful cases from his New Jersey base. In Cleveland, Meltzer had been pleasantly astounded when he used clozapine to treat tardive dyskinesia, the most devastating of the common neuroleptic side effects. In Basel, the Sandoz marketers were beginning to wonder whether clozapine's demise had been prematurely assumed. A revival seemed doubtful, however; all concerned parties agreed that the drug could only be reborn if the Food and Drug Administration could be convinced that it was reasonably safe for wide use.

Customarily, the FDA makes final decisions on controversial new drugs based on the recommendation of an advisory committee consisting of some dozen top-rated outside specialists in the field, and in 1982, upon inquiry from Sandoz, the neuroleptic drugs advisory committee indicated that possibly clozapine was not beyond retrieval.

Major new studies would be needed, and Honigfeld went to work with Meltzer and other clozapine aficionados. Sandoz was given further encouragement by a 1985 publicity bonanza. Dan Rather did a program on the *CBS Evening News* introducing clozapine as helpful for tardive dyskinesia. It was the sort of attention manufacturers bask in.

Additional consultations with the FDA finally led, in midwinter of 1986, to a conference at which Honigfeld, Meltzer, and two other investigators previewed initial results of "Study No. 30." It showed clozapine's value with 150 patients, half of whom had been given chlorpromazine for comparison purposes. Next came the go-ahead for a full-throttle investigation: a total of three hundred patients, some of whom would be treated with haloperidol (Haldol) for contrast.

There was a joker in this deck. The FDA wanted to approve clozapine, if at all, only for patients "with an unsatisfactory response to neuroleptic drugs." The medication absolutely had to prove itself as something altogether unprecedented. "The patients for trial Number 30 had to be the least likely to respond," Honigfeld said. "My heart sank."

He still had not cheered up by late 1987, when Sandoz sent the FDA one fat folder for each of the trial participants: 322 volumes. At last, promptly at 9 a.m. on April 26, 1989, the thirtieth meeting of the Psychopharmacologic Drugs Advisory Committee assembled to render a "go" or "no go" verdict for clozapine. Grouped around the horseshoe-shaped table at the foot of the combined conference rooms G and H in the high-rise FDA Parklawn Building in suburban Rockville, Maryland, the panel was called to order by the key figure of the all-day public proceeding: Dr. Paul Leber.

Leber was a former professor of psychiatry from New York who had converted to the much-maligned guild of Washington bureaucrats, though he could hardly have turned out less typical. Tall, erect, heavyset, he held his mobile face high, suggesting the loftiness of the British character-actor Robert Morley. Leber could flaunt his intellect, easily dropping quotes from Aristotle and John Stuart Mill at advisory committee sessions. Inquiries that he put to witnesses cut like knives. Powerhouse leaders of the pharmaceutical industry were awed by him as if he were a Supreme Court justice, for Leber's judgments could prove just as permanent and expensive.

"He's the smartest man in the government," I was advised by Skip Pope.

"The level of preparation was intense," Honigfeld remembered. Each committee witness who would be part of the eight-member Sandoz delegation rehearsed his testimony repeatedly and participated in a mock session, a full rehearsal of the committee meeting. In order to be ready to document replies to any safety question that might arise, Honigfeld prepared four trays filled with thirty-five-millimeter slides.

Internally, advance arguments were especially heated about the wording and layout of the proposed package insert, the user instruction sheet that would accompany all distributed pills. The insert had to reflect every kind of warning for adverse reactions. The most urgent alerts would be printed in heavy boxed type. The number of such heavyweight "black boxes" was invariably subject to debate. In the case of clozapine, the boxes were especially plentiful.

"What the committee was thinking was entirely unpredictable," Honigfeld recalled. He had been talking to Leber informally about clozapine for about five years. The FDA psychopharmacology chief had been friendly, even welcoming. He had made clear that the agency was not in principle wedded to continuing the ban on the drug. But he had never been specific.

The hearing started badly for Honigfeld. The FDA's safety review had been assigned to the agency's Dr. Richard E. Kapit and ran twenty-two pages in the 261-page transcript, longer than any other testimony. "The hazard of Clozaril outweighs the benefits," the doctor warned flatly. If 100,000 patients were treated for a year, "perhaps 900 would die from this iatrogenic disease [agranulocytosis]," he hypothesized. But then he made a mistake.

"He talked on and on," said Honigfeld, "blasting and blasting and blasting. After the first fifteen minutes I became very worried." But then it became a case of overkill. After piling one remote contingency on top of another, Kapit proposed that clozapine could not only set off the heat reaction known as hyperthermia but might encourage total global warming.

With that, his presentation was, in effect, over. The committee members knew that hyperthermia was indeed a rare aftereffect of clozapine, but the resulting fever was transitory, usually gone in seven to twenty-one days, and the idea of connecting it to global warming was absurd. So the committeemen laughed. So did the audience, mostly representatives of competing pharmaceutical companies with no interest in promoting clozapine. That put an end to Kapit's case and Honigfeld's worst worries.

Then Kapit's immediate superior spoke up with an upbeat view of the drug's safety problems and praised the drug's benefits. Whereupon the mighty Leber weighed in. He took note of the agranulocytosis crisis of 1975 as "very terrifying," but posed none of his customarily devastating questions. He seemed to hold a friendly view of the Sandoz application.

Kapit was not the only doctor holding strong reservations, but, one by one, the Sandoz witnesses dealt with them reasonably, and shortly before 4:45 p.m. the committee's genial chairman, Dr. Daniel E. Casey, said, "Call the question. In favor?"

There was a show of all hands.

"It is unanimous," said Leber, smiling.

Clozapine had become respectable. Meanwhile, less respectable acts of perilous experimentation were being revealed.

CHAPTER 17

The Symptoms Were
"Not Severe Enough"

AT 10:10 A.M., on May 23, 1994, in hearing room 2359-A of the Rayburn House Office Building in Washington, D.C., Gregory Aller Jr., twenty-nine and schizophrenic, took the witness stand before a congressional investigating subcommittee. Presiding as chairman was my older son, Representative Ron Wyden (Democrat, Oregon), a congressman for fifteen years before he was elected to the U.S. Senate in 1996. The purpose of the hearing, Ron announced, was to improve the protection of the mentally ill when they became test subjects in experiments with potentially dangerous medications.

"This issue is terribly complex," he continued, and the quiet, broad-faced Greg Aller quickly proved the point that, Ron told me later with considerable feeling, "we sure know about from our own family."

Greg began by telling the committee that he was felled by schizophrenia in April 1987, while studying for his college entrance exams. He saw a brilliant white light appearing above him: "Space aliens were directing this. They told me I was going to become Speaker of the House. Then President Bush and Vice President Quayle would die. I would unite our world with a dying alien planet."

A real and more frightening sequence of events ensued after he was referred to the clinic of UCLA's prestigious neuropsychiatric hospital. Greg testified: "I had the experience of becoming not a patient but a subject in high risk research. Though I signed a consent form, it turned out to be deceptive because it omitted what the research was really all about. . . . The consent forms were not legally valid under federal regulations because UCLA omitted foreseeable risks and alternative treatments. Over 100 persons participated in this research . . . that insured patients had severe or extremely severe relapses."

In graphic detail, Greg testified about his life during a deliberate long-term withdrawal of his treatment. His doctors were experimenting with an exploratory shot in the dark far riskier than the brief "washout" drug withdrawals experienced by Jeff during the same year.

The experiment on Greg began on a note of elation. He was given Prolixin, which almost magically banished his symptoms. He enrolled in Santa Monica College, made the dean's list, and worked fifteen hours a week. In 1989 his UCLA doctors asked him to go off the medication, ostensibly to prevent onset of tardive dyskinesia, but actually inviting relapse in order to investigate how well and how long patients could manage without medications.

Prompted by Greg's mother's concern about a potential relapse, the family and Greg met with the experiment's chief doctor. "He promised my parents that if I had a return of symptoms, the medication would be reinstated," Greg testified. "We trusted the doctors."

The consequences were disastrous. "This time my symptoms were much more severe than the symptoms of the onset of my schizophrenia," Greg told the subcommittee. "I was unable to do school work. I became manic and hyperactive. Some days I would hardly sleep at all. One night I woke up screaming, actually believing that I was sprouting another leg. I started to have paranoid delusions about government agents chasing me. I became violent with my father and threatened to kill him. . . . Later, I started hitchhiking to Washington to assassinate President Bush. . . .

"My doctor asked me if I felt I needed medication. Since I was paranoid at that time, I said I was fine, I didn't need medication."

Greg's doctors would not intervene, but his parents did. "From late 1989 to May 1990 my father called the project's staff, telling them that he thought I needed medication," Greg testified. Once the chief doctor said the symptoms might be "fluctuating and temporary," and they should wait. A case worker told Bob Aller that Greg's symptoms were "not severe enough." When the Allers met with two of the doctors, they were told that Greg's symptoms were mere "mood fluctuations."

On May 15, 1990, at his parents' very firm insistence, Greg received Prolixin again, and by the time of his congressional testimony he was studying
political science at UCLA. He had been lucky. Believing that the problems
with the university's psychiatric experiments were systemic, Greg's parents
had met with the vice chancellor of UCLA research and warned that murder
or suicide was likely. Five days later, Tony Lamadrid, a former UCLA student
and friend of Greg's from whom antipsychotic medication was withdrawn,
went to the roof of the nine-story Boelter Hall and jumped to his death.

Greg testified about this incident in Washington and described other
calamities. A woman patient released from UCLA and off medication was
raped by two men. A scientist's daughter, Elizabeth Balogh, suffered extremely
severe symptoms when her medication was withdrawn. Her parents called the
number they had been given for UCLA during the weekend and were told by a
recording that staff was available only from Monday to Friday.

The director of UCLA's neuropsychiatric hospital testified before the
committee that the university was "making several changes" but conceded no
neglect. "It is in the nature of the disease itself that there is a relapse," he said.
In the end, he held the afflicted responsible: "Some patients in the UCLA
study refused to go back on medication on recommendation."

The hospital lost its accreditation temporarily until the process of obtaining
informed consent from the mentally ill to join research projects was tightened.
Four top medical administrators resigned. The Allers sued. In the summer of
1997, the action was still pending. The complex ethical problem of how to
expose a few patients to risky experiments that might benefit others had become
the subject of new debate among researchers, bioethicists, and government
monitors.

"She and I are like guerrillas," Bob Aller had said grimly when he recommended that I contact Vera Hassner Sharav, the New York librarian–turned–
consumer activist who in 1990 had taken on the manufacturers of clozapine;
almost single-handedly, she had forced them to make the drug available at
somewhat less than exorbitant cost in the United States.

Guerrilla warfare against the establishment—the pharmaceutical houses,
the psychiatrists, and the public authorities supervising care for psychotic
patients—was a reasonable description of the campaigns launched by Sharav,
Aller, and a handful of other soulmates. They traded action tips and strategic
intelligence information; wrote investigative articles; formed alliances with
friendly reporters and lawyers; pressured researchers to raise ethical standards;

and, as self-appointed ombudsmen, watched over a large patient population that was constantly subject to exploitation by experimenters who at times risked patients' lives for the sake of publishing an intriguing paper.

Sharav, mindful of her schizophrenic son, also campaigned against the disorganized methods of the New York State mental health authorities in ministering to his needs and those of his fellow patients. "They're the fraternity of silence," she told me. "They're condemned and convicted."

While she and her fellow volunteers abhorred silence, they knew that research was essential to progress. They sided with ethical administrators like Dr. Herbert Pardes, now dean of Columbia University Medical School, who had declared, "We want research to advance, but we want it done right."

In Sharav's increasingly angry view, quite a few "protocols" were wrong, and some of the press were beginning to agree with her. When the headline "State Mental Patients Human Guinea Pigs" ran as the front-page banner in the February 3, 1993, *New York Newsday,* she was appalled but also delighted. Attention was being paid. By November 1, 1994, she had become the "quality of treatment chair" for the New York State Chapter of NAMI and was running a workshop that laid out numerous consumer complaints for the first time before a broad public. Among the charges:

- More than forty studies of systematic relapses, involving more than 2,481 patients, had passed muster by the erratically functioning Institutional Review Boards (IRBs) and were routinely published in medical journals. Several "especially egregious experiments" had been reviewed and given grants by the NIMH.

- Nontherapeutic studies with Haldol, not federally funded and therefore not subject to review by the government's Office for Protection from Research Risk (OPRR), were performed at New York State institutions without any outside knowledge and resulted in thirty-two suicides.

- Informed consent from patients, a legal requirement before research experiments may commence, sometimes was simply not obtained or was "waived."

As a case in point, Sharav cited a study of induced relapse entitled "L-Dopa Challenge and Relapse in Schizophrenia," conducted at the Bronx Veterans Administration Medical Center by a team from the Mount Sinai

Medical Center and published in the *American Journal of Psychiatry.* Its stated aim: "This study attempted to predict time to relapse in twenty-eight schizophrenic patients withdrawn from neuroleptics and challenged with L-Dopa for seven days, then followed until relapse." In plain English, helpless patients had their medications withdrawn to determine how long it would take for them to become seriously ill again. To ensure that they fell sick, they were given L-dopa, in the form of the medication Sinemet, which, according to standard literature, was like feeding sugar to diabetics.

Seven of the research subjects were not currently psychotic. Seven more were judged to be in remission. All twenty-eight relapsed into schizophrenia. All had signed consent forms that failed to disclose that relapse was likely and that the known side effects of Sinemet were severe.

Much later, Sharav complained to the director of the project. He defended it and wrote: "Talking to patients about psychosis or schizophrenia might cause unnecessary anxiety."

Five months before Sharav's seminar on case management, her son Ami, thirty-five, known as Jay, had died. Schizophrenic for seventeen years, he had nevertheless just received his B.A. in English literature from Fordham University. He collapsed in the hallway of Access House, a twenty-four-hour "intensive supportive" residence in lower Manhattan, and was left lying there for several crucial hours. Scattered in his pockets were some seventy clozapine tablets that he had deliberately failed to use. He had been taking clozapine sporadically, enough for death to have been caused by MNS—malignant neuroleptic syndrome. The prevalence of MNS was less than one in five hundred. Its "mechanism" isn't known, but in the end Jay's temperature shot up to 107 degrees.

His private psychiatrist, whom he had seen on Thursday, May 26, had found him well enough to go to his parents' home. On Friday, Vera and her husband, a college instructor in accountancy, reluctantly agreed to let him return to Access House after extracting repeated assurances from its managers that he would be monitored "extra closely" over the weekend. On Saturday morning, no case worker answered the phone. Agency supervisors assured the frantic parents: "If no one is answering the phone, it's because they are out making rounds." In fact, nobody had reported for work.

The ensuing official report by the New York State Commission on Quality Care for the Mentally Disabled and the Mental Hygiene Medical Review Board ran twenty-three pages, single spaced, plus an eighteen-page appendix of accounts from additional agencies. The very array of the ten "service entities" actually caused many of the problems resulting in the death of "Jacob Gordon," as the reports called Jay pseudonymously. They "failed to effectively communicate with each other," the main report conceded. And "while each saw a dimension of Mr. Gordon's life, no one knew the totality of his needs and assumed responsibility for addressing them."

Much space was devoted to blaming Jay and his mother, instead of the patient's disease. The young man didn't keep his room clean. He resisted his medications. And the "intensity of the ongoing interventions that Mrs. Gordon made on behalf of her son" exceeded all reason, according to Community Access, the agency that operated Access House. "Mrs. Gordon wasn't simply Jacob's mother; she was (and remains) a powerful and influential political force. . . . This influence becomes pervasive and counter-productive."

Sharav laughed bitterly. "The overinvolved mother?" she asked rhetorically when we talked. "I wasn't involved enough!"

"Don't give up!" Dr. Shamoo was shouting into the phone with a slight foreign accent as I entered his office at the University of Maryland School of Medicine in Baltimore. "Never give up! You've got to be their advocate!"

On the other end of the line, someone was evidently saying something about insurance coverage for the mentally ill.

"It's the law! I wrote it! They're violating it! They're lying! Do not take their word!"

Shamoo, fifty-three, an adviser to Vera Sharav on ethics, is a professor of biological chemistry who emigrated from Iraq as a political refugee twenty years ago. Shamoo's son, Abe, had been diagnosed schizoaffective at twenty-four in 1986. The family had spent nearly all its money, $300,000, on his care after the insurance coverage ran out, which showed Shamoo a wrong that needed to be set right.

"I said no one should go through this kind of hell," he told me, and in Maryland, according to a new law, no one suffers insurance discrimination any longer. After four years of Shamoo's wrestling in partnership with the Maryland branch of NAMI, the state became the first to mandate parity for all mentally ill.

Abe's years of hospitalizations, and swallowing "everything" that existed by way of treatments, paid off. The son was living independently and doing well back in college, thanks to clozapine. Meanwhile, Shamoo's role as advocate was expanding. As founder and editor in chief of the journal *Accountabil-*

ity in Research, he had been asked by NAMI officials to counsel Bob and Greg Aller in their campaign against UCLA. Ever since, Shamoo's writings and public appearances exposing washouts and induced relapses have proliferated. He was becoming feared.

Sometimes he was too controversial to serve his cause. At one of the annual meetings of the College of Neuropsychopharmacology in Puerto Rico ("the lion's den," Shamoo called it), he rose to compare the drug experimenters to the practitioners of the extermination policies of the Nazis, causing an understandable uproar of outrage.

I suspect it was the Aller case that prompted a representative sample of research doctors and government regulators to follow the call of Shamoo, as head of the University of Maryland's Center for Biological Ethics, to gather in January 1995 for a national conference in Baltimore on ethics in psychiatric research.

"Consensus on Ethics in Research Is Elusive," said the *New York Times* headline. The meetings agreed on little, except to offer seats on supervisory bodies to patient and consumer advocates. The opposing sides needed each other too much to resume ignoring each other, as they had done before the Aller case became public through my son Ron's congressional hearing and two investigative articles in *Time* magazine.*

Recently, Shamoo wrote about new medical evidence that sudden withdrawal of neuroleptic medications causes brain damage. His work became a chapter, written with Dr. Dianne N. Irving, in a book called *Health Care Ethics: Critical Issues for the 21st Century*. The battle could hardly be considered finished while patients like my Jeff floated through life without a toehold.

---

* The best continuing, no-nonsense coverage I found for these and other sensitive issues regarding the mentally ill is in *The Journal*, a nontechnical quarterly of CAMI, the California Alliance for the Mentally Ill, published at 1111 Howe Avenue, Sacramento, California, 95825. Its publisher and editor, the exceptionally able and compassionate Dan E. Weisburd, also cares for a longtime-schizophrenic son.

CHAPTER 18

Is There No Home for Jeff?

WHERE WAS Jeff to find a home during the interludes when he was out of the hospital? Where might he belong? How could he acquire a lifestyle that would let him exist more like an autonomous person, not a floater, a vagabond?

These had become pressing questions in the late 1970s when he was nearing the age of thirty. He was shunted back and forth between halfway houses, hospitals, and his mother's home, but increasingly, his professional caretakers found his behavior too disruptive and refused to keep him, and his mother could no longer cope with him. Eager to assert his self-reliance, he rented himself a room at the St. Clair Hotel in downtown San Jose, only to realize soon that this solution was grandiose, too expensive even before the sad old place was remodeled.

I had failed to manage my son in my New York apartment. When he lived with his more patient mother in Palo Alto, half an hour north of San Jose, ultimately Jeff's erratic comings and goings, his around-the-clock restlessness and unpredictability, his smoking in bed, and the pressures of Edith's full-time job left her nerves too strained to offer him further refuge.

It was the period when family values, popularized as "togetherness," were celebrated in TV sitcoms and on Madison Avenue. That was no help to us. In real life, the Norman Rockwell *Saturday Evening Post* idyll of "family" turned into another vexing Catch-22 for the Wydens. Jeff was driving his family crazy. At the same time, an influential school in mental health hypothesized, paradoxically, that it was families who were driving schizophrenics crazy in the first place.

By chance, at that moment in downtown San Jose, a Harvard-trained psychiatrist, Dr. Loren R. Mosher, had developed a program known as home-based moral psychiatry, meant to constitute a family substitute. At thirty-eight, this influential specialist wore two hats. He was the federal government's highest-ranking official for schizophrenia research, but he had also established Soteria House, in 1971, shortly before Jeff became ill. Soteria—Greek for "deliverance"—was quartered in a rambling, rundown residence in the same neighborhood where my son would periodically while away the next decades at numerous halfway houses.

The residents in the Soteria program were severely ill schizophrenic patients. The treatment consisted primarily of empathy and was administered by a staff of young enthusiasts recruited for their lack of professional background. Mosher rejected help from psychiatric colleagues because of his belief that schizophrenia was merely "disturbed and disturbing behavior," not an illness. He had picked up this delusion from the British guru with whom he had trained, R. D. Laing, some years before the doctor was drummed out of medicine.

Still, Mosher's program in San Jose was underwritten by Grant No. 20123 of the National Institute of Mental Health, which was convenient because in Washington the doctor was chief of the NIMH Center for the Study of Schizophrenia. Government grants are the fuel of major mental health investigations, and ninety percent of the money invested in schizophrenia originated in Mosher's center.

I had never heard of Soteria or Mosher during the 1970s, which was just as well because his pet project was not a success. By the early 1980s, NIMH refused to fund it further and eased Mosher out of the agency's mainstream and to outlying Montgomery County, Maryland.

"I would advise individuals with schizophrenia to avoid that county," wrote Dr. E. Fuller Torrey in reviewing Mosher's work in the consumer guide *Surviving Schizophrenia*. Instead of medications, wrote Torrey, Mosher used "love, understanding and a soft teddy bear."

Mosher's career curve makes a cautionary tale of changing fashions in psychiatry and proof that a doctorate in psychiatry, a creative mind, excellent intentions, and the highest sponsorship do not suffice for a serious attack upon the enigmatic disease. Commentators on NIMH operations attributed its lack of firm leadership in schizophrenia research to Mosher's ambiguous strivings for a better world, and Dr. Herbert Pardes, who had become the agency's director when Mosher left, moved to give it a harder, biological edge.

Pardes, a feisty New Yorker, did not think highly of some of the research in progress when he took the job. "They had a lot of work going that was bullshit," he told me.

While Mosher's abhorrence of antipsychotic drugs became a minority position, he still served in 1996 on the Scientific Advisory Board of the authoritative NIMH quarterly *Schizophrenia Bulletin,* which he had founded in 1961. His newest book, espousing his old ideas, *Community Mental Health,* was published in 1994 and was on the list of recommended reading at the World Health Organization. From 1991 to 1995 he was "principal investigator" and "principal researcher" on yet another grant of $1,287,604 dispensed by the NIMH. The project was confined to Montgomery County and was still looking into "Alternatives to Hospitalization."

Mosher reveled in his increasingly lonely opposition to antipsychotic medications and described himself, engagingly, as the quixotic "King Kong" of schizophrenia. His professional survival was testimony to psychiatry's helplessness. He was able to preach his failed gospel because many of his colleagues continued to feel insecure about their own agendas.

When Mosher was at the peak of his power, from the 1960s until the 1980s, especially during the period while I was shopping for Jeff's home away from home, the doctor spearheaded a movement whose views profoundly influenced the mental health professions and their many public and private institutions. These doctors had convinced themselves that the family was *the* root cause of schizophrenia. The most visible of the crusaders, in addition to Mosher, included Dr. Frieda Fromm-Reichmann of the Chestnut Lodge Clinic in Maryland; Dr. Theodore Lidz, professor of psychiatry at Yale; Laing, originally of London's Tavistock Clinic; and Dr. Gregory Bateson, an anthropologist who had worked among the families of natives in the Pacific with Margaret Mead.

The American family had taken quite a beating from psychiatrists by the 1970s. A 1976 technical treatise entitled *Treatment of Schizophrenia: Progress and Prospects* described the gyrations thus: "The interest psychiatrists have shown in the families of their patients has evolved from a posture of avoidance of contact with them to an interest in the so-called schizophrenogenic mother and finally to a study of deviant patterns of communication and interaction in families with a schizophrenic offspring." In this compilation, editors Louis Jolyon West and Don Flinn lauded Mosher's "recent innovative approaches" as "very promising indeed."

Mosher compiled a master list of "Characteristic Processes in Families with Psychotic Relatives." Among his categories were: "covert rejection," "lack of empathy," "inconsistency," and "contradictory expectations."

Fromm-Reichmann, a giant among her peers although she was only four feet nine inches tall, invented the schizophrenia-inducing (schizophrenogenic) mother. The doctor was the thinly disguised heroine in the best-selling novel *I Never Promised You a Rose Garden*. While her scholarly papers promoting intensive psychotherapy for schizophrenia enjoyed wide respect, critics contended that the symptoms of her *Rose Garden* patient suggested the less malignant diagnosis of hysteria.*

Lidz studied seventeen families for twelve years and concluded: "Schizophrenic patients virtually always grow up in seriously disturbed families. . . . One patient after another was subjected to a piling up of interfamily forces that were major forces in molding the misshapen personality."

Laing promoted the idea that schizophrenia was the sane reaction to an insane world, especially to families who picked on one member and victimized him or her as an emotional scapegoat.

Bateson proposed that schizophrenia was caused by parents who frustrated their offspring with "heads-I-win-tails-you-lose" messages.

These hypotheses, by now out of style and a source of embarrassment, were mainstays of therapists in the 1970s. No wonder Jeff's treatment team at Menninger treated his parents with suspicion. To their generation of healers, few fathers and mothers of schizophrenics were emotionally acceptable.

Mosher and his cohorts, in effect, denied the true villain. In practical terms, they were as blind as Jeff was when he turned doctors into scapegoats. Patient and doctors alike were shadowboxing. The true villain was the disease itself.

Of course I was not about to allow my son to join the hapless street people who shuffle homeless around our cities. Encouraged by my family therapist friend, Dr. R, and Rick Robinson, the biological psychiatrist who was

---

* In a painstakingly researched 1981 paper, "Diagnostic Discrepancy in Personal Accounts of Patients with 'Schizophrenia,' " Drs. Carol North and Remi Cadoret matched the schizophrenia diagnoses in five widely distributed autobiographical accounts against DSM-III diagnostic criteria and found them wanting. Given the clinical details available for "Deborah Blau," the patient in *I Never Promised You a Rose Garden*, the conclusion is inescapable that she was cured of her hysteria by an arrogant doctor's power of suggestion.

micro-managing Jeff's medications, I decided to set up a substitute family willing and qualified to create a sympathetic environment for Jeff.

As for Jeff at this point, he wrote a note dated "Monday, 4/18/83," dispatched from Crestwood Hospital, proclaiming his faith:

> I don't believe in—
>
> Crestwood Manor, this-or-that Manor, psychotherapy, medications, *A Clockwork Orange, The Graduate,* the Bible, the Great Rick Robinson, Edith Wyden or Peter Wyden, Taoism, Congressman Ron Wyden, vitamins. I just believe in me!!*

The last word was underlined three times. Whatever may have been wrong with his ego in childhood, there was no longer anything amiss. Had the need to overcome the adversities of his illness made him stronger?

Jeff still needed a home, and so for several weekends that spring I ran this ad in San Jose and Palo Alto newspapers:

> FOSTER HOME NEEDED
> For bright, thoughtful male, 31, under psychiatrist's supervision. Just needs friendly, caring environment.

No responses came. Most likely the specter of a psychiatric problem scared applicants away so decisively that they would not even bother to inquire about details of my son's condition or the pay.

By good fortune, Jeff managed the recruiting on his own. For a few weeks he had been trying to make his peace with a structured program operating at Murphy Manor, yet another halfway house. It offered a sophisticated staff with a small patient load. Jeff disdained the place as too regimented, but a bond of mutual affection developed between him and one of the social workers, Bernie. When this new friend, who was about thirty-five, heard what we were looking for, he volunteered himself, his wife, his small daughter, and his neat little subdivision home in the San Jose hills.

---

* *The Graduate* had long bugged him because of the vapid career advice whispered to the hero, the graduate, with whom Jeff identified: "Plastics!" The Bible and the word of Tao had become sources of solace that occupied many of his hours.

It was the best news of a bad year. Between March and mid-June, Jeff's condition seesawed so violently that he had to be admitted three times to Crestwood Hospital, his main escape hatch, to regain some measure of equilibrium. Fortunately, we were able to shield him from news of a possible economic disaster that was affecting *my* sleep for many nights. Keeping him in benign ignorance of such things was one of the advantages of Jeff's being out of touch with the world beyond his illness.

Having long been classified as one hundred percent disabled under Social Security rules, he was entitled to something over three hundred dollars a month in federal Supplemental Security Income, a stipend that was paid to his conservator at the Santa Clara County public guardian's office to help him keep Jeff afloat. In the early 1980s, the Reagan administration instituted "reviews," which the U.S. Supreme Court subsequently denounced as a "clandestine policy" of denying disability payments to the mentally ill. Hundreds of thousands like Jeff were being unjustly suspected of malingering. Half of those who lost their benefits regained them after appeals.

"People who are just clearly unable to function, let alone hold a job, are being put into the meat grinder of this process," I read in the *New York Times* from a speech by Senator John Heinz of Pennsylvania.

States and cities were suing the Social Security Administration. One victim cited in court by the New York authorities was a thirty-six-year-old paranoid schizophrenic who regularly hallucinated and had not worked in six years. He was a resident of a shelter and before that lived in Central Park. His benefits were canceled because his condition "prevented him from returning to his 'usual job,' but there are 'many other jobs' " he could do, theoretically.

I had visions of Jeff getting sucked into this meat grinder, which reached its most voracious stage in that frightening spring of 1983. Thank goodness, public outcry stopped the "reviewers" before they got around to him. I would have swallowed hard if he had been held accountable for a situation that was not remotely of his doing.

Realistic or not, from time to time I couldn't resist trying to pierce Jeff's armor with a few pellets of logic. Feeling like Willy Loman, the road-weary salesman who couldn't sell, I wrote Jeff on April 19:

> Whenever you find yourself back in the hospital, you blame your doctor
> or your mother or a policeman or the people in charge of whatever place

you happen to live in. You never seem to blame the true villain, which is your illness. . . . It won't help (it isn't even fair!) to blame these messengers with bad news for your condition and to think that they're hounding you into the hospital. Why should overcrowded hospitals take you in just on somebody's say-so? They've got all the business they can handle. . . . If you blame your helpers, you'll only make yourself bitter and depressed and block your insight into your true state.

Occasionally, perhaps to please me, Jeff would tell me that he understood and promised to change his thinking. This was one of those times. So on April 23, I wrote to him at Crestwood:

I'm really happy and much relieved to gather from our phone conversation that we're agreed: your illness itself is to blame for your problem, not the messengers . . . and the one thing that an objective historian can say about your problems for sure is that they are a very complex matter. They have to be complex, or else you wouldn't be back in the hospital so frequently, right?

I suggested that he start researching his illness by asking pointed questions of his doctors, which Jeff had never brought himself to do and would avoid doing now. The optimistic tone of my letter to him was a cheerleader's artifice, for at about the same time I was also flailing at his Dr. Robinson about loopholes in Jeff's nominally airtight support system.

"We must ask ourselves more explicitly how many more relapses and hospitalizations Jeff can stand before he goes into total sabotage or suicide or both," I wrote the doctor on April 20. "I was truly appalled when you reported Jeff's blood lithium level, when it was taken just before he was most recently hospitalized, was .4, so very substantially lower than the long-ago discovered minimum of 1. How did this really happen?"

Nobody knew. Jeff changed venue too frequently. His test levels changed too rapidly. To some of the lower-level helpers in the mental health system, he was becoming an annoyance—a too-frequent caller, too chronic, too much trouble. And so Bernie and his family looked like a life raft to me, far better than a passive foster-home setting.

Bernie was of the type that used to be called a live wire. He saw himself not only as a caretaker but as an assistant doctor. He would drive Jeff to his sessions with Robinson and sit in as a participant-observer so he could follow up on the doctor's instructions and treatment strategy. He determined when

Jeff became too agitated to be manageable at home, took him to the hospital, and visited him there.

Bernie saw Jeff as a challenge to his considerable energy and skills. He left him little sitting and brooding time. He kept in touch with me through progress reports in letters and tapes. He sent photos of Jeff looking pleased with himself. He took him shopping for new jeans and shoes. He drove him twenty-five miles to his mother's home for the weekend. He enrolled Jeff in vocational rehabilitation and kept in contact with the agency's staff. And he did not interfere when Jeff, wonder of wonders, dated a young woman in their neighborhood and admitted that he was having a good time. A good time! When had anybody last heard such a thing out of my son? Not since the early 1960s, more than twenty years before.

When I met Bernie at his home, I found him bright, largely self-taught, cheerfully outgoing, and loaded with enthusiasm and obvious affection for Jeff. His house was modest but meticulous. Jeff's designated room was cozy. Bernie's wife and little girl seemed warm, friendly, and intrigued by the idea of taking on a new family member. Robinson had a satisfactory chat with my new deputy. All systems were go, and on May 23 Bernie submitted an astonishingly insightful and detailed "proposal":

> Jeff will be provided with a family environment which will more effectively focus on him as an individual than the institutional and residential care facilities that have recently housed him. As a member of our household, Jeff will be able to overcome the institutional label of "mental patient" and progress toward establishing his own identity. I will initiate and coordinate a viable treatment plan for Jeff with his therapist, Dr. Rick Robinson. Emphasis will be on a no-fail approach to learning basic living skills. . . . I will provide Jeff with 24-hour daily care. Initially that will include 10–12 hours a day of active supervisions which will be gradually reduced to achieve a 40-hour week. As Jeff becomes more independent, we will work toward an eventual move to a private satellite housing program with minimal staff supervision.

Behold, an organized thinker with a solid plan. To me, it rang out like Beethoven's Fifth Symphony. But it wasn't cheap. Bernie asked me to sign a formal contract stipulating a fee of two thousand dollars a month. I agreed, with Jeff's mother consenting to pay half. I did append a warning that we could probably afford the arrangement for no more than six months.

Jeff was pleased by all the fussing on his behalf and looked forward to the friendly new faces, the privacy of a residential setting. In the end, of course, everything hinged on Bernie's therapeutic skill and his ability to hold his ingeniously designed refuge together.

During the first days of Jeff's stay, Bernie somehow found time to keep a journal that eventually ran to seventy-two pages. Excerpts show that he was working hard for his money:

6/1/83—Jeff combed his hair without being asked. . . . He asked if he could set the table. I thanked him. . . .

6/2—1 p.m.: Jeff has not returned from the store, he has been gone an hour. . . . 4:30: Still no Jeff. . . . 9:30: No sight of him. . . . I called Dr. Robinson; he agreed that Jeff was doing some testing. . . .

6/3—5:30 a.m.: Jeff's mother called. He had called her, rapping and raving. He was lost and cold on the highway. We drove out and picked Jeff up. . . . He said he was paying his rent and should be able to go where he wanted. . . . 10 p.m.: Jeff has been at my bedroom door four times now, for one reason or another, just like a kid. . . .

6/4—3:30 a.m.: I cracked his door open. There he was sitting in the dark with the ear-phones, listening to music. . . . He has 200 mg. Thorazine in him and he had not slept the night before. . . . 9 p.m.: He said if R.S. [Dr. Robinson] calls and ups his Thorazine, to tell him to go to hell.

6/6—8:30 p.m.: No Jeff. . . . He has no shoes and shirt. . . .

6/7—3:50 p.m.: Received a call from EPS [emergency psychiatric service] at Valley Medical Center. He was picked up by the police a while ago. . . . I attached a small bell to his door so I could hear him when he left his room. . . .

6/8—10 p.m.: I said, "Jeff, did you take your medication, all of it?" I could see the green pill on the floor. "Why do you think you could trick me?" He yelled at me very loudly that I could not tell him what to do and where to go. . . .

6/9—7:30 a.m.: He is showing a loss of appetite, decreased speech and has stopped joking. . . . 12:50 p.m.: Just received a telephone call from the San Jose police. They reported Jeff is at a 7-11 store. . . . 3:30 p.m.: In Dr. Robinson's office, Dr. R. said, "Jeff, you look upset." Jeff answered, "I am a D.J. I am what I play." Dr. R. asked him if he wanted to go back to Crestwood. Jeff didn't answer right away, but in a moment he said yes.

As if determined to spite me and my allies, the demons seemed to coax Jeff to turn more "brittle," as the doctors had begun to say. On June 17, I reached out to our senior adviser, Dr. Koran at Stanford, and complained about Jeff's sometimes frighteningly infantile behavior and his sometimes apparently deepening resistance to all medications on the hardly crazy grounds that they don't seem to help him. . . . During one brief period recently, Rick and I found Jeff in marvelous shape, better than ever, yet mere days later, despite very close supervision, he was, as Rick said, "grossly psychotic," acutely frightened and child-like, generally worse than Rick had ever seen him. . . . Somehow the valves seem to have been turned up on his illness. The extremes seem to be widening. He's better when he's well, worse when he's not.

It wouldn't be the last time that the mercurial habits of our demons caused puzzlement. The doctors ruminated vaguely about the "waxing and waning" of the disease and shrugged as if they had been asked to explain the weather. No wonder Jeff couldn't grasp what forces were buffeting him.

By midsummer he had been discharged from Crestwood for the last time that year and was back at Bernie's home, still, almost unbelievably, unwilling to concede that he was ill. Incorrigibly, I tried again to rise to the challenge and wrote him on July 30:

It has sometimes seemed to me that you deny your illness because you're understandably damned tired of it; or maybe you feel like being contrary. Lately, however, I've become convinced that you find it extremely difficult to acknowledge your illness because you cannot see it or feel it! This is true of most emotional illnesses and it's what makes them different from most physical illnesses, which you can track by pain or other observable symptoms. . . . You don't know how bad a shape you're in while you're in it. A small example: before your recent improvement (Hooray!), you kept telling me on the phone that they were about to shut off the water and the air in the hospital. Do you know that you believed this at the time? I imagine that you don't. . . . This makes it very easy for you to deny your illness. And that makes it damned near impossible for a doctor or a family to enlist your help in making you better. And without your help it's impossible to keep you out of the hospital—which is what you want.

While it was never discernible whether my lectures helped Jeff even remotely to clarify the tumult that, as I could tell, kept pounding over and over through his head, I did observe that he read my letters repeatedly, often kept them, thought about some of my offerings, and commented on them. But mostly it was Bernie's environment and energetic ministrations that produced relief and stability for him in the second half of 1983 and early 1984. I therefore did not go along when his mother hoped to renegotiate the costly home arrangement. On February 8, 1984, I renewed our contract after I wrote her:

> Imperfect as the setup may be, it works, and if it works, don't tinker! Jeff has been out of the hospital for a longer period than he has been in years; he takes showers and is neat and is getting used to going to some constructive activity each morning. . . . He is in a civilized, warm family environment. . . . So Bernie is not Dr. Freud and does not read Homer in the original Greek. The fact is that he is doing better with Jeff than the hospitals or me (when I had him) or you (when you had him). I say a prayer every day in hopes that Bernie won't get a job in Iowa.

To my delight, for once I was hearing no complaints from Jeff, not even about his daily trek to the Vocational Learning and Treatment Center (VLTC), where he had begun tutoring younger patients in reading classes. Bernie's family seemed content and stable, so I was startled to learn that Jeff's new father figure had already gone through two divorces in his twenties and had fathered three earlier children. Moreover, his two ex-wives were in contact with each other in Oregon and had agreed that their children should not visit their father, as in past years, as long as a mental patient was in the home.

I thought that Bernie's family life was none of my business and reveled in his continuing great news. On April 24 he reported:

> As you can see from the photos, Jeff is looking good. I took him in for a haircut. He enjoys this attention, getting his hair washed and styled. . . . Jeff is changing. He has adapted to all types of social situations, in and out of the house. I have extended his responsibilities around the house and his response has been positive. . . . In my one-to-one counseling sessions with Jeff, he has started talking about his phobias. This is a first. Rick also reported Jeff talking about his phobias and he sees this as a positive. Rick recently changed Jeff's medication with the addition of a new drug for phobias, called Xanax. Jeff was very excited about the new drug. I was surprised he wasn't talking about how many pills he was having to take now.

I was especially pleased about Jeff's good appearance, an important index of his self-esteem, not merely a matter of cosmetics. And on June 1 came encouraging corroboration from Jeff's vocational coordinator at the agency, where he was still tutoring:

When Jeff first entered VLTC he had very poor attendance and tardiness, rambling speech, poor self-esteem and constantly spoke off the subject. . . . Approximately one month later, Jeff began tutoring and had increased both his concentration and self-esteem. . . . It took until now before Jeff was able to begin speaking and listening more concretely. . . . With no complications regarding his medications, Jeff has demonstrated the ability to show improvement in his rehabilitation.

Feeling a need to see his children during the summer, Bernie decided to take them camping for two weeks in Oregon and sent me a detailed breakdown of the costs ("van rental," "camping fees," "emergency cash"). They added up to $1,670. Would I help to underwrite the venture by contributing $800? How could I refuse such a devoted effort to be a conscientious father?

The end of our idyll was nearing. That fall, Jeff reported a crescendo of discord in Bernie's household. It upset Jeff to listen to the arguments. I suspect they reminded him of the tensions between his mother and me. Before long, Bernie was getting his third divorce and had to sell Jeff's temporary home. We were all sad at the loss, and I never summoned enough nerve to start raising yet another substitute household. There was no telling when it, too, might implode and leave my brittle son stranded again.

CHAPTER 19

Rename It
"Nijinsky's Disease"

⎯⎯✑⎯⎯

"WELL, DOC, WHAT do you do with those *nuts* of yours?" This was a TV producer's sarcasm that welcomed Dr. Jerome Vaccaro when he arrived at a Los Angeles broadcasting studio to explain his research with schizophrenic outpatients as head of the Santa Monica Mental Health Center.

"Why do you want to write those *nasty* things about Jeff?" said one of my family members when I began work on this book.

As a public relations dilemma, schizophrenia was ever a disaster. "Illogical fear," as Senator Domenici had put it, was only one of the barriers giving the illness a reputation as dreaded as leprosy. Other obstacles were resignation that engendered hopelessness; and near-total ignorance—a NAMI poll found that fifty-five percent of the American public denied that mental illness existed.

Denial was rooted in intense repugnance. Schizophrenia never had a poster child. No telethons raised funds to combat it. Until NAMI began to make supportive sounds in the 1980s, the illness never mustered an advocate. It simply owned a burdensome history compounded by an intimidating, tongue-twisting name.

Labels induce stigma, as even academic theoreticians realized. (The authors of an editorial in *Biological Psychiatry* rightly proposed in 1985 that the condition be renamed "Nijinsky's Disease," honoring one of its most distinguished sufferers, the immortal Russian dancer Vaslav Nijinsky.)* The predicament of stigma—it is no exaggeration to call the effects disastrous—dates back, as did so much else in schizophrenia, to Emil Kraepelin. Along with the minutiae of his pioneering dissections, the revered scholar left behind a legacy of a most onerous sort that is still largely with us.

Kraepelin, at bottom, appraised schizophrenia as an essentially deteriorating, degenerative illness unresponsive to medical intervention, a sentence of death delayed. The rationale behind his extreme pessimism is still unclear. The editorial in *Biological Psychiatry* speculated—but considered it doubtful—that schizophrenics in 1900 may have been different, warranting a prognosis poorer than in modern times. More likely, the discouragement arose from the then-prevailing, generally defeatist psychiatric theory of psychosis and a hidden bias in the sampling of the patients who were undergoing such minute study at a time when helpful medications were half a century away.

"It is likely that the focus of Kraepelin's work was on the more severe or long-term institutional cases, especially those already on a chronic debilitating course," the editorial suggested. Kraepelin and his contemporaries simply "forgot about those who had long ago recovered and left the institution."

With his tunnel vision, the venerable professor argued in favor of hereditary predisposition ("seeds of decay" was his term), leading to his patients' inexorable decline and a final fate that the *Biological Psychiatry* editorial denounced as a "conceptual curse." Such was the long-term power of Kraepelin's influence that the public still refused to give credence to the results of the more benign modern "Vermont Study" of outcomes or the 1978 finding of the prominent researcher Martin Bleuler in Switzerland that only one-quarter to one-third of schizophrenics either fail to recover or need to deal with a mild chronic course of their condition.

"Sometimes it is easier to change genes than to change culture!" concluded the exasperated professors in *Biological Psychiatry*. At that, they had not ventured into Hollywood, where film culture was practicing psychiatry with vitriolic fury, further exacerbating the curse of mental illness. In one study, seventy-three percent of psychiatric patients on television were shown as violent; twenty-three percent were homicidal maniacs. Even well-designed hits

---

* The brilliant Nijinsky was able to describe himself slipping into madness: "I like to look closely in the mirror and I see only one eye."

produced for movie theaters rendered the world of psychotic patients so grotesquely evil that they qualified as dramatic malpractice.

Intentional or not, Jack Nicholson allowed himself to become a generation's symbol of psychiatry running amok and brutalizing psychotic patients. Playing on the public's ignorance and fear, the film version of psychedelic guru Ken Kesey's novel *One Flew over the Cuckoo's Nest* swept the 1975 Oscars, winning the awards for best picture, best actor, and best actress. The true winners were antipsychiatry prejudice and contempt.

In *Cuckoo's Nest*, an allegory of despicable authority battling plucky rebellion, Nicholson is Randle McMurphy, a healthy roustabout faking grinning insanity to wheedle himself out of a short jail stretch. Big Nurse Ratchet, the villain, hates him for sabotaging her control and the system. She punishes him by having him lobotomized. This inspires the hero, a schizophrenic Indian patient, Chief Broom, to do the "sane" thing: he breaks out and heads for freedom.

Similarly, Anthony Hopkins glamorized Dr. Hannibal Lecter, the psychiatrist who practiced cannibalism in *The Silence of the Lambs* (winning most major Oscars in 1992). *Sleeping with the Enemy,* according to one reviewer, begged the question, "What happens when a beautiful young woman marries her Prince Charming—and he turns out to be a psychotic monster?"

The "creative" variations on the tragic drama of psychosis are irresistible, financially rewarding, and profoundly damaging to the public's conception of hapless victims and their hard-pressed helpers. The portrayals were often inaccurate or flip. Half an hour of *Terminator 2* plays in a psychiatric hospital where the "doctor" explains, wrongly, that "violent acting out" is one of the "usual indicators" of schizoaffective disorder. And the TV *M*A*S*H* psychiatrist, Sidney Freedman, insults the villain, Colonel Flagg, by snorting, "I'd like to go on talking to you, Flagg, but with your schizophrenia, I'd have to charge you double."

In his impressively researched 1995 book *Media Madness,* Otto F. Wahl shows how *M*A*S*H,* which sometimes treated mental illness with understanding, resorted to dubious sport when psychiatrists called at the hospital unit on eleven occasions. Even the hero surgeon, Hawkeye (Alan Alda), cracked up in the final segment and wrote home that his "cheese has slipped off his cracker." The phrase was a screenwriter's reach for humor, perhaps projecting his own discomfort, but surely misplaced. In real life, Jeff at times resorted to defensive self-deprecation, but I don't believe he would stoop to smear himself with such an insolent caricature.

The relentless pounding of Hollywood's horror and lampooning drown

out the occasional sympathetic portrayals and reinforce the public view of
severe brain disorders as evil or comical lowlife behavior; the predominant
tone tends to brand the patients as hopeless misfits.

Clearly, this patient population sets off a high velocity of general anxiety
among presumably "normal" people, and underlying this discomfort festers
a nagging frustration: a psychic need for a cause or causes. Medicine has
assigned causes to diabetes, heart disease, cancer, and other chronic illnesses,
even leprosy. Severe mental disorders know no cause. Nothing is more frightening and open to abuse than the unknown.

In the face of this vacuum, the quest for the origin(s) of psychosis, antedat-
ing even Kraepelin, set frustrated researchers scrambling in errant directions.
First came the psychoanalysts and their expeditions into the allegedly twisted
minds of mothers. Or it was the patient's fault. Then behaviorists came to
blame family conduct, rather than biological triggers. This escalated in 1984
when Dr. Michael J. Goldstein, a UCLA psychologist, created a stir with his
ten-year study of sixty-five disturbed adolescent boys. He claimed that it "pro-
vides evidence that family attributes measured during adolescence are associated with the subsequent presence of schizophrenia or schizophrenia-related
disorders in the offspring once they entered young adulthood."

In an interview with Daniel Goleman, a qualified psychologist who writes
for the *New York Times,* Goldstein expressed himself more aggressively. "The
parents of these kids engaged in character assassination," he charged. "Instead
of criticizing what the child had done, they would make a personal attack, saying 'You're no good.' . . . The parents were also highly intrusive, telling the
kid what he thinks or feels, without regard to what the kid says. . . . These parents also spoke in a way that leaves the child feeling confused or uncertain. . . .
He doesn't know what to believe, with his shaken sense of reality."

These families supposedly created schizophrenic sons. "Under stress,"
Goldstein believed, "these children's thought processes are more easily
derailed."

The *Times* did not explore a related subject on this occasion—Goldstein is
also a leading proponent of a theory known as expressed emotion (EE), still
debated among researchers. It proposes a linkage between negative parental
behavior and full-blown schizophrenia in adult offspring, especially when they
return home after hospitalizations and conduct themselves in a less-than-
conventional manner. Most researchers are not greatly impressed by these
theories.

Alert to psychiatric fashions, Goleman on May 28, 1996, opened another *Times* dispatch from the schizophrenia battlefront with a striking salvo: "A dramatic change is afoot in the scientific understanding of schizophrenia." This was powerful language for the *Times,* and the occasion justified it.

Attention had finally shifted from such psychological theories as advanced by Goldstein to hard new physical findings by the likes of Dr. Daniel Weinberger, chief of the Clinical Brain Disorders Branch of NIMH. According to the Weinberger school, the roots in probably half of all schizophrenia cases lay buried in fetal brain abnormalities observable before birth and seen not long afterward in posthumous brain tissue procured from autopsies.

"The most consistent finding is that overall brain volume and cortical grey matter volume are reduced by five to ten per cent," Weinberger had written in the August 26, 1995, issue of the British journal *Lancet.* In the *Times,* Goleman described faulty wiring in the brains of schizophrenics. Neurons were frequently out of place in the prefrontal areas. Other abnormalities were also traced, usually beginning in the second trimester of fetal development.

A fresh study in *The Archives of General Psychiatry* supported the new discoveries. A coauthor, Dr. Steven G. Potkin of the University of California at Irvine, told Goleman: "There may be a wide range of causes, from a faulty genetic mechanism to environmental insults, like the mother having a virus that penetrates the placenta."*

Weinberger also cited a British Medical Research Council study of childhood neurological milestones showing subtle differences between infants who developed into normal adults and those who became schizophrenic.

"There were no gross abnormalities," Weinberger said, "but a lifelong pattern, on average, of delayed maturation of the [latter group's] brains. For instance, at six months, about a third of babies are two weeks or more late in sitting up. For those who later developed schizophrenia, two-thirds were late."

Still, nothing has allayed the abhorrence of the lay public for the repulsive and mysterious strangers in our midst, some of them lurking highly visible on streets, begging, huddled for warmth on steam grates in the pavements.

Perhaps no sizable minority was ever so conscientiously studied as the homeless. *Outcasts on Main Street,* the illustrated report published in 1992 by

---

* The hunt for the precise location of a gene responsible for schizophrenia has been long, relentless, and tedious in the extreme. By 1996 researchers at the University of Virginia and elsewhere had fixed its residence in the brain by the equivalent of its community and the probable specific street. They were still searching for the right house. It was speculated that, at most, twenty-five percent of schizophrenia cases might be caused by a gene defect; ultimately it may turn out to be only about five percent.

the Federal Task Force on Homelessness and Severe Mental Illness, listed 110 cooperating organizations and eighteen pages of recommendations.

"Homelessness in America must come to an end" were the opening words of the "action" section. The key failure appeared at first glance to be society's lack of will to spend enough money to pressure these anonymous sick people to take antipsychotic medications regularly. Since most of them deny that they are ill, this is a complex and expensive undertaking, but an NIMH team under Dr. Richard Jed Wyatt showed that with adequate will, enough funds, and dedicated social workers the task can be managed.

For more than two years, a team of public therapists focused intensively on the care of one hundred homeless New York street people; developed therapeutic relationships with them; made regular appointments with them to receive pills; tracked them down whenever they did not show up; and procured housing for those who could be persuaded to accept it. It worked. It also decreased costs by cutting down jail time and hospitalizations.

But the inner core of the homelessness dilemma, paradoxically, was not so much with the homeless as with the rest of us—the indifferent and ignorant who, until further notice, preferred to stay in that state. This perplexing message was drawn from an imaginative research project designed by Dr. Gerry Power, a communications authority at UCLA, reported in Dan Weisburd's *Journal*.

Power exposed nearly three hundred middle- and upper-middle-class men and women to eight different TV news segments depicting the homeless. The results of their transfer from mental hospitals to the streets documented an unexpected dehumanization.

"They have been shifted from an environment of complete invisibility to the openness of public spaces," Power wrote. There,

> they assume [another kind] of invisibility. They fade into the background and become permanent fixtures on park benches, routine sounds in doorways and familiar odors in bus stations. These daily reminders rarely take human form. They have lost the capacity to touch us. . . . They have become a natural part of the modern urban environment. Homeless mentally ill people are in many ways like human graffiti—a public display of all that is wrong in our society. Like graffiti, we rarely understand it and rarely care enough to try.

Where is the safety net so often (and glibly) cited in discussions of budgets for social services? Isn't such a catchall supposed to protect against "cracks in the system," the crevices into which abandoned souls sometimes tumble? I think of the nights when Jeff stormed up and down unlighted rural roads as a runaway without food or his pills.

It's not difficult in our culture to be swallowed up, to evaporate. Jeff was repeatedly very lucky. Steered by his family, the police rescued him again and again. But it *was* mostly blind luck. Floaters were more likely to wind up luckless, like Eric Dutch.

I first saw Eric's name in large type on a startling wanted poster tacked all over the walls at a meeting of NAMI parents at Yale University. "Missing— Endangered" it read over an appealing snapshot of a squinting young man with a broad, puckish grin. "Medical alert!" the text said. "Eric takes medication and becomes ill without it!!" His parents were offering a thousand dollars for information leading to his whereabouts. They described him as thirty-four years old, six feet two inches tall, weighing 170 pounds, with hazel eyes, brown hair, and an eight-inch scar on his left forearm. He was last seen in Middletown, Connecticut, home of Wesleyan University.

It took me weeks to summon the nerve to call the home number listed on the poster. About half a year had gone by since Eric's disappearance, in October 1994, from his room at the YMCA. I knew Middletown as a busy, civilized community on the Connecticut River. His parents lived nearby and were apparently caring, alert, and reasonably affluent people, well organized in their outreach for help.

My nervousness proved justified. The woman answering the phone identified herself tensely as Eric's mother, Elaine. I could sense her anxiety rising the moment I said I was calling about her son, although I instantly added that I had no news about him. Yes, she had had numerous calls about "sightings," referring to the reports in the manner of UFO observers speaking of unidentified flying objects. Six calls had come from the area of Westerly, Rhode Island, others from as far as San Diego.

Eric's history resembled my son's. He had been schizophrenic for half his life and taking clozapine for four years. His disappearance had been triggered when his psychiatrist moved away, Mrs. Dutch said. The doctor's successor "didn't know" anything about him, Eric complained. He felt lost.

In the fall of 1996, I checked with the state police. The trooper who had worked on the case recalled it immediately. A year before, a workman trimming trees in a heavily wooded section had come across a dry storm drain that Eric had turned into a hideaway. "It looked like a place of refuge," the officer said. "There were only skeletal remains."

The lives of schizophrenics in less developed, poorer lands are as vexing as in rich America. The rate of *incidence* seems to hold at about one percent of the population even in the most underdeveloped nations, as confirmed by the experts at the Division of Mental Health for the World Health Organization (WHO) in Geneva.

"The differences are surprisingly low," said Walter H. Gulbinat, chief statistician for the agency's several worldwide studies. "The concept of the healthy savage is a myth."

The data on *outcomes,* however, reveal a surprise. WHO's 1992 study of 1,379 patients in ten countries arrived at this conclusion after the participants were examined at intervals three times: "On five out of six course and outcome dimensions patients in the developing countries had a markedly better prognosis than patients in the developed countries."

When I expressed amazement to the mental health division's senior medical officer, Dr. Jose Manoel Bertolote, he explained the apparent paradox: "It's in the way civilizations handle the illness. The less resources, the better the prognosis." He mentioned India and the Eskimos of northern Canada as outstanding examples of superior outcomes. Other experts would later add China, Colombia, and Nigeria.

"The U.S. and Germany are not the best environments," Dr. Bertolote said. "You don't find the closeness of community, the belief in a social network of support."

Dr. Arthur Kleinman, a Harvard professor, psychiatrist, and also an anthropologist with decades of experience conducting cross-cultural studies in Africa and Asia, did not challenge the WHO statistics on incidence and prognoses, but would not confirm the reported reasons for better outcome in poor societies.

"Nobody knows why there is a difference," he said. "Is it because families stick with them? That's all hypothesis."

The negative attitude many (perhaps most) Caucasian Americans display toward their schizophrenic kin is a fact, however. Kleinman and his associates conducted a study in Seattle that demonstrated this lack of supportiveness, and, according to my own impression, the touted American worship of "family values" rarely stands up well under stress of severe mental illness.

"We value a hyperindividualism in this country," Kleinman said. "The dominant stream in our society finds schizophrenics burdensome and 'you can't do anything about it anyway.'"

The prevailing defeatism seems to me of a piece with the ubiquitous burnout I have encountered among families and therapists enmeshed in coping with hard-to-manage schizophrenia patients. For every doctor like Bill Wirshing of the Brentwood VA Hospital, who "loved" the disease, there were more who deserted it, depressed and frustrated. Among kinfolk, the burnout phenomenon is notorious. "Five years," snapped Dr. Vaccaro in Santa Monica when I asked how long it took most relatives to abandon schizophrenia patients. And in all of Jeff's hospitals and halfway houses, I have noticed that visitors are rarities.

Among the industrialized nations, the Japanese are, as in so many other respects, the people with the most idiosyncratic reactions. They consume huge quantities of neuroleptic drugs—thirty percent of total world sales, $434 million worth in 1995, compared with $632 million for all European countries combined—yet have no unusual benefits to show for their expensive effort.

"There is no evidence that they are doing better or worse," said Kleinman, who spent much time working in Japan.

The Japanese are adept, however, at extracting maximum service from severely limited therapeutic resources. For 120 million people, the country offers only 8,000 psychiatrists, no psychologists, and no social workers. The doctors' fee per patient is only thirty-three dollars in hospitals and thirty-nine dollars at outpatient clinics. Salaries are based on dollar volume, so the higher the drug prices, the better the doctors' income.

As a result of the pressures, the doctors are kept frantically busy, often seeing fifty patients a day and overloading the hospitals with severe cases, forty-five percent of whom stay locked up for more than five years at a stretch. Even analysts usually see patients for only ten minutes or less per session. To make up for the haste, the recommended attitude of therapists is to generate the most empathy and highest possible therapeutic quality, making the most of each moment. In practice, loyalty to doctors runs low, and patients fire them at a high rate.

By stunning contrast, the government system for treating schizophrenia in France produces near-perfect stability, though with no appreciably better results. As explained to me by Dr. Jean-Noel Beuzen, a psychiatrist and former consultant to the system in Paris, the French doctors—possibly because neuroleptics were invented in their country—like to fashion "cocktails," using two or three neuroleptics at a time, each to target specific symptoms, such as hallucinations and delusions.

Uniquely, the country has been divided since 1838 into *secteurs*, districts where therapeutic teams are assigned to patients for as long as their illness requires. Continuity of care by the same treaters progresses through convalescence, including night hospitalizations for patients who work during the day. (French care may not have brought better health to Jeff, but it would have helped mine by not making me chase down each new treater whenever the American system forced my son to change venue.)

Openness to innovation, particularly neuroleptics, also tends to vary from country to country, again with little or no change in outcomes for patients. A new drug like Olanzapine was expected to be received among psychiatrists in the United Kingdom much as in relatively venturesome America. According to Dr. Andrew Wood, the research director at Eli Lilly's Erl Wood Research Park, a leafy corporate center about an hour south of London, antimedication crusaders like America's Dr. Peter Breggin were not unknown but had made little headway in stirring up sales resistance.

The German market presented an altogether different tradition and obstacles. "Neuroleptics have a poor reputation," I was told by a research psychiatrist who helped to direct clinical trials with some five hundred Olanzapine patients at twenty German treatment centers, and the unfriendly climate had been solidly reflected in a fourteen-page cover story that appeared in the spring of 1980 in the newsmagazine *Der Spiegel*. With a circulation of more than one million and a reputation for uncovering scandals, the magazine exerted an influence in turning public opinion against the antipsychotic medications before clozapine would be difficult to exaggerate.

"Pills in Psychiatry" was the headline across the cover; underneath, in very large type, "The Gentle Murder." The frightening tone of the text lived up to that billing.

"A growing number of psychiatry critics assert that the majority of patients were not being cured," it said, "but were chemically mistreated and condemned, through a kind of brainwashing, to an existence as emotional and physical cripples." Inflammatory quotes from doctors—such as "psychiatric Holocaust," "zombies," "prophylactic annihilation," "passive euthanasia"— conveyed the proposition that "murder" was indeed afoot and that its execution was not necessarily "gentle."

The article jarred readers into awareness of the incendiary—and peculiarly German—historical underpinnings for the objections to antipsychotics. It alluded to the discredited "racial hygiene" movement of the 1920s and the Nazis who condemned "life unworthy of life." The seeds of these teachings were said to be still flourishing. Also reported was a recent reminder of the terrible past, released by the German Society for Social Psychiatry on the fortieth anniversary of Hitler's takeover. "We still are close to the era of National Socialism," the statement said.

Evidently, *Der Spiegel* preferred the traditional German affinity for gentle talking therapy to the harsher intervention by chemical agents. Freud still did well in German-speaking territory.

After 1980 the reluctance to accept antipsychotic medications did not much soften. Remoxipride, the first important new compound in twenty years, imploded in disaster. Clozapine brought great promise for some but was seen to bring fresh dangers to others. Risperidone did not live up to its early billing. Psychoanalysts remained well entrenched.

Among the population at large, negative views of psychopharmacology were subject to remarkably powerful and rigid expression. A carefully designed, unique 1995 public opinion survey of 2,100 middle- and upper-middle-class Germans, conducted by a team led by Professor Otto Benkert, found "strong rejection" and "incomprehending fear" of biological treatments for severe mental illness.* The majority of the population had "only relatively little knowledge" of psychopharmaceuticals. Generally, psychic illnesses were "wrongly assessed." The medications were widely seen as addictive and as leading to "loss of control." Their side effects were viewed as "dramatic while their efficacious effects were not perceived." Talk therapies were "widely seen as more acceptable." Overall, psychopharmacology was characterized as an "inarticulate" science, lacking in comprehensible foundation or credible rationale. "The system must deliver provable concepts and categories" to become plausible. Thus far it seemed to have "no basis in fact."

So vehement was the German public's apparent refusal to grant recognition to biological psychiatry that I made inquiries about the survey's senior author, Benkert. His survey project had been prompted by the shabby treatment of biological psychiatry in the media, Hanns Hippius, the clozapine pioneer from Munich University Hospital, reported. Fortunately, the condemnations have been abating as more users of the medication find relief.

Still understandably cautious, the German representatives for Eli Lilly described the current neuroleptics market as "conservative" and the psychopharmacological treatment of the country's approximately 500,000 schizophrenics "still very inadequate." The outlook for Olanzapine seemed relatively

---

* *Psychopharmaka im Widerstreit* (*Psychopharmaceuticals in Controversy*), by Professor Dr. Otto Benkert, Psychiatric Clinic of the Johannes Gutenberg University, Mainz, and others (Springer Verlag, 1995).

favorable. The nursing personnel at the psychiatric clinic of Munich University Hospital were said to be "enthusiastic" because patients, much like those I sampled in the United States, found the medication more tolerable than earlier varieties.

"We are not expecting a problem," said Dr. Fred Rappard, one of the Eli Lilly research psychiatrists, perhaps too optimistically. "The pressure of the suffering is too great. And no serious doctor can manage schizophrenia without medications." It was astonishing to look back on how far the doctors had come. Surely all this was a long way from the few alternatives available for Jeff as recently as the mideighties.

CHAPTER 20

Shock

JEFF WAS unrecognizable. He was snarling, darting about, unwilling to listen, unable to hold still, his face distorted in terror. I saw him hit a nurse and throw a chair as he struggled desperately to fight off the male attendants of El Camino Hospital in the Silicon Valley between Palo Alto and San Jose. His mother and I were watching as leather straps tied our son tightly onto a narrow cot. He bucked, thrashed, screamed, and could not be calmed because he was permitted no medication of any kind.

A few days previously, he had been shooting baskets with his visiting brother on the hospital's basketball court. In the interim, on orders of the doctors, he had been taken off his usual medications, the washout being medically essential as preparation for electroconvulsive shock treatments.

Shakily, we had reached June 1987, and Jeff had steadily deteriorated, in and out of hospitals, in and out of his mother's home. He had fired his loyal and very competent psychiatrist Rick Robinson. To safeguard Jeff's kidneys, Robinson had prescribed Depakote instead of lithium for manic depression, and the new drug had made Jeff nauseous—and furious—and he went back to taking lithium. Dr. Reed Kaplan, Robinson's partner, another experienced specialist in psychopharmacology, had taken over.

Kaplan was quick and unquenchable. Motivated by a case of schizophrenia in his own family, he was a crisp mix of caution and gung-ho boldness, small and a bit cocky. I always pictured him, like the Red Baron, in the open cockpit of a fighter plane, a red muffler fluttering in the winds. As was so typical for doctors dealing with Jeff's ailment, Kaplan and his good friend and partner Robinson differed about the diagnosis of this patient for whom both had developed an abiding liking. Robinson thought he was *primarily* manic-depressive (or bipolar). Kaplan thought he was predominantly schizophrenic.

"He was chronically depressed," Kaplan recalled. "He was hallucinatory and delusional. And everything psychopharmacological had failed." And that was after the dosages of most medications had been pushed to the limit.

Kaplan did not tolerate failure easily. He therefore proposed the shock treatments as a last resort, and of course the suggestion rocked our family. The mere thought of the treatment made me freeze. It was too much like electrocution. Artificially induced convulsions? That sounded like a form of medieval torture. A year before, at the suggestion of my friend Dr. R, who still wondered whether Jeff might be suffering from what was once called hopeless "process schizophrenia," in which case nothing could be lost, had sent me for a briefing to a New York specialist who was said to be the nation's leading expert on ECT. He came across to me as callous as a concentration camp boss, instantly hateful and untrustworthy.

More to the point, I had read a detailed "Annals of Medicine" article in a 1974 issue of *The New Yorker* by Berton Rouché, the magazine's brilliant investigator of medical mysteries, about a woman economist who underwent ECT treatments for a disabling depression. Two years later, much of her memory was still gone. "It makes me feel so stupid," she said. "I almost wish I were back resting and vegetating."

Still, I didn't want my squeamishness to deprive Jeff of treatment that might help him. ECT had been in use with thousands of patients, usually for severe depression, since April 1938, when two Italian psychiatrists first applied it without apparent problems to a schizophrenic patient in Rome, although I could find no record of the long-term outcome or aftereffects of that treatment. Over the years results had been controversial but considered generally useful. Most memory loss, though not all, was trivialized as minor and temporary. The operational techniques had been refined; the number of treatments had been reduced, usually to twelve (it often used to be one hundred); and the amount of electric current had been cut to an average of one hundred volts administered for one-tenth to five-tenths of a second.

Overriding to me were Jeff's feelings about his worsening state. He was no longer questioning that he was ill. He informed me that a fellow patient had told him how much she had been helped by shock treatments and that he was convinced he needed them. "The way things are going it's inevitable," he told me. I did not want Jeff to feel his despair was ignored. He told his mother he wanted the treatments immediately.

I was still not convinced that the likely benefits were worth the risk of a permanent memory loss, and so Kaplan arranged for an evaluation of Jeff's overall status at the federal government's National Institute of Mental Health in suburban Washington. The checkup was to last three days. Instead, it took fourteen. When his mother, brother, and I gathered for a final meeting with several of the NIMH doctors who had been examining Jeff in relays, the message that we took away was simple: Jeff was a very, very sick fellow. We were to go with God, take him back to California, and follow the local doctors' orders. The verdict on electroshock was something like a shrug of the shoulders. No one overtly opposed it.

Kaplan interpreted this outcome as a mandate to proceed. So did Rick Robinson, still taking a friendly interest. He thought that my fears were overreactive. He had administered shock treatments lots of times, he said. There wasn't much to them. Some of his patients had driven themselves to the hospital and home again after some rest.

El Camino was a large, modern general hospital in suburban Mountain View where Kaplan normally cared for his patients. Jeff had been in and out of its isolated "psych" ward repeatedly and had found the atmosphere welcoming. He even enjoyed his long talks with the psychiatrist who gave the shock treatments, a most pleasantly reassuring former priest. I also found him sympathetic.

The orientation paper we were given on "procedures of electroconvulsive therapy," three single-spaced, typewritten pages excerpted from Task Force Report 14 of the American Psychiatric Association, was less encouraging, its kid-glove wording notwithstanding:

> Treatment consists of passing a small, carefully controlled electric current between two electrodes applied to the head. . . . Prior to each treatment, the patient receives an injection to reduce secretions in the mouth. . . . The patient is given an anesthetic in the vein which leads to sleep within a matter of minutes. He/she is then given a second medication in the vein which produces muscular relaxation. The patient should experience no discomfort or pain during the treatment; he/she does not feel the electric current and most individuals have no memory of the treatment. When the treatment is given, the patient, who is already asleep, has generalized muscular contractions of a convulsive nature. These contractions, which have

been modified and "softened" by the second medication in the vein, last approximately 60 seconds. Minutes later, the patient slowly awakens and may experience temporary confusion similar to that seen in patients emerging from any type of brief anesthesia. . . . Headache, mild muscle soreness or nausea sometimes occur. . . . Haziness of memory may develop. This memory impairment is usually temporary.

"Usually" is a word that I had grown to mistrust since Jeff's symptoms and reactions rarely seemed to fall into any "usual" range. Withal, it would have been mulish and primitive of me to continue my stalling. Although everybody in the family had signed on to going ahead, more anguish developed. We had not counted on the capability of the California bureaucracy to make a heartrending decision even more nerve-racking than necessary.

Skittishness about ECT, much like mine, had left the authorities increasingly gun-shy about authorizing the treatments. Particularly in California, a civil rights movement by (and on behalf of) mental patients was crusading against involuntary measures restricting rights of dysfunctional citizens like Jeff. Santa Clara County maintained a patients' rights advocate, a lawyer, whom Jeff had discovered and had contacted on several occasions when he felt that officialdom was ignoring his vision of his interests.

For a patient such as my son, who, like a great many other schizophrenics, was legally a ward of the county, a judge's explicit authorization was required to permit ECT. Regrettably, the application on behalf of Jeff pushed the bureaucracy into temporary paralysis. Its medical and judicial arms were not synchronized. The hospital had withdrawn Jeff's protective medications, but the judge had not issued an OK to proceed with the treatments. In the language of psychiatry, Jeff had "regressed" and "decompensated." In my language, he was bucking in restraints and screaming.

The records do not show how long the stalemate of the authorities kept him in this state. I seem to have blocked the details. The deadlock certainly continued for a number of days. The fact that I was at hand to blast the system out of inaction was not as significant, however, as the mere presence of a family advocate like myself on an occasion such as this. Many schizophrenics lack such a spokesman. Also, Jeff would not have commanded a forceful, timely intervention if I had heeded the well-meant advice of some of my medical and family advisers and removed myself from the day-to-day management of Jeff's managers—never mind that the managers were not a unified command and were sometimes at loggerheads.

How "appropriate" it had once seemed to let doctors be doctors, to leave the patient to the mercies of persons in authority who were nominally responsible; how appropriate and how wrong, how devastating the consequences could be.

When my phone appeals to various officials yielded nothing, I sent this telegram to the judge, signed by Edith and myself:

> You may be unaware of intolerable hardship inadvertently imposed on my son Jeffrey Wyden, a ward of the Santa Clara Public Guardian's Office, by delay in okaying electric shock treatments for him at El Camino Hospital. As County Counselor Susan Chapman has been advised, four Palo Alto psychiatrists recommend these treatments urgently. So do three teams of doctors at the National Institute of Mental Health in Washington. Currently my son is unintentionally subjected to unnecessary torment because medications had to be withdrawn which would render electroshock treatments ineffective. Jeff's parents plead with you to stop delays at once. Society has created a terrible dilemma for this helpless person. Regulations designed to help are hurting him terribly. We owe it to him to get him out of this trap right now.

That worked. Jeff was given a series of twelve shock treatments in June. The treatments were uneventful, the aftermath unexpected: electrifying, simply wonderful. His mind cleared. His spirits soared. Almost immediately, out came the "old Jeff," witty, sharp, self-assured. It was like a liberating magic trick. I have a letter from him, assuring me that my fears had been groundless, written in a large, clear, relaxed script, much different from the constricted little curls to which I had grown accustomed from his letters in recent years. I was dumbfounded.

Years later, Jeff talked about his memory of another encounter that confirmed his grasp on reality at the time of his shock treatments. He was bantering at El Camino with Rick Robinson, who sometimes filled in for Reed Kaplan. Jeff brought up Mark Vonnegut and his book. Jeff had read it and remembered that young Vonnegut had also been subject to ECT treatment.

"I was scared to death of it," Vonnegut had written. But also: "It probably did me some good."

Finding himself in the same situation, Jeff told Robinson that he had Vonnegut's writings once again on his mind, not only the autobiography but also an article that Vonnegut had written for *Harper's* magazine entitled "Why I Want to Bite R.D. Laing." Robinson also remembered reading the article, and the two of them enjoyed a snicker about Laing's eventual fall from grace.

Right after his ECT, Jeff also sent me a photo taken in the sunshiny garden on the hospital grounds. He is leaning back, relaxed, against a pillar, smiling the quizzical grin of old times, clean-shaved except for a neatly trimmed mustache, wearing a pristine white shirt and neat trousers, holding the inevitable cigarette. A decade later, I still pull that photo out of the files when I'm feeling low. It shows that not everything turns out badly, not even in schizophrenia. At least not consistently.

Within three months, though, Jeff was on the way back to the hospital. His genie had whooshed back into the bottle.

Nearly a decade after Jeff's two-week stay among the schizophrenia establishment at NIMH Washington, second thoughts stirred in my head. Shouldn't these specialists have at least mentioned that clozapine was at that very time revolutionizing schizophrenia treatment? They had said not a word, even though I had read the then-already-ancient news about the medication's extraordinary effectiveness in the *New York Times* three days before we checked Jeff into NIMH.

I don't know why I didn't take the initiative and ask about the drug. I suppose that the tentative tone of the *Times* article left me less than alert. Consider, too, that I wasn't a doctor on the case. When I queried NIMH in the midnineties about their failure to bring up clozapine, a social worker who had reviewed Jeff's file replied: "I cannot answer the question as to why you were not alerted to its existence."

This stimulated my interest in Jeff's NIMH file, and I was able to review it with the help of a doctor who had never met Jeff and had not been involved in his case in 1987. The report, six pages, single spaced, noted at least one remarkable initiative taken by the Washington experts while Jeff was in their care. It concerned lithium, which everyone had long regarded as indispensable to regulate his mood swings. "Lithium was discontinued," the report stated in describing Jeff's stay at NIMH. No details were given.

Regarding the usefulness of ECT, the doctors were less definitive. "It is felt that Jeffrey may benefit from a course of electro-convulsive therapy," their report stated on page six. Two lines farther, it seemed to disagree with itself: "There is no clear indication for electro-convulsive therapy at this time."

The doctor who helped me untangle what happened to Jeff in Washington was not so ambiguous. "He went to the wrong shop," this specialist said.

"These were not schizophrenia people. They worked with ECT strictly for depression. They had no more relevance to Jeff than the man on the moon."

This caused me to turn again to the NIMH case file. At the top it quoted Jeff: "CHIEF COMPLAINT: 'I'm here to see if shock treatments will help me.' " This was the solution to the riddle of the Washington crew's irrelevance. It was the patient's fault. He happened to phrase his needs too vaguely.

As I retrace the chaos that followed Jeff's experiment with ECT in the summer of 1987, I am disappointed at the sluggishness of my perception. Fifteen years into his illness, it had not yet dawned on me how formidable a character I was dealing with when it came to my son's responses to his "brittle" fate. The sequence of glitches during the course of that season finally lifted the fog from me. A note that I wrote on December 15 to "all concerned with Jeff's illness—re: his latest relapse" tracked his spin downward, step-by-step, including a cast of (once again) mostly new psychiatrists and citing new treatment places:

> It was a tragic and avoidable shame that Dr. Les Becker's careful and effective work, in consultation with Dr. Reed Kaplan, during Jeff's recent stay at East Valley Pavilion [a branch of Valley Medical Center] went down the drain when Jeff left there. . . . When Jeff left for SART [a halfway house] I tried at once to communicate with the medical person there, Dr. X, that Jeff had a most complex history. . . . I wrote a detailed cautionary letter and later sent him a telegram, once again pleading with him to contact Dr. Kaplan for background information. For unknown reasons, Dr. X and Dr. Kaplan did not talk until . . . the cat was out of the bag; Jeff was on the way to becoming manic. Jeff's mother had said so to the SART staff. . . . Disaster became predictable, but nobody did anything. . . . I don't know how long it was between whatever day Jeff was last seen by a physician at SART and the time he was transferred to Samaripa house, sounding high to me on the phone, but it clearly was too long. Nor do I know Jeff's medications prescribed at SART . . . except that Jeff talked the doctor there into giving him Elavil, which Dr. Kaplan says is definitely contraindicated for him.

More and more, the establishment seemed no longer to regard Jeff as a person. He kept "falling through the cracks." For the overworked people who controlled his day-to-day life, he had become flotsam, all but inanimate. I suppose that one should perhaps have been quiet and grateful that the public mental health system commanded so many places where doctors bothered with unproductive citizens like Jeff at all. But while they were at it, why did they have to stop just short of doing the full job and then shoot themselves and Jeff in the foot again and again? Was he just too inconvenient? Did they possibly want, unconsciously, to kick him, to punish him for nasty behavior? I confronted the attitude of the treaters in my December 15 note to all hands as diplomatically as my anger allowed:

> Like others, I get furious and resentful when Jeff levels preposterous charges against me, insults me, hangs up on me, etc. I hope that some of the professionals involved in his treatment *won't start holding his illness against him*. Let me put it to everybody straight: what if *you* had been f———d over by the System, as he was in the above sequence of events and for years before that, over and over and over again, and as disastrously as Jeff has been? Wouldn't you be contemptuous and insulting and obnoxious in your helpless state, just as Jeff is? I think Jeff is a true hero. It's remarkable that he hasn't treated us all much worse than he has.

A hero, yes. The frustrating events of that autumn had succeeded in letting me see my son plainly. I think this helped him and me. Ever since, I have confronted him with himself as a gallant warrior when we hit crises.

"Jeff, you're my hero!" I say to him.

"Really?" he asks, smiling, wanting to believe.

The long course of my education was inching ahead, the teacher now mostly Andrew Abarbanel, M.D., of Los Altos, California. Andy's background was in psychoanalysis, starting out at McLean Hospital at Harvard Medical School (he also held a Ph.D. in physics). The stereotypical analyst style—glum, neutral, the reactions confined to an occasional "hm"—was alien to him. He was recommended by Rick Robinson, who sensed Jeff's need for an outlet into which he might pour his brooding and intellectualizing. Robinson had been finding him by then sufficiently insightful to possibly benefit from talk therapy, even though the medications had brought him only on-again-off-again periods of stability.

I've been profiting from Andy since November 19, 1985, when he first wrote cautiously of his hope that Jeff might "cement an alliance" with him, since "people like to understand themselves." He appended a note unprecedented in my experience: "Please feel free to call or write at any time, and I'll do the same." I tested him by writing on November 30:

> Edith finds Jeff extremely lethargic, even by his low standards. He is interested in absolutely nothing, not in TV, not in glancing at a paper, not in going to his Oakland relatives, whom he likes, for Thanksgiving. . . . I told Dr. Koran some weeks ago that I am greatly distressed that Jeff is getting so little out of life and seems so unhappy; that I can't imagine what he is living for. Koran said, "Is that your perception or his?" A neat question, and for a while I thought perhaps Jeff "feels no pain," that I'm suffering more than Jeff is, which is Koran's phrase. On reflection, though, I think this is Koran's thoughtful way of trying to make me feel better, not an assessment of Jeff's frame of mind. I now get very little out of him on the phone, which is not normal, and his mother keeps volunteering how unhappy he clearly is. . . . Granted he has been disabled for a very long time, but he is not a quadriplegic, after all. Yet he pretty much lives like one, and it is clear from his occasional scathing remarks about his condition that he knows it and suffers from it every minute of the day. Please don't misunderstand. My expectations for Jeff could hardly be more modest. All I wish for him is that he regain some feeling for having something to wake up for in the morning.

This rumination set off a written and telephone dialogue that is still a work in progress. Andy became a travel guide to my son's world. He showed me how he managed to insinuate himself into that world as a friend, using the climbing tools of psychotherapy to hack a path through the alien rock formations in Jeff's head. I had never comprehended the inner workings of his obstinate obsession with Annie, the pointless pursuit then in its eleventh year. Andy laid the dynamics bare when he wrote me on February 18, 1986, about Jeff's "remnants" from "developmentally early forms of thought":

> The separation of his wishes and agendas and those of the rest of the world isn't very good. He is bewildered that people don't just do what he wants. . . . My hope for him is that in therapy the underlying cognitive miswirings can be re-wired so that he can come to some comfort with others as independent centers of actions and agendas.

Comfort level was important to Andy, including the comfort of Jeff's father. He picked out my wavelength as well as Jeff's in the same letter:

I know how distressing it is for you to experience what is going on with Jeff, and what is likely to go on for a long time. Your interest is enlightened but has to be practical. That is, what the hell am I doing for Jeff—that's the central problem for you. For me, the question is always, what the hell *can* I do for my patients.

In the same letter, Andy volunteered a glimpse into how he had come to learn, working with psychotics who were often considered impervious to reason:

My training at McLean was all in the shadow of Alfred Stanton, grand old man of psychotherapy with very disturbed patients. He told me as I left New England that I should be the representative here of how to treat disturbed patients with psychotherapy, and I am learning much more from my patients as time goes by.

I complained to Andy that Jeff was still scoffing at the flawless reasoning of the lectures that I tended to deliver in an authoritative, fatherly style. Logic and common sense, as I've said, rarely made a dent in his armor. "*Jawohl, Herr Kommandant!*" he often barked at me in his imitation of Sergeant Schulz, the Nazi guard in the prisoner-of-war camp of his favorite TV series, *Hogan's Heroes*. Obviously, Andy employed a different tone. On December 19, 1986, he disclosed his method:

I call it "The Modified Stanton." Alfred Stanton, 6′3″, white-haired and my hero, used to say, "I always try not to scare them. I act a little dull, slow and boring." I told him I couldn't do that, that I'm too interesting. I think he was amused. . . . With Jeff I just accept outwardly what he says. . . . I would recommend something of the same general approach: treat what he says with benign acceptance.

In time I discovered that Andy's personal "Modified Stanton" was very modified indeed. Stanton was an analyst, an inspired one. "Teach your patient how his bloomin' mind works," this Harvard professor told his residents. "Listen and allow the patient to tell you what he thinks and feels. Understand the experience rather than try to change him. If someone calls you superficial, say 'Thank you.' " The transference with his students was so finely tuned that, according to legend, everyone at McLean Hospital smoked Stanton's brand of cigarettes.

Once Andy had heard Stanton reluctantly concede that a patient's improvement was not due to his analytic work. "Maybe it's the lithium," he said. But generally the professor did not welcome medication. When the new *DSM-III* manual did not recommend psychotherapy for psychotics, Stanton was quoted as grumbling, "It's a giant step . . . backward."

Andy started working with patients on his own in California shortly before Stanton's death in 1983, and the disdain of his student days toward medications promptly changed. By the time my son became his patient, he was using pills extensively. And they were not enough. Throughout his year with Bernie, Jeff saw Andy irregularly and with little success, despite precautions. Andy's antennae were sharp, and he was quick to pull away when Jeff became agitated, as he so frequently did. Years later, when I sat in on one of their sessions, I watched how Jeff got prickly and Andy simply grinned, got up, and said to Jeff, "Come on, let's go to the bagel place." Which we did, thereby probably short-circuiting a major fury.

Sometimes, bagel parties did not pacify sufficiently. It wasn't a surprise that Jeff celebrated the advent of 1988 by firing Andy. On January 21, Andy, typically, commented that the patient is always right:

> Jeff is indeed sick of me. And he's pretty manicky. He doesn't want me to come back until he says so. I think that makes sense; that is, he is upset enough now not to make any real sense out of my being there seeing him, to insult me for an hour, walk out and smoke. Ultimately that sort of treatment doesn't help. It will just make him guilty, and me tired. . . . Jeff always does call me after firing me. In his increased agitation, he can't tell me from you, he's mad at both of us for controlling him.

At about the same time, Jeff sent me a note from East Valley Pavilion that did not blame Andy for anything. Jeff explained the move this way:

> I don't see that I need "psychotherapy" any longer. As the novel *Portnoy's Complaint* pointed out, many people who "see" psychoanalysts such as Andy become dependent bellyachers.

Jeff could be a champion bellyacher, but he did not wish to be considered dependent. In another note of that period, he wrote:

> Have a seat, pour yourself a drink and brace yourself for the latest news. I'm considering firing some more doctors, in my own atrocious way.

He was still hospitalized at the time, but my records fail to show which doctors he wanted out of his life at that moment. Curiously, the last note went on to casually quote Jerry DeFraites on the value of lithium. Jeff hadn't seen Dr. DeFraites for about a decade, but any doctor whose opinion he wished to cite was always instantly whisked into Jeff's thinking as if he were still standing by as part of the current medical retinue. Such a summons was especially likely if Jeff had retained a fondness for the remembered doctor, and he had very much liked DeFraites, a resident at Stanford during his brief time as Jeff's psychiatrist.

DeFraites was another rare gem like Andy. He listened. He conveyed to Jeff that Jeff was important. "You have to be somebody who values psychosis," the doctor told me recently. "Your patient is trying to tell you something. It can't be seen as the ravings of a madman." The patient was merely using a difficult foreign language.

Like Andy, DeFraites found humility useful. After Stanford, he had administered double-blind drug tests for schizophrenics at NIMH. Half of them were being given placebos. "It was an ego-bruising experience," he recalled with a chuckle. "When they broke the blind, the patients who got the medication were the ones who improved, not the ones with whom you'd been doing psychotherapeutic work two or three times a week."

DeFraites elevated the issue of side effects to rank as most important in a schizophrenic patient's perception of his priorities. Twenty years after its publication, the doctor cited for me from memory some portions of a letter that an associate had written to the *American Journal of Psychiatry*. The letter writer was Dr. Kenneth S. Kendler, then a medical student at Stanford, currently a leading researcher on the genetics of schizophrenia. Kendler reported the devastating effects that had hit him personally when, as an experiment, he administered Haldol to himself.* DeFraites clearly wished he had written that letter.

---

* Here is how Kendler described his self-induced *akathisia*, which Jeff experienced involuntarily for months:

> At 9:00 p.m. I received 1 mg of haloperidol intramuscularly. I felt drowsy by 9:15. By 9:30 the drowsiness had dissipated and was replaced by a diffuse, slowly increasing anxiety. My uneasiness soon began to focus on the idea that I could not possibly sit still for the rest of the experiment. I imagined walking outside: the idea of walking was particularly attractive. I could not concentrate on what I had been reading. . . . I found myself pacing up and down the lab, shaking and wringing my hands. Whenever I stopped moving, the anxiety increased. . . . I walked very quickly to my bicycle which brought some relief from the anxiety. At home, I walked rapidly several times around the apartment complex and then ran up and down the long driveway. Once inside my apartment, I did a little jig, moving my arms and legs quickly. . . . To have something to do, I gladly washed a large pile of

"A workable doctor-patient relationship can be established with the schiz-ophrenic patient," wrote the unduly revered analyst Dr. Frieda Fromm-Reichmann. "If and when this seems impossible, it is due to the doctor's personality difficulties, not the patient's psychopathology."

Most psychiatrists would vehemently deny this proposition.

---

dishes that were not mine—normally not my favorite activity. I was able to get to sleep by 2:00 a.m., two hours past my usual bedtime. . . . With the possible exception of going on stage on an opening night, I cannot remember any feeling of anxiety so intense. Second, the sense of a foreign influence forcing me to move was dramatic. . . . I was pacing and wringing my hands. . . . I believe that warning patients of the possibility of this reaction is particularly important. The sense of a foreign force driving one to move, with the con-comitant anxiety, might be extremely disconcerting to an uninformed patient who is already struggling with psychosis.

CHAPTER 21

Three Breakthroughs

T HE HISTORIES of pharmacology are full of what the chroniclers describe
as "Eureka!" moments—defining markers of watershed victories won after
years or decades of laboratory chores, toil, and hope, expectations dashed,
questioned, pushed ahead by millimeters, or exploded in disaster, possibly
even death, for the experimenters.

When I learned in 1994 that at least three brand-new antipsychotic medications, all of them reportedly superior to clozapine, the current standard for
treating schizophrenia, were racing toward approval by the Food and Drug
Administration, I decided to trace these potential successors to the "Eureka!"
moments of their inception, to more fully understand them, to see how confident I would be in their use for Jeff. I came to understand how incredible the
achievements were and what remarkable good these drugs would do.

In October 1989, Dr. Nick Tye, Eli Lilly's chief biochemist at Erl Wood
Research Park outside London, had felt severely depressed. In 1982 he and his
colleagues had synthesized an experimental antipsychotic, known only as No.
170053. Tye was persuaded beyond the slightest doubt that this chemical relative
of clozapine was safe and superior to the Sandoz product that the worldwide
psychopharmacology industry was determined to improve upon. The stakes
were high. Publicity, honors, and a long-lasting financial bonanza were possible.

To his mounting frustration, No. 170053 rested in suspended animation. His management was hesitant to commit $400 million or more to develop it. In the fall of 1989, however, his mood and his career were lifted. He was among some forty Eli Lilly research people assembled for a major conference in an auditorium at home base in Indiana. Speaking to them was an executive whom Tye knew well, Dr. Melvin Perelman, formerly the director of Erl Wood, now president of Eli Lilly central nervous system (CNS) research after more than thirty years with the firm. Perelman was discussing Tye's compound, the drug that would eventually be named Olanzapine and ultimately Zyprexa.

"That's our Manhattan Project," Tye heard Perelman announce, to his enormous delight. Tye was old enough to remember that "Manhattan Project" had been the code name for the World War II scientific and industrial feat that brought forth the first atomic bomb and changed the world.

Dr. Jeffrey Goldstein, the short and exuberant chief of electrophysiological pharmacology for the British-owned Zeneca Pharmaceuticals in the suburban outskirts of Wilmington, Delaware, had been modifying Perlapine, a clozapine derivative, since 1984. Tests with laboratory rats had convinced him that his new compound, U-24207, was an effective antipsychotic and structurally sufficiently different from clozapine to be patentable, but his superiors wanted specific laboratory evidence before committing themselves.

One warm afternoon in the summer of 1985, Goldstein, excited and triumphant, rushed into the office of his boss, Ralph Childs, the director of pharmacology. Childs was at his desk. *His* boss, Mort Goldberg, the vice president for research, was standing next to him. Both looked surprised. Goldstein was obviously pregnant with big news.

"Hey, Ralph," he said, "the drug worked in the electrophysiological model!"

Both of his bosses hurried toward him, arms outstretched in congratulations.

"I think we have a drug," Goldberg said. They had given birth to Seroquel.

For Drs. John Hyttel and Jörn Arndt, the "Eureka!" moment arrived in 1987. As directors of pharmacology research for the old and respected A. S. Lundbeck Company on the industrial periphery of Copenhagen, Denmark, they were well aware of the American competition for a clozapine successor. They were puzzled by one aspect of the drug: Why did it work without side effects? They were still asking the question when I talked with them in 1995.

Their hunt for the right chemical "profile" had proceeded regardless. They zeroed in on some one hundred likely compounds and tested them with their rats. One substance, LU 23-174, matched their precise profile needs. "It was serendipity," the doctors told me. That drug would come to be called Sertindole.

It took eighteen months to get the medication patented and to negotiate secrecy agreements with eight American pharmaceutical companies. Little Lundbeck needed a rich partner for further development and, above all, the financing to bring its invention to market. "It was like making a marriage match," said Dr. Hyttel after Lundbeck had arrived at a partnership deal with Abbott Laboratories in Chicago, which customarily invested nearly one billion dollars a year in new product research and development.

I was early for my appointment with Dr. William Wirshing in Building 210 of the Brentwood Veterans Administration Hospital, a look-alike little community in gleaming white. Its hilly streets were laid out in a pleasant flow, much like those of Bel Air, a ghetto of Los Angeles's wealthy, not far away.

Schizophrenic patients were cared for in Building 210. More than a dozen of them were milling expectantly around the front door, waiting to be called. It was medication time. All were men, young or middle-aged, shoulders stooped, heads down, and they were silent. Their clothes seemed slept-in. Their faces looked gray and were barely visible under lush beards and long, mostly unkempt hair. These silent figures seemed to wish to hide. The same illness united them; it also kept each of them separate, alone.

It occurred to me that until recently Jeff could not have been admitted to this group. In the hierarchy of schizophrenics, he had not ranked as much recovered as these men. Unlike Jeff, they were not locked up. When Jeff was hospitalized, it was at Crestwood in San Jose, a prisonlike, locked facility where I was sluiced through a set of escape-proof double doors. This usually took time because the attendants were few and kept busy coping with their bedlam and therefore sometimes slow to hear the bell intruding from the calm outside.

I spent most of my visiting hours walking in large circles with Jeff. We hiked around and around the fenced-in yard with its trampled-down grass and its sea of crushed cigarette butts. Jeff kept bumming lights for his smokes from our fellow walkers, who moved slowly in the same circular route to nowhere.

It was a ritual that never seemed to cease. The chronic craving for the nicotine in tobacco was an unforgiving force that held Jeff and the other walkers captive. Risk of fire outlawed all matches, so the walkers depended on one another to keep alive the eternal flame of their carcinogenic diversion. Like the patients waiting in front of Dr. Wirshing's building in Brentwood, Jeff's people at Crestwood had nothing to say to each other except for an occasional muttered "thanks" when a light was passed on.

I had been told that Bill Wirshing, thirty-eight, was one of the new breed of scientist-psychiatrists pushing research in schizophrenia to its outer edge. And in room 5, his laboratory in the bare stone basement of Building 210, amid the clutter of mysterious technical equipment, the lanky, fast-moving doctor explained himself. Having come to psychiatry research via his original field of study, engineering, Wirshing was measuring the patterns of disabling muscle contractions in tardive dyskinesia for the first time with electronic precision.

"The trouble with psychiatry is that we do it with the ears," he said. "Psychiatrists are terrible at observing. I hope my machinery will take the place of the eyes."

It was tedious labor to which the doctor brought the same warmth that other schizophrenia researchers had demonstrated. "I love the illness," Wirshing declared, "and I love the guys who are struggling with it." Which sounded strange until I made the connection to Jeff and my perception of him as a hero.

This was how Wirshing came to introduce me to John Guy, fifty-four, his patient for eight years. "He was the most delusional I've seen," the doctor remembered. Diagnosed as paranoid schizophrenic in Florida, where he was selling insurance until he was twenty-eight, John had an IQ of 140 and had studied mechanical engineering at Georgia Tech University. During the Cuban Missile Crisis, he served with the air force in Alaska and flew behind Soviet lines, communicating with U.S. nuclear submarines.

After fourteen months in Chattahoochee State Hospital, his schizophrenia took the usual confused course. "I was just existing," Guy told me, "I didn't know what I was doing." His hallucinations were vivid: "The KGB was after me; I could see their gunfire flashing." Desperate, he overdosed on his Prolixin medication. Sometimes Wirshing heard from him from South America, once from the emergency room of a hospital in Dallas. Their interest in tardive dyskinesia had brought them together. Wirshing was studying the condition; Guy would have given almost anything to get rid of it and to stop taking the Haldol that was causing it.

TD is an all-too-visible and grotesque illness, and sometime after we met and Guy had relaxed with me, he imitated how the disease had affected him when he walked. Somehow he was able to move, although his joints seemed to be manipulated by a mad puppeteer; he was constantly bent so far backward by muscle contractions that I couldn't figure out how he kept himself from toppling.

At the time of his demonstration, we were spending Sunday morning in his two-bedroom apartment in a neat, small row house on a quiet street of central Los Angeles. John was moving normally, effortlessly, and spoke of his past life with animation, humor, and only a trace of resentment at his lot over the decades. It was difficult to reconcile what I was seeing in the fall of 1995 with what I knew of his life up to eighteen months ago.

Eighteen months was the length of time that Wirshing had been giving him the experimental drug Olanzapine, which I was researching. John, open-faced, ruddy, a bit overweight, casually dressed, was not given to excessive talk. "It turned me around," he said. "I feel great. I used to have terrible headaches. I haven't had a headache in nearly two years." I knew that this was an understated account. Wirshing had briefed me on the scope of John's turn-around: he had become his boss, in addition to continuing as his doctor, when needed.

John was working thirty-five hours a week for the VA laboratory run by Wirshing and a staff of professionals. He was operating the communications system, routing the extensive traffic of calls and faxes between doctors and patients. He made appointments, evaluated requests for cancellations, and channeled emergencies.

"He's solid as a rock," Wirshing said, "assessing the importance of calls, knowing when to interrupt." Nor was John shaken by events that would have been exceptionally difficult for a paranoid schizophrenic (or anyone with paranoid tendencies). Shortly before I met the two men, $1,500 had been stolen from the laboratory, setting off a sizable, unsuccessful investigation. As Wirshing saw this delicate situation, John was telling himself, "I know the doc knows I didn't do it." To which the doctor added with some pride, "He's my assistant."

John, in turn, was comfortable and determined in his telephone dealings with patients. He knew all of them by first name, and they knew that he had been one of them until not long ago. When a patient phoned and reported,

"I'm throwing things at people who aren't there," John talked to the man about anger and said, "I felt that way." Whenever someone wanted to cancel an appointment, John tried to set up another date right away. If that wouldn't work, he made sure that the patient spoke with a doctor. John was truly Wirshing's right hand—thanks to Olanzapine, his own strong will, and a young doctor-engineer who fell in love with schizophrenia.

Nor did John confine himself to the world of the ill and the formerly ill. I had noticed in Wirshing's hectic laboratory that the walls were filled with large, vivid paintings. The painter was John. He had taken up art during a hospitalization in 1979 and had been refining his technique steadily ever since. Mostly he did landscapes and biblical scenes.

When I saw him at his home, he took me into his spare bedroom—a remarkable sight. More than a dozen new works were in various stages of progress, and painting had ceased to be just a hobby. "I've sold quite a few," John said shyly. When I pressed him a bit, he disclosed that two of his works hung in the Vatican, four were on loan to the Metropolitan Museum of Art, and one had fetched $2,500.

"That's just one case," said Jeff dismissively when I related to him John's experience with Olanzapine. Still dubious about all medications, Jeff was not about to let himself be impressed by an experimental new drug still not widely in use and not authorized for general distribution. So I told him about my trip to the UCLA Harbor Medical Center in Torrance and Dr. Jambur Ananth.

A professor of psychiatry at UCLA, trained by the best researchers in the field, Ananth had been working with schizophrenic patients for more than twenty years. As soon as I mentioned Olanzapine, his manner was transformed. He smiled broadly and turned into an eager raconteur of stories about his eighty patients who had been testing Olanzapine for a year or more.

"It's definitely a revolution," he said. "You wouldn't even think they are patients." Moreover, nobody recognized the striking change in their condition better than the sufferers themselves. "The patients become advocates for the new drugs," Ananth said. "They like to take them. One patient tells another, 'I feel so good.'"

The doctor's elation was not limited to Olanzapine. He had not worked with two of the other new drugs, Sertindole and Seroquel, but he had patients on a still-newer experimental medication, Ziprasidone, from the Pfizer pharmaceutical firm, and had found it just as effective and also nearly free of side effects. As a veteran clinician weighed down by past disappointments, Ananth could not quite trust his good fortune. So he was tempering his elation with contrarian caution.

"Will the new drugs make the chronicity of the illness go away? No," he said. "Will they be a cure? No. They are palliatives, but they've taken us one step further." And for many of his patients, the step was long indeed.

Ananth told me of Jim, twenty-three, who had never interacted with anyone until he suddenly badly beat up a fellow patient. On Olanzapine, Jim had started to live with his parents, met a girlfriend, and worked at a full-time job as an electronic repairman for twelve dollars an hour.

Ron, thirty-two, had been hearing voices almost nonstop for years. After seven months on Olanzapine, he was busy filling out job applications. "My mind came back," he told the doctor.

Another patient's mother wrote Ananth an eight-page letter. Her son had survived miraculously after jumping from a sixth-floor window. He was going to college after a year on Olanzapine. "My son is reborn," the mother wrote.

Jeff shrugged off Dr. Ananth's eighty patients much as he had dismissed John Guy's rebirth. None of these people seemed to him to have much relevance to his own potential convalescence. Why were so many dramatic case histories not persuasive to him, seemingly not even of interest? Why couldn't he identify with them? I could only guess that we were faced with yet another example of logic not striking him as logical. He still lived in a place different from the world of the relatively well. His mind was not in tune with ours.

To satisfy my own mind, if not Jeff's, I decided to pursue the Olanzapine trail in still more detail and talk privately to patients who had been taking the drug for some time. So in the summer of 1996, I had myself introduced to two women by their doctors; one patient in Los Angeles, the other in New York. The former had been taking Olanzapine for three years, the other for two. Both were astoundingly cheerful and well.

Marion in California began hearing weird voices at age seventeen and was taken to a hospital. "Ah, we have a friendly schizophrenic here!" she remembered a doctor calling out. She was given Haldol. "It was awful," Marion said. "I had tremors, drooling. I had a feeling I was not being there and I was still hearing voices." They told her she was "somebody great, a chosen person."

Marion managed to reach her senior year in college, with the first of fifteen hospitalizations along the way. In between, she spent months on the streets and in shelters. As a determined optimist, she denied her schizophrenia diagnosis and called herself manic-depressive. The doctors believed her and put her on lithium, but her delusions persisted. "The sidewalks seemed to be roller-coasting in waves," she told me.

With her good looks, infectious smile, and bubbly personality, she found a loving husband, a school administrator. They had a son, who was a police officer, twenty-eight and married when I met Marion, and a daughter, twenty-five, a police-radio dispatcher, but Marion's persisting symptoms broke up the marriage.

The experimental Olanzapine that Marion was given at UCLA Harbor Medical Center enabled her to return to college for her degree in psychology, and she was looking for a husband. Work remained problematic. At a secretarial job she couldn't concentrate sufficiently. As a restaurant chef ("I love to cook"), the pace was frantic and the waitresses' abbreviations on the food orders were too difficult to make out fast enough.

"Mostly, I feel peaceful, but sometimes I still get panicky and feel vulnerable," Marion said. Her therapist, Michael W. Smith, medical director of the Harbor UCLA outpatient clinic, believed that her remaining symptoms were residual effects attributable to the severity and length of her illness—Marion was by now forty-nine—and would gradually subside. Her case worker, Yoshi Arai, said he believed that Olanzapine would be most beneficial to patients for whom such negative symptoms as vocational handicaps were dominant.

Marion was seeing her doctor only once every two months these days, and so was Helen, thirty-four, whom I met in Manhattan. She had started classes at a community college in Massachusetts during 1985 when she heard voices telling her to drink a lot of beer and go to New York. She drifted into alcoholism, got minor trouble with the police, and vainly asked the judge for help. "They wouldn't let me see a psychiatrist," she said. "They said I was imagining things."

Obeying her voices, Helen went to New York and spent four years as a homeless vagrant. She slept on park benches, occasionally in a Salvation Army shelter, and most often in "the hole," a dark space in the basement of the Port Authority Bus Terminal. The voices kept urging her to drink.

Drunk, chain-smoking, and suffering from scabies, Helen was eventually picked up and taken to a municipal hotel for the homeless. A psychiatrist put her on lithium and Atavan, then on Trilafon, which made her throw up. Shaking with anxiety and akithisia (she knew this term for restlessness), she did little better on Prolixin. Stelazine dehydrated her. And then her fortunes shifted to forward gear at long last. She was sent to the director of the schizophrenia program at St. Luke's–Roosevelt Hospital Center, which is part of Columbia University. He was prescribing Olanzapine for the Eli Lilly clinical trials.

By coincidence, the doctor's name was Peter J. Weiden. At forty, he had already published an impressive body of research in scientific journals. I had liked this psychiatrist when he lectured at a seminar for a convention of the American Psychiatric Association. He was extroverted, apple-cheeked, and the only doctor I ever met who took off his jacket and rolled up his shirt sleeves before speaking to a professional audience. The manner and the dress code matched.

Helen was still wide-eyed about Olanzapine. "It's done wonders," she told me. "It got me out of bed."

She had stopped drinking. She had not had a cigarette for a year and two months. She was still very heavy but had just lost three pounds. She lived in a snug room of a well-kept publicly supported apartment project and worked full-time in the laundry of a big corporation's employee gym. She considered this very temporary employment and was attending horticulture classes at an agency called Transitional Employment Training, planning to work on flower arrangements for a floral shop.

"I'm the kind of person who wants to accomplish something," she said. The words came out sounding perfectly natural.

Helen was the first of some twenty patients whom Weiden treated for Lilly after he volunteered for the Olanzapine trials. His original expectations were not high. He had heard that the trial subjects had initially been undermedicated, so first results were not impressive. Once the dosage was adjusted, the medication performed well beyond Weiden's hopes.

"It knocked my socks off," was how he put it. "I couldn't believe how much better the patients did."

What happened to Helen?

"She started looking like a person," Dr. Weiden said. "I could understand what she was saying. She started making sense. She had been so thought-disordered!"

On a wellness scale of one to ten, she originally rated about three. Soon she rated five. Progress, though modest at first, was relatively excellent. "It was the best I've ever seen," said Dr. Weiden. "Whether you're living independently or not is a huge thing in someone's life. Sustained benefits leave a profound emotional effect."

At the same time, I checked on still another Olanzapine patient, a twenty-nine-year-old man at my friend Skip Pope's McLean Hospital, in whom I had taken an interest since the previous spring. He had been incapacitated for a decade with delusions, hallucinations, and other symptoms more profound than Jeff had experienced. When my son was vainly offered participation in the Olanzapine trials, Skip had arranged for me to share the cost of the preparatory paperwork with the father of his hospital charge. By the time I inquired in the summer, the patient lived in his own apartment, worked part-time with retarded children, and was back finishing college.

"He truly has his old personality back," the family told Skip.

I finally felt reassured. The future of Olanzapine seemed reasonably secure.

In the race to have their drugs formally approved by the FDA and brought to market, Olanzapine's principal rival, Sertindole, seemed also to be progressing well, so its developers, the researchers at Abbott Laboratories, suggested that I meet Gordie in Milwaukee. Schizophrenic for seventeen years, Gordie was recovering after less than a year on the Abbott drug. I found him as spiffy as any executive, wearing a light blue three-piece suit, dignified, heavyset, no longer the diamond in the rough who had worked as a shredder operator in a scrap yard for nine years before going berserk. He remembered the bar where it happened. There seemed to be no triggering cause.

"I ordered a six-pack to go," he said. "Then I sent a card table into the TV. I had no voice. People were looking at me, trying to stop me. I kicked some of them and went home. I threw a suitcase into a cab and took the Greyhound bus to my friend's house in Green Bay. I stayed three days watching TV until the oxygen ran out in that house."

Gordie was reliving his experience now, relating the mad sequence calmly, logically, speaking in an animated but extremely low voice. I had difficulty hearing him.

"I was running across an open field," he said, "and began ripping off all my clothes, screaming and hollering, 'Go home!' I grabbed a big stick and ran down the middle of the main highway. A car kept coming at me, and I drove the stick through the windshield. I was running again. I got to the airport and wanted to steal a plane. Police surrounded me. I remembered my name. Then I was in a bright orange jumpsuit and was taken to the Brown County mental hospital. I thought I died and went to heaven."

Gordie had no idea why he was in that hospital and did not find out for more than a year that he had schizophrenia. Ultimately, he went through at least six hospitalizations. At various times he was given Thorazine, Haldol, Cogentin, Mellaril, and lithium. What he remembered best was his meanness and that he would rarely talk.

Nevertheless, Gordie found a girl. It didn't last long. So he rented a room, read comic books, watched cartoons on TV, paced and paced and paced the floor, and never went to bed. When he slept, it was at the kitchen table, his head between his arms. He heard voices telling him, "Don't let nobody in your house," and "You don't need no friends, all your friends are dead," and he heard Jesus "rebuke evil spirits and the devil."

Eventually, Gordie became an outpatient at the Milwaukee Veterans Hospital, and in 1994 the doctors there asked him whether he wanted to try a new experimental medication, Sertindole.

"I told them I would try anything," he said, "but I didn't want to come to the hospital. I was afraid of talking to anybody." Ultimately, he persuaded his ex-wife, who had divorced him almost twenty years before, to bring him to the doctors. There was a five-day washout period, with no medications. Gordie had been warned of that and felt prepared. He had great hopes for the new medicine.

"I was like an animal in a cage," he told me, "threatening people. But I didn't touch anybody. I could feel everything happening all over again, but I knew there was a good lock on the door." The new drug worked quickly. "I saw some change in the first week," Gordie said. "After three weeks I stopped shaking. I was waking up and feeling well."

Soon he was getting restful sleep in his apartment and began to clean the place regularly. He still smoked two packs of cigarettes daily, but his appetite returned, and he gained sixty pounds. He planned to surprise his family for Thanksgiving, especially his nieces and nephews. He was applying for jobs and eventually went to work as a custodian in an office building. And he grinned broadly when he reported, "I can have sex again."

I still had trouble hearing Gordie and asked whether his voice had always been so soft. Gordie said no, that he was still getting used to talking to people. He had been out of the habit too long.

When Mel Perelman anointed Olanzapine in 1989 as Lilly's "Manhattan Project," the drug was a dozing orphan. Its erratic history, already stretching back fifteen years, had consistently been out of tune with the industry's public relations terminology. In tracing the creation of any new medication, spokesmen customarily suggested that an orderly "drug development process" was at work. The phrase was a euphemism. Like clozapine, Olanzapine was the winner of two dogfights, first among its corporate creators and then, for a much longer stretch, in worldwide industrial competition. In the antigovernment climate of the 1990s, it was fashionable for pharmaceutical lobbyists to attack the Food and Drug Administration for dawdling. Supposedly, bureaucratic chicanery kept new medications from suffering patients. All told, Olanzapine's gestation did last twenty-two years; demonstrably, however, bureaucracy had little to do with the delay. In actuality, the drug was not "developed." It kept lurching on, sometimes driven, sometimes held back, by all manner of forces.

Clozapine was the most influential of these determinants. Its revolutionary composition motivated an Indian-born scientist for Eli Lilly in Britain, Chakardvasti Brandei, who envisioned the engineering of a "few adjustments" of the clozapine molecule. Colleagues told him such a drug would not differ sufficiently from clozapine to be patentable. But in May 1974, mostly to humor him, he was permitted to go ahead anyway, and the resulting product was significantly different from clozapine. It produced such severe blood toxicity that it had to be abandoned.

By then, Nick Tye and his team were also spurred on by clozapine. Paradoxically, the 1975 agranulocytosis epidemic in Finland increased the pressure for a clozapine-like drug. Clearly there was a market for it, and the formula for an effective drug existed. Only the toxicity plaguing the competitors at Sandoz in Switzerland had to be eliminated. Tye ran tests on more than two hundred compounds, and one of the last, synthesized by his lab in 1980, showed promise—briefly. Tested on healthy volunteers, it caused potentially fatal liver damage and was promptly scrapped.

Tye was not disheartened. Setbacks are routine events in all labs; successes rarities. The clozapine model still intrigued him, and its promise kept him going until, on April 29, 1982, Olanzapine was born in Tye's test tubes. Large-scale animal tests produced no significant extrapyramidal side effects and no agranulocytosis.

Now Eli Lilly management in Indianapolis pronounced itself, as one senior insider recalled, "ambivalent." In their minds, clozapine was a negative influence. The nagging reservation persisted: anything similar to clozapine would eventually produce agranulocytosis. But Tye's rats and dogs stayed well, even when exposed to "huge" doses of Olanzapine. So finally, on September 10, 1986, the company safety committee authorized human tests on a dozen healthy volunteers at St. Mary's Hospital in London. When that went off smoothly, the first psychotic patients were tested, again without difficulties, on December 9, 1988.

Enthusiasm failed to develop in Indianapolis. At issue was the gamble of spending what turned out eventually to run into about half a billion dollars. And the drug still lacked an internal advocate in the corporate headquarters with rank and clout, like Perelman.

"No one was prepared to take it on," Tye told me. "We weren't getting support in Indianapolis. Schizophrenia was a new area for Lilly. It wasn't a CNS company, and other products had priority. We didn't have the people who understood schizophrenia, and it was expensive." Yet after nearly a decade of rejections, Tye refused to give up on his antischizophrenia compound.

Ironically, the company had a history of risk taking. Its first gambler was the founder, Colonel Eli Lilly, a former Confederate artillery officer who had gone bankrupt planting cotton and had briefly run a drugstore. In 1876, with capital of $1,400, he took another chance and set up a tiny laboratory in downtown Indianapolis to manufacture "ethical drugs," the kind dispensed by physicians, rather than quacks.

The colonel had found his calling. Discerning quickly that talent was the crucial ingredient for generating profits, he organized a sterling research department by 1886 and, unprecedentedly, placed a full-time chemist in charge. He encouraged his staff to search for new products outside the firm as well, and one of his associates soon discovered the company's first winner in a medical journal. Called Succus Alterans, it worked for some cases of venereal disease and made the colonel a million dollars by 1890.

In 1922 attention to research brought Lilly its first world-class coup. Biochemical research was headed by Dr. George Henry Alexander Clowes (pronounced "clews"), a minister's son from Britain with irrepressible curiosity, educated at Göttingen and the Sorbonne. He met Dr. Frederick Banting, a shy, impecunious instructor in surgery at a provincial medical school in London, Ontario. Banting would discover insulin for the treatment of diabetes, and in May 1922, Clowes signed an exclusive agreement to make the drug and commit an initial $250,000 toward the creation of an insulin monopoly for Eli Lilly. By 1996 Lilly was still one of the two major insulin manufacturers in the world; annual sales stood at $665 million.

The company has grown explosively. Total sales were $6.7 billion in 1995, net income $2.2 billion. Assets were valued at $14.4 billion. Employment stood at twenty-eight thousand. The star in this lineup was a revolutionary medication born of Eli Lilly research: the antidepressant Prozac, developed in 1972 and first marketed in 1987. From 1994 to 1995, its worldwide sales grew twenty-four percent to exceed a stunning $2 billion, causing the firm's net income to jump by seventy-eight percent.

The overnight success of Prozac turned Lilly into a CNS company. Sales tripled between 1988 and 1989. Prozac was not received as a mere pill; it was a cultural phenomenon. Magazines produced cover stories with headlines such as "How Science Will Let You Change Your Personality with a Pill" (*Newsweek*). Patients reported feeling "better than well." *Listening to Prozac,* by Peter Kramer, became a best-seller.

The backlash was severe: a small minority of patients became violent and suicidal, and Lilly had to defend 150 lawsuits. The drug nevertheless remained irresistible for millions. In the United States alone, an estimated 11.2 million suffered from depression (anxiety was the only more prevalent psychological malaise), and the record was impressive: more than sixty-five percent of the patients receiving prescriptions for Prozac found their symptoms fully relieved in two to six weeks.

The lever of the Prozac revolution was not only in the drug's makeup, which was radically different from earlier antidepressants; the difference was also in the dosage. To go on a regimen of Prozac meant taking one standard-strength pill once a day. Previous medications had to be taken more often and at varying strengths, which caused many patients to be undermedicated by their understandably cautious doctors.

The effect of Prozac on the Lilly organization as a whole was seismic. The publicity whirl drew the firm into national consciousness. Employee morale soared sky-high. The influx of so much unexpected corporate income loosened purse strings for staff expansion and numerous new products as well as extensive aggressive promotion campaigns. The development of Olanzapine was also to be given a boost.

Not until 1994 was one of the drug's most tragic failures revealed. It hit close to home. Randall L. Tobias, the company's chairman and CEO, himself a diabetic, disclosed that his wife, Marilyn, who had suffered from depression for more than twenty years, had committed suicide. Prozac had not worked for her.

Prozac had its godfather in Dr. Solomon Snyder. It is intriguing to speculate whether Prozac would have come into existence if, in 1971, Lilly hadn't invited Snyder from Johns Hopkins University in Baltimore (where he is now chairman of neurosciences) to its Indianapolis laboratories to receive an award and give a lecture.

"Snyder is one of the great minds in modern biological psychiatry," wrote Peter Kramer in his book on Prozac. "Most major developments in American biological psychiatry rely to some degree on an element of Snyder's work." And Snyder probably knows as much about mapping the brain as anyone.

The territory is daunting. The neurons (nerve cells) that make the human brain work number some hundred billion. They communicate at exchanges called synapses, of which there are more than ten trillion. The chemical messengers communicating between the neurons are called neurotransmitters, and these were the topic of Snyder's seminal talk in Indianapolis.

More specifically, he lectured on a research tool he had invented, which he named the "synoptosome." He prepared it by grinding up rat brains. When he exposed it to a neurotransmitter he could see how much of it was taken up. This came to be known as "binding and grinding." The Lilly researchers, pushing to make a better antidepressant, had not known of this possibility. After they met Snyder, they applied it at once, with historic clinical results.

"This procedure almost defied belief," wrote Kramer. "You could more or less blenderize a brain and then divide out a portion that worked the way live nerve endings work." For Snyder, this was but a first step. Two years later, he and an associate were first to find a site (receptor) in the brain that a specific neurotransmitter plugs into. And in 1990, Snyder and his team cultured human brain cells in their laboratory, thereby creating a long-sought research tool: a human cell line on which to experiment.

Since new knowledge of the brain is regarded as the cornerstone of schizophrenia, Snyder's technique became as basic to the research into the disease as the ladder in the construction industry. Nobody had moved so close to a brain cell before, much less cultured one. Snyder's method was direct. He used the brains of deceased children who had been operated on for epilepsy at Johns Hopkins Hospital.

One question has run through Snyder's professional life: What exactly causes schizophrenia? The elusive answer was the end point for most of his investigations. When I looked him up, Snyder, fifty-seven, sounded as tentative in 1996 as one of his medical students. "We know so little," he said sadly. "There's a screw loose, but we don't know which screw."

By 1994 clozapine had triggered not only the industrial horse race between Eli Lilly, Abbott Laboratories, and Zeneca Pharmaceuticals, but additional companies in the United States, Europe, and Japan were rushing to bring other efficacious pills to market. Careers were on the line, as were corporate reputations, profits as reflected in stock prices on Wall Street, domination of a global market, and the ethics of the pharmaceutical industry as viewed by an increasingly critical public.

Widespread shoddy and criminal practices in this business had been the subject of headline-making government investigations for decades.* Gradually, most of these were being brought under control. The charge of profiteering through price gouging, however, remained very much alive and was massively documented.†

Arguably, pharmaceuticals are America's most profitable business. Prescription drug prices shot up 147 percent from the early 1980s to the early 1990s (compared to an overall price level increase of about 50 percent). The price of one of Jeff's medications, Cogentin, used mostly against spasticity in Alzheimer's and neuroleptic side effects, soared 208 percent in the decade.

In response, the American drug industry points to a total outlay of $18.9 billion in 1997 for research and development and argues that its price structure is mandated by the need to recoup this speculative investment and the cost of "dry holes." Also, profits must provide incentives to undertake new gambles.

I hope that competition among the new generations of antipsychotics will keep prices relatively reasonable. But a good word is indicated for the profit motive that moves a market economy. Without these forces, there would almost certainly be no clozapine, no Olanzapine, and the rest. Suffering patients like Jeff would suffer more.

Patients were foremost on the mind of Randy Tobias, the Lilly CEO, when he turned unexpectedly personal in a speech to a 1994 national conference on a seemingly dry topic, "Using Outcomes to Improve Care."

Before a sizable cast of the mental health establishment, he shredded his privacy and spoke feelingly about the tragic "outcome" for just one patient—his wife, Marilyn, recently deceased after twenty-eight years of marriage. Sparing neither himself nor his audience, he related how she had been misdiagnosed and mismedicated for two decades until finally Eli Lilly's own Prozac had failed her. Olanzapine and other future medications would have to do better.

---

* For a dispassionate compilation, see *Corporate Crime in the Pharmaceutical Industry*, by John Braithwaite (Routledge & Kegan Paul, 1984).

† For details, see *Making Medicine—Making Money*, by Donald Drake and Marian Uhlman (Andrews & McMeel, 1993).

CHAPTER 22

In the Pipeline

THE COMPANIES that had pumped more than one billion dollars into the rush to bring out Olanzapine, Sertindole, and Seroquel were only forerunners. Their three entries had not yet been launched into the market when at least eight additional large American pharmaceutical houses were driving still more antischizophrenia drugs through fast-track development toward FDA clearance.

"It's an explosion," Dr. Nina B. Schooler of Pittsburgh University, smiling in delight, told a ballroom filled with clearly pleased doctors assembled for the 1996 meeting of the American Psychiatric Association in New York.

Expectations were running particularly high for another clozapine cousin, Ziprasidone, due for release in 1998. The manufacturer, Pfizer, enjoyed an enviable reputation, and the reports from the clinical trials sounded rosy. Only relatively mild problems were reported: headache, insomnia, some agitation—none of the disabling side effects.

In the end, however, the race for market dominance might not go to the giants. There might be room for small, innovative entrepreneurs. Especially intriguing were the seventy million dollars that Schering-Plough Corporation decided to gamble on the know-how of a Yale professor named John Tallman of Branford, Connecticut.

Tallman was not one of the brash, aggressive, young pirates-in-a-hurry who start up many high-risk technology companies; nor was he the prototypically authoritarian captain of industry. Seemingly relaxed at forty-nine, he had been around: a dozen years as biochemist at NIMH in Washington, then eight years of researching and teaching at Yale, slowly acquiring self-confidence and expertise as he watched drug manufacturers struggle.

"You get to the point where you say, 'I can make better drugs than that,' " Tallman told me, not at all boastfully. So in 1989, he quit the university, recruited a few corporate executives, and amassed three million dollars to start Neurogen, a public company headquartered near the Long Island Sound beaches north of New Haven.

Tallman decided to deal first with the leading emotional scourge of the age, anxiety. Twenty-five million Americans were paying for a great many medications, all causing sedation. In partnership with Pfizer, Tallman and his coworkers, numbering about one hundred by then, developed NGD 91-1. It worked for anxiety without sedation, according to initial trials on 150 test subjects.

From there, Neurogen turned to the schizophrenia market and focused on an unexploited gap in dopamine territory, the D4 receptor, the most complex of the D1 to D5 range. It had not been discovered until 1990. Tallman came up with NGD 94-1, which showed high selectivity only for the D4 receptor. Belief was growing that this receptor was directly implicated in schizophrenia. It worked on a long-suspected site in the brain, and autopsied schizophrenic patients revealed elevated levels—from 200 to 600 percent—of D4. Clozapine also acted disproportionately upon it.

Tallman spent a year talking with about a dozen pharmaceutical houses in search of a rich partner. "There were those who were kicking our tires," he said. "Eventually we did better than that." Schering-Plough gave Neurogen fourteen million dollars up front in a deal that would eventually cost them seventy million dollars plus all the costs of clinical development.

"They'll lose it all," said one researcher, possibly in envy, possibly soured by decades of watching similar development deals crumble.

Already, the research wheel had spun on, moving beyond Tallman. All over the country, senior researchers were getting restless. They talked about "getting off the dopamine treadmill" and eyed entirely different routes into the schizophrenic brain. When I spoke with the grand old man of D4, Philip B. Seaman, professor of biochemistry at the University of Toronto, the discoverer of this receptor, he also sounded impatient.

"We're treating the smoke, not the fire," he told me.

"Prodromal" was a hot-button word among schizophrenia researchers in early 1996. It comes from the Greek word *prodromos,* meaning the forerunner of an event, and referred to newly intensified efforts to identify the earliest signs of schizophrenia's onset. The ambition was spreading to devise methods to head off the disease, to learn how to prevent it in its earliest acute (florid) phase.

This possibility had been haunting me for a quarter of a century. As early as 1972, I had begun retracing hints of abnormalities in Jeff's behavior as a teen, his stage fright, school phobia, and what I suppose the experts would now call social withdrawal. When I lampooned his reclusiveness then as "moofing," it made me feel edgy because it represented a change of his personality. Did my premonition have any practical predictive value?

Emil Kraepelin had hypothesized in 1919 that the seeds of schizophrenia were lodged in far more people than developed a clinical case of the disease. The impatient pioneer Harry Stack Sullivan fulminated as long ago as 1927 that psychiatrists "see too many [patients in the] end-stage and deal with too few of the pre-psychotic." In 1938 a groundbreaking article, "Early Schizophrenia," in the *American Journal of Psychiatry,* did suggest prodromal symptoms such as anxiety, irritability, depression, boredom, loss of energy, inability to concentrate, social withdrawal, and change in sense of self, but these categories were too broad to be of much value in treating patients.

Large-scale "anecdotal" studies began in the 1970s and separated five stages of onset, the first two nonpsychotic: (1) overextension, a sense of being overwhelmed by great stress; (2) restricted consciousness, including boredom and social withdrawal; (3) disinhibition, the appearance of previously repressed urges; (4) psychotic disorganization, leading to loss of self-control; (5) psychotic resolution, including delusions and massive denial of illness and responsibility.

By 1996 several studies had documented that early detection and quick intervention with neuroleptics softened the impact of symptoms and shortened the course of the disease. But not much progress had been made in narrowing definitions of early symptoms to usable specifics. I asked Dr. Richard Jed Wyatt of NIMH, the author of one study, what he thought about Jeff's "moofing." Was it indicative of a later psychosis? He smiled and shrugged. There was no way of being certain.

The dimensions of the prodromal stage in schizophrenia were being defined a bit better. Writing in the government's *Schizophrenia Bulletin,* Drs. A. R. Yung and Patrick D. McGorry of the Early Psychosis and Prevention Centre in Parkville, Victoria, Australia, defined it—still rather generally—as a "period of pre-psychotic disturbance, representing a deviation from a person's previous experience and behavior."

These investigators had compiled fifteen major studies of the prodromal stage, conducted all over the world between 1938 and 1994, and they elicited thirty-one supposedly distinct "symptoms and signs." The researchers were not happy with their inventory. "Some items such as odd or bizarre ideation or markedly peculiar behavior cannot be measured at all," they conceded. "Psychiatric attention and intervention could occur in people who will not go on to develop psychotic behaviors," they said; this would trigger serious ethical concerns similar to those encountered when genetic counseling triggers predictions.

"Warning the individual of the risk of developing a psychosis must be balanced with the potentially stigmatizing and anxiety-provoking effect of such information," the researchers cautioned. Time would be necessary to devise techniques to deal with this developing source of anxiety because the "paucity of methodologically sound research of individual psychotic prodromes" remained a handicap. Yung and McGorry called yet again for further "rigorous and systematic data collection of first-episode psychosis."

At least one model program of collecting such data had already registered success, and a report of the results created a stir at the convention of the American Psychiatric Association in the midsummer of 1996. Beginning in 1984, Dr. Ian Faloon, a New Zealand psychiatrist working in Buckingham, England, had distributed a ten-question basic-screening inventory and his own checklist of prodromal signs for schizophrenia. The lists were used by primary-care doctors, and the outcome was dramatic.

Earlier, a study had found an annual schizophrenia incidence of 7.4 per 100,000 in the local population. When the lists came into use, the incidence dropped to 0.75 per 100,000. A relatively large number of prospective acute cases had been headed off by early detection.

The Faloon checklist included generalized symptoms that had long been suspected, but also some innovative, more narrowly defined categories: inappropriate, or loss of, expression of feelings; speech that is difficult to follow; marked lack of speech and thoughts; marked preoccupation with odd ideas; persistent feelings of unreality; and changes in the way things appear, sound, or smell. Whenever such symptoms aroused suspicion, a program of patient and family education, stress management, and neuroleptic medication was instituted "without delay."

"False positives" could occur and become the occasional price of vigilance, but the cost of delay in instituting treatment was now known to be higher. Clearly, the doctors had come a long way since Jeff was at Menninger in 1972, when the staff at first dared only to "observe" him and then used very little or no medication. With quick and informed action, it was possible to prevent the worst and longest suffering. Prodromal treatment was no longer wishful thinking.

"Psychosocial" had become another buzzword for schizophrenia patients. It related to efforts at recovery and rehabilitation and had traditionally languished in unfashionable limbo.

"The work isn't glamorous enough," explained Larry Koran, the Stanford professor. "It requires psychiatrists to function within a team. It involves behavior modification, so it looks mechanical and not intellectual."

He might have added that the topic had long seemed remote because only lately had a significant number of patients become active candidates for recovery and rehabilitation. Not only had a change begun with the successes of medications like Haldol and clozapine, but the number of patients emerging from hospitals and halfway houses would doubtless further increase dramatically as more effective drugs took hold.

"How are we going to manage all that new sanity?" I kept asking the experts, thinking of the reentry adjustment I hoped Jeff would one day face, along with hundreds of thousands of other patients floundering in the no-man's-land between madness and functionality. That question led me to Robert Paul Liberman, M.D.

Liberman, nearly sixty, is a psychiatry professor at the UCLA School of Medicine. Thirty years of bumping up against infuriating resistance from his clients left him somewhat brusque and impatient but with his persistence undiminished. He is a protean operator, issuing a stream of books, articles, videocassettes, "modules," and lectures loaded with upbeat case histories. He shuttled between his four headquarters scattered across the Los Angeles area: at the university in Westwood; the Veterans Administration Hospital in Brentwood; the Camarillo State Hospital, his original base, forty miles north; and his isolated lakeside home in Thousand Oaks.

Behavior modification had been Liberman's original gospel, and this step-by-step teaching method was unpopular with patients and staff alike when the professor set out at Camarillo in the early 1970s.

"I used to round up the patients," he said, not entirely without bitterness. "They were busy smoking. There was also a lack of administrative support. The custodial approach was easier." The staff had to be rounded up, too. The motivators had to be motivated: "It required a vision and the belief that it really worked."

His 1972 paper describing his methods for practicing behavior modification outlined techniques that had nothing in common with the exercises prescribed for Jeff by his doctors at about the same time. Although Liberman's subjects were mental patients, they were treated more like hard-core criminals. A discussion of one technique, "extinction," began like this: "The treatment intervention was the nurse abruptly leaving the patient and terminating the interview at the first indication of delusional speech."

Another core lesson for "social learning" was the "token economy." As Liberman's paper described it: "Instead of receiving food, bed, privileges, and small luxuries like cigarettes free of charge, the patient must work at a higher level of functioning in order to earn tokens that he can exchange for the good things of life. . . . Failure to engage in socially appropriate behavior leads . . . to punishment . . . tokens are taken away. . . . The patient subsists in a 'welfare state.' He may eat his meals on a steel tray rather than using more pleasant dinnerware."

These days, a dozen large hospitals around the country employ the Liberman model. It no longer mentions punishments or a token economy and doesn't make staffs behave like prison guards.

"I was a doubter," said Dr. C. C. Beebe, a staff psychiatrist at the South Carolina State Hospital in Columbia. "Out of 120 patients I deliberately chose the eight I thought would be the most difficult to reach by the Liberman model. After three months I was very delighted by the changes I saw. This is such a pleasant, positive experience. The patients become relaxed and happy and enjoy what they are doing."

"Now, I love to lead groups," reported a social worker, Noni Richards. "I have seen patients get out of the hospital for the first time in ten years."

"We give them encouragement by clapping, patting them on the back, or giving them a hug, making eye contact and giving them a direct compliment," said a program director, Rosalind Smith.

Their tool kit consisted of unequivocally structured modules that broke down Liberman's program into slow, repetitive mini-steps: "symptom management," "medication management," "recreation for leisure," "basic conversation skills," and "community reentry." There was no prison ambience. Respect, patience, and recognition of the patients' individual learning curves made the program work. Perhaps most important, the incremental steps were meant to help patients minister to their difficulties on their own.

Time, however, was a problem. Not every treater could muster enough of it. Liberman estimated that a year was usually required for his model to meaningfully affect patients, and this assessment may be optimistic. Jerry Hogarty, a social worker in the field, at Pittsburgh University since 1968, reported great success with four hundred patients, mostly living at home. But three years of expert involvement were required; the mostly encouraging improvements did not begin to emerge until two years had been invested.

Money was too short as well. At Boston University's nonprofit Center for Psychiatric Rehabilitation, courses in "assisted education" had to be curtailed. Not enough students could afford the tuition of $16,000 a year for learning to work with computers. Psychologist Bill Anthony of the Boston group, arguably the brightest thinker in the psychosocial arena, believed that his specialty was in a state of "revolution." Probably so, but who would pay for it? Skilled help was hard to find. Fragmentation hurt, too: the experts in Los Angeles, Boston, Pittsburgh, and half a dozen other centers did not seem eager to communicate with one another or to move in unison.

Psychosocial operations may be too diverse even for Liberman. His encyclopedic "modules" could not cover patients of all mental states and every stage of convalescence. When I sent Liberman three hundred dollars for the module that seemed most appropriate for Jeff's status, my advisers told me it wouldn't help. I would have to turn elsewhere for Jeff.

I had heard that Lilly had put a team under Dr. Peter J. Weiden of Columbia to work on a series of educational booklets to help patients and treaters. The publication of the texts was to coincide with the launch of Olanzapine. The first five pamphlets were already prepared: *Understanding Your Illness, Helping Yourself to Prevent Relapse, Managing Crisis and Emergency Situations, Getting the Best Results from Your Medicine,* and *You and Your Treatment Team.*

I was skeptical. If all the literature I'd read had accomplished its goals, there would be no schizophrenia. These guides were different. They were direct but not directive. The tone was informal and not patronizing. Instead of preaching, the texts offered interactive sections inviting specific reactions from readers. Throughout, patients were gently coaxed to examine themselves and find their own ways out of their problems. There were no simple answers; one size didn't fit all.

It was a unique home library, and the compilers had begun their labors with Liberman. "Liberman made the major breakthrough," said Weiden. "We tried a new level of effort for how to reach people at various stages. We're like a clothing store. We expanded the selection, the scope, the choice of sizes."

Browsing through his shop, I came across *Building a Road to Recovery*. It started off: "Choosing to build a road to recovery can be a very positive step. Things can begin to move to a more normal state, but it will probably be a new 'normal.' You may have to work out new ways to do many of the things you used to do. Going back to school or getting a job may not be best for you right away. . . . Think about the kinds of activities you might like to do. On the lines below, list the ones you'd like to do when you're feeling better."

Six vacant lines followed and then: "Which activity might you like to do first?"

I sent the pages to Jeff, but he wasn't well enough to concentrate sufficiently, not even on ideas that could help him. More than ever, I knew that he and I and the afflicted all over the world had a crucial stake in the outcome of the hectic competition among the new medications in progress that were going through the obstacle course of clinical testing.

CHAPTER 23

"That Could Have Killed the Drug Right There"

THE LIFESAVING idea was first tested on May 20, 1747, aboard the British sailing ship *Salisbury*. The guinea pigs were twelve sailors who had come down with scurvy. According to the records of their Scottish ship's surgeon, James Lind, his patients were suffering from "putrid gums," "spots," "weakness of their knees," and lassitude so severe that their likely fate appeared to be death, the common outcome for scurvy.

Lind divided his charges into groups and fed each a different dietary supplement. He tried vinegar, apple cider, seawater, diluted sulfuric acid, garlic, mustard, horseradish, and citrus fruit. Ten of the men failed to improve. The two who ate lemons and oranges became immediately and visibly better. The cure for deadly scurvy was at hand.

In principle, the regimen known these days as "controlled clinical trials" differs little from Lind's ingenious experiment. For Dr. Charles M. Beasley Jr., the clinical trials for Olanzapine varied considerably, but mostly just in scope and complexity: as the Eli Lilly research psychiatrist in charge of running the tests, Beasley commanded a force of more than 4,200 physicians, study coordinators, research nurses, monitors, pharmacologists, systems programmers, statisticians, and other specialists, distributed over 174 medical centers in seventeen countries.

Beasley was well acquainted with the difficulty of doing research with schizophrenic patients. He never forgot Rick, a young man at the University of Cincinnati Medical School, one of his first charges during his residency on the research ward. Rick was severely psychotic; he was also crippled by tardive dystonia, the most disabling form of tardive dyskinesia.

"He was twisted like a pretzel and could barely walk," the doctor recalled.

A specially engineered wheelchair was constructed to make Rick more comfortable. Also, he was taken off his antipsychotic medications, which could prove to be a no-win decision. Rick would almost certainly turn more psychotic without the pills. On the other hand, they were clearly aggravating his physical problems.

The patient became so disturbed and violent that the hospital staff could no longer care for him safely. Rick was transferred to a state hospital and was calmed with antipsychotics. Whereupon he escaped one night and was killed when he was hit by a car; the death could have been a suicide; nobody could say.

Participants in the Olanzapine trials had one characteristic in common with Rick. To a greater or lesser degree, they felt desperate about their illness; otherwise they would hardly have agreed to sign informed-consent forms and join a venture that was necessarily perilous on two counts. The effects of the experimental new medication on a sizable number of human subjects were unknown. Furthermore, luck might consign any one of them to taking a placebo, which could worsen their condition, perhaps severely.

It became a truism of clinical trials that test subjects tended to be worse off than patients in the general population who would take the medication once it was approved by the FDA. So Beasley's research patients were not a flock of passive objects quietly waiting to be experimented upon. They were volatile sufferers who might at any point try to stop taking their medication; resort to alcohol or drugs; turn violent or suicidal; or be plunged into all manner of psychiatric or physical emergencies.

Beasley and his associates were aware of the hurdles facing their trial, but they could not predict the intensity of the efforts that it would take to clear them. "Nobody realized the implementation complexity," Beasley said in his understated manner.

Until his retirement in 1993 after thirty-six years with Eli Lilly, Mel Perelman oversaw Olanzapine's progress intently from the top floor, the twelfth, considered hallowed turf, of Lilly's stately main building in Indianapolis. Here the highest-ranking executives deliberated company policy in the hush of their individual suites. And from here, in the tradition of Eli Lilly, the organization stockpiled fresh talent—a "schizophrenia company," virtually a new firm, was added onto the corporate structure.

Only Beasley was a relative old-timer in this crew. He had been aboard since 1987, working on Prozac. His new boss, Dr. Gary D. Tollefson, austere and fastidious, had participated in the Prozac clinical trials while still chairman of psychiatry at a St. Paul, Minnesota, hospital. To run the business end of central nervous system work, Robert N. Postlethwait was recruited in 1993 from his post as Lilly's vice president for Europe. That same year, Lilly added its highest-ranking psychiatrist, Dr. Steven M. Paul, long the scientific director of the National Institute of Mental Health in Washington.

Beasley signaled the onset of Olanzapine's gestation as a commercial product on November 21, 1991, when the first "double-blind, placebo-controlled efficacy dose" was dispensed. The two-year trial ran in two tracks. In North America, 335 schizophrenic patients received Olanzapine; another 68 were given placebos for comparison purposes. In Western Europe, Israel, South Africa, and Australia, 431 patients were placed on so low an Olanzapine dosage that the researchers classified it as a placebo substitute.

Results of the North American trials pleased Beasley and his people. No agranulocytosis or significant extrapyramidal side effects were reported. Some mild sedation and occasional insomnia could be dismissed as insignificant. Liver reactions, which had been feared the most, appeared but proved transitory.

The international trial, however, was a failure by the standards of the governmental regulatory agencies, and for a bizarre reason. The mini-dosage was needlessly strong. "There was too much efficacy of the substitute," Beasley explained. "We didn't know that it was as potent as it was."

"Dosage"—the term was familiar and smacked of habit. ("Take as directed.") Neuroleptics could not be dispensed automatically; all patients developed different tolerances. As I learned from Jeff, all may require adjustment periodically. Trial and error was the standard method. Daniel Casey of Veterans Affairs has defined the ideal dosage this way: "Just enough and not too much."

An unscheduled third study with a full dosage of Olanzapine was needed, and so Beasley set out by plane to sign up teams of investigators to run the new tests on an accelerated schedule. He was paying substantial fees, because no slippage could be tolerated.

"The inducement was to overpromise," said Beasley. "I had to ask old friends to look me in the eye and had to tell them, 'If you mess up, you'll never work for us again.' " In under a week, he stopped in Boston, Worcester, New Haven, Tampa, San Francisco, Napa, and San Diego. "They were very intense personal contacts," Beasley said. "We had given ourselves a year for the study. It took seven months."

Although the results replicated the first study, Beasley considered them inconclusive. Drug testing had made him an inveterate skeptic, and his wariness ran deep. "I hope I'm never moved to become a true believer in anything," he told me. He thought the chances for Olanzapine at that point were up in the air: "If you ask me to bet money, I'd say fifty-fifty."

In addition to the Finnish epidemic that struck clozapine, another cloud hung over Lilly and all competitors: Remoxipride; it never left Beasley's mind as Olanzapine entered the late (Phase III) stages of the tests.

Developed by the large Swedish manufacturer Astra and licensed in America to Merck and Company, Remoxipride was reported in European medical journals in February 1993 to demonstrate a "good and often rapid anti-psychotic effect with few and mild adverse effects." By fall, the drug had been used by some fifty thousand patients in fifteen European countries, and clinical trials were progressing well in the United States. Suddenly, in November, eight cases of aplastic anemia were reported, most of them in Great Britain. Two patients died. No ill effects were reported in the United States, yet Astra and Merck—in excessive haste, according to some industry sources— permanently withdrew the drug from the market.

Beasley and his colleagues wondered at one bad moment whether Olanzapine was suffering the same fate. One of their test patients at a major New York hospital registered a steep decline in his white cell blood count. "That could have killed the drug right there," Beasley said. When the blind was broken, it turned out that the patient had been taking Haldol and his condition could be reversed.

Beasley's task kept him totally accessible. Crises concerning "notable patients" were reported to him at once. Some patients suffered seizures and guidance was needed: Could they be kept in the study? The flow of quick decisions did not abate for more than three years.

Once all five trials had ended, nine Olanzapine patients had committed suicide for a variety of reasons (another suicide victim was taking a placebo). In view of this group's volatility, these totals were considered benign. The dropout rate, averaging about fifty percent throughout the industry, was kept in tolerable limits, ranging as low as thirty-four percent in one of the European trials.

In all, Olanzapine was administered to some 3,200 meticulously screened patients, all severely psychotic. For comparison purposes, another 810 were given Haldol and a further 236 received nonactive placebo pills. Technically described as a dopamine and serotonin antagonist, Olanzapine was found safe without blood tests and worked for 79.3 percent of the patients who tried it.

October 1, 1995, became the date ingrained in the minds of all ninety-five members of the "Heavyweight Team" colocated in Building 48. It was the end point of numerous overlapping Olanzapine "timelines," the day when the formal New Drug Application (NDA) had to go off to the Food and Drug Administration in Washington. The date was splashed all over the walls in multicolor banners. It was meant to become an obsession, and it did.

The NDA was not one document. It was ninety-one large boxes containing one and a half million pieces of paper and a stack of computer CD-ROMs. The total represented the results of all "core studies."

The "Heavyweight" label, an invention of a Harvard management guru, signified that the Olanzapine workers—specialists who normally performed tasks with many different goals at widely scattered locations—formed an autonomous elite force indoctrinated with a single goal. They were transformed into all but a separate company, and their focus was made graphically plain. Each day, they faced an enormous poster consolidating a final "Olanzapine Timeline." It was divided into categories called "Milestones Achieved," "Milestones Remaining," and "Days Remaining," and was updated as each day passed.

As his Washington deadline neared, Beasley was keeping an increasingly anxious eye on Lilly's competitors. He could get many of his technical questions about competing drugs answered simply by poring over excerpts of late research results from all manufacturers; these were customarily pinned onto display boards at crowded "poster sessions" in the exhibition halls of professional meetings. Doctors, nurses, hospital people, suppliers, and researchers showed intense curiosity at these sessions because once a drug was patented, not much was left to guesswork. Competing manufacturers had to balance their scientists' wish to retain some of their secrets against the drive of their marketers to impress the trade and future customers with the promise of their upcoming products.

As further reinforcement, the psychiatrists in charge convened a panel presentation calling all of these medications part of a "major breakthrough." A newsletter from NARSAD described Olanzapine as "unique" and offering "considerable positive effect to the patient." The *Wall Street Journal* reported that "Olanzapine has the potential to become a major new mental-health therapy." In a lapse from his usual circumspection, Beasley ventured his view that half a billion dollars was the likely minimum annual sales figure for his drug, and that it might eventually reach two billion.

Gossip made the rounds quickly at the meetings, and psychological warfare raged wherever interested parties got together. Beasley knew that his competitors were spreading mean-spirited word that Olanzapine's liver complications were more troublesome than Lilly had disclosed. His colleagues, in turn, professed worry over the forty percent of male Sertindole users who were said to experience "dry ejaculations."*

Meanwhile, at Lilly's manufacturing plant in Kinsale, Ireland, speed and pressure in the production of Olanzapine were changed so that the drug in the form of crystals would not explode in the factory. It had been discovered that the first crystals were too large. They were tamed when "slurry milling" during their suspension in a liquid turned the crystals into a powder whose particles were of a safe size.

The Indianapolis Heavyweights beat their own deadline. They assembled in the courtyard on the morning of September 21 to watch their ninety-one boxes being loaded onto a twelve-wheeler truck. The men had put on coats and ties. Randy Tobias, their chairman and CEO, addressed them: "I hope you're very, very proud of yourselves—you deserve to be." And when the loaded truck pulled out, those gathered together waved little black-and-white checkered flags of the kind flashed at the Indianapolis speedway races—and they cheered.

A full week later the rival Sertindole team chartered a jet to haul its NDA papers to Washington. The dimensions of Abbott's New Drug Application for Sertindole—two copies of 814 volumes, each averaging three hundred pages—hardly warranted the hiring of an entire jet; the principal motivation was to save time. The Abbott Venture Group knew that in the race with the Eli Lilly Heavyweight Team even a few hours might be of value.

The Sertindole licensing agreement with the inventors, Lundbeck, from

---

* This is a benign sexual condition in which erections and orgasms are normal, but little or no ejaculate is expelled.

Denmark, had been hurriedly signed when all parties were assembled in Kyoto, Japan, for a psychopharmacology convention in July 1991. Ever since, the Abbott crew had been scampering to compensate for their late start. Their aggressive stance toward the Lilly competitors was undisguised. "The Prozac patent runs out in 2001," said a marketing man. "If they don't have a winner by then, they're going to have a lot of people with tin cups out."

Abbott's best weapon was its unorthodox boss—a woman, still a rarity in the pharmaceuticals industry. Terri Sebree, thirty-seven, held no advanced college degree and had made her way through the corporate ranks. She was relentless. For five years she rose daily at 5 a.m.—except Saturday, which she designated "family day"—and began work at Abbott Park, north of Chicago, by 6 o'clock. Administering clinical trials at more than 150 centers under a tight deadline, she knew she had to inspire loyalty and fear.

"You're going to delay getting the drug on the market," she threatened whenever an investigator was about to deliver data past the deadline. "We may have to shut your site down."

Terri had another side. If an emergency call on her home phone in the middle of the night awakened her seven-year-old daughter, the mother patiently explained what was happening. And her staff—it numbered only twenty-five—was driven by her gentle definition of the Venture Group's mission. "Schizophrenia researchers have to be special," she said. "They have to be angels. They have to be very caring."

For effective marketing, Sebree knew she had to showcase some distinctive characteristics for Sertindole. So even the basic composition of her clinical test sample was designed to be unique. Of the 1,446 schizophrenics who received Sertindole and also the 1,000 comparison subjects who were given Haldol, as well as another 500 who took a placebo, some twenty-five percent were women. The easier availability of male subjects from veterans' hospitals resulted in a female component of only five to ten percent in most trials. Sebree considered such a ratio unacceptable.

Needing an orderly system to pinpoint the original clinical state of each trial participant and then to track the impact of Sertindole, the Abbott crew created a method to "standardize the rating scales." Faced with having to train more than four hundred evaluators, mostly physicians, in the complexities of conducting clinical trials, they retained a leading authority on the subspecialty of testing: Dr. Luis Ramirez, a Case Western Reserve University psychiatrist.

Ramirez started by lecturing the trainees about how to rapidly establish rapport with the severely ill test population. After showing the doctors some of his ten different taped sample interviews with schizophrenics, each running twenty to thirty-five minutes, he briefed his raters on how to use the six-point scale they were to apply to classify the symptoms of the trial participants. Each of the six ratings was known as an anchoring point—an allusion to the ocean of diagnostic uncertainties. The physician-evaluators were then equipped to conduct standardized interviews lasting twenty to forty minutes with all test subjects, both before and after they went through the trial. Nobody had devised a more exacting system for measuring clinical trial outcomes.

The Abbott forces also whipped up a positive spin to counteract Sertindole's disadvantages. While about half of their test subjects dropped out, the manufacturer insisted, not implausibly, that patients quit the trials because they started feeling too well. The "dry ejaculation" side effect was trivialized as "reduced ejaculate volume." Only one-fifth of patients were affected by it, and critics were reminded that older medications produced retrograde ejaculations that propelled seminal fluid painfully into the bladder, a much more serious problem.

As the results of clinical trials for all the new medications accumulated, it became clear that low sedation was Sertindole's outstanding advantage. Elimination of drowsiness—common with neuroleptics—would not only improve the quality of patients' lives in general; it empowered them to embark on a career or return to school, which represented a significant advance.

As a marketing dress rehearsal, the Sebree team convened a "SWOT Analysis" session. The objective was to assess strengths, weaknesses, opportunities, and threats that confronted the impending launch of Sertindole. On the day preceding the annual convention of the American College of Neuropsychopharmacology in San Juan, Puerto Rico, in early December 1995, a panel of seven authorities delivered their confidential verdicts on the full set of data they had received from Abbott a week earlier.

The group included some of the field's most knowledgeable hands-on researchers, such leaders as Dr. David Pickar of the National Institute of Mental Health and Dr. Casey of Veterans Affairs. All day, the experts grilled Sebree and her team. They praised, cautioned, weighed statistics, and searched for ways to put the new drug's best foot forward while downplaying its drawbacks.

Out of this brainstorming came Sertindole's "laser" strategy. In addition to emphasizing the no-sedation advantage, the Sebree group would put out word to the psychiatric community that the medication worked much like a laser beam. Unlike its competitors, it would not "swamp" the brain at multiple receptors but would target the most therapeutic sites.

Conceivably, the Lilly Heavyweights could ultimately still be outmaneuvered.

The Zeneca doctors developing Seroquel, the third breakthrough drug, knew they were running far behind their schedule and were more than six months behind their competitors. "They're rookies," said one researcher in describing the beleaguered group in Delaware.

It showed. Executives kept being removed and replaced by more rookies. Decisions were postponed. At times the toilers in the lower echelons wondered how firmly their leaders were committed to the company's entry into the unaccustomed central nervous system market. Lateness of itself was not devastating, however. Patients' responses to any drug were unpredictable; there might well be room for more than one new medication.

This was Seroquel's opportunity, and the Zeneca developers were relieved when their New Drug Application went to the FDA on July 29, 1996, with general sale expected late in 1997. The clinical trials had involved 3,197 patients and 382 principal investigators worldwide. The dropout rate was 58.4 percent—relatively high but not considered excessive. Headache, somnolence, and dizziness were reported, but in acceptable numbers. No serious effects on the heart or sexual function had to be investigated. If the Zeneca people were jittery, they didn't show it. The uncertainties of schizophrenia had left the field open.

The public debut of Pfizer's Ziprasidone was likely in the second half of 1998, with the special sales pitch that the medication would lead to less weight gain than all its competitors.

Abbott's Sertindole, however, developed a more complicated history.

CHAPTER 24

Last-Minute Hurdles

THE RUMOR HAD been circulating for more than a month: Sertindole, now trade-named Serlect, was in serious trouble. The problem was no longer merely an annoyance, such as occasional sedation and nasal congestion, previously reported, or even the dry ejaculation that troubled some of the male subjects in the clinical trials. (Gordie, the Sertindole patient in Milwaukee, had, typically, been so ecstatic to regain his vigorous sex drive that decreased ejaculation did not bother him as long as he had his orgasms back.)

Now the issue was Q T prolongation,* a cardiac irregularity that could cause sudden death. The FDA's Psychopharmacological Drug Advisory Committee, whose recommendations the agency almost always followed, would have to rule at its next meeting on delicate details of how Sertindole should be presented to prescribing psychiatrists. Should the drug be downgraded as a "second line" rather than a "first line" medication? Should EKGs be required before and during its use? Should a warning about possible Q T prolongation be required on the descriptive package insert in each box of pills? And would such a warning have to be printed in the boldface type most damaging to sales and perhaps also set off with an ominous black box?

---

* The letters "Q" and "T" stand for sequential reference points in an electrocardiogram (EKG) as its zigzag pattern tracks the contractions and relaxation of the heartbeat.

These choices between alarming and reassuring signals to the physician-customers would be fateful, especially if the competing medication, Eli Lilly's Olanzapine, was about to be licensed without any caveats, as rumor had it. Hundreds of millions of dollars, potentially billions, were at stake. The FDA was no longer allowed to hold up a New Drug Application for more than a year. Ten months had passed.

Shortly after 8:30 a.m. on July 15, 1996, the chairman of the advisory committee, Dr. Dan Casey, called its forty-seventh meeting to order in the Plaza ballroom of the Holiday Inn in Silver Spring, Maryland. These meetings tended to attract about fifty people. Today, some three hundred visibly expectant drug-industry functionaries crowded the ballroom. The air-conditioning was overworked, as usual, so most of the men were in shirtsleeves. A large section of chairs was marked as reserved for representatives of the companies with the most at stake: the drug's American manufacturer, Abbott Laboratories, and its licenser, Lundbeck.

At the far-left front, where the Sertindole team had assembled near the microphone, sober-faced, professional-looking dignitaries in very dark suits were poised to go into action. None had taken their jackets off. Seated in the center of that sponsoring delegation was Eva Steiness, the dignified Danish director of the Sertindole team, looking grim in a starched white blouse. Nearby was Terri Sebree, the administrator who managed the clinical tests for Sertindole and had just left Abbott for a better job with a clinical-testing company. Lined up to the right of her were the tight-lipped top brass for Seroquel, third in line in the sweepstakes for new antipsychotics and still lagging behind their schedule to file a New Drug Application with the FDA. Also scattered around the room were marketing executives from Lilly and lobbyists from NAMI.

Attention centered on the nine psychiatrist committee members—six men, three women—seated around a spacious horseshoe-shaped table. Each faced a pile of briefing papers prepared for them in advance by staff. Lined up to the near right, as if to assure clear shooting toward the cluster of the Sertindole dark suits at the opposite end of the battleground, were the heavyweights from the FDA: the huge, booming Dr. Raymond Lipicky, director of the Division for Cardio-Renal Drugs, and Dr. Tom Laughren, second in command for psychopharmacology. The decision maker for the day's proceedings, Dr. Paul Leber, director for psychopharmacology, lounged in the front corner.

A printed agenda made clear that Lipicky would be matched against the dark suits up front, principally Dr. Edward Pritchett, chief for cardiology and clinical pharmacology at Duke University Medical Center. The agenda listed him as head of an "independent expert cardiology committee," but it was easy to guess that he had been recruited as chief defense counsel for the Abbott forces.

Tom Laughren launched the first salvo. The FDA examiners had cited evidence of "certain serious cardiovascular events." There was a record, he remarked pointedly, of "deaths in the database that are not readily explained." His tone was one of dry scientific inquiry.

The cluster of Sertindole's representatives was set astir. Striding to the microphone, Dr. Pritchett seemed nine feet tall. Addressing the room with a small, pleasant smile, he managed to sound cordial and professorial at the same time, not a small achievement. Various consultants and Abbott medical staff ducked in and out of his presentation. Doctors rushed forward with supporting material freshly retrieved from computers handheld in the Abbott delegation. "It's getting crowded up here," said Dr. Pritchett through a tight smile.

The 2,194 patients who had participated in the clinical trials had been subjected to a total of some ten thousand electrocardiograms, the manufacturer's people said. "Incredible scrutiny," one of the outside cardiology professors called the effort. Dr. Pritchett conceded that the "theoretical possibility" did exist of "serious cardiovascular outcome." But he emphasized the "theoretical" nature of the threat. There had been twenty-seven deaths in the clinical test population, yes, including thirteen unexpected "sudden deaths." However, no one could judge with certainty that any of these events were attributable to the medication that was on trial in the Holiday Inn ballroom.

Four of the deaths had been somewhat "suspicious," Pritchett conceded, but were evidently not due to the controversial Q T prolongation factor. In only one case was such a cause "not possible to exclude." That was the death of a forty-one-year-old woman who had been under treatment for a year because of hypertension and was suffering from so many other risk factors that the true cause of her demise could not be reliably singled out.

Well past the scheduled lunch hour, Dr. Lipicky rose and pronounced in a deep bass: "I think this is a dangerous drug." To a lay audience, that might have sounded like an ominous, possibly fatal, verdict, but his listeners were not ruffled. They dealt with few medications that were *not* dangerous. Moreover, Lipicky seemed to backtrack right away.

"It can cause death," he said, "but that is my assertion; it is not fact."

While he offered no overt indication that he was seriously disturbed at the permissive direction taken by the meeting, Leber, as he often did, clothed his doubts in a philosophical bon mot.

"The absence of evidence is not evidence of absence," he said, raising his voice slightly.

He would have a whole afternoon to protect the FDA's collective backside in the event that Sertindole was to be approved and later found to be deadly. Everyone in the ballroom probably remembered that the deaths caused by Remoxipride did not set in until after more than fifty thousand Europeans had been taking the highly praised drug.

Casey led the meeting adroitly, clearly eager for a full airing of all relevant points, but opening the afternoon session, he steered toward closure. He posed two crisp questions: (1) Was a signal of serious cardiac danger flashing at the committee? (2) How do the drug's benefits measure up against its risks?

Addressing the second point, the highly respected researcher Dr. Carol Tamminga, speaking as an Abbott consultant, pointed out that eight commonly used drugs for disorders of the central nervous system caused more frequent Q T prolongation than did Sertindole.

"We detected a signal of sudden death," said Leber. "We want to find out about it. If there is a signal affecting this drug, we want to know." The emphasis on the last four words was marked.

Pritchett, countering for Abbott, remained the voice of reasonableness. "You're asking questions to which no one has the answer," he said, still in his nondefensive, almost-apologetic manner. "I'm trying to tell you what reassured *me*."

Some of the exchanges between the Sertindole people and the FDA were testy, yet the overall tone was civil, the flashes of rancor brief. Dr. Lipicky conceded, "I see not a single case that proves anything. It's very tenuous. There is nothing with predictive value."

Eight hours of verbal fencing having passed, it was up to Casey to draw the bottom line. He tried. "There is a signal," he said, "but we don't know what to do with it." It really wasn't much of a signal, and it could not be pinned on Sertindole alone. Measured against cardiac risks faced daily by the general population, the risk of Sertindole for desperately ill people seemed tolerable, lack of evidence in either direction notwithstanding. Accordingly, the committee's vote was unanimous in favor of the drug's efficacy, and only two members voted against it for reasons of safety.

Now it was up to the FDA lawyers to haggle over the remaining details with the Abbott lawyers, but an acrimonious stalemate developed. As morbid industry wits made their rounds, they referred to Sertindole as "Certain Death," a gross exaggeration. An Abbott manager said, "The company is being dragged through the mud." Still, as the uncertainty about cautionary labeling language for the drug in the United States dragged on, the medication was clearly being downgraded. In the early fall of 1997, the phrasing of the prospective warnings had still not been agreed upon with the FDA.

The European licensing authorities reflected the discomfort of the American regulators. The British were first to permit the drug's sale but asked that doctors administer benchmark electrocardiograms before starting patients on Sertindole. Most other Europeans followed suit, except for France and Sweden, where further reviews were ordered. No such impediments, however, were likely to delay the final verdict for the front-runner in the race for the rich schizophrenia market: Olanzapine.

The untroubled outlook for Olanzapine should have been grounds for Jeff and me to cheer. Instead, it had become a new source for suspense and conflict between us. The stalemate was making me edgy. In the spring of 1996, I had arranged for Jeff to become part of the Olanzapine clinical trials. Skip Pope had handled the paperwork and had urged Jeff to give the medication a try. So had I, Jeff's mother, his doctor in San Jose, and his conservator.

Jeff had agreed, but he balked at the last moment. To keep the clinical test records "clean," he would have been required to submit to a two-day washout, without medications, during the transition from clozapine. The prospect scared him, and he could not be budged. Olanzapine would have to wait until it was no longer an experimental drug; then the washout would not be necessary. I hoped it would not be a long wait, but I felt frustrated, to say the least, and I launched a new campaign.

On June 12, I wrote him:

> You may not recall, but when Skip Pope was trying to arrange for you to get Olanzapine a few months ago, I was sharing the cost of the considerable paperwork with another father. He had a son, a patient at McLean Hospital, ill for ten years with delusions, hallucinations, totally incapacitated with schizophrenia, evidently a lot sicker than you. Well, this young man did start on Olanzapine, now lives in his own apartment, works part-time with retarded children, and is back in college to finish studying for his

degree. His family has been telling Skip: "He truly has his old personality back."

Jeff did not reply.

With schizophrenia, surprises never end. On May 24, 1996, I was talking with Dr. Michael W. Smith, director of the Adult Psychiatry Outpatient Clinic at UCLA Harbor Medical Center in Torrance, California. He was briefing me about two female patients on Olanzapine who had agreed to be interviewed by me.

"Has anybody talked to you about the P450 enzymes?" the doctor asked, suddenly appearing to veer away from his Olanzapine patients.

"The what?" I asked.

"This is about drug interactions," said Smith, smiling tolerantly.

"Oh, that," I said. "Each time I see my doctors these days I have to recite a list of all the medications I take, even aspirin. They watch everything really closely."

"Oh, yeah?" said the doctor. "How about over-the-counter stuff like anti-histamines? How about grapefruit juice?"

Patiently, he explained the current emergence of a brand-new medical specialty. The complexity of this field had become known only lately, slowly, as new, increasingly complicated, and more-potent drugs were developed and turned out to affect different people in a great variety of ways because individuals metabolize enzymes—proteins functioning as biochemical catalysts—at different speeds. The interactions were complex: grapefruit juice often triggers a reaction when consumed along with some medications. Prescribed dosages must be tailored to the reactions of particular patients. "Patients get erroneously dismissed as nonresponders," Smith said.

Differences between Caucasians and blacks and some ethnic groups can be marked for antipsychotic medications. "The Japanese are slower metabolizers and need lower doses," said Smith, who also ran the Research Center for the Psychobiology of Ethnicity. "They take Haldol at one-tenth the dosage of whites. The Chinese need much less clozapine than we do. Koreans have more side effects. And smoking cigarettes can speed enzymes."

Smith produced a table from a 1996 issue of the *Journal of Clinical Psychiatry* entitled "Drugs Metabolized by P450 Enzymes." It listed seventy-nine medications scattered across five types of P450 enzymes. Haldol, risperidone, and clozapine were included. So were such routine items as caffeine, codeine, and two antihistamines. Olanzapine and Sertindole were too new to be mentioned. When I queried Daniel Casey about these puzzles, he sent me a seventeen-page article from the *1996 Annual of Drug Therapy* entitled "Brussels Sprouts and Psychopharmacology," and described my latest field of inquiry as "nascent emerging."

In the summer of 1996, most psychiatrists were still slow to metabolize all this knowledge.

"Most of us know the working hypothesis of competition between medications," Skip Pope said. "We don't worry about all the technical niceties. The question is: Does a patient have a reasonable level of drugs in his system? If he is on Prozac, for instance, he needs less clozapine."

Reasonable levels can usually be determined by blood tests, Skip explained. If the most therapeutic blood plasma levels are not known for a medication, prescribing doctors operate "empirically," relying on patients as they report how they feel. "We usually don't need the fancy details," said Skip.

When I asked Dr. Beasley in Indianapolis whether the P450 enzymes made any difference in prescribing Olanzapine specifically, he replied carefully: "Statistically yes, clinically no." Would any details about possible drug interactions appear on the package insert for Olanzapine? "Oh, yes," he said, "quite a lot!"

To do something constructive while we waited for Olanzapine to reach the marketplace, I continued my campaign for the drug with Jeff, hoping to eliminate his past objections. On July 18 I wrote him:

> Everyone is convinced that Olanzapine is very likely to help change your condition. . . . My interviews with (by now quite a few) Olanzapine patients demonstrate this. These people are in fact a whole lot improved. Their good old personalities are being restored and they're enjoying life and told me so in considerable detail.
>
> It's not definite exactly when the Food and Drug Administration will OK Olanzapine for general sale. It is definite, however, that access to the medication will NOT entail the transition complications that you disliked the last time around when the medicine was experimental and you would have had to go through some intermediate steps when switching from the old to the new pills. All these complications will fall away once Olanzapine is no longer experimental. That may be as early as September or October or not too long thereafter.

As yet, I was reserving for the moment of Jeff's final decision making the one argument that I thought would clinch the sale. Skip had come up with language that I thought would work because it was incontrovertible: it would be unethical to leave Jeff on the highly toxic clozapine once the more benign new drug was available. Who could resist that proposition?

CHAPTER 25

Jeff Now

"HOW'S JEFF DOING these days?" friends often ask me because they have gathered that I don't mind talking about his illness. I tell them I'm proud that someone so enduring is my charge. Jeff is my buddy, not only my hero. I'm his historian, and nowadays, happily, life is finally looking up for him. What better news is there to talk about than this upturn after years of crises?

"He's better than he has ever been since 1972," I say cautiously. "He'd be on his way to his own apartment and a job if it weren't for the negative symptoms."

"The what?"

For more than twenty years of Jeff's illness I didn't know exactly what these symptoms were. They don't usually become a consideration until after a patient's more obtrusive "positive" signs ebb away and turn largely or completely into remission. Thus only the experienced have occasion to learn much about negative symptoms. Yet for the Wydens, and more often than not for other families like ours, they are the difference between functionality and dysfunction. And as so often in schizophrenia, this issue is misleadingly named. While a diagnosis of "negative" normally calls for a champagne celebration, in schizophrenia it refers to the most baffling, most stubborn, and usually the most debilitating and difficult-to-treat residue of the disease.

I've never had to deal with a phenomenon more frustrating. Jeff looks and sounds outwardly pretty well, but his negative symptoms keep him down:

chair-borne, preoccupied, absorbed in "moofing." The researchers call it a deficit disorder. Its very tranquillity is mystifying and unsettling. It's one of the black holes of psychiatry.

Predictably, the markers were first identified in a gross way by Emil Kraepelin. It was also he who separated the characteristics from the equally mislabeled "positive" signs. The latter have undergone no appreciable change since Kraepelin offered his first list of hallmarks: hallucinations, delusions, suspiciousness (fear of persecution), agitation (undue excitement), and thought disorganization. The negatives, in contrast, have been mired for decades in controversy that seems to proliferate as additional studies pile up at laboratories throughout the world.

"It's a mess," diagnosed Fuller Torrey.

Kraepelin's outstanding misapprehension has been corrected by the combined wisdom of the research establishment. No longer is it gospel that schizophrenia means hopeless deterioration, a progressively downhill course. Some reduction of cognitive skills has been noted among chronic patients, but the average decline in IQ over many years is only five points.

Otherwise, Kraepelin's guideposts have stood up remarkably well for close to a century. As early as 1919, he enumerated the "weakening of those emotional activities which permanently form the mainsprings of volition," leading to "emotional dullness, failure of mental activities, loss of mastery over volition, of endeavor, and of ability for independent action."

These convolutions bear fair resemblance to the catalog of negative symptoms used by Daniel Casey when he now addresses professional audiences: flat affect, emotional withdrawal, apathy or avolition, alogia (lack of spontaneity in speech), and anhedonia (inability to experience pleasure).

Other lists propounded by various contemporary authorities differ in their shadings, but not greatly. A compilation in the *American Psychiatric Glossary* of the American Psychiatric Press specifies: "Impaired ability to focus or sustain attention on a particular task, difficulty in initiating or following through on tasks, loss of fluency and spontaneity of verbal expression, impaired ability to experience pleasure, to form emotional attachment to others, and blunted affect." Still other sources list such features as apathetic immobility, inattention, and disorientation. Throughout, the prime common ground is lack of motivation and will and inability to concentrate—precisely the stultifying handicaps that make Jeff's life so boring and lonely.

As I learned from exuberant patients taking clozapine, Sertindole, and Olanzapine, some negative symptoms—and sometimes even all of them—can be brought under control to a greater or lesser extent in some people, even patients who have been severely and chronically ill. But rebirths, including the ability to work, to live independently, and to maintain meaningful relationships, are not common. To what extent and how often Olanzapine and upcoming medications will make inroads on the dead weight of negative symptoms remains largely untested as I write.

"It depends on what drug company representative you talk to," says Fuller Torrey.

In their attempts to slice their way through the labyrinth and create some order among the behavioral nuances, various systematizers fashioned "scales." There are eight rating scales, including PANSS (Positive and Negative Symptom Scale), SANS (Scale for Assessing Negative Symptoms), SAPS (Scale for Assessing Positive Symptoms), and BPRS (Brief Psychiatric Rating Scale). Unfortunately, assigned ratings depend considerably on subjective impressions and inferences of individual raters, so confusion is inevitable.

"There is little uniformity in which specific symptoms are considered as negative," wrote one leading scholar, Dr. Nina R. Schooler of Pittsburgh University. "As yet there is no 'golden standard' against which to judge the criteria, if any, that define valid subgroups."

Some ingenious informal road signs do exist, though many people are unaware of them. "Does he ever pick up the phone to call you?" I was asked by Herb Meltzer, the clozapine authority of Case Western Reserve University, when I complained that I couldn't place Jeff in the literature.

Spontaneity is a useful, simple indicator. Too bad that Jeff phoned (constantly) when he was in deepest trouble and, in recent years, only once every few months when he feels an urgent need of cash.

Throughout the summer of 1996 I was in suspended animation. When, I wondered, would the FDA permit doctors to write prescriptions for Olanzapine? Would Jeff reverse himself and accept the medication?

July 15—Sertindole had run into rough winds with the FDA advisory committee; Olanzapine would win the medication race.

July 16—Rumor had it that the FDA was approving Olanzapine without any advisory committee hearing because there were no substantive problems to discuss. However, no announcement had come from Eli Lilly.

July 23—Charles Beasley denied that FDA approval was in hand, but laughed heartily (a little nervously?) throughout our conversation. Was he being candid or discreet?

August 12—I faxed Skip Pope at McLean: "When Jeff's mother visited him last week, Jeff launched into a forty-five-minute monologue that he knew Olanzapine to be no good, that clozapine was the one and only—he's probably just scared of rocking the boat. I still like your stance that it'll soon be unethical to continue Jeff on clozapine but am beginning to think that this may, unreasonably, still not be sufficiently persuasive."

August 19—Beasley called on other business. "What's up with Olanzapine?" I asked. "Soon," he said, "soon."

August 20—A family friend reported Jeff volunteering a possible change of mind about Olanzapine when they had dinner in San Jose. "I guess it's inevitable," Jeff told him. That was news, but I wasn't ready to accept this as my frightened son's final word.

September 3—The *Wall Street Journal* said the FDA has sent Eli Lilly a letter calling Olanzapine "approvable." Lilly's stock rose $2.50 to $59.75, but there was no word about any date when "approvable" will turn to "approved." I was advised this could happen in two weeks or not until the end of October. I couldn't discover the cause of the delay.

September 19—I asked Beasley about Olanzapine again. "*Very* soon," he said.

By the autumn of 1996, my optimism had firmed into conviction: Jeff would soon acquire a new life. There were preconditions, of course. First, we urgently needed Olanzapine or possibly some similar soon-to-be-released basic medication; even so, the period when Jeff began taking it would be suspenseful. Jeff would need to tolerate it in sufficiently strong dosage to stabilize him without such bizarre side effects as vomiting. It would also have to give him as much control over his negative symptoms as I had seen with the Olanzapine patients I had interviewed in California and New York. Skip stood ready to help Dr. Kerschenbaum manage this high-wire act.

Harder to control, Jeff's body would have to continue to stand up under the stresses imposed every day by the actions and interactions of his various medications. Unless his physiology could process all the chemicals, the artfully calibrated system of his lifelines could conceivably slide into imbalance. The impending elimination of the highly toxic clozapine would help. (I had become as eager to drop the drug as I had once been to get hold of it.)

We had lately gone through another worrisome medication scare. Routine blood tests had signaled for the second time that perhaps Jeff's kidneys were having difficulty tolerating the lithium he continued to need. The nephrologists at Stanford Hospital examined him again. Luckily, they said he could continue on this potent drug, subject to regular future monitoring.

Luck. Who doesn't need some luck? We would get our share. We were on a roll, and Jeff was tough. There *was* life after twenty-five years of schizophrenia. As I watched my son get ready to move on, I kept thinking of a missile shuddering on its pad, not quite ready for liftoff. How to nudge it along? For years, I'd tried to dream up projects to help Jeff with his reentry from the encapsulated universe of his disease. Nothing seemed to make much difference. I'd never thought of a typewriter, but Karen Wrinkle did.

I was visiting in San Jose and was asked to come along the day Karen, Jeff's social worker, took him to a huge warehouse discount store to buy the little machine. Karen was one of the very few helpers over the years who had managed to attune herself to Jeff's wavelength. Jeff obviously thought Karen was wonderful, although he never said so, perhaps not even to himself.

Karen had made it her business to learn about our family, so she realized that the clacking of my typewriter had traditionally produced our income and held us together. When I had been an editor on magazines in New York, one of the favorite adventures for Jeff and Ron had been to come to my office and bang on my huge manual machine. My typewriter was our family coat of arms, our lifeline. Jeff, of course, had not forgotten, and at the discount warehouse he was as excited as he had ever shown himself over anything other than his standard complaints. He and Karen discussed the merits of various models and poked them appropriately. She knew that Jeff had frequently (if tentatively) given indications of wanting to be a writer someday. The typewriter would, I hoped, become a link to a vocational future. He took it to his halfway house, beaming.

So far, it hasn't helped a lot. My hints that I would appreciate a short letter on the new acquisition brought no response. Months later, casually—as I have learned to proceed so as to avoid raising resistance—I inquired how he was faring with the typewriter. Well, it had not yet been removed from its packing case. Jeff claimed he worried that he might mishandle it and cause damage. I suggested that the world is loaded with repair places, but logic, as so many times before, was not relevant. Jeff was fearful of the outside world, probably even fearful—as has been suggested by various psychiatrists for years—of getting well and maybe stumbling embarrassingly along the way.

About six months later, after more of my reminders, a very brief, businesslike note came from my son, perfectly typed. It was like Christmas in July, but there was no repeat performance.

At the time, Jeff's clozapine dosage had already been cut roughly in half, to two hundred milligrams, a distinct sign of progress. He still urinated excessively, puffed two packs of cigarettes a day, downed innumerable Cokes, and often trembled so that he had to pick up a glass with both hands. He remained almost inactive. But, providentially, another project materialized that produced great animation in him: this book.

Jeff greeted the project with totally unaccustomed enthusiasm. Psychologically, I suppose, the work was ideally positioned, halfway between his old world and the new. It allowed him to rummage again among some of his old bugaboos, about his pills and his doctors. He loved the detailed attention and was excited by the thought that his memories would help other sick people and their families. And so we embarked on a series of interviews, which have enriched this book greatly. Jeff's memory filled in many gaps and corrected some of my impressions. The required interview technique was fascinating. It reminded me of how gently I had to interview Hiroshima survivors about their memories of the atomic bomb. Many of the memories were similarly painful. It was necessary to proceed very slowly, gently.

Jeff and I talked for only five to ten minutes at a time. Setting his own pace, Jeff would break off, sometimes in midsentence, bolt out of my hotel room, and disappear to pace outside and have "a smoke." Or two. Sometimes he wouldn't reappear for half an hour. But he didn't once hesitate to expose himself to further questioning. He recounted amazing incidents from twenty and more years ago. Whenever practical, I corroborated his impressions with other eyewitnesses. I never found Jeff to distort the facts.

I can report other changes in him that indicate he is better. Most of them are subtle. He is no longer afflicted with "blunted affect." The fog is slowly, slowly lifting. Some bits of evidence:

- I used to hear interminable generalized agonizing from him, clichés like "I'm worried about my future." Now Jeff invokes structure. At age forty-six, he wants to get a grip on the long, deep black hole in his résumé. "It's been twenty-one years since I drove a car," he says. And, "I haven't been on a plane in ten years." And, "I've been in San Jose for eighteen years."

- He always used to measure life by the string of dates of his hospitalizations. Now the date of his last hospitalization is a firm signpost toward wellness. He announces, "I've been out of the hospital since I left Crestwood on February 16, 1993."

- He used to account for his days with such nonspecific complaints as "I've been feeling anxious a lot." Recently, he was able to say, "What I usually do these days is sit around wasting time."

- His conversation used to be weighed down with hugely deprecating negative quotations from his doctors, going back decades. Now Jeff remembered one psychiatrist who told him, "You have energy and intelligence!" It was like getting a new face.

- Whenever I asked, "What would you like to do tomorrow?" the response from Jeff was invariably, "I dunno." The last time I visited him he said, "Could we go look at the campus in Santa Cruz? I've never been there."

- The world's focus no longer rests totally upon himself. He volunteers, "How's the book going?" And when the baby daughter of his doctor, Andy Abarbanel, became ill and Jeff got angry because Andy had to cancel an appointment, he quickly softened when he heard what had caused it. "He was a different guy than he'd ever been," Andy said. "He was very tender. It was very touching. He has the emotional machinery to respond."

Maybe I've been too preoccupied with too many loose ends. Maybe I've blocked out some hindrances because deep down I feared nothing could be done about them. Maybe it takes unduly long for the coin to drop. Maybe the experts need to learn how to convey crucial thoughts succinctly enough for laypeople to absorb. Still, in my cautious euphoria of midsummer 1996, I wrote Jeff to propose a next step he could take in his reentry efforts:

All experts agree: inactivity—lack of purposeful regular activity—is of itself not good for you. Right now there is nothing more constructive for you to consider: You could help yourself by simply stepping up your daily physical and mental activity in a conscious way, as best you can. Remember how your hero JFK said, "But let us begin!" . . . Frequent, vigorous walking (not just ambling) is great for all of us, especially if it has a purpose and a definite destination. Using your bike regularly and vigorously would be great. Writing for your own fun on your new typewriter would be useful. . . . You seem to be pretty bored. I recognize that you still can't do much about this now. But you can do a little more. And then a little more, if you recognize the value of it. All it takes is for you to make up your very formidable mind that this is something important.

The letter brought immediate action from Jeff. His report was encouraging if ultimately frustrating for us both. He had walked three hours round-trip to the local Goodwill office to apply for volunteer work. The people who worked there welcomed him pleasantly and wanted him to get started on some clerical chores immediately, he said, but he felt he had to turn the opportunity down. He would have had to sit at a desk to concentrate on paperwork for six hours at a stretch, and he didn't think he could stay focused that long.

The exploration was a measure of his eagerness to move ahead and the limits of his current medication in its present dosage. I was not discouraged. The task before my son was, on reflection, difficult for an outsider to fathom. He was being asked to reengineer his lifestyle and to reinvent his identity. How many of us could maintain motivation long enough to accomplish a makeover of such magnitude, even without negative symptoms?

The present Jeff would die hard, and nothing illustrated the barrier more vividly than two symbols: the cap and the beard. They had become integral to his self-image. The beard was luxuriant and scruffy and made him look like a religious fanatic or a Manson-style serial killer. The baseball cap was dark, greasy beyond description, and he forced it down to cover his face as if he were seeking a partial disguise. It reminded me of the headgear that we bought so many years before to ward off rain while touring the Tivoli amusement park in Copenhagen. He wore that neutral-colored cap in the same way then.

If Jeff was to rejoin the everyday world, the beard and the cap would have to go. Their departure would signify major progress, since the present Jeff was quite unreasonably clinging to both. He made that clear when I gently suggested that he would look much more handsome without them. The beard and the cap, however, were among his moorings. There were others.

It pains and shames me every day to think about the manner in which I have to let Jeff live. To be straight, Jeff is a welfare client. He lives at the poverty level, utterly dependent upon the good graces of the (too easily defamed) bureaucrats in Washington, Sacramento, and San Jose. His environment hovers on the brink of destitution, and it is far from all that he needs. It is barren and is slowing down his recovery.

If Jeff's caregivers were to receive this assessment as an insult, I would be further upset. My admiration and gratitude for their efforts on Jeff's behalf only increase as I watch them strain to stretch their shrinking assets. Years ago, Santa Clara County had been known as Santa Claus County among California mental health workers. Coverage by social workers was adequate; occupational therapists performed well; board-and-care homes ran rehabilitation programs. But the pressures today threaten to overwhelm the system.

Administrators scheme to invent new emergency strategies to rob Peter so he can pay Paul. "Do you fire a social worker to get more medication?" I was asked rhetorically by Dr. Soleng Tom, the director of the county mental health system. His patient load stood at 4,000 and was increasing. His budget was down from $120 million to $90 million a year, and $6 million more had to be eliminated. Staff had been cut by twenty percent. The best locked hospital facility (eighty-five beds) had to be closed. Dr. Kerschenbaum's patient load of 175 was nothing unusual; another doctor handled 254.

At first glance, Jeff's halfway house, Jordan Hall, on South 13th Street, one of seventeen near the center of town, appears comfortable and serene. The California sunshine makes even slums look respectable, and the Jordan Hall neighborhood is triste but no slum. The "civilian" residences in Jeff's vicinity are old, large, not always meticulously maintained, but decent looking. Upon closer inspection, however, the building that Jeff literally calls home appears quite different.

Usually, twenty-one middle-aged men subsist here, two crammed into each small room. Two toilets serve all. Since most patients are heavy cigarette users, and smoking is forbidden in the house, life centers around the little, prosaic backyard. Remains of ancient lawn furniture are usually occupied by expressionless males staring ahead. Sometimes someone peers over the solid man-high fence at an unwelcoming outside world. Few of the men ever say a word, although they do perk up, sometimes smile a little, and call out a greeting when a rare visitor penetrates their domain.

I have never seen lonelier people.

Some were already familiar faces in 1988, when Jeff was a resident for five months between hospitalizations, as he now recalls precisely. Yet he knows next to nothing about his fellow dwellers, except for matter-of-fact fragments that on occasion I find moving ("John taught math for twenty-one years"). Here, living at closest quarters does not encourage communication. Jeff could tell me little about Bill, with whom he had shared a room for three years: "He's from Alaska, I think." "He's forty-four, I think."

"They're very guarded," said Jo Ann Cloutier, the administrator, off and on, since 1975. "Sometimes you see them chuckling to themselves when they're enjoying something, but they don't share. I can tell they're afraid of making friendships."

The three-times-a-day ritual of getting in line for the distribution of antipsychotic medications—the employees make sure that they are actually swallowed—is the central event at Jordan Hall, and Jo Ann tolerates no deviation.

"I tell them that our licensing people say you can't live here if you don't take your meds," she said. "If necessary, we sit down and talk to them. I tell them to make their doctor aware of problems. I say, 'You have to communicate! Your doctor only knows what you tell him.' "

Obvious? Not if you are imprisoned by schizophrenia's negative symptoms. It was the same message that I had been trying to drill into Jeff again and again: no doctor can divine what's on your mind.

Jo Ann longs for her charges whenever other commitments pull her away for a time. "It just keeps calling me back," she said. "These guys are my family." She bakes birthday cakes for them and maintains a bed for herself in the basement. "If we're having problems, I can't just take off." The county's deteriorating support for her charges depresses her. "They used to eat a lot more beef," she says, and the attending dentists drive her furious. "They don't think of treating teeth," she said, "all they want to do is pull."

Through all the years, it has remained hard for me to believe, much less accept, that I must leave a son in such conditions, that his mother and I are reduced to beggars who can't be choosers. There are no alternatives. The facts are hard and unequivocal. Until Jeff can produce some income and his need of medical support is greatly reduced, the cost of his care is such that it would soon wipe us out, which would help no one.

I attempt to console myself by remembering that I pay my taxes promptly; that I lost three years of my life to military service during World War II and did not cash in on government benefits available to veterans when it was over; that I paid hundreds of thousands of dollars to Jeff's doctors and hospitals as long as I could; that I'm still supplementing the government efforts with more thousands of my own and working as best I can to get Jeff off his dole.

On October 1, at last, lightning struck in time for the 11 p.m. local TV news. Olanzapine was approved by the FDA. It would be available at pharmacies by the week's end. The next morning, the *New York Times* headline confirmed: "FDA Approves Schizophrenia Drug, Offering Hope for Many." A leading expert, Alan Schatzberg, head of psychiatry at Stanford, was quoted: "It's a potential breakthrough of tremendous magnitude." I felt relieved and vindicated, having picked the winner in the medication race two years earlier.

CHAPTER 26

On the Road to Wellness

FROM JEFF'S CARETAKERS in Santa Clara County comes only silence. It looks as if we're in for more bureaucratic foot-dragging, just as when clozapine was introduced. I decide to keep a diary of the lurch toward the Olanzapine finish line.

December 9—A confidential source tells me that a hornet's nest is erupting among the county pharmaceutical chiefs. Turf control is at stake, also relationships with drug suppliers and reallocation of big money—the annual local bill for clozapine is running at about a million dollars plus another $500,000 for risperidone. The cautious and badly pinched county authorities are feuding with the eager Eli Lilly representatives. The switching of patients from clozapine and risperidone to Olanzapine brings uncharted problems, and Abbott agents have secured a strong toehold on behalf of their still-unapproved Sertindole.

January 8, 1997—Skip Pope hears from San Jose that Olanzapine use has finally been authorized by the local authorities on a selective basis. An official memo spells out six hurdles toward case-by-case approval of "applications."

January 11—Dr. Kerschenbaum goes on indeterminate sick leave—a sad loss at a critical point. His replacement, Dr. John Almogela, is reportedly a very different personality.

February 2—Chaos. I mobilize Jeff's conservator, Henry Russell, who finds Almogela "overwhelmed" by his increased workload. The doctor does not voice opposition to Olanzapine, but has been told little about it. He sees most patients only once a month and protests that he doesn't have Jeff's records. I make sure that he gets them with a digestible summary prepared by Skip Pope. Russell says that the medication switch is up to Jeff. Jeff says he hears Olanzapine will make him drowsy. A well-informed source—the regional Eli Lilly representative—assures Jeff that his fear is groundless and tells him again that Olanzapine is much like clozapine, only safer and more effective. Jeff is undecided and upset. I report to Skip Pope: "He sounds worse than I've heard him in years, manic and very frightened." The absence of Dr. Kerschenbaum's accustomed and caring ways is not helping.

February 7—The timing seems ripe for me to fly to San Jose. Perhaps I can reassure Jeff and help break his impasse. I explain Olanzapine to Jeff once more and reassure him. He agrees to switch. I shake his hand ceremoniously and say, "So we have a deal, right?" He agrees, but the next day he complains to the administrator of his halfway house: "Every time I go on a new medication, I wind up in the hospital. I don't want to upset the applecart." In a ten-minute meeting with Dr. Almogela I explain that years ago Jeff was indeed often hospitalized after doctors ineptly switched his medications; these dreaded events remain seared in his mind as if they just occurred. The doctor's desk is stacked with papers. I espy Jeff's case history on top, unopened, and ask whether it would be acceptable for Skip Pope to keep in touch with the doctor. He agrees. This closes a vital loop—now Skip can diplomatically keep his hand on the proceedings.

February 10—Still in San Jose, I commit a grave error by getting drawn into a shouting argument with Jeff about his smoking two packs of cigarettes a day (a routine craving for many patients like himself). He had asked for spending money. I said I feel guilty giving him money regularly, knowing it will go for cigarettes. In my anxiety, I overlook that this is hardly the time to add to Jeff's pressures. He is furious, breaks off all conversation. I fly home.

February 18—As I do frequently, I brief Jeff's brother, Ron, on the latest bumps of my toboggan ride. He hasn't heard me so depressed in a long time and is a bit alarmed. "Don't give up!" he says. "Don't give up!" I say, "Don't worry, I won't! Not when we're so close."

February 19—Skip Pope reports he rechecked with the conservator, who finds Jeff in a "go" mood for Olanzapine. Is the unanimity of his counselors sinking in?

February 28—Jeff's social worker, Karen McCreddin, whom he likes because she is soft-spoken and respects his person and views, reports that Jeff has signed an informed-consent form for going on Olanzapine. He still isn't actually taking the pill, which has to be introduced very gently.

March 11—Jeff is taking the minimum 5 milligrams of Olanzapine. His clozapine dosage has been scaled down to 150 milligrams. The recommended therapeutic Olanzapine dosage is 10 to 20 milligrams. Meanwhile Olanzapine is enjoying the most successful medication launch in history: sales this year are projected at $450 million, $850 million next year.

March 17—I call Jeff, but he won't come to the phone. "Tell him I'm not here," he shouts to the housemate who is taking the call. This has never happened before.

March 18—Jeff is taking 10 milligrams Olanzapine, 125 milligrams clozapine. McCreddin finds him suddenly "agitated," also "hostile" to his housemates. I have read about the relapsing and "decompensating" of a few patients when newly introduced to Olanzapine, so my heart moves into my throat. Skip muses that perhaps the Olanzapine should be stopped for ten days. My instinct urges me not to retreat; my interviewing has convinced me that Olanzapine is worth a gamble. And if the dosage was reduced, the battle might be lost: Jeff and his caretakers might never agree to increase it again.

March 21—Skip Pope hears from Laura Mechling, the county's "Health Care Analyst Psychiatric Medication Oversight Coordinator," that Jeff remains on 10 milligrams Olanzapine; his clozapine is reduced further, to 100. It's like following the stock market. Jeff is still irritable, but Mechling finds this common while a patient's system becomes accustomed to the new medication. Nobody seems worried but me, but he hasn't hung up on anyone else.

March 22—McCreddin is neutral about his dosages. "Jeff is an adult," she lectures me. "These are his decisions." I keep quiet but disagree. Jeff didn't go to medical school; he cannot be expected to know which medications and dosages are right for him.

March 24—I'm told by Eli Lilly that clozapine is very sedating; Olanzapine is not. A switch away from sedation sometimes triggers its opposite, agitation—temporarily. Skip and I talk about my long-term expectations for Jeff. McCreddin keeps insisting they're too high, although I've told her I'm shooting for no more than a private room for Jeff, a private bath, and a few hours of constructive activity daily. Skip comes to my relief with a challenge: "I say, 'Why don't we have high expectations and see what happens?' "

March 26—Dr. Peter Weiden, who has written papers on clozapine-Olanzapine switching, cuts through the fog of Jeff's agitation. "It's not an

Olanzapine reaction," he says. "It's undermedication. Ten milligrams plus a little clozapine is pissing in the wind." This portends another clash with Jeff, who habitually wants all medications reduced or eliminated in memory of old pills that caused him grief long ago.

March 27—I suspect that Jeff is feeling lonely and won't hang up on his brother. I suggest to Ron that they have a gentle, noncommittal chat; that Ron refrain from asking questions or giving Jeff advice, or even bringing up medication problems unless Jeff does. In case Ron sees an opening, Jeff should be flatly told that he is undermedicated, not overmedicated. Ron must have handled this mission lovingly because it worked. Jeff grew chatty with him and agrees to consider twenty milligrams of Olanzapine, which he needs. Is he already getting better, after all?

April 8—Sounding pleased and somewhat surprised, Karen reports that Jeff is getting "steadily better," a wonderful relief. He is more lucid and less irritable. Skip recommends to Almogela that Olanzapine be increased from ten to fifteen milligrams, then to twenty milligrams the following week, and the clozapine phased out. I'm elated.

April 21—We've lucked into a policy that turns out to be scientifically sound: More Olanzapine works better. Talking to the director of a university hospital clinic in Germany, I learn that dosages of thirty and forty milligrams are not uncommon there; no negative reactions are reported. Jeff is still taking fifteen milligrams.

April 23—More evidence that Jeff is discovering an improved self: he has requested—and been granted—a new roommate at his halfway house. His partner of several years is not doing as well as Jeff, and they no longer make a neat match. It's another intriguing sign of improvement, especially since Jeff made the first move. The act of taking the initiative has generally been an impossibility for him.

May 5—I make a routine call to Jeff. "How're you feeling?" I ask. "Crummy!" he grumbles. "Gee, I'm awful sorry to hear that!" Jeff isn't buying sympathy. "Are you really?" he snaps sarcastically and hangs up. That hurts.

May 6—Karen is reassuring. Jeff is experiencing some inner turmoil but mostly to the good. He is coming out of his cocoon, questioning Karen about such "psychosocial" subjects as how to get along better with other people. Paradoxically, Karen recommends that I keep my distance for a while. I guess I stir up too many emotions in him.

May 13—I call Jo Ann Cloutier, the administrator of Jeff's halfway house, who reports Jeff is disappointed with Olanzapine. He had bought into it, but it makes him feel inebriated and like a guinea pig, he says. He's disgusted, which feeds my worst fear: that he might go on strike and forswear all medications. That would be hard to recover from, a psychotic break.

May 14—Dr. Almogela is on vacation, and the county system is too short staffed to provide a replacement. I feel Jeff should be checked by a doctor promptly, possibly for an adjustment of his medication. Who? Andy Abarbanel and Rick Robinson were fired by Jeff. Reed Kaplan is superb with medications but a bit too gung ho in manner for Jeff's present mood. What about Larry Koran at Stanford, who assembled the superb summary of Jeff's case in 1981? His gentle, quiet, but incisive manner would fit. The doctor has always liked Jeff, who has never fired him and, in fact, hasn't seen him in a decade. Perfect! I'm glad that I've been in attendance long enough to provide an institutional memory. Special dispensation is required from Henry Russell, the conservator, to bring in an outside consultant. As always, he is agreeable. Koran is willing to see Jeff at 12:30 p.m. tomorrow.

May 15—It's a ten-strike! Koran spends a full, relaxed hour with Jeff, asks a lot of questions, and concentrates hard on Jeff's answers. Jeff responds at once to this respectful, detailed attention. "He was organized, very articulate, and able to summarize," Karen McCreddin reports proudly. Koran tells Jeff that he needs twenty milligrams of Olanzapine; that his discomfort is temporary; and that it will take three to four months for the drug's full benefit to appear. I've noticed before: it's hard to think of a logical alternative whenever Koran builds up slowly toward a treatment recommendation. Jeff is surprised, but goes along, and the doctor makes an immediate call to get the new dosage started the next morning. "You can rest easy," he tells me. "Jeff's in pretty good shape."

May 16—It's great to see my confidence in Koran so dramatically justified; I'm also a shade bitter. I write him, "I'm both profoundly grateful to you and saddened that there was no way to get Jeff equivalent care right along. If that had been possible, I'm convinced he'd be convalescing a lot faster and more comfortably." Repeat lesson: The quality of psychiatric care varies to a frightening degree.

May 28—Skip reports Jeff feeling "drunk" and anxious. "If this is going to be my life, I hope it'll be short," he tells Karen ominously. Shortly afterward, he calls her back and volunteers he's already feeling better. Skip thinks the sensation of inebriation may be caused by the old-fashioned chloral hydrate which Jeff is allowed to take to sleep better.

May 29—Will Jeff hang up on me again? I decide to take a chance and find him fairly relaxed and with his sense of humor operating. "I've had three gins and tonic," he announces. After a while he concedes that his "inebriation" problem has improved. He is thinking more clearly and, for the first time, tackling life issues maturely. He wants to know how he became ill. "Nobody knows," I tell him. "It's mostly bad luck." He mutters about his luck as any ordinary person might. I remind him of Koran's warning that it might require three or more months for the Olanzapine to take hold. "My life always starts some other time," says Jeff, but he sounds as if he thinks his day will come. I cannot believe he is forty-six years old.

October 1—The ugly years have been whisked away like a dilapidated stage set. I'm in San Jose for the first time in six months and the changes in Jeff are difficult to believe. "He's like . . . like . . . a civilian!" I burst out at Karen, the social worker. She smiles, which she never did before.

Jeff looks taller, leaner, straighter. His hands don't shake. The mental hospital slouch is gone. The scabrous visor cap, the last visible evidence of hopelessness, has vanished. The beard is still in place, but it is fluffy, neatly brushed, no longer a pirate's relic. Jeff combs it frequently.

"Do you think you could get me a watch?" he asks as we settle into a rental car. "I'd like to get my days organized."

Come again? This was breathtaking. For a quarter of a century Jeff's days had been devoid of just about all structure. Even much of his nourishment came from irregular snacks at convenience stores. Only the 8 p.m. collective pill-taking ritual, the principal dispensing time, was a fixed daily anchor.

The need to organize was prompted by a central event that Jeff had scheduled himself, three mornings a week, firmly at nine o'clock, when previously he would have been sleeping. Now he felt drawn to the basement of the Grace Baptist Church, two blocks from his house. There, the City of San Jose operated a therapeutic recreation center for the recovering disabled, physical and mental, with a variety of programs scheduled at certain times.

I had never heard of the place, but it had become the focus of Jeff's days. He would read in its library, but mostly he was actually talking with the people he met there. Some were college-educated kindred spirits; all had known him for years. In his pre-Olanzapine isolation he had very rarely conversed with anyone. Now his shell had dropped away. He was chatting, trading gossip, obviously feeling comfortable "on the outside."

We went to Macy's and got him a Swiss Swatch watch, which he began to wear—and to consult—right away. So when would his new wings let him fly greater distances? "I've been very impressed with his stick-to-itiveness," Karen said. "He wouldn't be going to the center three days a week if he weren't on the road. . . ." And when she saw me still looking expectant, she said, "He needs to be the driver."

Afterword

by Jeff Wyden

A S T H I S B O O K S H O W S, I have undergone psychiatric routines since 1972 that are hard to imagine in terms of the trauma that they caused me. Then, late in 1973, a doctor whom I would include in the competent category told me that I could expect to be all right in a couple of years but that I would have to be "careful."

I hope readers will have gathered that my being careful—and mental patients in general being careful—cannot lead to good results unless the many medical personnel are also careful in the way in which they deal with patients.

Other doctors advised me to be "patient," no pun intended. This was also reasonable advice, I supposed, but I did not find it easy to follow for twenty-six years. Now I hope it is OK for me to live just a bit less carefully and that I will no longer have to remain quite so patient.

A Financial Disclosure

IN THESE cynical times, it should be said that neither I nor any member of my family has ever owned, now owns, or intends to acquire any stock in any pharmaceutical or allied enterprise.

P.W.

Notes

Overview of the Literature

The History of Psychiatry, by Franz G. Alexander and Sheldon T. Selesnick (1966), remains an excellent, if partly outdated and pro-Freudian, source. *A History of Psychiatry*, by Edward Shorter (1997), is outstanding, if anti-Freudian and not quite as up-to-date as the year of publication suggests.

The best quick briefing on the disease is "Schizophrenia," by William T. Carpenter Jr. and Robert W. Buchanan, in the *New England Journal of Medicine* (March 10, 1994). By far the best reference book—penetrating, complete, and readable—is *Surviving Schizophrenia* (third edition), by E. Fuller Torrey (1995); I cannot recommend this work highly enough. The four-part series "Advancing on Schizophrenia," in the *New York Times* (1986), by Philip M. Boffey, Erik Ekholm, Harold M. Schmeck Jr., and Daniel Goleman, is insightful, thorough, and suffers very little from age.

Psychopharmacology, as a distinct specialty, is not well covered in up-to-date, integrated format. *The Psychopharmacologists*, a far-ranging collection of detailed interviews with leading researchers, assembled by David Healy (1996), is revealing and fresh. A second volume is due in 1998. *Discoveries in Biological Psychiatry*, a collection of valuable original biographical articles by the pioneer investigators, edited by Frank J. Ayd Jr. and Barry Blackwell (1970), is the indispensable basic resource. *Chlorpromazine in Psychiatry*, by Judith P. Swazey (1974), covers its specialty elegantly. *Origins of Psychopharmacology: From CPZ to LSD*, by Anne E. Caldwell, is good coverage but stops in 1970.

Two masterful, invaluable papers track the revolt of the biological psychiatrists and their eventual victory over the psychodynamic Freudians: "Neurosis, Psychodynamics, and DSM-III," by Robert L. Spitzer and Ronald Bayer, in the *Archives of General Psychiatry* (February 1985), and "DSM-III and the Transformation of American Psychiatry: A History," by Mitchell Wilson, in the *American Journal of Psychiatry* (March 1993).

For the history minded, the reprints of forty-four articles by great names of psychiatry in the sesquicentennial anniversary supplement of the *Journal of the American Psychiatric Association* (1994) is a stirring flashback to groundbreaking events and personalities.

For current developments, the *New York Times* and the monthly *Psychiatric Times* generally do the most alert job, especially the *Times* writer Daniel Goleman. The bulky quarterly *Schizophrenia Bulletin* of the National Institute of Mental Health, while largely too technical for general readers and not always current, has lately become more accessible to news and to unconventional studies. It is trying harder to keep up with the pace of research and hold up a mirror to what is preoccupying the scientists.

CHAPTER 1

The Onset

Conditions in the Kansas mental hospitals were sketched in my series of articles beginning in the *Wichita Eagle* on October 15, 1948. The reforms initiated by the 1948–1949 Kansas legislature and Karl Menninger's role are traced in Lawrence J. Friedman's meticulous *Menninger: The Family and the Clinic*. Luckily, Dr. Vincent J. D'Andrea was still practicing at the Stanford University student health center; my contemporaneous interviews with him were invaluable. The indispensable personal correspondence and records quoted throughout the book remain in my possession.

CHAPTER 2

Diagnosis: School Phobia

The literature on school phobia, especially its possible aftermath, remains frustratingly vague. The psychological sophistication of my late mother, Helen, unusual for her age and lack of formal background, was most helpful in our understanding of Jeff's mentality during his teens. Details on the Los Angeles Suicide Prevention Center come from my August 19, 1961, *Saturday Evening Post* article, "Suicide." Suicide in schizophrenia is discussed in E. Fuller Torrey's *Surviving Schizophrenia*, pages 271–73. Behaviorism and behavior therapy originated in the literature of J. B. Watson and B. F. Skinner; my own education in this field began with George R. Bach, the behaviorist psychologist with whom I coauthored *The Intimate Enemy*.

CHAPTER 3

Meltdown

Interviews with Dr. Vincent J. D'Andrea, Dr. Lorrin Koran, Jeff, and his mother, Edith, form much of the basis for this chapter. Memories of my relationships with Karl Menninger and Franklin Murphy, stretching over thirty years, informed my references to them. Details of Dr. Karl's travail with Freud in Vienna and Menninger's passion for Freud's teachings appear in Lawrence J. Friedman's *Menninger: The Family and the Clinic*, pages 108–10. Freud's candid letter to István Hollós, abjuring psychotics, is in Peter Gay's *Freud: A Life for Our Times*, page 537.

CHAPTER 4

What Really Ails Jeff Wyden?

The Menninger Clinic's case notes for 1972 to 1974 were of obvious crucial help in pinning down details of symptoms, treatments, Jeff's reactions, and, most particularly, the motivations and mind-set of the treatment team. The 1988 quote from *Nature* and other basic data about the disease come from the superb briefing paper "Schizophrenia," by William T. Carpenter Jr. and Robert W. Buchanan, in the *New England Journal of Medicine* (1994). Skip Pope and Joseph F. Lipinsky Jr.'s July 1978 article in the *Archives of General Psychiatry* on schizophrenia versus manic-depression diagnosis is one of the most widely quoted statements in the contemporary literature on psychosis. Its caveats have been generally accepted; its practical applications to patients like Jeff are in doubt. Pope's authority notwithstanding, he is the only one of Jeff's innumerable doctors who ever labeled him unqualifiedly "manic-depressive."

The basic document for the John Hinckley case is the careful, surprisingly even-handed history by the would-be assassin's parents, Jack and JoAnn Hinckley, *Breaking Points*. The transcript of their candid interview on ABC's *20/20* program, "There but for the Grace of God," of April 28, 1983, was also helpful. The *New York Times* article of September 20, 1996, "Hinckley Tries, Again, to Gain Some Freedom," updates the complexities of the case usefully. Hinckley's latest lawyer, Barry Levine, was accessible and eloquent in two telephone interviews. Dr. Carpenter tried to be helpful with two letters, but felt confined by doctor-patient confidentiality.

The diagnosis of Rosemary Kennedy presented a dilemma when I began researching. Fuller Torrey had raised the possibility that she had been schizophrenic as well as retarded. Laurence Leamer's exhaustive *The Kennedy Women* fanned the suspicions. Fortuitously, the affidavit from Dr. James Watts that Ronald Kessler obtained for his Joseph P. Kennedy biography, *The Sins of the Father*, settled the case. Watts had performed the surgery half a century ago. Kessler had performed a stunning research tour de force, demonstrating once again that a stubborn reporter's shoe leather is history's stoutest ally. The literature on the triumvirate of frontal lobotomy, Egas Moniz—its inventor—and its chief surgeons, Walter Freeman and James Watts, is extensive but not very revealing. By far the most authoritative history, a work of remarkable diligence and fair-mindedness, is more recent: *Great and Desperate Cures*, by Elliot S. Valenstein (1986).

While much of the huge literature on Marilyn Monroe is self-serving or bizarre, *Goddess*, by Anthony Summers, represents exemplary reporting. My quotations are of judgments he elicited from dozens of eyewitnesses. His material on Dr. Greenson is unique. Not everyone will accept the case for a schizophrenia diagnosis as conclusive. I do. I found my conversations with Bob Litman and Arthur Miller persuasive.

CHAPTER 5

The Godfather: Emil Kraepelin

Though dead for more than seventy years, Kraepelin as a figure in history remains a work in progress, spurred anew by the belated discovery of his remarkably bland memoirs. These *Lebenserinnerungen* were finally published in 1983 by a team at Munich University headed by one of his successors, Hanns Hippius. I was extended many hours of generous assistance by Hippius and his colleague Paul Hoff, author of a technical 1994 Kraepelin monograph. They led me to a walking encyclopedia in the Munich suburbs, Frau Alma Kreuter, nearly ninety years old, with personal memories of Kraepelin. She passed me onto a grandson, Professor Hans-Peter Dürr. Appreciative assessments of Kraepelin's scientific contributions appear even in writings of such psychoanalytic-minded adversaries as Silvano Arieti and Gregory Zilboorg. For Kraepelin's hypernationalism, see Paul Weindling's *Health, Race and German Politics Between National*

Unification and Nazism; more of the same, as well as Kraepelin's little-known American connections, is in Matthias M. Weber's *Ernst Rüdin*, the informative biography of the godfather's collaborator and future Nazi ideologue. The most informative sources on the feud between Kraepelin and Freud are *Kraepelin und Freud*, by Kurt Kolle, a Kraepelin student and successor; the searching essay by the psychiatrist Jacob Wyrsch in *Der Nervenarzt* (1956); and some intriguing inside glimpses in *Helene Deutsch*, by Paul Roazen. The most insightful appraisal, "Two Faces of Emil Kraepelin," by the British psychiatrist Michael Shepherd, did not appear until 1995, almost seventy years after Kraepelin's death.

CHAPTER 6

The Menninger Wars

The account of the Menninger encounters relies on the clinic's case file of Jeff and the memories of Jeff and myself; the clinical case study by Dr. Lorrin Koran in 1981; and Lawrence Friedman's biography of the Menningers, *Menninger*. Henri Laborit's role in the Thorazine discovery is still unjustly downplayed in much of the literature, subordinate to contributions of enterprising but later doctors and developers. I relied on Judith P. Swazey's history, *Chlorpromazine*; and *The Miracle Finders*, by Donald Robinson, a diligent American medical writer who interviewed Laborit in the 1970s; and *Madness and the Brain*, by Solomon Snyder.

CHAPTER 7

The Revolutionaries

Mike Gorman's graphic *Reader's Digest* book condensation *Oklahoma Attacks Its Snake Pits* remains instructive. His *Every Other Bed* helped me set the scene for reform in the mid-1950s. *The Mad among Us*, by Gerald N. Grob, supplied useful context. *The Mentally Ill in America*, by Albert Deutsch, delves into older history in greater detail. During several interviews in New York and Puerto Rico, Frank Ayd Jr. was an encyclopedic source. I found his 1991 lecture, "The Early History of Modern Psychopharmacology," authoritative, and I also drew from *In the Beginning*, the privately published volume on the origin of the American College of Neuropsychopharmacology. "Profiles in Psychiatry: Frank J. Ayd, Jr.," by Sandra Somers, illuminates those early days. Several interviews with Oakley Ray, of the college staff in Nashville, Tennessee, were invariably productive. So were the hours of interviewing the peppery Dr. Paul Janssen in Beerse, Belgium, supported by documentation from his in-house books, *Breakthrough*, by Harry Schwartz, and *Dr. Paul*, by Janssen Pharmaceutica. For Janssen's early successes I used his own account, "The Butyrohenone Story," in Ayd and Blackwell's *Discoveries in Biological Psychiatry*, pages 165–79.

CHAPTER 8

The Restored

The Mark Vonnegut story is in his *Eden Express*; "Why I Want to Bite R.D. Laing" in *Harper's* (April 1974); and interviews conducted by me in 1996 and Otto Friedrich in 1974.

The latter is in Friedrich's wise and beautifully reported history *Going Crazy* (1975). I interviewed Dr. Frese in Ohio. Background on him is in *NAMI Advocate*, May/June 1995, page 21. The Dr. North data come from her book *Welcome, Silence*. Lori Schiller set down her dramatic experiences in *The Quiet Room*. Linda Woods's recovery is in the *New York Times* (1995). The John Nash recovery was reported by Sylvia Nasar, also in the *Times* (1994). The first-person accounts of patients that appear in each issue of the *Schizophrenia Bulletin* convey the feel of the schizophrenia experience. Access to the Olanzapine success stories came through Dr. Michael W. Smith of UCLA and Dr. Peter J. Weiden of Columbia.

CHAPTER 9

"An Arrogant View of Their Mission"

For the Rosehan caper, probably the most widely discussed experiment in psychology, I drew on the original text in *Science*. For the battles and triumph of the biological psychiatrists, I used the summaries by Mitchell Wilson ("DSM-III") and Robert L. Spitzer with Ronald Bayer ("Neurosis"); *The Selling of DSM*, by Stuart A. Kirk and Herb Kutchins; and the monumental *Disorders of Personality: DSM-IV and Beyond* (second edition), by Theodore Millon, which includes a veritable encyclopedia of accessible historical and personality sketches (818 pages). Interviews with Melvin Sabshin and Robert Spitzer were the most valuable. "Rewriting the Dictionary of Madness," by Ann Japenga, in the *Los Angeles Times Magazine*, puts forth an interesting but extreme version of a negative view.

CHAPTER 10

The Shattered

Michael Wechsler's tragedy was chronicled in his father's book, *In a Darkness*, by James A. Wechsler, but I relied on the insightful account in *Going Crazy*. The Frumkin/Mason odyssey was felicitously and exhaustively detailed, twice, in *The New Yorker* by Susan Sheehan.

CHAPTER 11

Freud Is Dead, Freud Lives!

Much of this chapter of necessity relies on my memory, supported by the recollections of Dr. D'Andrea and Jeff. Appraisals of Freud are, of course, almost limitless and still proliferating; it is an industry. For a pro-Freudian view, I relied on the reasonably objective *Freud*, by Peter Gay. The best-researched, nonapoplectic, but negative view is in *Freud and His Followers* and *Brother Animal*, by Paul Roazen. The brief assessments in *Going Crazy* (page 72 and following) are highly perceptive. *Freudian Fraud*, by E. Fuller Torrey, is an intriguingly global, somewhat overwrought perspective. For the contemporary controversies, I used "Is Freud Finished?" by John Elson in *Time*; "The Trouble with Sigmund," by John Leland in *Newsweek*; and "Freud May Be Dead, but His Critics Still Kick," by Dinita Smith in the *New York Times*. Two volumes by Nathan G. Hale Jr., *Freud and the Americans* and *The Rise and Crisis of Psychoanalysis in the United States*, are scholarly, far ranging, and accessible, and bring Freud and his influence closer to home.

CHAPTER 12

Antiheroes

The Milton Wexler incident is related by him in chapter 10 of *Psychotherapy of Schizophrenia*, edited by John Gunderson and Loren R. Mosher. For a treatment of John Rosen, I consulted the chapter "John Rosen and Direct Psychoanalysis" in *Against Therapy*, by Jeffrey Moussaieff Masson. Nathan G. Hale Jr. deals with Rosen evenhandedly in *The Rise and Crisis of Psychoanalysis*, vol. 2, pages 264–67. A sample from Rosen's hand is "The Survival Function of Schizophrenia," in the May 1950 *Bulletin of the Menninger Clinic*. A sympathetic picture of Rosen is in *Treatment of Schizophrenia*, Louis Jolyon West and Don E. Flinn, editors, pages 111–16. Correspondence between Rosen and Karl Menninger is in the Menninger Clinic archives.

For Henry Cotton's career, I relied on "Desperate Remedies: A Gothic Tale of Madness and Modern Medicine," by Andrew Scull, in *Lectures on the History of Psychiatry*, 1990, the Squibb Series. There is nothing satisfactory on Adolf Meyer; Gerald N. Grob makes a largely abortive attempt to capture this strange but influential figure in *The Mad among Us*.

Peter R. Breggin has produced a virtual library of his own, beginning with *Psychiatric Drugs: Hazard to the Brain* (1983). I used *Toxic Psychiatry* (1991) and *Talking Back to Prozac* (1994). For the April 2, 1987, Oprah Winfrey show I used the transcript from Radio and TV Reports, Inc., of Chevy Chase, Maryland. For news stories about reactions to this show, see especially "Doctor Says Md. Medical Panel Cleared Him," by Susan Schmidt, in the *Washington Post*, September 23, 1987, page A22. From the considerable literature on Ewen Cameron, I relied largely on the most complete and up-to-date account, *Journey into Madness*, by Gordon Thomas.

CHAPTER 13

Out of It

This chapter relied mainly on correspondence and interviews with Jeff and conversations with Edith Wyden; Drs. Koran, Rick Robinson, Reed Kaplan; and the late Dr. R. Dr. Koran's 1981 evaluation of Jeff is in my files. The revised and up-to-date version of H. L. Newbold's theories and practice (1993) is detailed in *Dr. Newbold's Nutrition for Your Nerves*.

CHAPTER 14

"So Many Wonderful, Wonderful People"

Interviews were the principal sources: Pete and Nancy Domenici; Ron Wyden; Robert, Connie, and Joe Litman; Fuller Torrey; David Pickar; Richard Jed Wyatt; Jay Neugeboren. The personal role of Senator Domenici and other politicians is sketched in "When Politics Becomes Personal," by Laura Blumenfeld, in the *Washington Post*. Karl Menninger's 1926 paper, "Influenza and Schizophrenia," is reprinted in the 1994 sesquicentennial anniversary issue of the *American Journal of Psychiatry*. "Stalking the Schizovirus," by E. Fuller Torrey and Robert H. Yolken, is in vol. 14, no. 2 (1988) of *Schizophrenia Bulletin*. "Could Schizophrenia Be a Viral Zoonosis Transmitted from House Cats?" is in vol. 21, no. 2 (1995) of the *Bulletin*. From Torrey's prodigious output I was particularly struck by his groundbreaking if inconclusive *Schizophrenia and Civiliza-*

tion (1980) and drew often from the much-needed Appendix A in his *Surviving Schizo-phrenia:* "Ten Best and Ten Worst Readings on Schizophrenia." Details on Meggin Hollister are in the *Los Angeles Times,* by Renee Tawa, and in *People,* by Patrick Rogers.

CHAPTER 15

Clozapine I: The Twenty-Five-Year Marathon

For its first phase, the reconstruction of clozapine's travail depended principally on interviews with Skip Pope, Herb Meltzer, Vera Hassner Sharav, Meltzer's born-again alumni (Kevin Buchberger and Brandon Fitch), and, in San Jose, Michael Kerschenbaum and Henry Russell. The Sandoz bureaucracy in the United States responded lethargically at best, with the exceptions of Drs. Marion Finkel and Daniel Hauser. Mrs. Sharav (then Hassner) told her story, "The Clozapine Saga," in *The Journal* (California Association for the Mentally Ill), vol. 4, no. 1, 1993. The Virginia Street Project vanished without a trace known to me. Caremark left a long paper trail. I relied largely on Daniel Goleman's "Outcry Grows over Method of Selling New Drug," in the *New York Times,* and "Caremark International to Plead Guilty in Kickback Inquiry, Pay $159 Million," by Thomas M. Burton, in the *Wall Street Journal.* For some of the overall clozapine story, I relied on the 1993 article "Penetrating the Secrets of Schizophrenia," in the *Sandoz Bulletin* by Herb Meltzer, and the comprehensive 1992 cover story in *Time* magazine, "Awakening," July 6, 1992, pages 52–60.

CHAPTER 16

Clozapine II: Death and Resurrection

I discussed the Finnish epidemic with Dr. Idänpään-Heikkila in Geneva, Dr. Hanns Hippius in Munich, and Dr. Botond Berde in Basel, and all agreed that the facts will remain elusive. The best, if unsatisfying, study is by H. A. Amsler et al., in *Acta Psychiatrica Scandinavia* (1977).

Much of the rest of this chapter is also based on interviews, especially with Gil Honigfeld, Hanns Hippius, Daniel Casey, and Michael Kerschenbaum, as well as Paul Leber, Botond Berde, Lou Gerbino, Dr. J. Schmutz, Morton Mintz, Skip Pope, and Soleng Tom. The late Nathan Kline is inadequately captured in the literature. The best biographical evaluation is in *The Miracle Finders,* by Donald Robinson, who actually got Kline to sit still for an interview. The Food and Drug Administration holds documents about its years of legal wrestling with Kline and the October 11, 1979, Senate hearings. *Preclinical and Clinical Hearing, Testing by the Pharmaceutical Industry, 1979,* pages 33–34, contains hilarious recollections of FDA attempts to tame the doctor. Hippius contributed "The History of Clozapine" to *Psychopharmacology* in 1989. The final approval phase of clozapine is detailed in the dramatic 261-page transcript of the thirtieth meeting of the FDA Psychopharmacologic Drugs Advisory Committee on April 26, 1989. Subsequent years brought an avalanche of appraisals of the drug's value and uses. Arguably most interesting are two articles in the *American Journal of Psychiatry* of June 1995: "Patient Response and Resource Management: Another View of Clozapine Treatment of Schizophrenia," by William T. Carpenter Jr. et al., and "Clozapine: Is Another View Valid?" by Herbert Y. Meltzer. For Sandoz's corporate history, see the special 1986 issue of *Sandoz Bulletin, 100 Jahre fuer ein Leben mit Zukunft (100 Years for Life with a Future)* and *Sandoz*

Ltd. 1986–1996, which the company produced in English translation. The LSD story is told by its inventor, Albert Hofmann, in chapter 7 of Frank Ayd's *Discoveries in Biological Psychiatry* and brought up-to-date in *LSD: Still with Us after All These Years,* by Leigh A. Henderson and William J. Glass.

CHAPTER 17

The Symptoms Were "Not Severe Enough"

Interviews: Dan Weisburd, Bob Aller, Ron Wyden, Jim Willwerth, Vera Hassner Sharav, and Adil Shamoo. Weisburd's touching tribute to his son David, entitled "DJW," is in the CAMI *Journal.* The Ron Wyden House hearings on informed consent are in serial No. 103-85, May 23, 1994. The best journalistic summaries of the UCLA controversy are "Witness in Fine Print" and "Tinkering with Madness," both by Jim Willwerth, in *Time,* and "For the Sake of Science," by Joy Horowitz, in the *Los Angeles Times Magazine.* The tragedy of Sharav's son Ami is traced by his father, Itzhak Sharav, in "Ami's Race with Death," in the *New York Times,* also by *In the Matter of Jacob Gordon,* in the August 1995 report by the New York State Commission on Quality of Care for the Mentally Disabled. The issue entitled *Ethics* of CAMI's *Journal,* vol. 5, no. 1, 1994, contains a wealth of outstanding contributions, including a discussion of drug washouts in "Our Responsibilities toward Persons with Mental Illness As Human Subjects in Research," by Dr. Shamoo. His January 1995 Baltimore conference on ethics is adroitly covered by Philip J. Hilts in "Consensus on Ethics in Research Is Elusive" for the *New York Times.* The proceedings of the conference were published by Dr. Shamoo at the University of Maryland School of Medicine, 108 N. Greene Street, Baltimore, MD 21201.

CHAPTER 18

Is There No Home for Jeff?

Interviews: Fuller Torrey, Herbert Pardes, Connie Litman, Rick Robinson, and, of course, Jeff. Vintage Loren Mosher is his *Community Mental Health,* coauthored with Lorenzo Burti, 1994 edition. Details of Mosher's early work in California are from "Soteria: Evaluation of a Home-Based Treatment for Schizophrenia," by Mosher et al., in *American Journal of Orthopsychiatry,* 1975. Details on Fromm-Reichmann are from Nathan Hale's second volume on Freud, pages 186–87. She and the rest of the antimothers school (Lidz, Bateson, etc.) are sensibly drawn in Maryellen Walsh's *Schiz-o-phre-nia.* The R. D. Laing material comes mostly from Otto Friedrich's *Going Crazy* (pages 99–104). Of the many recent writings, I used *R.D. Laing* by his son, Adrian Charles Laing, and *The Wing of Madness,* by Daniel Burston. The Reagan administration's abortive campaign to deprive the mentally disabled of Social Security benefits was repeatedly covered by the *New York Times* in April 1983, especially in an editorial, "Why Drive Troubled People Crazy?" April 20. My file of communications with Bernie is large.

CHAPTER 19

Rename It "Nijinsky's Disease"

Interviews: Jerome Vaccaro, Lonnie Edenfield, Richard Jed Wyatt, Laurie Flynn, Elaine Dutch, Walter B. Gulbinat, Jose Manoel Bertolote, J. A. Costa e Silva, Norman

Sartorius, Arthur Kleinman, Charles Beasley Jr., Jean-Noel Beuzen, Andrew Wood, Otto Benkert, Fred Rappard. The editorial "Degeneration Theory and the Stigma of Schizophrenia" appeared in *Biological Psychiatry* in 1985. The national poll on stigma was conducted for NAMI by Belden and Russonello in January 1996. Kleinman is coauthor of *World Mental Health*; I drew from chapter 2, "Mental Illness and Psychiatric Services," and from his *Rethinking Psychiatry*. His work and other useful data are discussed in the chapter "Disordered States" of *The Trouble with Medicine*, by Melvin Konner. The ten-country WHO study is in Monograph Supplement 20 of *Psychological Medicine*.

From the large literature on homelessness, I used *Nowhere to Go*, by Fuller Torrey; "Imminent Danger," by Dan Hurley, in *Psychology Today*; *Outcasts on Main Street*, by the Federal Task Force on Homelessness and Severe Mental Illness. A revealing profile of Dr. Richard Jed Wyatt, "Seeking to Understand—and Change—the Course of Schizophrenia," by Janet Farrar Worthington, is in the winter 1994/1995 *NARSAD Newsletter*. The NAMI search service for missing and homeless persons, operated by Lonnie Edenfield, is in Warner Robin, Georgia, at (912) 328-3555. For German practices, the Otto Benkert study is seminal. For Japan, I drew on "Zen and the Art of Psychotherapy," by Yutaka Ono and Douglas Berger, and "The Japanese Mental Health System and Family Movement," by Iwao Oshima and Kazuyo Nakai.

For the role of media, I used *Media Madness*, by Otto F. Wahl, and the issue on media and mental illness in the CAMI *Journal*, vol. 4, no. 1, 1993, especially "Movie Madness," by Steven E. Hyler et al.; "The Movies and the Mentally Ill," by Frederick J. Frese; and "A Real Take on Mental Illness," by Stuart Fischoff.

CHAPTER 20
Shock

Interviews: Reed Kaplan, Rick Robinson, Andy Abarbanel, Jeff Wyden, Edith Wyden, Jerry DeFraites, David A. Sack, Matthew Rudorfer. The literature on electroconvulsive therapy electroshock (ETC) is very large, beginning with its pioneers, Ugo Cerletti and Lothar Kalinowsky. I used "As Empty As Eve," by Berton Rouché, from the "Annals of Medicine" section of *The New Yorker* (1974), and "Short Sharp Shocks," by Gene Stone, in *New York* magazine. *USA Today* of December 6, 1995, contains four thoroughly researched contemporary contributions: "Patients Often Aren't Informed of Full Danger"; "For Patients, Treatment's Value Varies"; "Stunningly Quick Results Often Fade Just As Fast"; and "Doctor's Financial Stake in Electroshock Therapy."

CHAPTER 21
Three Breakthroughs

Interviews: Nick Tye, Melvin Perelman, Jeffrey Goldstein, Jes Gerlach, John Hyttel, Jörn Arndt, Terri Sebree, Charles Schulz, Lisa Arvinitis, Bill Wirshing, John Guy, Jeff Wyden, Jambur Ananth, Gordie, Kristin Phillips, Solomon Snyder, August Watanabe. For Banting's discovery, I used *Banting's Miracle*, by Seale Harris. The insulin story and other Eli Lilly history are from *All in a Century*, by E. J. Kahn Jr., and *The Merchants of Life*, by Tom Mahoney. Lilly's explosive growth, triggered by Prozac, is documented in its 1995 annual report. For details on Prozac, see *Listening to Prozac*, by Peter Kramer, and *Talking Back to Prozac*, by Peter Breggin. *The Merchants of Life* by Tom Mahoney puts the pharmaceutical industry's best foot forward. The worst is in *Corporate Crime in the Phar-*

maceutical Industry, by John Braithwaite. Several exemplary exposés by Morton Mintz make the negative case reliably, especially *The Therapeutic Nightmare.* For the industry's profits, I used *Making Medicine—Making Money,* by Donald Drake and Marian Uhlman. The Randall Tobias tragedy is in "Private Pain," by Donna Heimansohn.

CHAPTER 22
In the Pipeline

Interviews: John Tallman, Philip Seeman, Richard Jed Wyatt, Robert Paul Liberman, William Anthony, Peter J. Weiden. "Dopamine Receptors and Psychosis," by Philip Seeman, in *Scientific American,* was my basic briefing, especially for the elusive D4 receptor. The Neurogen annual report for 1994 is informative. "Early Intervention in Schizophrenia," by Marvin I. Herz, is a history of prevention by a pioneer. *Psychiatric News* for July 5, 1996, page 4, contains unusually valuable material on this subject. "The Prodromal Phase of First-Episode Psychosis," by Alison R. Yung and Patrick D. McGorry, was helpful. "After the Awakening, the Real Therapy Must Begin," by James Willwerth, is an incisive introduction to psychosocial rehabilitation. The issue on recovery of the CAMI *Journal* (vol. 5, no. 3, 1994) covers the entire subject well. From the output of Robert Paul Liberman, I found the self-published *Recovery from Schizophrenia: The Road to Recovery Is Paved with Social and Independent Living Skills* most helpful. Details on career counseling, educational support, and employment support for persons aged seventeen to fifty-five with a history of mental problems are available from Larry Kohn, Center for Psychiatric Rehabilitation, Boston University, 730 Commonwealth Avenue, Boston, MA 02215.

CHAPTER 23
"That Could Have Killed the Drug Right There"

This material relies principally on repeated conversations with Charles M. Beasley Jr. and interviews with Gary D. Tollefson, Steven M. Paul, Robert N. Postlethwait, Karin A. Graffeo, Vin Rampey, Terri Sebree, Daniel E. Casey, Jeff Goldstein, Dan Carlson, and Steven Strand. The tests for scurvy are covered in *The Aspirin Wars* by Charles C. Mann and Mark L. Plummer. Early reports on Remoxipride are in "A Long-Term Study of Remoxipride in Chronic Schizophrenic Patients," by H. Vartiainen et al.; "Remoxipride in the Treatment of Psychoses," by Lars Eriksson; and "Experiences of Long-Term Treatment with Remoxipride: Efficacy and Tolerability, by Jan Wallinder et al.

CHAPTER 24
Last-Minute Hurdles

Interviews: Daniel E. Casey, Dan Carlson, Jeff Wyden, Michael W. Smith, Yoshi Arai. My chief source for drug interactions was "The P450 Family," by Alan J. Gelenberg, in *Biological Therapies in Psychiatry Newsletter,* especially the crucial table on page 30. "Ethnicity and Psychopharmacology," by Keh-Ming Lin et al., and "Brussels Sprouts and Psychopharmacology," by James W. Jefferson and John H. Greist, are useful.

CHAPTER 25
Jeff Now

Interviews: Jeff Wyden, Michael Kerschenbaum, Skip Pope, Karen McCreddin, Jo Ann Cloutier, Karen Wrinkle, Soleng Tom, Alex Mitchell, Ron Wyden, Dan Casey, Herb Meltzer, Fuller Torrey, Robert Paul Liberman, Peter J. Weiden. Fuller Torrey explains negative symptoms in fourteen lines in his *Surviving Schizophrenia,* third edition, pages 89–90. William T. Carpenter Jr. and Robert W. Buchanan do the job with more scientific documentation, including Emil Kraepelin's original assessment, in their essay "Schizophrenia." "Negative Symptoms in Schizophrenia: Assessment of the Effect of Risperidone," by Nina R. Schooler, is actually not limited to risperidone. The various confusing assessment scales are explained in "New Agents for Treating Negative Symptoms," by Lewis Opler. "Olanzapine: A New 'Atypical' Antipsychotic," by Peter J. Weiden, is a rounded profile; his and Mark Olfson's "Switching Antipsychotic Medications," copes carefully with an intricate undertaking as of January 1997.

Bibliography

Abbott Laboratories. *Safety and Dose Response of Three Doses of Sertindole and Three Doses of Haldol in Schizophrenic Patients.* Study M-93-113. Abbott Laboratories, 1995.

Alexander, Franz G., and Sheldon T. Selesnick. *The History of Psychiatry.* Harper, 1966.

Aller, Gregory, Jr. *Problems in Securing Informed Consent in Experimental Trials of Unapproved Drugs and Devices: Hearing before the Subcommittee on Regulation, Business Opportunities and Technology* [UCLA]. House of Representatives, May 23, 1994, 4–39.

American College of Neuropsychopharmacology. *In the Beginning . . . the Origins of the American College of Neuropsychopharmacology.* ACNP, 1990.

American Psychiatric Association. *Practice Guideline for Treatment of Patients with Schizophrenia.* APA Office of Research, May 1996.

———. *Quick Reference to the Diagnostic Criteria from DSM-IV.* APA, 1994.

Amsler, H. A. "Agranulocytosis in Patients Treated with Clozapine: A Study of the Finnish Epidemic." *Acta Psychiatrica Scandinavia* 56 (1977): 241–48.

Anderson, Carol M., Douglas J. Reiss, and Gerard E. Hogarty. *Schizophrenia and the Family.* Guilford, 1986.

Andreasen, Nancy C., and William T. Carpenter Jr. "Diagnosis and Classification of Schizophrenia." *Schizophrenia Bulletin* (National Institute of Mental Health), 19, no. 2 (1993): 199–211.

Anthony, William A. *Community Support Systems: Lessons for Managed Care.* Center for Psychiatric Rehabilitation, Boston University, 1996.

———. "Psychiatric Rehabilitation: Key Issues and Future Policy." *Health Affairs* (Fall 1992): 164–70.

Anthony, William A., et al. "Relationships between Symptomatology, Work Skills and Future Vocational Performance." *Psychiatric Services* 6, no. 4 (April 1995): 353–58.

Arieti, Silvano. *Interpretation of Schizophrenia.* 2nd ed. Basic, 1974.

————. "Treatment of Schizophrenia: Progress and Prospects." In *Interpretation of Schizophrenia.* 2nd ed. 1974.

Arno, Peter S., and Karyn L. Feiden. *Against the Odds.* HarperCollins, 1992.

Associated Press. "Court-Ordered Study Condemns Illinois's Psychiatric Hospitals." *New York Times,* December 22, 1995.

————. "Cutoffs for Mentally Ill Bring Moratorium Plea." *New York Times,* April 10, 1983.

————. "FDA Approves Schizophrenia Drug, Offering Hope for Many" [Olanzapine]. *New York Times,* October 2, 1996.

————. " 'Killer Bureaucrats': Ads Say FDA Stalls Vital Drugs." *Waterbury* [Conn.] *Republican,* January 30, 1995.

————. "Panel Endorses Schizophrenia Drug" [Sertindole]. *New York Times,* July 16, 1996.

————. "Tests Show New Drug to Be of Help for Some Severe Schizophrenics" [clozapine]. *New York Times,* May 15, 1987.

Ayd, Frank J., Jr. "The Early History of Modern Psychopharmacology." *Neuropsychopharmacology* 5, no. 2 (1991): 71–83.

Ayd, Frank J., Jr., and Barry Blackwell, eds. *Discoveries in Biological Psychiatry.* Lippincott, 1970.

Backlar, Patricia. *The Family Face of Schizophrenia.* Tarcher Putnam, 1994.

Ban, T. A., and Hanns Hippius, eds. *Thirty Years CINP* [Collegium Internationale Neuro-Psychopharma Cologicum]. Springer, 1988.

Begley, Sharon. "One Pill Makes You Larger and One Pill Makes You Small." *Newsweek,* February 7, 1994, 37–43.

Bender, Kenneth J. "FDA Evaluates Antipsychotic Research." *Psychiatric Times* (October 1995): 1, 27–29.

————. "New Antipsychotics: Concept to Late-Stage Development." Supplement to *Psychiatric Times* (May 1996): 1–4.

Benkert, Otto, H. M. P. Kepplinger, and K. Sobota. *Psychopharmaka im Widerstreit* [*Psychopharmaceuticals in Controversy*]. Springer, 1995.

Bennett, Amanda. "Back from Hell: Lori Schiller Emerges from The Torments of Schizophrenia." *Wall Street Journal,* October 14, 1992.

Birmingham, Stephen. *Our Crowd* [James Loeb]. Harper, 1967.

Blakeslee, Sandra. "How Brain May Weigh the World with Simple Dopamine System." *New York Times,* March 19, 1996.

Bleuler, Eugen. *Dementia Praecox or the Group of Schizophrenias.* International Universities, 1950.

Blumenfeld, Laura. "When Politics Becomes Personal" [Sen. Domenici]. *Washington Post,* June 19, 1996.

Boffey, Philip M. "Schizophrenia: Insights Fail to Halt Rising Toll." *New York Times,* March 16, 1986.

Boodman, Sandra G. "The Mystery of Chestnut Lodge." *Washington Post Magazine,* October 8, 1989, 18–43.

Bovard, James. "First Step to an FDA Cure: Dump Kessler." *Wall Street Journal,* December 8, 1994.

Braceland, Francis. "Kraepelin, His System and His Influence." *American Journal of Psychiatry* 113 (1957): 871–76.

Braithwaite, John. *Corporate Crime in the Pharmaceutical Industry.* Routledge & Kegan Paul, 1984.

Breggin, Peter R. "Brain Damage, Dementia, and Persistent Cognitive Dysfunction Associated with Neuroleptic Drugs: Evidence, Etiology, Implications." *Journal of Mind and Behavior* 101, no. 3–4 (1990): 425–64.

———. "Psychiatry Doesn't Help Mental Health Cause." Letter to the Editor. *New York Times,* March 9, 1995.

———. *Psychiatric Drugs: Hazard to the Brain.* Springer, 1983.

———. *Talking Back to Prozac.* St. Martin's, 1994.

———. *Toxic Psychiatry.* St. Martin's, 1991.

Brimeyer, Jerome R. *Doctor's Orders* [Olanzapine]. Lehman Brothers, January 1996.

Brooke, James. "Hinckley Tries, Again, to Gain Some Freedom." *New York Times,* September 30, 1996.

Brown, Alan S., and Ezra S. Susser. "Prenatal Risk Factors in Schizophrenia." *Psychiatric Times* (January 1996): 21–23.

Buchanan, Robert W., and William T. Carpenter Jr. "Domains of Psychopathology." *Journal of Nervous and Mental Disease* 182, no. 4 (April 1994): 193–204.

Burke, Ross David. *When the Music's Over: My Journey into Schizophrenia.* Basic, 1995.

Burston, Daniel. *The Wing of Madness: The Life and Work of R. D. Laing.* Harvard, 1996.

Burton, Thomas M. "Caremark International to Plead Guilty in Kickback Inquiry, Pay $159 Million. *Wall Street Journal,* June 16, 1995.

———. "FDA Clears Lilly's Schizophrenia Drug As Fight Looms with Market Leader J & J" [Olanzapine/risperidone]. *Wall Street Journal,* October 2, 1996.

———. "Lilly's Drug for Schizophrenia Shown to Have Edge on Current Therapies" [Olanzapine]. *Wall Street Journal,* December 15, 1995.

———. "Risk vs. Benefit: FDA Weighs Antipsychotic" [Sertindole]. *Wall Street Journal,* October 14, 1996.

Caldwell, Anne E. *Origins of Psychopharmacology: From CPZ to LSD.* Charles C. Thomas, 1970.

California Alliance for the Mentally Ill. *Families Know.* California Department of Mental Health, 1993.

———. *In the Community.* California Department of Mental Health, 1993.

———. *Out of the Hospital.* California Department of Mental Health, 1993.

Caplan, Paula J. *They Say You're Crazy.* Addison Wesley, 1995.

Carpenter, William T., Jr., and Robert W. Buchanan. "Schizophrenia." *New England Journal of Medicine* 330 (March 10, 1994): 681–90.

Carpenter, William T., Jr., Douglas W. Heinrichs, and Althea M. I. Wagman. "Deficit and Nondeficit Forms of Schizophrenia: The Concept." *American Journal of Psychiatry* 145, no. 5 (May 1988): 578–83.

Carpenter, William T., Jr., Robert R. Conley, Robert W. Buchanan, Alan Breier, and Carol A. Tamminga. "Patient Response and Resource Management: Another View of Clozapine Treatment of Schizophrenia." *American Journal of Psychiatry* 152, no. 6 (June 1995): 827–32.

Cauchon, Dennis. "Doctor's Financial Stake in Electroshock Therapy." *USA Today,* December 6, 1995.

————. "Shock Therapy: Controversy and Questions." *USA Today,* December 6, 1995.

Chernow, Ron. *The Warburgs* [James Loeb]. Random, 1995.

Clay, John. *R. D. Laing—A Divided Self.* Hodder & Stoughton, 1996.

Clements, Mark. "What We Say about Mental Illness." *Parade,* October 31, 1993, 4–6.

Coleman, Ray. *Lennon.* McGraw-Hill, 1984.

Covan, Frederick L. *Crazy All the Time.* Fawcett, 1994.

Craft, Susan F. *The Liberman Model: Setting Patients Up to Succeed.* Focus on Mental Health Issues, South Carolina Department of Mental Health, December 1995.

Crossen, Cynthia. "Fright by the Numbers: Alarming Disease Data Are Frequently Flawed." *Wall Street Journal,* April 7, 1994.

Crow, T. J. "Brain Changes and Negative Symptoms in Schizophrenia." *Psychopathology* 28 (1995): 18–21.

————. "The Demise of the Kraepelian Binary Concept and the Aetiological Unity of the Psychoses." In *Negative versus Positive Schizophrenia,* ed. A. Maneros et al., 425–40. Springer, 1991.

Dain, Norman. "Critics and Dissenters: Reflections on 'Anti-Psychiatry' in the United States." *Journal of the History of the Behavioral Sciences* 25 (January 1989): 3–25.

Davis, John M., and Philip G. Janicak. "Risperidone: A New, Novel (and Better?) Antipsychotic." *Psychiatric Annals* 26, no. 2 (February 1996): 78–85.

DeBoest, Henry F. *The Train Trip That Was a Turning Point* [insulin]. *Nation's Business,* January 1971.

Deutsch, Albert. *The Mentally Ill in America.* Columbia, 1949.

Domenici, Pete V. *Severe Mental Illnesses: Misunderstanding and Discrimination.* Testimony before Senate Committee on Finance, May 10, 1994.

Drake, Donald, and Marian Uhlman. *Making Medicine—Making Money.* Andrews & McMeel, 1993.

Dubovsky, Steven. "How Safe Are New Psychotropic Medications?" *Journal Watch for Psychiatry* 1, no. 9 (October 1995).

"Dumping the Disabled" [editorial]. *New York Times,* February 19, 1983.

Duncan, Erika. "A Summation from the Patron Saint of Sociology" [Robert Merton]. *New York Times,* April 16, 1995, Sunday Long Island section.

Durden-Smith, Jo. "Baltimore's Dr. Solomon Snyder and the Chemical Cure for Madness." *Baltimore Magazine,* December 1978, 62–65, 121–123.

Eckholm, Erik. "Schizophrenia's Victims Include Strained Families." *New York Times*, March 17, 1986.

Edgerton, Jane E., ed. *American Psychiatric Glossary*. 7th ed. American Psychiatric Press, 1994.

Eisenberg, Leon. "The Social Construction of the Human Brain." *American Journal of Psychiatry* (November 1995): 1,563–73.

Eli Lilly & Co. "Ireland Scales Up by Slurring Its Work" [Olanzapine]. *Focus* 3, no. 6 (1995): 15.

———. "A Renaissance of Hope: Olanzapine May Offer Millions a New Chance." *Essentials* (June 1993): 12–15.

———. "Tollefson Leads the Way for Promising Schizophrenia Treatment" (Olanzapine). *Lilly Update* 3, no. 15 (April 14, 1995).

Elson, John. "Is Freud Finished?" *Time*, July 6, 1992, 60.

Eriksson, Lars. "Remoxipride in the Treatment of Psychoses." *Progress in Neuropsychopharmacology and Biological Psychiatry* 18 (1994): 619–23.

Eronen, Marku, et al. "Schizophrenia and Homicidal Behavior." *Schizophrenia Bulletin* 22, no. 1 (1996): 83–89.

Falloon, Ian. "Model Program Successful" [early detection]. *Psychiatric News* (July 5, 1996): 4.

Federal Task Force on Homelessness and Severe Mental Illness. *Outcasts on Main Street*. National Institute of Mental Health, 1992.

Feinberg, Mark. "Being Normal." *Boston Globe Magazine*, November 20, 1988.

Fenno, Richard. "Emergence of a Senate Leader: Pete Domenici and the Reagan Budget." *Congressional Quarterly* (1991).

Fieve, Ronald R. *Moodswing*. Bantam, 1976.

———. *Prozac*. Avon, 1994.

Fisher, Jeffrey A. *2000: Breakthroughs in Health, Medicine and Longevity by the Year 2000 and Beyond*. Simon and Schuster, 1992.

Fisher, Seymour, and Roger P. Greenberg, eds. *The Limits of Biological Treatments for Psychological Distress*. Lawrence Erlbaum, 1989.

Fitzpatrick, Jackie. "Advocates at Work in Often Hostile World." *New York Times*, December 3, 1995.

Flach, Frederic. *Rickie* (biography). Fawcett, 1990.

Foderado, Lisa W. "Mentally Ill Gaining New Rights with the Ill As Their Own Lobby." *New York Times*, October 14, 1995.

———. "A Voyage to Bedlam and Part Way Back" [Michael Laudor]. *New York Times*, November 9, 1995.

Food and Drug Administration. *In the Matters of Nathan S. Kline, M.D.* Regulatory Hearing, Commissioner's Decision, November 13, 1980, 1–39.

———. "Transcript of Proceedings" [clozapine]. 30th meeting of the Psychopharmacologic Drugs Advisory Committee, April 26, 1989.

Frances, Allen, Michael B. First, and Harold Alan Pincus. "DSM-IV: Its Value and Limitations." *Harvard Mental Health Letter,* June 1995, 4–6.

Freedman, Robert, et al. "Schizophrenia and Nicotine Receptors." *Harvard Review of Psychiatry* 2, no. 4 (Nov.–Dec. 1994): 179–92.

Friedenberg, Edgar Z. *r. d. laing.* Viking, 1973.

Friedman, Lawrence J. *Menninger: The Family and the Clinic.* Knopf, 1990.

Friedrich, Otto. *Going Crazy.* Simon and Schuster, 1975.

Gay, Peter. *Freud: A Life for Our Times.* Norton, 1995.

Gelenberg, Alan J. "Clozapine: Adverse Effects, Interactions and Withdrawal Symptoms." *Biological Therapies in Psychiatry Newsletter* (June 1996): 21–23.

———. "Clozapine for Smokers with Schizophrenia." *Biological Therapies in Psychiatry Newsletter* 18, no. 10 (October 1995).

———. "New Antipsychotics." *Biological Therapies in Psychiatry Newsletter* (December 1996): 45–47.

———. "The P450 Family." *Biological Therapies in Psychiatry Newsletter* 18, no. 8 (August 1995): 29–31.

Goldman, Albert. *The Lives of John Lennon.* Bantam, 1989.

Goldstein, Jeffrey M., et al. "Seroquel: Electrophysiological Profile of a Potential Atypical Antipsychotic." *Psychopharmacology* 112 (1993): 293–98.

Goleman, Daniel. "Amino Acid Offers Hope of Relieving Minor Symptoms of Schizophrenia." *New York Times,* September 7, 1994.

———. "Evidence Mounting for Role of Fetal Damage in Schizophrenia." *New York Times,* May 28, 1996.

———. "Focus on Day-to-Day Support Offers Hope to Schizophrenics." *New York Times,* March 19, 1986.

———. "Free Expression or Irresponsibility? Psychiatrist Faces a Hearing Today" [Peter Breggin]. *New York Times,* September 22, 1987.

———. "Hallucinating Patients Give Doctors a Clue." *New York Times,* November 9, 1995.

———. "Outcry Grows over Method of Selling New Drug" [clozapine]. *New York Times,* September 27, 1990.

———. "Provoking Patient's Worst Fears to Determine the Brain's Role." *New York Times,* June 13, 1995.

———. "Research on Brain Leads to Pursuit of Designer Drugs." *New York Times,* November 19, 1996.

———. "Schizophrenia: Early Signs Found." *New York Times,* December 11, 1984.

Gorman, Christine. "Prozac's Worst Enemy" [Peter Breggin]. *Time,* October 10, 1994, 64.

Gorman, Mike. *Every Other Bed.* World, 1956.

———. "Oklahoma Attacks Its Snake Pits." *Reader's Digest,* September 1948, 139–60.

"Gorman, Mike." In *Current Biography* (October 1956): 20–21.

Greenberg, Joanne [Hannah Green]. *I Never Promised You a Rose Garden*. Penguin, 1964.

Grinfeld, Michael Jonathan. "JCAHO Downgrades UCLA Neuropsychiatric Hospital." *Psychiatric Times* 12, no. 60 (June 1995).

———. "L.A. County to Reassess Human Subjects Research Policies" [UCLA]. *Psychiatric Times* (December 1995).

———. "Patient Death Prompts Hospital Investigation" [UCLA]. *Psychiatric Times* (August 1995).

Grob, Gerald N. *The Mad among Us*. Free Press, 1994.

Gruson, Lindsey. "Nathan Kline, Developer of Antidepressants, Dies." *New York Times*, February 14, 1983.

Gunderson, John, and Loren R. Mosher. *Psychotherapy of Schizophrenia*. Jason Aronson, 1975.

Hale, Nathan G., Jr. *Freud and the Americans (1867–1917)*. Oxford, 1971.

———. *The Rise and Crisis of Psychoanalysis in the United States: Freud and the Americans. 1917–1985*. Oxford, 1995.

Harris, Seale. *Banting's Miracle*. Lippincott, 1946.

Hassner, Vera. "The Clozapine Saga." *The Journal* 4, no. 1 (1993): 47–49.

———. "What Is Ethical? What Is Not?" *The Journal* 5, no. 1 (1994): 4–5.

Hayley, J. *Leaving Home*. McGraw-Hill, 1980.

Healy, David. *The Psychopharmacologists*. Chapman & Hall, 1996.

Heimansohn, Donna. "Private Pain" [Randall Tobias]. *Indianapolis Monthly*, January 1995, 80–128.

Henderson, Leigh A., and William J. Glass. *LSD: Still with Us after All These Years*. Lexington, 1994.

Herz, Marvin I. "Early Intervention in Schizophrenia." In *Psychosocial Treatment of Schizophrenia*, 25–43. Vol. 4 of *Handbook of Schizophrenia*. Elsevier, 1990.

Higgs, Robert. *How FDA Is Causing a Technological Exodus*. Competitive Enterprise Institute, February 1995.

Hilts, Philip J. "Consensus on Ethics in Research Is Elusive." *New York Times*, January 15, 1995.

———. "FDA Becomes Target of Empowerment Groups." *New York Times*, February 12, 1995.

Hinckley, Jack, and JoAnn Hinckley. *Breaking Points*. Zondervan, 1985.

———. "There but for the Grace of God." Interview by ABC on *20/20*. Journal Graphics Script, April 28, 1983.

Hippius, Hanns. "The History of Clozapine." *Psychopharmacology* 99 (1989): 3–5.

Hippius, Hanns, et al. *Murnau and the History of Psychiatry. New Results in Depression Research*. Springer, 1986.

Hoff, Paul. *Emil Kraepelin und die Psychiatrie Als Klinische Wissenschaft* [*Emil Kraepelin and Psychiatry As Clinical Science*]. Springer, 1994.

Horowitz, Joy. "For the Sake of Science" [UCLA]. *Los Angeles Times Magazine*, September 11, 1994, 16–23.

Hunt, Morton. *Mental Hospital*. Pyramid, 1961.

Hurley, Dan. "Imminent Danger" [homelessness]. *Psychology Today*, June/July 1994, 55–68.

Hyler, Steven E., Glen O. Gabbard, and Irving Schneider. "Movie Madness." *The Journal* 4, no. 1 (1992): 4–7.

Isaac, Rael Jean, and D. J. Jaffe. "Mental Illness, Public Safety." *New York Times*, December 23, 1995.

Isometsa, Erkki T., et al. "The Last Appointment before Suicide: Is Suicide Intent Communicated?" *American Journal of Psychiatry* 152, no. 60 (June 1995): 919–21.

Janov, Arthur. *The Primal Scream*. Putnam, 1970.

Janssen Pharmaceutica. *Dr. Paul*. Janssen Pharmaceutica, 1993.

Japenga, Ann. "The Heresy of Peter Breggin." *Hippocrates* (May 1995): 41–46.

————. "Rewriting the Dictionary of Madness" [*DSM-IV*]. *Los Angeles Times Magazine*, June 5, 1994.

Jay, Sarah. "Helping the Medicine Go Down, for a Start." *New York Times*, November 23, 1995.

Jefferson, James W., and John H. Greist. "Brussels Sprouts and Psychopharmacology" [P450 enzyme]. *Psychiatric Clinics of North America: Annual of Drug Therapy* 3 (1995): 205–22.

Journal of Clinical Psychiatry. *Update on Serotonin/Dopamine Antagonists in Psychiatry* 12, no. 2. Monograph Series. Physicians Post-Graduate Press, August 1994.

Journal Watch for Psychiatry. "Discontinuing Neuroleptics in Schizophrenia: Good News or Bad News?" *Massachusetts Medical Society* 1, no. 4 (May 1995): 1.

Kahn, E. J., Jr. *All in a Century: The First 100 Years of Eli Lilly & Co.* 3rd ed. Eli Lilly, 1989.

Kaiser, David. "Not by Chemicals Alone: A Hard Look at Psychiatric Medicine." *Psychiatric Times* (December 1996): 42–44.

Kane, John M. "Enormous Ethical Challenges." *The Journal* 5, no. 1 (1994): 28–29.

————. "Risperidone: New Horizons for the Schizophrenic Patient." Supplement to *Journal of Clinical Psychiatry* 55, no. 5 (May 1994).

Kane, John M., and Stephen R. Marder. "Psychopharmacologic Treatment of Schizophrenia." *Schizophrenia Bulletin* 19, no. 2 (1993): 287–302.

Kaplan, Arline. "Progress in Psychoses." Supplement to *Psychiatric Times* (October 1996): 1–4.

Kaplan, Arline, ed. "Progress in Psychoses: From Pathophysiology Research to Treatment." Supplement to *Psychiatric Times* (November 1995): 1–4.

Karp, David. A. *Speaking of Sadness*. Oxford, 1996.

Kasanin, Jacob. "The Acute Schizoaffective Psychoses." *American Journal of Psychiatry* 13 (1933): 97–126.

Kempker, Kerstin, and Peter Lehmann, eds. *Statt Psychiatrie* [*Instead of Psychiatry*]. Anti-Psychiatrie Verlag, Berlin, 1993.

Kendler, Kenneth S. "A Medical Student's Experience with Akathisia." *American Journal of Psychiatry* 133, no. 4 (1976): 454–55.

Kendler, Kenneth S., and Scott R. Diehl. "The Genetics of Schizophrenia: A Current Genetic-Epidemiologic Perspective." *Schizophrenia Bulletin* 19, no. 2 (1993): 261–86.

Kessler, David A. "Drug Promotion and Scientific Exchange." *New England Journal of Medicine* 325, no. 3 (1991): 201–3.

Kessler, Ronald. *The Sins of the Father* [Joseph and Rosemary Kennedy]. Warner, 1996.

King, Ralph J., Jr., and Stephen D. Moore. "Basel's Drug Giants Are Placing Huge Bets on U.S. Biotech Firms." *Wall Street Journal*, November 29, 1995.

Kirk, Stuart A., and Herb Kutchins. *The Selling of DSM*. Aldine de Gruyter, 1992.

Klee, Ernst. *Was Sie Taten, Was Sie Wurden* [*What They Did, What They Became*] [Ernst Rüdin]. Fischer, 1988.

Kleinman, Arthur. *Rethinking Psychiatry*. Free Press, 1988.

Kline, Nathan S. *From Sad to Glad*. Putnam, 1974.

"Kline, Nathan S." In *Current Biography* (1965): 227–30.

Kolle, Kurt. *Kraepelin und Freud*. George Thieme, 1957.

Konner, Melvin. *The Trouble with Medicine*. Penguin/BBC, 1994.

Kopelowicz, Alex, and Robert Paul Liberman. "Self-Management Approaches for Seriously Mentally Ill Persons." *Directions in Psychiatry* 14, no. 17 (August 24, 1994): 1–7.

Koran, Lorrin M., ed. *The Nation's Psychiatrists*. APA, 1987.

———. *Psychiatric Consultation and Case Summary Re. Mr. Jeffrey Wyden*. Stanford University Medical Center, March 10, 1981, 1–5.

Kraepelin, Emil. *Lebenserinnerungen* [*Reminiscences of My Life*]. Springer, 1983.

———. *One Hundred Years of Psychiatry*. Citadel, 1918.

Kramer, Peter D. *Listening to Prozac*. Viking, 1993.

Kruief, Paul de. *Microbe Hunters*. Harcourt Brace, 1926/1954.

Kucharski, Anastasia. "History of Frontal Lobotomy in the United States, 1935–1955." *Neurosurgery* 14, no. 6 (1984): 765–72.

Kudlien, Friedolf, and Christian Andree. "Sauerbruch und der Nationalsozialismus" [Kraepelin]. *Medizinhistorisches Journal* (1979): 201–22.

Kutchins, Herb, and Stuart A. Kirk. "DSM-IV: Does Bigger and Newer Mean Better?" *Harvard Mental Health Letter* (May 1995): 4–5.

Laing, Adrian Charles. *R. D. Laing—a Biography*. Peter Owen, 1995.

Laing, R. D. *The Divided Self*. Penguin, 1990.

Lampert, Mark. "The Right Formula" (interview). *Barrons*, May 22, 1995, 29.

Leamer, Laurence. *The Kennedy Women*. Ballantine, 1994.

Lehmann, Christine. "Family Testimony Reveals Human Dimension of UCLA Schizophrenia Research Controversy." *Psychiatric News* (March 17, 1995).

————. "UCLA Required to Change Certain Research Procedures after Allegations of Harm to Study Subjects." *Psychiatric News* (March 3, 1995).

Lehmann, Peter. *Der Chemische Knebel* [*The Chemical Gag*]. 3rd ed. Anti-Psychiatrie Verlag Berlin, 1993.

Leland, John. "The Trouble with Sigmund." *Newsweek,* December 18, 1995, 62.

Levy, Doug, and Anita Manning. "Drug Firm Rx: Be First" [cover story]. *USA Today,* July 11, 1995, 1–2.

Liberman, Robert Paul. *Recovery from Schizophrenia: The Road to Recovery Is Paved with Social and Independent Living Skills.* Clinical Research Center for Schizophrenia and Psychiatric Rehabilitation, UCLA School of Medicine, n.d., 1–4.

Liberman, Robert Paul, ed. *Psychiatric Rehabilitation of Chronic Mental Patients.* American Psychiatric Press, 1988.

Liberman, Robert Paul, and Alex Kopelowicz. "Recovery from Schizophrenia: Is the Time Right?" *The Journal* 5, no. 3 (1994): 67–69.

Liddle, Peter, William T. Carpenter Jr., and Tim Crow. "Syndromes of Schizophrenia." *British Journal of Psychiatry* 165 (1994): 721–27.

Lidz, Theodore. "A Developmental Theory." In *Schizophrenia: Science and Practice,* ed. John C. Shershow, 69–95. Harvard, 1978.

Lidz, Theodore, et al. *Schizophrenia and the Family.* 2nd ed. International Universities, 1985.

Lieberman, Jeffrey A., et al. "Clozapine: Guidelines for Clinical Management." *Journal of Clinical Psychiatry* 50, no. 9 (September 1989): 329–38.

Lief, Alfred. *The Commonsense Psychiatry of Dr. Adolf Meyer: 52 Selected Papers.* McGraw-Hill, 1946.

Lifton, Robert Jay. *The Nazi Doctors.* Basic Books, 1986.

Lin, Keh-Ming, et al. "Ethnicity and Psychopharmacology." *Cultural Psychiatry* 18, no. 3 (December 1995): 635–47.

————. "Studies of Drug Response in Multiethnic Populations." *Applied Clinical Trials* 3, no. 10 (October 1994).

McCormick, Gene E. *Insulin: A Hope for Life.* Eli Lilly & Co., 1979, 1–8.

McFadden, Robert D. "Psychiatrist Barred from Administering Experimental Drugs." *New York Times,* May 25, 1982.

McGinley, Laurie. "GOP Takes Aim at FDA, Seeking to Ease Way for Approval of New Drugs, Medical Products." *Wall Street Journal,* December 12, 1994.

McGlashan, Thomas. "Course of Schizophrenia Can Be Improved through Early Identification, Intervention." Interview. *Psychiatric News* (July 5, 1996): 4.

McTaggart, Lynn. "Putting the Drug Tester to the Test." *New York Times Magazine,* December 7, 1980.

Mahoney, Tom. *The Merchants of Life.* Harper, 1959.

Mann, Charles C., and Mark L. Plummer. *The Aspirin Wars* [clinical trials]. Knopf, 1991.

Marder, Stephen R., and Theodore Van Putten. "Who Should Receive Clozapine?" *Archives of General Psychiatry* 45 (September 1988): 865–67.

Marks, John D. *The Search for the Manchurian Candidate*. Times Books, 1986.

Masserman, Jules H. *A Psychiatric Odyssey*. Science House, 1971.

Masson, Jeffrey Moussaieff. *Against Therapy*. Atheneum, 1988.

Maxmen, Jerrold S. *The New Psychiatry*. Morrow, 1985.

"Medical Ethics in the Dock" [editorial]. *New York Times*, March 14, 1994.

Medina, John. "The Genes of Schizophrenia." *Psychiatric Times* (March 1996): 31–32.

Medline, Elaine. "A Bible for Shrinks" [*DSM-IV*]. *Los Angeles Times*, May 21, 1994.

Meise, Ullrich, et al. "Autopsychotic Maintenance Treatment of Schizophrenia Patients: Is There a Consensus?" *Schizophrenia Bulletin* 20, no. 1 (1994): 215–25.

Meltzer, Herbert Y. "Clozapine: Is Another View Valid?" [editorial]. *American Journal of Psychiatry* 152, no. 6 (June 1995): 821–32.

———. "New Drugs for the Treatment of Schizophrenia." *Psychiatric Clinics of North America* 16, no. 2 (June 1993): 365–85.

———. "Penetrating the Secrets of Schizophrenia: The History of Clozapine Therapy." *Sandoz Bulletin* (1993).

Meltzer, Herbert Y., et al. "Cost Effectiveness of Clozapine in Neuroleptic-Resistant Schizophrenia." *American Journal of Psychiatry* 150, no. 11 (November 1993): 1,630–38.

Mender, Donald. *The Myth of Neuropsychiatry*. Plenum, 1994.

Menninger, Karl A. "Influenza and Schizophrenia" [1926]. Supplement to *American Journal of Psychiatry* 151-6 (June 1994): 183–87.

Merton, Robert K. "Behavior Patterns of Scientists." *American Scientist* 57, no. 1 (1969): 1–23.

Meyer, Adolf. "In Memoriam Emil Kraepelin" [1927]. Supplement to *American Journal of Psychiatry* 151-6 (June 1994): 112–24.

Mezzich, Juan E., et al. "Making Room for Culture in Psychiatry." *Primary Psychiatry* (November/December 1995): 40–45.

Migler, Bernard M., et al. "Seroquel: Behavioral Effects in Conventional and Novel Tests for Atypical Antipsychotic Drug." *Psychopharmacology* 112 (1993): 299–307.

Miller, Alexander L., Roderick K. Mahurin, Dawn I. Velligan, and James W. Maas. "Negative Symptoms of Schizophrenia: Where Do We Go from Here?" [editorial]. *Biological Psychiatry* 37, no. 10 (May 15, 1995).

Millon, Theodore. *Disorders of Personality: DSM-IV and Beyond*. 2nd ed. Wiley, 1996.

Mintz, Lois Imber, Robert Paul Liberman, David J. Miklovitz, and Jim Mintz. "Expressed Emotion: A Call for Partnership among Relatives, Patients and Professionals." *Schizophrenia Bulletin* 13, no. 2 (1987): 227–35.

Mintz, Morton. *At Any Cost*. Pantheon, 1985.

———. "The Cure That Could Kill You: FDA Reforms Are Bad Medicine." *Washington Post*, July 14, 1996.

———. *The Therapeutic Nightmare*. Houghton Mifflin, 1965.

Modestin, Jiri, and Roland Ammann. "Mental Disorder and Criminality: Male Schizophrenia." *Schizophrenia Bulletin* 22, no. 1 (1996): 69–82.

Moore, Nicholas A., and Nicholas C. Tye. "The Behavioral Pharmacology of Olanza-pine, a Novel 'Atypical' Antipsychotic Agent." *Journal of Pharmacology and Experimental Therapeutics* 262, no. 2 (1992): 545–51.

Mosher, Loren R., and Alma Z. Menn. "The Surrogate 'Family,' an Alternative to Hospi-talization." In *Schizophrenia: Science and Practice*, ed. John C. Shershow, 223–39. Harvard, 1978.

Mosher, Loren R., Alama Menn, and Susan M. Matthews. "Soteria: Evaluation of a Home-Based Treatment for Schizophrenia." *American Journal of Orthopsychiatry* 45, no. 3 (April 1975): 455–67.

Mosher, Loren R., and Lorenzo Burti. *Community Mental Health*. Norton, 1994.

Naber, D., et al. "Clinical Management of Clozapine Patients in Relation to Efficacy and Side Effects." *British Journal of Psychiatry* 166, supplement 17 (1992): 54–59.

NARSAD. "Which of These Researchers Will Unlock the Secret of Severe Mental Ill-ness?" [advertisement]. *New York Times* May 23, 1994.

Nasar, Sylvia. "The Lost Years of a Nobel Laureate" [John Nash]. *New York Times*, November 13, 1994.

National Alliance for the Mentally Ill. *Highlights from a National Survey*. NAMI, January 1996.

Nesse, Randolph M., and George C. Williams. "Genes and Disease: Defects, Quirks and Compromises." In *Why We Get Sick*, 91–120. Times Books, 1994.

Neugeboren, Jay. *Imagining Robert*. Morrow, 1997.

Neurogen Corp. *Annual Report 1994*. Neurogen, 1994.

Newbold, H. L. *Dr. Newbold's Nutrition for Your Nerves*. Keats, 1993.

New York State Commission on Quality of Care for the Mentally Disabled. *In the Matter of Jacob Gordon*. August 1995.

Noel, Barbara, with Kathryn Watterson. *You Must Be Dreaming* [Jules Masserman]. Posei-don, 1992.

North, Carol. *Welcome, Silence*. Simon and Schuster, 1987.

North, Carol, and Remi Cadoret. "Diagnostic Discrepancy in Personal Accounts of Patients with Schizophrenia." *Archives of General Psychiatry* 38 (February 1981): 133–37.

Oaks, David. "Is the Doctor Crazy?" *Dendron, Mad Underground News* (Fall 1993): 6.

O'Brien, Barbara. *Operators and Things: The Inner Life of a Schizophrenic*. A. S. Barnes, 1958/1975.

O'Callaghan, E., et al. "Schizophrenia after Prenatal Exposure to 1957 A2 Influenza Epi-demic." *Lancet* 337 (May 25, 1991): 1,248–50.

Ono, Yutaka, and Douglas Berger. "Zen and the Art of Psychotherapy." *Journal of Prac-tical Psychiatry and Behavioral Health* (November 1995): 203–10.

Opler, Lewis. "New Agents for Treating Negative Symptoms." *Psychiatric Annals* 25, no. 4 (May 1995): 301–4.

Oprah Winfrey Show, April 2, 1987. "Inappropriate Treatment for Psychiatric Problems" [Peter Breggin]. Transcript, Radio and TV Reports, Washington, D.C.

Oshima, Iwao, and Kazuyo Nakai. "The Japanese Mental Health System and Family Movement." *New Directions for Mental Health Services,* no. 60 (Winter 1993): 13–23.

Pear, Robert. "Congressional Leaders Agree on New Insurance Proposals." *New York Times,* September 20, 1996.

————. "Lawyers and Lobbyists Help Guide Effort by Republicans to Speed Drug Approvals." *New York Times,* March 4, 1996.

————. "U.S. Seeks to Review More Disability Cases." *New York Times,* March 19, 1996.

Pfeiffer, Carl C., et al. *The Schizophrenias—Yours and Mine.* Pyramid, 1970.

Pickar, David. "Prospects for Pharmacotherapy of Schizophrenia." *Lancet* 4 (March 1995): 557–62.

Pies, Ronald. "Schizoaffective Disorder: Mixing Mood and Madness." *Psychiatric Times* (January 1996): 26–28.

Pies, Ronald, ed. "The Neurobiology of Schizophrenia." Supplement to *Psychiatric Times* (March 1996): 1–4.

Pollen, Daniel A. *Hanna's Heirs* [Kraepelin]. Oxford, 1993.

Pope, Harrison G., Jr., and Joseph F. Lipinsky Jr. "Diagnosis in Schizophrenia and Manic-Depressive Illness: A Reassessment." *Archives of General Psychiatry* 35 (July 1978): 811–828.

Pope, Harrison G., Jr., Bruce M. Cohen, and Joseph F. Lipinsky Jr. *Is Schizophrenia a Meaningful Diagnosis?* McLean Hospital, n.d.

Pope, Harrison G., Jr., et al. "Clozapine in the Treatment of Psychotic Mood Disorders, Schizoaffective Disorder, and Schizophrenia." Draft copy, McLean Hospital, n.d., 1–9.

Posvoll, Edward M. *The Seduction of Madness.* HarperCollins, 1990.

Power, Gerry. "Making the Invisible More Visible: Homeless Mentally Ill People in the News." *The Journal* 4, no. 1 (1991): 23–26.

Proctor, Robert. *Racial Hygiene.* Harvard, 1988.

Pryor, David. *Statement on Clozapine Marketing.* House of Representatives, Subcommittee on Hospitals and Health Care, June 28, 1990.

Raught, Joyce T. "Investigating New Treatments for Schizophrenia: A Profile of Nina R. Schooler." *NARSAD Research Newsletter* (Summer 1996): 1–5.

Ray, Oakley, and Charles Ksir. *Drugs, Society and Human Behavior.* 6th ed. Mosby, 1993.

Reality Lost and Regained: Autobiography of a Schizophrenic Girl, with Analytic Interpretation by Marguerite Sechehaye. New American Library, 1970.

Reed, Susan. "Waking to Nightmare" [Jules Masserman]. *People,* December 7, 1992.

Restak, Richard M. *Receptors.* Bantam, 1994.

Roazen, Paul. *Brother Animal: The Story of Freud and Tausk.* Knopf, 1969.

————. *Freud and His Followers.* Knopf, 1975.

————. *Helene Deutsch: A Psychoanalyst's Life* [Kraepelin]. Anchor, 1985.

Robinson, Donald. *The Miracle Finders.* McKay, 1976.

Roder, Thomas, and Volker Kubillus. *Die Manner Hinter Hitler* [*Hippius and Rudin*]. Pi-Verlag fur Politik and Gesellschaft, 1994.

Rogers, Patrick. "A Sense of Purpose" [Meggin Hollister]. *People,* July 15, 1996, 139–42.

Rosen, John N. "The Survival Function of Schizophrenia." *Bulletin of the Menninger Clinic* 14, no. 3 (May 1950): 81–91.

Rosenhan, D. L. "On Being Sane in Insane Places." *Science* 179 (January 1973): 179–258.

Rotrosen, John, and Leonard Adler. "The Importance of Side Effects in the Development of New Antipsychotic Drugs." *Psychiatric Annals* 25, no. 5 (May 1995): 306–10.

Rouché, Berton. "Annals of Medicine: As Empty As Eve" [electroshock]. *New Yorker,* September 9, 1974, 85–100.

Rycroft, Charles. *A Critical Dictionary of Psychoanalysis.* Penguin, 1968.

Sabshin, Melvin. "Turning Points in 20th Century American Psychiatry." *American Journal of Psychiatry* 147, no. 10 (October 1990): 1267–73.

Sandoz, A. G. *Sandoz: 100 Jahre fuer ein Leben mit Zukunft [100 Years for Life with a Future].* Special issue of *Sandoz Bulletin,* 22 (1986).

Sandoz Pharmaceutical Corp. *Agranulocytosis—Fact Sheet.* Sandoz, 1994.

———. "Politics vs. Patient Safety . . . Clozaril: What Are the Issues?" [advertisement]. *New York Times,* January 2, 1991.

———. *Sandoz Ltd. 1886–1986.* Sandoz, Basle, 1986.

Sartorius, Norman, et al. *Schizophrenia: Manifestations Incidence and Course in Different Cultures—A World Health Organization Ten-Country Study.* Psychological Medicine, Monograph Supplement 20. Cambridge University Press, 1992.

Sass, Louis A. *Madness and Modernism.* Basic, 1992.

Sayers, Janet. *Mothers of Psychoanalysis* [Helene Deutsch and Emil Kraepelin]. Norton, 1991.

Scheifler-Roberts, Patricia, and Robert W. Mullaly. *Medication Maze.* Intuition, 1985.

Schiller, Lori, and Amanda Bennett. *The Quiet Room: A Journey Out of the Torment of Madness.* Warner, 1994.

Schmeck, Harold M., Jr. "Schizophrenia Focus Shifts to Dramatic Changes in Brain." *New York Times,* March 18, 1995.

Schmidbauer, Wolfgang. *Hilflose Helfer [Helpless Helpers].* Rohwohlt, 1994.

Schmidt, Susan. "Doctor Says Md. Medical Panel Cleared Him" [Peter Breggin]. *Washington Post,* September 23, 1987.

———. "Psychiatrist's TV Comments Prompt Md. Probe" [Peter Breggin]. *Washington Post,* September 19, 1987.

Schmutz, Jean, and E. Eichenberger. "Clozapine." *Chronicles of Drug Discovery* 1 (1982): 39–59.

Schneider, Kurt. "Kraepelin und die Gegenwaertige Psychiatrie" ("Kraepelin and Contemporary Psychiatry"). *Fortschritte der Neurologie-Psychiatrie* 24, no. 1 (1956): 1–7.

Schooler, Nina R. "Negative Symptoms in Schizophrenia: Assessment of the Effect of Risperidone." Supplement to *Journal of Clinical Psychiatry* 55, no. 5 (May 1994): 22–28.

Schwartz, Harry. *Breakthrough: The Discovery of Modern Medicines at Janssen.* Skyline, 1989.

Schwartz, John. "FDA Often Blamed for Problems That Aren't Agency's Fault." *Washington Post,* July 15, 1996.

Schweder, Richard A. "It's Time to Reinvent Freud." *New York Times,* December 15, 1995.

SCRIP World Pharmaceutical News. "Merck Withdraws U.S. NDA for Roxiam" [Rempoxipride]. *SCRIP,* January 18, 1994.

Scull, Andrew. "Desperate Remedies: A Gothic Tale of Madness and Modern Medicine" [Henry A. Cotton]. In *Lectures on the History of Psychiatry.* The Squibb Series. Gaskell, 1990.

Seeman, Philip. "Dopamine Receptors and Psychosis." *Scientific American* (Sept./Oct., 1995): 2–11.

Shamoo, Adil E. "Ethical Considerations in Medication-Free Research on the Mentally Ill." Paper delivered at Annual Meeting of the American College of Neuropsychopharmacology, San Juan, Puerto Rico, December 13, 1994.

―――. "Our Responsibilities toward Persons with Mental Illness As Human Subjects in Research." *The Journal* 5, no. 1 (1994): 14–16.

Sharav, Itzhak. "Ami's Race with Death." *New York Times,* February 3, 1995.

Sharav, Vera Hassner. "Independent Family Advocates Challenge the Fraternity of Silence." Alliance for the Mentally Ill, New York State, n.d., 1–10.

Sheehan, Susan. "The Last Days of Sylvia Frumkin." *New Yorker,* February 20 and 27, 1995, 200–11.

Shenk, Joshua Wolf. "Warning: Cutting the FDA Could Be Hazardous to Your Health." *Washington Monthly* (January/February 1996): 17–23.

Shepherd, Michael. "Two Faces of Emil Kraepelin." *British Journal of Psychiatry* 167 (1995): 174–83.

Shetler, Harriet, ed. "A History of the National Alliance for the Mentally Ill." National Alliance for the Mentally Ill, n.d. 1–33.

Shorter, Edward. *The Health Century.* Doubleday, 1987.

―――. *A History of Psychiatry.* Wiley, 1997.

Shrine, Jim. "Neurogen Partners with Schering Plough in $70M Deal." *Bio World Today* (June 16, 1995): 1.

Smith, Dinita. "Freud May Be Dead, but His Critics Still Kick." *New York Times,* December 10, 1995.

Snyder, Solomon H. *Madness and the Brain.* McGraw-Hill, 1974.

Social Security Administration, Office of Supplemental Security Income. *Red Book on Work Incentives.* SSA pub. no. 64-030. August 1994.

Solomon, Jolie. "Breaking the Silence." *Newsweek,* May 20, 1996, 20–21.

Somers, Sandra. "Profiles in Psychiatry: Frank J. Ayd, Jr. *Psychiatric Times* (November 1996): 55.

Sperling, A. P. *Psychology for the Millions*. Frederick Fell, 1946.

Gentle Murder. No. 12: 98–124. *Der Spiegel*, 1980.

Spilker, Bert. *Multinational Pharmaceutical Companies: Principles and Practices*. 2nd ed. Raven, 1989.

Spitzer, Robert L., and Ronald Bayer. "Neurosis, Psychodynamics, and DSM-III." *Archives of General Psychiatry* 42 (February 1985): 187–96.

Stanton, Alfred H. "Intensive Psychotherapy with Schizophrenic Patients: A Preliminary Manual." *McLean Hospital Journal* 9, no. 1 (1984): 1–30.

Stanton, Josephine M. "Weight Gain Associated with Neuroleptic Medication: A Review." *Schizophrenia Bulletin* 21, no. 3 (1995).

Stille, G., and K. Fischer-Cornelssen. "Die Entwicklung von Clozapine (Leponex)—Ein Mysterium?" [The Development of Clozapine—A Mystery]. In *Pharmakopsychiatrie im Wandel der Zeit*, ed. O. K. Linde. Tilia Verlag, 1988.

Stone, Gene. "Short Sharp Shocks" [electroshock]. *New York*, November 14, 1994, 55–59.

Stratenwerty, Irene. "Hör Mal, Wer da Spricht" ["Listen to Who Is Talking"]. *Die Zeit* (October 27, 1995): 22.

Sullivan, Harry Stack. "The Onset of Schizophrenia" [1927]. Supplement to *American Journal of Psychiatry* 151-6 (June 1994): 134–39.

Summers, Anthony. *Goddess* [Marilyn Monroe]. Macmillan, 1985.

Susser, Ezra S., et al. "Schizophrenia after Prenatal Exposure to the Dutch Hunger Winter of 1944–1945. *Archives of General Psychiatry* 49 (December 1992): 983–88.

Swazey, Judith P. *Chlorpromazine in Psychiatry*. MIT, 1974.

Swerdlow, Joel L. "Quiet Miracles of the Brain." *National Geographic*, June 1995, 2–41.

Tamminga, Carol A. "The New Generation of Antipsychotic Drugs." *NARSAD Research Newsletter* (Winter, 1996): 4–6.

Tawa, Renee. "Unraveling a Cruel Mystery of the Mind" [Meggin Hollister]. *Los Angeles Times*, April 29, 1996.

Thomas, Gordon. *Journey into Madness* [Ewen Cameron]. Bantam, 1989.

Tienari, Pekka, et al. "The Finnish Adoptive Family Study of Schizophrenia: Possible Joint Effects of Genetic Vulnerability and Family Interaction." In *Understanding Major Mental Disorders*. Family Process Press, 1987, 33–52.

Time. "Way Out of Reach [clozapine]." October 1, 1990, 79.

Torrey, E. Fuller. *Freudian Fraud: The Malignant Effect of Freud's Theory on American Thought and Culture*. HarperCollins, 1992.

———. *Nowhere to Go: The Tragic Odyssey of the Homeless Mentally Ill*. Harper, 1988.

———. *Out of the Shadows*. Wiley, 1996.

———. *Schizophrenia and Civilization*. Jason Aronson, 1980.

———. *Surviving Schizophrenia*. 3rd. ed. HarperCollins, 1995.

Torrey, E. Fuller, and Robert H. Yolken. "Could Schizophrenia Be a Viral Zoonosis Transmitted from House Cats?" *Schizophrenia Bulletin* 21, no. 2 (1995): 167–72.

————. "Viruses, Schizophrenia and Bipolar Disorder." In *Clinical Microbiology Review* (January 1995).

Torrey, E. Fuller, Anne E. Bowler, Edward H. Taylor, and Irving I. Gottesman. *Schizophrenia and Manic Depressive Disorder.* Basic, 1994.

————. "Stalking the Schizovirus." *Schizophrenia Bulletin* 14, no. 2 (1988): 223–29.

Tosteson, Daniel C. "Lithium and Mania." *Scientific American* (April 1981): 164–75.

Toufexis, Anastasia. "Brain Work" [hallucinations]. *Time,* September 20, 1995, 101.

Tsuang, Ming T., and John C. Simpson. *Nosology/Epidemiology and Genetics of Schizophrenia.* Vol. 3 of *Handbook of Schizophrenia.* Elsevier, 1988.

U.S. Senate Subcommittee on Health and Scientific Research. *Preclinical and Clinical Hearing, Testing by the Pharmaceutical Industry, 1979.* U.S. Senate, October 11, 1979.

Valenstein, Elliot S. *Great and Desperate Cures.* Basic, 1986.

Van Putten, Theodore, and Stephen R. Marder. "Behavioral Toxicity of Antipsychotic Drugs." Supplement to *Journal of Clinical Psychiatry* 48, no. 9 (September 1987): 13–18.

Vartiainen, Heikki, et al. "A Long-Term Study of Remoxipride in Chronic Schizophrenic Patients." *Acta Psychiatrica Scandinavia* 87 (1993): 114–17.

Vietor, Richard R. *Schizophrenia—a Major New Market Opportunity.* Merrill Lynch, November 1994.

Vonnegut, Mark. *The Eden Express.* Praeger, 1975.

————. "Why I Want to Bite R. D. Laing." *Harper's* (April 1974).

Wahl, Otto F. *Media Madness,* Rutgers, 1995.

Wallinder, Jan. "Experiences of Long-Term Treatment with Remoxipride: Efficacy and Tolerability." *Acta Psychiatrica Scandinavia* 82, no. 358 (1990): 158–63.

Wallis, Claudia, and James Willwerth. "Awakenings" [clozapine]. *Time,* July 6, 1992, 53–60.

Walsh, Maryellen. *Schiz-o-phre-nia. Straight Talk for Family and Friends.* Warner, 1985.

Weber, Matthias M. *Ernst Rüdin.* Springer, 1993.

Wechsler, James A. *In a Darkness.* Norton, 1972.

Weiden, Peter J. "Olanzapine: A New 'Atypical' Antipsychotic." *Journal of Practical Psychiatry and Behavioral Health* (January 1997): 49–51.

Weiden, Peter J., and Mark Olfson. "Cost of Relapse in Schizophrenia." *Schizophrenia Bulletin* 21, no. 3 (1995): 419–30.

Weiden, Peter J., et al. "Switching Antipsychotic Medications." *Journal of Clinical Psychiatry* (January 1997).

Weinberger, Daniel E. "From Neuropathology to Neurodevelopment." *Lancet* (August 26, 1995): 552–57.

Weindling, Paul. *Health, Race and German Politics Between National Unification and Nazism, 1870–1945.* Cambridge, 1989.

Weinstein, Sharon. Letter to the editor [Alfred H. Stanton]. *McLean Hospital Journal.*

Werth, Barry. *The Billion Dollar Molecule.* Simon and Schuster, 1994.

West, Louis Jolyon, and Don E. Flinn, eds. *Treatment of Schizophrenia: Progress and Prospects.* Grune & Stratton, 1976.

Wexler, Bruce E. "Beyond the Kraepelian Dichotomy" [editorial]. *Biological Psychiatry* 31 (1922): 539–41.

"Why Drive Troubled People Crazy?" [editorial]. *New York Times,* April 20, 1983.

Willwerth, James. "After the Awakening, the Real Therapy Must Begin." *Time,* July 6, 1992, 56.

———. "Tinkering with Madness" [UCLA]. *Time,* August 30, 1993, 40–42.

———. "Witness in Fine Print" [UCLA]. *Time,* November 7, 1993, 62–63.

Wilson, Mitchell. "DSM-III and the Transformation of American Psychiatry: A History." *American Journal of Psychiatry* 150, no. 30 (March 1993): 399–410.

Winslow, Ron. "Schizophrenia Groups Seeking Access to Drug" [clozapine]. *Wall Street Journal,* October 5, 1990.

The Wolf Man. *The Wolf Man.* Hill & Wang, 1991.

Woolis, Rebecca. *When Someone You Love Has Mental Illness.* Tarcher, 1992.

World Health Organization. *The ICD-10 Classification of Mental and Behavioural Disorders.* Division of Mental Health, Geneva, 1994.

———. "Remoxipride: Aplastic Aenaemia." *WHO Drug Information* 8, no. 2 (1994): 69.

———. *Schizophrenia: Information for Families.* Division of Mental Health, Geneva, WHO/MNH/MND, 92.8, n.d.

———. *WHO Activities in the Area of Biological Psychiatry during the Period 1990–1994.* Division of Mental Health, Geneva, 1994.

Worthington, Janet Farrar. "Seeking to Understand—and Change—the Course of Schizophrenia: A Profile of Richard Jed Wyatt." *NARSAD Newsletter* (Winter 1994/1995): 1–5.

Wright, Robert. "The Evolution of Despair." *Time,* August 28, 1995, 32–38.

Wyatt, Richard Jed. "Risks of Withdrawing Antipsychotic Medications." *Archives of General Psychiatry* 52 (March 1995).

Wyden, Peter. "Medical Men Eyeing Sterilization Program at Winfield Hospital." *Wichita Eagle,* October 18, 1948.

———. "Topeka Has Extremes in Mental Hospitals: VA Shows How State Could Humanize." *Wichita Eagle,* October 24, 1948.

Wynne, Lyman C. "The Family Left Out and the Family Included: Two Outcomes for Schizophrenia." In *Stories of Medical Family Therapy,* ed. Susan H. McDaniel et al. Basic Books, 1996.

Wyrsch, Jacob. "Ueber die Bedeutung von Freud und Kraepelin fuer die Psychiatrie" ["About the Significance of Freud and Kraepelin for Psychiatry"]. *Der Nervenarzt* 27, no. 12 (December 20, 1956): 530–35.

Yolken, Robert H., and E. Fuller Torrey. "Viruses, Schizophrenia and Bipolar Disorder." *Clinical Microbiology Reviews* 8, no. 1 (January 1995): 131–45.

Yung, Alison R., and Patrick D. McGorry. "The Prodromal Phase of First-Episode Psychosis." *Schizophrenia Bulletin* 22, no. 2 (1996): 353–70.

Zehentbauer, Josef. *Psycho-Pillen*. AG SPAK, 1993.

Zilboorg, Gregory. *A History of Medical Psychology*. Norton, 1941.

Zubin, Joseph, Gerald Oppenheimer, and Richard Neugebauer. "Degeneration Theory and the Stigma of Schizophrenia" [editorial]. *Biological Psychiatry* 20 (1985): 1,145–48.

Zugibe, Frederick T. "Sudden Death Related to the Use of Psychotropic Drugs." *Legal Medicine* (1980): 75–90.

Zukin, Stephen R., et al. "Ameliorations of Negative Symptoms by Glycine." *American Journal of Psychiatry* 151, no. 8 (August 1994): 1,234–36.

Acknowledgments

LIFE USED TO UNFOLD for psychiatrists in leisurely fifty-minute segments, with most patients appearing once or more every week. In the frantic universe of the new biological psychiatry, even the most psychotic patients are treated in sessions of half an hour, sometimes a quarter of an hour or even less. Not infrequently, they are seen only once a month. So the uncounted hours of pro bono time that I was given by my principal advisers add up to a priceless gift. My gratitude is beyond measure, and my faith in the basic goodness of humankind received a welcome boost.

In addition to Skip Pope of McLean Hospital, my most generous psychiatric helpers were Charles M. Beasley Jr., of Eli Lilly and Company; Daniel E. Casey, of the Portland (Oregon) Veterans Affairs Medical Center; E. Fuller Torrey, of the National Institute of Mental Health; Terri Sebree, then of Abbott Laboratories; and Peter J. Weiden, of St. Luke's–Roosevelt Hospital Center and Columbia University.

From Jeff's many treatment teams I must single out Andy Abarbanel, Jo Ann Cloutier, Vincent J. D'Andrea, Alexis Horozan, Reed Kaplan, Michael Kerschenbaum, Lorrin Koran, Karen McCreddin, Rick Robinson, Henry Russell, and Karen Wrinkle.

Of the patients' advocates, nobody could have opened more doors than the indefatigable Laurie Flynn, of the National Alliance for the Mentally Ill; and the voices of Bob Aller, Pete and Nancy Domenici, Adil Shamoo, Vera Sharav, and Dan Weisburd made themselves heard with their customary insistence.

Guardian angels from the Eli Lilly Heavyweights included Karin Graffeo, Jim Lancaster, Alex Mitchell, Jeff Newton, Steven Paul, Fred Rappard, Gary Tollefson, Nick Tye, and Gus Watanabe.

Jonathan B. Segal, who edited and edited and edited this book, is a startling exception to the rule that today's editors have turned in their pencils. He reorganized the structure of the entire project and improved the text considerably, line by line, in many other ways.

Some of the researchers and historians who contributed well beyond any call of duty were Jambur Ananth, Frank J. Ayd Jr., Arvid Carlsson, Will T. Carpenter Jr., Jonathan Cole, Jeff Goldstein, David Healy, Hanns Hippius, Paul Hoff, Gil Honigfeld, Paul Janssen, John Kane, Robert Paul Liberman, Bob Litman, Herb Meltzer, David Pickar,

Oakley Ray, Mel Sabshin, Sol Snyder, Bob Spitzer, Carol Tamminga, Mauricio Tohen, and Jerome Vaccaro.

And the family. When Jeff behaved at his most disruptive, his mother, Edith, living alone, cared for him in her home for years, far longer and more patiently than I did in mine. His brother, Ron, who must spend much of his life on the road, constantly shuttling between Washington, D.C., and his Oregon constituency, was invariably and instantly at hand with enterprising ideas and activist support—unfailingly cheerful and emphatic. And I would not have made it without my wife, Elaine.

The same needs to be said of my son and partner Jeff. Without his uncanny ability to recall and convey details of his life, large and small, and to share his feelings to an extraordinary degree, this would be a much shallower book. We have always complemented each other, he and I. His illness did little to weaken that bond, and never for long. At times, he shouted at me in frustration and fury, and I at him. Still, my respect and admiration for his fortitude never wavered. I know of nobody who can muster greater inner strength, more will to overcome, and a sharper rapier for puncturing pomposity, including mine. His mock-submissive *"Jawohl, Herr Kommandant!"* rings often in my ears.

He always will be—I need to say it again—my hero.

PETER WYDEN
Ridgefield, Connecticut
June 1997

Index

mental retardation, 48–52
Merck and Company, 252
Metropolitan Hospital, New York, 3, 128
Meyer, Dr. Adolf, 51, 57, 63, 116–17
Miller, Arthur, 55*n*.
Millon, Dr. Theodore, 94–5, 97; *Disorders of Personality*, 97; *Modern Psychopathology*, 95
Milwaukee Veterans Hospital, 235
Minus Triple P, 78
misdiagnosis of schizophrenia, 44–5 and *n*., 46–55, 93
MNS (malignant neuroleptic syndrome), 185
Moban, 101
Moniz, Dr. Egas, 49–50
Monroe, Marilyn, 52–5 and *n*., 145
Montana, 118
Montana Alliance for the Mentally Ill, 118
Mosher, Dr. Loren, 118, 189–91; *Community Mental Health*, 190
Moss, Daphne, 166
motivation, lack of, 11–16, 77–8, 220, 243, 267, 272, 273
multiple personality disorder, 40, 41
Munich, 61, 115, 172, 173
Munich University Hospital, 56, 58, 172, 210, 211
Murphy, Dr. Franklin D., 36
muscle spasms, 84, 90, 156, 229

narcissism, 108
NARSAD Artworks, 152
Nash, John Forbes, 89–90
National Alliance for Research on Schizophrenia and Depression (NARSAD), 152, 254
National Alliance for the Mentally Ill (NAMI), 42, 47, 79–83, 120, 144–5, 184, 200, 206; birth of, 79; NIMH collaboration, 81–3; pharmaceutical industry and, 81–3
National Association of Psychiatric Survivors (NAPS), 121*n*.
National Institute of Mental Health (NIMH), 23, 76, 90, 119, 120, 149, 162, 184, 204, 205, 242, 251, 256; evaluation of patients at, 214, 217–18; NAMI

collaboration, 81–3; schizophrenia research, 189, 190, 223
National Mental Health Association (NMHA), 80
National Mental Health Committee, 72
Nature, 41
Navane, 164
Nazism, 60, 63, 173, 187, 209–10
negative symptoms, 77–8, 266–8, 275; scales of, 268; *see also specific symptoms*
Neugeboren, Jay, 152–3; *Imagining Robert*, 152
Neugeboren, Robert, 152–3
Neurogen, 242
neuropathologists, 42
neurosis, 105, 107; Freudian concept of, 96–7; terminology, 96–7
neurotransmitters, 239
Newbold, Dr. H. L., 127–8; *Mega-Nutrients for Your Nerves*, 127; *Vitamin C Against Cancer*, 127
New Drug Application (NDA), 253–7, 259
New England Journal of Medicine, 160
New Jersey, 115–17
New Mexico, 143, 144, 145
Newsweek, 107, 238
New York, 126–9, 137*n*., 159, 174, 205, 232
New Yorker, The, 100, 102, 213
New York Hospital–Cornell Medical Center, 33, 88
New York Newsday, 184
New York Post, 99
New York State Alliance for the Mentally Ill, 159, 160
New York State Commission on Quality Care for the Mentally Disabled, 185
New York State mental health system, 76, 184–6
New York Times, The, 22, 24, 48, 79, 84, 89, 90, 121, 152, 154, 157–60, 187, 193, 203–4, 217, 275
NGD 91-1, 242
NGD 94-1, 242
niacin, 127, 128, 163
Nicholson, Jack, 202
Nijinsky, Vaslav, 201 and *n*.
1996 Annual of Drug Therapy, 264
No. 170053, 225–6
no-drugs philosophies, 35, 118–23, 209–11

PETER WYDEN was born in Berlin and came to the United States in 1937. He wrote for the U.S. Army's Psychological Warfare division, the *Wichita Eagle*, the *St. Louis Post-Dispatch*, and *Newsweek*. After serving as an editor of the *Saturday Evening Post* and *McCall's* and as executive editor of *Ladies' Home Journal*, he operated Wyden Books, a New York publishing house, for ten years. He is author of fourteen nonfiction books on contemporary issues, including *Day One: Before Hiroshima and After*; *Bay of Pigs: The Untold Story*; and *Stella*. He and his wife, Elaine, a library director, live in Ridgefield, Connecticut, and Château d'Oex, Switzerland.

A NOTE ON THE TYPE

THIS BOOK was set in Fournier, a typeface named for Pierre Simon Fournier *fils* (1712–1768), a celebrated French type designer. Coming from a family of typefounders, Fournier was an extraordinarily prolific designer of typefaces and of typographic ornaments. He was also the author of the important *Manuel typographique* (1764–1766), in which he attempted to work out a system standardizing type measurement in points, a system that is still in use internationally.

Fournier's type is considered transitional in that it drew its inspiration from the old style, yet was ingeniously innovational, providing for an elegant, legible appearance. In 1925 his type was revived by the Monotype Corporation of London.

Composed by North Market Street Graphics,
Lancaster, Pennsylvania
Printed and bound by Berryville Graphics,
Berryville, Virginia
Designed by Cassandra J. Pappas